TRAVELING
SPIRIT MASTERS

◆ ◆ ◆

TRAVELING
SPIRIT MASTERS
MOROCCAN GNAWA
TRANCE AND MUSIC
IN THE GLOBAL
MARKETPLACE

◆ ◆ ◆

DEBORAH KAPCHAN

WESLEYAN UNIVERSITY PRESS

Middletown, Connecticut

Published by Wesleyan University Press, Middletown, CT 06459

www.wesleyan.edu/wespress

5 4 3 2 1

The publisher gratefully acknowledges assistance from the
Lloyd Hibbert Publication Endowment Fund of the American
Musicological Society.

Chapter Eleven is based on the article "Possessing Gnawa Culture,"
which was published in *Music and Anthropology* in 2002.

Library of Congress Cataloging-in-Publication Data

Kapchan, Deborah A. (Deborah Anne)

Traveling spirit masters : Moroccan Gnawa trance and music in the
global marketplace / Deborah Kapchan.

p.   cm. — (Music/culture)

Includes bibliographical references and index.

ISBN-13: 978-0-8195-6851-9 (cloth : alk. paper)

ISBN-10: 0-8195-6851-1 (cloth : alk. paper)

ISBN-13: 978-0-8195-6852-6 (pbk. : alk. paper)

ISBN-10: 0-8195-6852-X (pbk. : alk. paper)

1. Music, Influence of.   2. Music—Physiological effect.

3. Trance music—Morocco.   4. Islamic music—Morocco.

5. Gnawa (Brotherhood)   I. Title.

ML3920.K15   2007

306.4'842292764—dc22   2007016405

to yahya

whose name derives from "life"

and who gave me his for many happy years

to jonathan

who made me live again

and to camille aumasson

(1903–1997)

and marvin kapchan

(1930–2004)

whose lives live on in memory

"This world is a stage or marketplace passed
by pilgrims on their way to the next. It is
here that they are to provide themselves with
provisions for the way; or, to put it plainly,
man acquires here, by the use of his bodily
senses, some knowledge of the works of God,
and, through them, of God Himself . . ."

al-Ghazzali,
The Alchemy of Happiness

CONTENTS

◆ ◆ ◆

ILLUSTRATIONS

◆ ◆ ◆

TRANSCRIPTION AND TRANSLITERATION

◆ ◆ ◆

Moroccan Arabic (MA) is largely a nonwritten dialect of Arabic that differs considerably from other dialects, even in the vernacular recitation of sacred texts and formulae. This is largely due to the saturation of Moroccan Arabic with the Hamitic language of the Berbers (or Amazighi people) who were the inhabitants of Morocco when the Arabs colonized the country in the sixth century, converting virtually all the Berbers, some of whom were Christians, others Jews, and others animists. Through intermarriage and long cohabitation, Moroccan Arabic has acquired both syntactic constructions and vocabulary words from Berber. It has also incorporated words from Spanish and French, the two European colonizing languages (Heath 1987).

Arabic is a triconsonantal language. In Moroccan Arabic these consonants are sometimes inverted (so that la 'a na—to curse or damn—becomes na 'a la in Moroccan). Moroccan Arabic is also known for the shortening of vowels that are long in other dialects of Arabic (muqaddima in classical Arabic becomes mqaddema in Moroccan and mu'allim becomes m'allem). I have remained faithful to transcription of the phonemics of Moroccan Arabic. For consonants I have followed the system used by the *International Journal of Middle Eastern Studies*. For vowels, however, I have diverged from this system. Moroccan Arabic does not employ long vowels as in classical Arabic (CA). Rather there are what Jeffrey Heath refers to as "full vowels" (a, i, u). Unlike those in classical Arabic, they "have no one-to-one relationship to shorter counterparts, and . . . are not especially prolonged phonetically. They do, however, commonly reflect CA long vowels . . . in inherited vocabulary" (Heath 1987: 23). In general, full vowels represent the phonemic rendering of the Moroccan vowel system. In addition to these, there are short vowels that are usually word-medial in Moroccan Arabic and change according to their environment. For the sake of simplicity, I have used the letter "e" to represent sounds that most approximate the schwa (usually pronounced as the "e" in "bet"). The shortening of vowels means that words like ṭarīq in classical Arabic are pronounced ṭreq (with a short "o" as in not). Ay is a diphthong, as in Mulay, similar to the English pronunciation of "they."

The consonants not found in English are rendered as follows:

Adapted from Kapchan 1996.

gh is a voiced uvular fricative, pronounced like a French "r"

kh is a voiceless uvular fricative, similar to the last consonant in Bach

š, is the letter *sheen* in classical Arabic, as in the English "shine"

sh should be pronounced as an s followed by the h; thus *ṣaḥḥa* (health) in classical Arabic loses its initial vowel and becomes *ṣha* in Moroccan Arabic

' is a voiced pharyngeal fricative, corresponding to the letter *ʿayn* in classical Arabic

' is a glottal stop, the Arabic letter *hamza*

dh represents the Arabic letter *dhal*, as in the English "that." It usually becomes a "d" in Moroccan Arabic

The emphatic consonants in Arabic are shown with a dot under the letter they most resemble in English: thus, ḍ, ṣ, ṭ, ḥ

Unless otherwise noted, plurals are marked with an "s"

Following convention, I have maintained the transcriptions of place names and proper names that are known by particular spellings (often the French spellings, like the Chellah Gardens, for what in Arabic is *shella*). This means that some words are preceded by the article "el" (as in the name El *Gourd*) in-stead of "al" or simply "l" and emphatic markings are absent. When quoting a previous transcription from Moroccan Arabic in English or French it has been my policy not to change anything.

Whereas Heath follows strict morphological rules in his use of hyphen-ation, I use hyphens in the following cases:

1. To indicate definite articles before nouns: *al-ḥal*, the state
2. To indicate prepositions: *b-ṣha*, with health or to your health
3. To indicate possessives: *dawi ḥal-i*, heal my state [heal state my]
4. To indicate the object of a verb: *šift-ha*, saw [past first-person singular] her
5. To indicate verbal prefixes marking duration and gender: *kay-mši*, he goes; *kat-mši*, she goes; *ghadi y-mši*, he will go; *ghadiya t- mši*, she will go; etc.

In presenting the discourse in this manuscript, I have tried to remain faithful to the music of Moroccan Arabic. In most cases conventional punctuation and typeface—commas, periods, dashes, italics, etc.—are sufficient to alert the reader to regular rhythms, repetition, parallelism, and rhymes. Where neces-sary, ellipses (. . .) indicate where discourse has been deleted. In poetic tran-scriptions, line breaks indicate pauses or rests; loud or stressed words are written in CAPITAL letters; and vowels that are drawn out are indicated by a colon after the vowel (ha:rd = haaaaard). All other information relevant to the keying of the performances is enclosed in square brackets. With the exception of casual conversations recounted in the more narrative chapters, all the discourse analyzed in the book was recorded and transcribed. Unless otherwise noted, all texts were originally spoken in Moroccan Arabic.

TRAVELING SPIRIT MASTERS

INTRODUCTION
INITIATION

Many years ago I became entranced with Morocco. Only now—twenty years later—am I able to write about trance. And that, only with the help of the spirits.

Trance is a transcultural phenomenon, but all trance takes place within a cultural framework. The performance of trance, like any performance, is highly contextual and must be understood in its specificity. This book lifts off of the Gnawa possession trance ceremonies in Morocco. It is not a book about the Gnawa, however;[1] rather, in these pages I explore the power of trance, the way it circulates globally, and its relation to music and gendered subjectivity. I also ask detailed questions about its enactment. How is trance cued or "keyed" (Bauman 1977; Hymes 1974)? What is the role of gesture in the transition into trance? How are emotion and somatic memory embedded in narrations about trance? What role do the senses play in this dramatic performance of otherness? And how and why is "trance"—and sacred music more generally—becoming a transnational category of the sacred?[2]

Studies on trance have existed since at least the colonial era, and it is possible to read the history of social theory and its tropes through them. Adeline Masquelier sets them out clearly: possession as pathology, possession as a means of healing social contradictions (functionalism), possession as therapy, possession as protest and resistance, and more recently, possession as theater, possession as cultural text, possession as situated expression of local identity and gendered subjectivity, and possession as embodied history (Masquelier 2001: 11–20).[3] If there is a theoretical paradigm informing this work, it is found at the fructuous intersection of aesthetics, poetics, and performance. Although focusing on the embodied aesthetic technique—the poetics—of trance more than the spirits and the cosmology that inhere in it or even the history that informs it (Lambek 1981; Stoller 1995), these are all of a piece; indeed, it is impossible to pull apart the affective and aesthetic strands of Gnawa trance.

The Gnawa heal those afflicted with spirit possession in Morocco through all-night ceremonies (lilat, pl.) that placate the spirits with music, incense, colors, and animal sacrifice. The Gnawa play music that induces trance (jadba) through the regular rhythms of heavy metal castanets (qraqab) and the bass melodies provided by the hajhuj, a three-stringed instrument tuned in an octave and a fifth. But the Gnawa have also become very popular on the world music market, collaborating with African American jazz musicians, American rock and roll musicians, and French recording artists, while also participating in festivals all over Europe and touring occasionally in the United States. In my observation of the recontextualization of what is, in origin if not in essence, spiritual music (musiqa ruḥaniyya, as one Gnawa master called it)—music intended to heal—my primary question has been this: what travels? How do aesthetic styles associated with the sacred inhabit new, nonsacred contexts, and what does this amalgam produce in the global circulation of sounds and meanings? These questions necessarily imply others related to cultural property, to style as an icon of identity, and to appropriation and power in the global music market (Erlmann 1996, 1999; Feld 1995; Meintjes 2003; Stokes 1994). Such phenomena, of course, are particular to this moment in history, determined in part by the conjuncture of late capitalism and aesthetics with experiences of time and space. "World music," notes anthropologist and ethnomusicologist Veit Erlmann, "is a new aesthetic form of the global imagination, an emergent way of capturing the present historical moment and the total reconfiguration of space and cultural identity characterizing societies around the globe" (1996: 469). While the music I analyze here is not limited to "world music," it nonetheless expresses a unique relation to the global imagination.

Traveling Spirit Masters is organized into two parts: "The Culture of Possession" and "Possessing Culture." In these sections I employ the verb "to possess" in two ways. In the first definition, a spirit possesses another—one is possessed by an incorporeal being who animates the limbs, causes the mouth to move, and the vocal chords to sound. Colors are often related to states of possession; auras appear; incense, or other smells accompany the transition from being one's self to being embodied by a spirit, "inhabited" by another. Unlike the spirit itself, the relationship is a corporeal one; the senses, their synapses and responses, are infused with difference. Like barium shot into the bloodstream, the body becomes magnetized, transparently dense. Possession requires an alchemical reaction, a transmutation of subtle and dense matter as two different substances encounter and change each other. This is not unlike the process of ethnography (Crapanzano 2004: 5–6; Lambek 1993).

But one can also possess culture like one possesses an object—a car, a coat, or a pet. This relation involves an exchange—money for goods in the case of a commodity or food and shelter for affection and companionship—the inalienable gifts that are shared but never lost (Weiner 1992). Possessing an object does not require the possessor to be reflexive and conscious of her possessiveness. To possess *culture*, however, is often qualitatively different. In order to possess culture—to really "own" it, to own up to it—one must "come to terms" with it; that is, one must debate and create the terms of culture, to define it, to be self-possessed, to be possessed by an idea of culture. Such metacultural definitions become particularly salient at moments when naturalized historical assumptions about racial, gender, and cultural identities are in flux.[4]

Part I, "The Culture of Possession," delineates how a cultural imagination takes material form intersubjectively, in the body and senses, in sound, image, and word. Taking place in Morocco (that is, locally), this half of the book explores the ritual life of the Gnawa. I examine Gnawa practices in Morocco as they are performed and narrated by the Gnawa themselves and particularly by the women practitioners and the female overseers of the ceremonies (*mqaddemat*). Although the sexual division of labor is codified among the Gnawa— men are musicians, and women comprise the majority of the possessed— close analysis reveals a complexity and flexibility of gendered power relations and ritual responsibilities that, with increasing commodification, are transforming rapidly.[5] Chapter one, "Emplacement," sets out the ritual world of the Gnawa in Rabat, exploring their historical relation to slavery and their place in the contemporary imagination. Here I analyze the term *tagnawit*, the concept that the Gnawa use to distinguish between authentic and inauthentic performance in a community whose practices are changing radically in response to the global music market. In chapter two, "Intoxication," I analyze what Marcel Mauss called the "mixture of sentiments" that produce the discursive world of the Gnawa (where discourse refers to practices as well as narratives), paying particular attention to the intersections of sentiment with sensate experience and the power of these linkages (or networks) to generate a cultural imaginary (cooke and Lawrence 2005; J. Goodman 2005; Ossman 2002; Silverstein 2004). I describe the roles of magic, of Eros, and of trauma and healing that define the ritual lives of the Gnawa and that eventually allow them to restructure relations of subjugation by "working the spirits." Chapter three, "Gesture and Word in Trance Time," continues the discussion of affect—particularly the expression of grief, but extends this analysis to the body in trance. In this chapter, I analyze the bodily metaphors of Gnawa trance (inhabitation, falling, rising, standing), their relation to the codified gestures of trance performance, and their intersections with the poetics of trance in narratives of possession (producing what I call "entranced narratives"). Chapter four, "Working the Spirits," is a close analysis of one narrative of possession in which the theme of mediation is dominant. The woman recounting this story falls into trance upon hearing the Gnawa on television and eventually consults a medium who is also a television producer. Analyzing her use of pronouns, repetition, sound symbolism, reported speech, and rhythm, we see how the poetics of trance create a particular form of modern female subjectivity. In chapter five, I enter the realm of "Dreams and Visions," both my own and those of Gnawa master Si Mohammed Chaouqi. This chapter makes evident the porosity between the interior life of the individual and the exterior life of public ritual and discourse.

In the second half of the book, "Possessing Culture," I explore the worlds created when the Gnawa, their music, and their beliefs travel to France and the United States. In this section, I delineate how the Gnawa and their European and African American collaborators come to inhabit new terrains and to "possess culture," particularly the culture of trance. Chapter six is an ethnographic description of daily life for Si Mohammed Chaouqi in the Chellah Gardens, where the Gnawa are tourist attractions more than ritual specialists. Chapter seven, "Money and the Spirit," extends this conversation, analyzing the role of sacred music on the world music market, the collaborations of the Gnawa with African American pianist and composer Randy Weston, and the way discourses of Gnawa identity respond to the figure of Moroccan pop star Hassan Hakmoun. I also ask implicit questions about how the history of French scholarship on the Gnawa has shaped their representations and spiraled back to influence their own discourses. Chapter eight recounts my experiences when traveling in France with the Gnawa. This chapter provides an ethnographic example of what George Marcus calls "a multi-sited research imaginary" that reaches across the boundaries of geography, class, and race (1998: 14). In chapter nine, "Narratives of Epiphany: Indexing Global Links," I analyze the contemporary fascination with trance experience through the narratives of three performers—Si Mohammed Chaouqi, Randy Weston, and a group of Breton musicians who collaborated with the Gnawa on the festival circuit in Brittany. All of these musicians played a piece that invoked the spirit Sidi

Musa, yet each of their narratives demonstrates very different relations to trance and trance experience. Their comparison elucidates the way particular discourses combine to form a transnational imagination around trance, as well as the way differences (for example, "Celtitude" versus "Négritude") are glossed over by global representations. In chapter ten, "Displaying Sound, Creating History in Dar Gnawa," I demonstrate how discourses of history and race are reconfigured through the collaborations between Randy Weston and Gnawa master Abdellah El Gourd. El Gourd, who has been playing with Weston since Weston lived in Tangier in the 1960s, has transformed his house into a public institute (nadi) called Dar Gnawa, the House of Gnawa. His highly self-conscious display of Gnawa heritage reconfigures lines of genealogical influence and participates fully in the creation of a transnational Gnawa identity in the African diaspora. This chapter is followed by a conclusion that ties together the theoretical implications of this work under the rubric of fetishization and the transglobal musical imagination. An epilogue follows that.

While part I demonstrates how dreams, visions, and spirits take material form, the emphasis in part II is on how material and aesthetic forms themselves travel and inhabit each other, producing hybrid cultural imaginations. The book in its entirety documents processes of trans(e)location—spiritual, musical, physical, and geographical.

Entrancement is also an entrance—a door to another world. ("Who will open the door?" the Gnawa ask when eliciting the first offerings of the ceremony.) I walked through that door in 1982 when I first went to and lived in Morocco until 1985. At that time I remember thinking that Morocco was a veritable culture of trance—whether observed in the possession ceremonies of the Gnawa or the devotional practices of al-ḥaḍra (literally "presence") among the many Sufi practitioners there (the 'Aissawa, the Darqawa, the Tijani, the Hamadsha, and the Boutshishi, to name just the most visible paths). My own experiences with the Gnawa began in September 1994 when I lived in the capital of Rabat for twelve months on a research grant and began to attend ritual ceremonies regularly with the m'allem or "master" Si Mohammed Chaouqi.[6] While I had no intention of becoming a Gnawiya at the time, in retrospect I see that during the twelve initial months of fieldwork I passed through the phases that many initiates in the Gnawa world recognize—notably, affliction, divination, propitiation, and finally relief and empowerment. The spirits have their way. Trance thus became not just an object of study for me, but also a vehicle of knowledge, an ontology of difference that at times possessed me viscerally, in the very habits of my body and spirit.

Although my introduction into the ceremonial world of the Gnawa was through the m'allem Si Mohammed, I eventually got to know the female community who employ them, as well as the mqaddemat (pl.),[7] the women "overseers" who work with them. Indeed, women play an extremely important role in the Gnawa culture, despite the fact that they do not carry the title of "master." Eventually I was to meet master musicians in other cities and their families and followers. I am indebted to all of these people for generously accepting me into their fold. My experiences with the Gnawa have continued over many summers, as well as during twenty-two months of extended research leave—and they continue still. By the end of the book, the story travels with the Gnawa from Morocco to Paris to Brittany and eventually to New York, New Jersey, and Texas. The "traveling spirit masters" that I refer to are not just the Gnawa, however, not just the musicians who collaborate with them, but also the women and men who trance to them, as well as the spirits that inhabit them all.

Spirits inhabit the bodies of their hosts, but cultural worlds also inhabit us, and as people and their sounds, images, and words travel, we are inhabited by more and by different worlds. These worlds live in us at all levels of human experience—in our imaginations, to be sure, but also in our bodies, our perceptions, and our interpretations. To quote novelist Michael Ondaatje, "Jung was absolutely right about one thing. We are occupied by gods. The mistake is to identify with the god occupying you" (2000: 230). This book stands as evidence that we not only identify with the gods occupying us (and they are many), but the gods themselves change names, genders, and demeanors as they encounter each other in the bodies of their moving and mutable hosts. The people in this book are all inhabited by spirits—some cultural, some musical, some localized, and some traveling the globe. As these spirits rise up in the occupied body, they themselves transform, and we divine the complex process of transmutation that takes place when imagination materializes, when image lodges in flesh and tries to speak.

What does it mean to be owned by a presence that is not the self but that nonetheless has its residence within the confines of the flesh? This question proceeds naturally from the phenomenon of possession, but it may also be posed about the experiences arising from the transfer and adaptation of local rituals and musical styles to the global arena. The incarnation of one musical aesthetic in a different cultural body affects its substance and its agency. This book explores how.

Inhabiting and being inhabited by a cultural imaginary is not a process that

FIGURE 1: Deviation: The Gnawa in a theater piece in Saint Brieuc, Brittany.
Photograph, Deborah Kapchan

takes you from point A to point B. To the contrary, there are many detours, many "deviations" along the way. The double entendre of "deviation," as both detour and transgression, stands for some of the peregrinations that are charted in this manuscript (see figure 1). Stefania Pandolfo refers to the ethnographic process as a journey (a *riḥla* in Arabic): "Riḥla," she says, "is the narrative form of a kind of travel that opens a metaphysical journey, but that is also made by walking: an investment of libidinal energy, an expenditure of the body, and of oneself" (1997: 20). She asks the reader to "surrender the viewer's position" in order to embrace "that of the walker—the position of a *marcheur*," that is, to give oneself over to the perambulations of evocation, memory, and experience (1997: 21). In this work I take inspiration from that (re)quest.

As an ethnography of North African expressive culture, this work distinguishes itself from previous scholarly works on Morocco by analyzing how Moroccan cultural practices influence and interact with other, nonlocal cultures, contributing to emergent aesthetic and ideological formations at the global level.[8] It also contributes to the literature on Islamic practices in their specificity.[9] Focusing particularly on the intersection of the imagination with sound, movement, olfaction, and language, I analyze how aesthetic expression intersects with the imagination as a "social force" that transfigures local and global identities. I also analyze how Moroccan Gnawa music is commodified and packaged as "trance music" to foreign audiences and how the Gnawa and their African American and European collaborators together create a schismogenetic dance of identity in the global public sphere.[10] Attending to the materialization of the ephemeral and, contrariwise, with how forms—musical, visual, gestural, and poetic—affect and effect cultural imaginations, this book examines the subtle dance of desire as it possesses and is possessed by "traveling spirit masters" on both sides of the Atlantic.

◆ PART I ◆
THE CULTURE OF
POSSESSION

◆ ◆ ◆

EMPLACEMENT

"*aji l-hna, glis-i hna, hna qadam-i. Ha, ha dir l-micro hna.* Come here, sit here, here next to me. Here, here, put the microphone here."

The master Gnawa musician, or *m'allem*, Si Mohammed, motioned for me to take a seat on the floor next to him. Blankets had been lain down for us and pillows protected our backs from the cold of the mosaic walls. There were pillars in the high-ceilinged room that branched up to a flat, open roof at least ten meters above our heads. The black night sky claimed the view over the center of the room; because I was against the lower wall, however, I only saw the women and children hanging over the edges of the roof above, looking down on the ceremony and on the participants.

Women had been arriving for several hours now, each in a caftan that shimmered in synthetic golds and silvers, blues and oranges. Some sat on the floor, observing the crowd and waiting for the ceremony to begin. Others chatted with their acquaintances, their hands covering their mouths as they recounted the neighborhood news or a marital scandal. The cookies and tea that a few young girls were circulating on trays made the waiting more tolerable. Many of the women accumulated the sweets on their napkins in order to take them home to their children or grandchildren—sesame and almond paste mixed with honey and flour and rose water, baked on huge pans at the public oven, now piled high and displayed on Chinese ceramic plates decorated with peacocks. The odor of fresh mint steamed from the slender tea glasses as the tray was proffered.

Finally at about 11:15 the master musician got up. He and the rest of the group retrieved their drums from an alcove, slung them around their torsos and proceeded into the street. The woman overseer of the ceremony, the *mqaddema,* an attractive divorcée, led the guests; she carried a brass tray laden with ceramic bowls filled with different kinds of incense—black and white benzoin, myrrh, sandalwood, chips of amber, and musk—each scent intended for a different spirit or jinn. There was a bowl of henna paste for auspiciousness, a bowl of milk, and a plate of fresh dates. And burning candles. On the way out

FIGURE 2: Invoking the spirits in the beginning of a divination ceremony.
Photograph, Deborah Kapchan

the master glanced at the mqaddema's slender calves in white lacy stockings, evident below her caftan, which was tucked up into her belt for easier movement.
"Ah, when I was young," he sighed. Then the Gnawa went out through the
front door. The guests followed them into the street. The mqaddema carefully
placed the tray in the middle of the tarred road in front of the m'allem and
backed away as the Gnawa began to circle around it, banging on the painted
snare drums with carved sticks, invoking the presence of the spirits. The late
spring night held a slight chill for women in caftans. Shutters and windows
along the street opened, neighbors emerged from their dwellings; some joined
the crowd, while others stood on the lintels or peered over the roofs. The young
girls who had emerged with the guests now held lit candles as the Gnawa
danced and spun, each separately and then in unison, inviting the spirits to
rise up in the bodies of those whom they favored among the crowd.

We did not have long to wait. A young man in jeans and a t-shirt let out a
painful bellow; he flailed his arms and "was thrown" to the ground. Those
around him panicked, fearing the violence of his jerks. When it was clear that
he had not split his skull on the concrete, however, they moved away, watching him carefully but allowing him to writhe and roll in the gutter. Malika, the
mqaddema, looked to Si Mohammed for instructions, but he simply nodded, by

which everyone understood that the boy should be left alone. Soon after, the Gnawa finished playing and started the procession back into the house, the guests filing after them, removing their shoes as they stepped over the threshold. The young man was left outside, in the care of his cohorts.

Once inside, the Gnawa set down their snare drums and took up heavy iron cymbals (qraqab, pl.). They sat close together along one side of the room. The m'allem picked up his three-stringed hajhuj, and they all began singing a pentatonic homage to the spirits of Bambara, the sub-Saharan spirits who represent their origins: "fangaru fangari," the Gnawa began. One of the Gnawa got up and did a ceremonial dance to the Bambara spirits, mimicking a hunter shooting game animals with a shotgun.

Upon completion of this song, the Gnawa sang the formula that follows each of their invocations to the jinn throughout the nightlong ceremony or lila; namely the praising of the Prophet Muhammad with the words:

llāh ṣallī 'alā rasūl allāh,	God pray for the messenger of God,
llāh ṣallī 'alā rasūl allāh,	God pray for the messenger of God,
llāh ṣallī 'alā sayyidinā muḥammad.[1]	God pray for our lord Mohammed.

FIGURE 3: Woman in trance being attended to by another.
Photograph by Ariane Smolderen

Emplacement | 13

"Who will open the door?" asked the Gnawi who had been dancing. "Who will say 'In the name of God [let's begin]'?"

A woman seated across from me held out a ten-dirham note to the Gnawi, who, accepting it, held the note up and said loudly, "A *faṭḥa* [invocation] for our sister Asma. God bless our sister who gave us this blessing [*baraka*]. May she come and go protected. Bless her in her travels. Her sons, God grant them success. Bless her loved ones near and far. Grant her health. Grant her abundance. May God cover her [sins]." To each blessing, the seated Gnawa added "Amen" in chorus. Once finished, the solicitations continued: "Who will open the door? Who will say 'In the name of God'?"

When the Gnawi had collected money from about four or five women, he placed it on the tray of incense in front of the *m'allem*. A hot brazier was also there, ready to receive the gums and resins that the spirits required. After relinquishing the money, the Gnawi pinched some incense from a bowl, threw it on the hot coals, and took his place among the others. As the incense melted and bubbled, smoke rose up before the *m'allem*, and he began once again to play. Before long he invoked the Muslim spirit of Sidi Abdelqadr Jilani as well as other holy men of Islam. Sidi Abdelqadr Jilani was a saint who lived in Persia in between 1077 and 1166 A.D. and whose teachings founded a Sufi sect— the Qadiriyya—which has now disseminated throughout the Middle East and Muslim Africa.

My tape recorder was behind a pillow next to me, so I could change the tape when necessary, and the microphone was clipped to Si Mohammed's *jellaba*. The music was loud, the iron castanets clapping hard and frantic; my hearing had already grown fuzzy, muffling the decibels and making it tolerable. Several women had gotten up and were moving their heads rhythmically from side to side or up and down to the music, their hands clasped behind their backs or less frequently held up over their heads, their bare feet beating the raffia-carpeted ground in a regular and hard pulse. White smoke rose up around them as one of the Gnawa held the brazier under their faces, the musk adhering to their sweaty and glowing skin. The Gnawa sped up their rhythm, then broke off their cymbals, leaving only the sound of the *hajhuj* to carry the beat.

"Allah, Allah," one trancer cried, her thorax lifted like a face to heaven.

The Gnawa began clapping. Then the *m'allem* played the final bars of the song, and the trancers fell into the arms of surrounding women and were pulled to the sides of the room. They were sprinkled with orange-blossom water from ornate metal canisters with long spouts. These spouted vessels were also inserted into their mouths. The water dripped from their brows, spilling out of their lips. Each remained in the embrace of another, someone who hadn't been in trance, who stroked them and kissed them until they came to (see figure 3).

The Gnawa again solicited money, giving blessings in return. Soon it was the black pantheon, Sidi Mimun's *nuba* ("turn" or moment to manifest), and soon after Lalla Mimuna, the spirit who Si Mohammed described as Sidi Mimun's sister and the mother of Aisha Qandisha, the most powerful of female *jinn*. Knives appeared and the trancers seemed to thrust them into their bellies. They struck their arms and legs with the blades and ran them along their tongues. Blood ran also, dripping on the patches of blue tile where the mats separated, dripping on the clothing of the trancers. I turned my head away, imagining the cut in the thick flesh of tongue. After the black spirits, the blue arrived: Sidi Musa, the spirit of the sea. People balanced bowls of water containing anise seeds on their heads, and one woman lay face down on the floor and made swimming motions with her arms. As the Gnawa passed on to the *samawiyyin*, the sky spirits, a few women pulled scarves tightly around their necks, cutting off the circulation; their lips turned blue, their eyes rolled back into their heads.[2] I watched with anxiety for their expiration, but they did not lose consciousness, eventually falling to the floor and releasing their hold on the scarves. Many women were up on the floor now, their arms beating the air like desperate wings or lifted above their heads as if in ascension, their eyes floating back into their heads in an attitude of rapture. The Gnawa again stopped their cymbals, leaving only the *hajhuj* to accompany the incense in the air. Some women screamed; others cried out for God. When the segment was over the musicians took a break, retiring into a side room and leaving the guests by themselves.

I changed the tape.

The woman next to me noticed and asked what I was doing. I told her I was doing research on the Gnawa.

"b-saḥ? Really?" she said. "You're not from here? You're not Moroccan?"

"No, an American," I said. "But I've lived here for years."

"The wonders of God!" she said. And then the music began again, and we both turned our attention back to the floor.

The spirits in red were next—Sidi Hamu, the spirit of the slaughterhouse, the spirit who demands blood.[3] Before Si Mohammed had even played a few bars, a woman went into violent contortions. Those around her jumped up and moved out of the way. The *mqaddema* flew to her side and shepherded her toward the brazier. The afflicted woman remained on her hands and knees while

Emplacement | 15

the *mqaddema* wafted the incense up into her nostrils, her head hanging low and loose. Slowly she began to raise and lower her hands, patting, then striking the ground, her head thrown to the left and right. The *mqaddema* began to help her to her feet, but the spirit pushed her away. Throwing a red veil over her head and tying a red scarf around her waist, the *mqaddema* held the woman from behind, as she jerked against the weight of her supporter. By now others were up and trancing next to her. A Gnawi was passing out bunches of lit candles. The entranced woman accepted a bundle with each hand and passed them under her neck, then under her open mouth. A young man had taken off his shirt and was passing his bundle of flames across his chest and under his arms. Hot wax dripped and solidified on his body making his skin seem as if it were flaking and peeling off. At the end of this set, the trancers stood still, stunned in the sudden silence, while the *mqaddema* gathered the candles and passed them around to the onlookers—*baraka*, blessing. I was instructed to blow mine out, which I did, placing it in my bag behind the pillows, near the tape recorder.

The woman to my left again began to converse with me.

"Those women who were screaming, they aren't really possessed. Those who were screaming were only pretending," she said.

"How do you know?" I asked.

"Because Aisha [Qandisha, the *jinniyya*] told me. She spoke to me and said, 'all those that are screaming are not mine. I don't scream. The ones that scream do not belong to me,' she told me. Aisha doesn't scream."

"*Wash antiya maskuna*; are you inhabited?" I asked.

"By Aisha," she answered. "That's how I know. She talks with me. I have her *baraka*. I once fell from a fourth-story roof and wasn't hurt."

"You fell four stories?" I repeated, surprised.

"Without a scratch," she affirmed. "Aisha protects me. She comes to me. I see her before me."

The musicians were filing back into the room now. The dawn was not far away. It was time to invoke Aisha Qandisha, the *jinniya* of the threshold, the seductress, the demanding dominatrix. The lights were turned out as the Gnawa started singing,

ah aiša qandisha
O Aisha Qandisha
ah aiša l-gnawiyya
O Aisha the Gnawi

ah aiša wawisha
O Aisha, little Aisha

ha hiya aiša jat
Here Aisha has come
ha hiya aiša jat
Here Aisha has come

The *mqaddema* turned off the lights in the courtyard. Women moaned in the darkness. The room was now dense with gyrating bodies, legs stamping the floor, arms thrown above their heads, swaying above them like branches. Suddenly the woman next to me flung herself forward onto the floor and quickly got up, her silhouette revealing carefully practiced moves; trancing madly and purposefully, she was clearly not a novice. I stayed put, watching, ready to fend off anyone who might lose control and tumble into my lap.

The cycle of songs to Aisha Qandisha lasted quite a while. Many women who had been seated all night now got up to trance. The scented air was palpable, the heat of moving bodies settled like a morning blanket on the room. The sky above our heads was growing lighter, the darkness giving way to dawn, as the spirits (jnun, pl.) retired into their parallel realm. The songs ended, the trancers collapsed. Women bustled about in the kitchen, preparing to serve the *harira* soup and coffee that would be our breakfast.

"You see?" said my neighbor, having returned to my side. "That's Aisha. Aisha came and left."

"*shift-ha*," I answered. "I saw her." And indeed I had.

RELIGION, SLAVERY, AND MASTERY

The trans-Saharan slave trade brought hundreds of thousands of slaves to Morocco (Mohammed Ennaji 1994, 1999). Indeed, "Morocco was probably the largest single market for imported black slaves in the Arab Maghrib" (Wright 2002: 55). Beginning in force in the eighth century and not ending until the twentieth century, the largest influx of slaves were brought by Sultan Moulay Ismail, who brought massive numbers of slaves from sub-Saharan Africa for his army, as well as women to bear more sons to the soldiers (Wright 2002). From countries as far away as modern Sudan, Nigeria, Niger, Guinea, Mali, and Senegal, the slaves came from many countries that were already Islamicized and that had traditional possession ceremonies already in place—populations such as the Bori (Erlmann and Magagi 1989; Masquelier 2001), the

Songhay (Rouch 1960, 1998), 2003; Stoller 1989a, 1992), and others. Words—and especially names—in Bambara, the language of modern-day Mali and part of the Manding family of West African languages, still sprinkle the songs of the Gnawa, as do invocations to the spirits of the Fulani and the Hausa.

Spirits in Morocco are called al-mluk—"the owners" (from the verb ma-la-ka, to own).[4] There is a relationship of power within the body of the possessed, which is often a conflicted one until the possessed submits to the possessor. Spirits cannot be exorcised in Moroccan belief. They inhabit the host and "rule over the head." Indeed, a possessed person is said to be maskun—"inhabited" by the spirits (also referred to as jinn, s., jnun, pl.). The body becomes a residence in which the spirits dwell and that they also change irreversibly. These spirits may be benevolent or tyrannical, but they are always powerful, and they "follow" (taba') the subject, afflicting her with poor health and misfortune until she acknowledges and "accepts" their power (kat-qabl 'ali-hum), placating them with animal sacrifice, music, incense, and trancing. Only then may the possessed subject enter into a relationship of desire with her possessor(s). This is why propitiation is so important. If the body is not a welcoming host, the tenant will cause troubles for a lifetime. Conversely, by placating the spirit, one also partakes in his or her power. Accommodation is necessary for coexistence, but the possessed person is not diminished by being inhabited; she may even come to master the spirits that reside within her, to "work" them in the Gnawa idiom. Working the spirits is nothing other than learning to manage the state of being multiply possessed, learning to master the shifts in emotion and identity that occur in the course of spirit possession. Given the history of Gnawa enslavement in Morocco, the metonymic relations between the state of being possessed by a spirit and the historical state of being possessed by an owner are clear. Insofar as spirit possession evokes somatic memories of historical slavery among the Gnawa, learning to work or control the spirits is a potentially liberating endeavor, leading one out of victimhood to mastery.

While the origins of the Gnawa are in sub-Saharan Africa, the origin of the word "Gnawa" is less clear. Some say the word comes from a transmutation of the word "Guinea," which at one time in Morocco was used to refer to the countries south of the Sahara.[5] Ethnopsychiatrist and Gnawa scholar Abdel-hafid Chlyeh notes that Al-Zuhri, a geographer and historian of the twelfth century, called the citizens of the kingdom of Ghana the Djinawa (1998: 17). As Ghana was the empire conquered by the Almoravides in the sixteenth century, this is a likely etymology.[6] Thomas Hale in his study of griots and griottes advances the theory that the word "griot" and the word "gnawa" are related, as are the populations (1998),[7] while anthropologist Viviana Pâques notes the possible derivation from the Berber, *igri ignawan*, meaning "the field of cloudy skies," a paraphrase, she says, for the star Aldebaran from which the Gnawa are said to hail (1976).[8] The Gnawa, who are Muslim, claim descent from Bilal, the only black companion of the Prophet, who was a freed Abyssinian slave, a Christian convert to Islam, and the first muezzin, that is, the person to call the faithful to prayer from the minarets of medina mosques. Not all of the black African populations in Morocco are Gnawa. Although many came as slaves during the twelfth and sixteenth centuries,[9] others—speakers of Tashilhit— have been cultivators and traders in the south of Morocco since at least the third century (Becker 2002; El Hamel 2002).

Before the twelfth century, slaves in Morocco "were of all races. There were slaves taken from the northern shores of the Mediterranean, and from the northern shores of the Black Sea. They were also imported from central Asia" (El Hamel 2002: 37). Moroccan historian Chouki El Hamel notes, however, that after the twelfth century,

> Slave raiding in western sub-Saharan Africa increased and became even more common when the slave supply of purchases and captives of war from areas of Europe such as the Iberian Peninsula, the Caucasus, and the Black Sea began to dwindle once the jihads fought by Islamic sultanates and principalities died down. (2002: 37)

At this time, slaves were brought primarily from sub-Saharan and East Africa.[10] It is generally acknowledged that the largest migrations came during the reign of the Saadians between the fifteenth and sixteenth centuries when they conquered Timbuktu and the Songhay empire and sent much of the population of this already Islamicized nation (with its own beliefs in possession and propitiation practices) to Morocco. At the same time, the Portuguese were running a slave trade between sub-Saharan Africa and the Moroccan port cities. Indeed Pâques, an anthropologist who has worked with the Gnawa for more than forty years, notes that some Gnawa still distinguish among themselves between those who came by the ports (by sea from West Africa) and those who came over the Sahara, mostly from the Songhay Empire (1991: 25). Many of the latter slaves were employed in the service of the sultanate when the Alaouite dynasty overthrew the Saadians in the 1500s and established the holy lineage that still rules Morocco today.[11] These slaves had a certain status because of their ties to the palace. Indeed, according to Pâques, the "Gnawa of the [Sultan's] Palace in effect provided oral instruction to all the other Gnawa, whether or not they were of Saharan origin" (1991).[12] Si Mohammed Chaouqi, the Gnawa master that I worked with in 1994 and 1995 and have worked with ever since, was born within the palace walls. Si Mohammed (also called *al-'abdi*, "the slave") remembers his grandmother as a tall black *mqaddema* (overseer or leader) who eventually apprenticed him to a Gnawa master.

The history of the Gnawa in slavery, though not well documented, is important to mention at the outset, for despite the fact that the Gnawa reside in Africa, they are a transplanted and minority population in Morocco with little historical memory of a sub-Saharan homeland (Becker 2002; Mohammed Ennaji 1999; Lovejoy 2004; Pâques 1991).[13] The Gnawa *lila* or ritual ceremony is one context where at least the names of sub-Saharan spirits and ancestors are preserved. The repetition of these African names—Baba Madani, Fulani, Busunana, Malgatu, Mamario—is one way that links with a sub-Saharan past are remembered and commemorated. They are the *ulad al-Bambara*, the sons of Bambara. Vocalizing the names of the ancestors both honors and invokes them, preserving their memory by acknowledging their presence in history and in the ritual present. While ritual expressions aimed to heal the possessed through music exist in many parts of Africa and the African diaspora, only some arise from historical conditions of slavery, and of those, possession ceremonies in North Africa seem to make the slave experience most salient in their performances.[14] Apart from the ceremony, however, the position of the Gnawa in the contemporary Moroccan social hierarchy has, until recently, relied as much on the forgetting of this subjugated past as on its constant and implicit presence.[15] The Gnawa are traditionally in the category of *ša'b*, the popular class, and have catered primarily to that class.[16] Their current popularity on the world music market, however, is changing this class orientation, and it is now chic to invite the Gnawa to the poshest of hoi polloi gatherings among Moroccan urbanites. Nonetheless, most Gnawa musicians still live in modest, if not humble, lodgings.

The connections between the actual slavery of the Gnawa and the metaphorical and mimetic re-enactments of subjugation that I describe here are clearly not coincidental.[17] The practice of slavery was not eradicated until the early twentieth century in Morocco (Becker 2002; Mohammed Ennaji 1994, 1999). Indeed, Moroccan historian Mohammed Ennaji estimates that until then approximately 20,000 people a year were forcibly brought to Morocco from Sudan and sub-Saharan Africa (1999). The spirit possession ceremonies of the Gnawa are metonymic performances in which somatic memories of slavery are invoked and symbolically mastered (Fuson 2001; Hell 2000; Pâques

1991). They are an example of "the ways in which closeness to the ineffable terrors of slavery was kept alive—carefully cultivated—in ritualized, social forms" (Gilroy 1993: 73). While the connections between trance and colonialism are documented in many traditions,[18] the contribution of this work is not simply to illustrate the relation of power, politics, and trance in the Moroccan example, but to analyze the power of the voice, gesture, and other media, to restructure historically determined relations of power via the aesthetic and affective modalities of trance. These emotional restructurations work for the Gnawa as they do for enthusiastic audiences and trancers in the West, though clearly in very different ways.

GNAWA IN THE POPULAR IMAGINATION

The Gnawa became popular in post-Independence Morocco as contributors to the popular music groups Nas al-Ghiwan and Jil Jilala, adding an African aesthetic to the music and helping to create a particularly Moroccan sound. In the 1960s, international revolutionary discourses were prevalent in the mentality of the Moroccan intelligentsia—the Black Panthers and Reggae music were held up as examples of liberation discourses (see the magazine Souffles). The Gnawa thus represented the slavery experience and the existence of racism in Morocco, but they were also the connection to authentic aesthetics and political activism. Indeed, Abraham Serfaty, the noted Jewish writer and critic of the government at this time who was jailed and subsequently exiled until 1999, wrote about the intimacy of aesthetics and politics in African art and life, drawing inspiration from Leroi Jones and the Black Panthers. On the occasion of the Pan-African Festival, held in Algiers, Algeria, in 1969, Serfaty wrote:

> In the face of this pretend "culture" of the slave masters where "the triumph of the economic spirit over the imagination" provoked "a schism between art and life," the black slaves preserved the essence of African culture where "it was, and will always be inconceivable to separate music, dance, singing or any other artistic endeavor from the existence of man and his cult of gods." (Serfaty 1969: 32–33, quoting Leroi Jones, The People of the Blues, translation mine)[19]

The Gnawa became symbols (often despite themselves) of the "essence of African culture." They became Morocco's link to the African diaspora and the international struggles for racial equality. That the struggles of African Americans played such a large role in postcolonial North Africa speaks to the recursivity of influence in the African diaspora more generally.[20] The Gnawa were also sought out by American and British rock and roll stars of the time, like Jimi Hendrix, Robert Plant, and others, to say nothing of the African American artists who collaborated with them—Randy Weston, Pharoah Saunders, and Archie Shepp. These collaborations transfigured racial identities in the public sphere on both sides of the Atlantic.

TAGNAWIT: GNAWA KNOWLEDGE AND PRACTICE TODAY

Don Cherry, the late African American jazz trumpeter who, before he died, cut an album with Gnawa musician Hassan Hakmoun, was fond of saying that there are three kinds of music in the world—folk music, classical music, and devotional music (Rudolph 2001). In its inception, Gnawa music falls into the latter category; it is sacred music by dint of its words, which praise and solicit blessings from God, the Prophet, particular Islamic saints, as well as a pantheon of both sub-Saharan and North African, Islamic and non-Islamic spirits. The music is considered so powerful that at one time it was thought that singing the songs outside of the ceremonial context would incite the wrath of the spirits, who would then exact retribution in the form of afflicting the transgressor. Today, however, Gnawa musicians either aver that they only commercialize the praise songs to dead saints (called the mdaḥ) and not the invocations to the spirits, or that their intention (niya) mediates the relation between sound and spirit, thus neutralizing the effects that the desacralization of the music might cause. One Gnawi m'allem, Si Abbass Baska Larfaoui, dismissed the entire division between ritual contexts (lilat) and performances done for non-Muslim and foreign audiences (frajat), saying that Gnawa music is for healing, and it does its work wherever it is and among whoever hears and needs it. He went on to say that the Gnawa were not doctors, only musicians, and it was the spirits that had spiritual and healing power via the music. "Gnawa-ness is like a woman," he told me. "If you treat her well, she treats you well, and if you are not good to her, she's not good to you."

Gnawa-ness is an awkward translation of the word tagnawit, which may be more loosely translated as "Gnawa authenticity," "Gnawa identity," or even "Gnawa culture." It stands for Gnawa knowledge as practiced, its epistemology. The word is a Berber syntactical construction that has been incorporated into Moroccan Arabic syntax. Adding the Berber prefix "ta" and the suffix "t" to an Arabic root makes a noun of identity (a nisba, made by adding "i" to the end of a noun, as in "Gnawi") into a noun of attribution. Thus huwa Gnawi means, "he is a Gnawa" whereas 'and-u tagnawit means that "he possesses [the qualities, or attributes of] Gnawa-ness." *Tagnawit is the word the Gnawa use to differentiate "authentic" Gnawa-ness from the "inauthentic."* Those possessing *tagnawit* are most often born into a Gnawa milieu and come up through the ranks, learning the ritual in all its complexity by observation, participation, and slow initiation. Those who do not possess *tagnawit* are the popularizers who, for purposes of commercialization, have adopted the Gnawa identity and music but know little of its deeper ritual significance, its history in the bones. "Had-ši f-dam-nah," Younis Chaouqi, a young Gnawi, told me, "It's in our blood." "Khalq-nah fi-h; we were born into it," Tangier m'allem Abdellah El Gourd explained. To say that "tagnawit is like a woman," on the other hand, is to acknowledge that the culture and traditions of the Gnawa have an independent (and sexualized) agency. The master does not create *tagnawit*; he only interacts with it. In this sense, being a Gnawi is a dialogic enterprise—the Gnawi enters into a relationship with the spirits via the music, who enter into a relationship with the possessed, who, themselves, have a relationship with all these entities.[21] Close analysis and comparison of the performances of the Gnawa in Moroccan ritual contexts, on the one hand, and in nightclubs and concert halls, on the other, shows that the rules for recontextualization of the music are fluid and even more various than any of these articulations imply. The boundaries of *tagnawit* are never easily drawn, even though they are continually evoked and contested.

Today not all Gnawa have a history in slavery (due to apprenticeships by non-Gnawa), yet this part of their past remains prominent in representations by scholars (Pâques 1991), music producers, and only sometimes by the Gnawa themselves. Foregrounding the history of Gnawa slavery links them to the larger African diaspora. In liner notes and popular music criticism, the Gnawa become the embodiment of the "blues" on the African side of the Atlantic. They often wear dreadlocks when performing in public, a symbol associated with the protest and liberation music of reggae in the eyes of the public. Of course one is never actually liberated of or by the spirits in Gnawa ceremonies, as the spirits are permanent inhabitants of their hosts. In the spiraling of *tagnawit* into the world music market, however, trance is represented more as a medium of liberation than a symbol of possession. In this manuscript I track these transformations.

◆ 2 ◆
INTOXICATION
◆ ◆ ◆

We have now arrived at the conclusion that there are affective states,
generators of illusions, to be found at the root of magic, and that these
states are not individual, but derive from a mixture of sentiments
appertaining to both individuals and society as a whole.
—Marcel Mauss (1972 [1902]: 159)

Published in 1902, this quote by Marcel Mauss brings us face-to-face with the power of emotion to create shared belief, as well as the power of shared belief to be performative—that is, to materialize collective sentiment. According to Mauss, shared affective states create the effects of magic; what's more, these are *mixed* sentiments, by which we may infer that emotions of different provenance (abjection, desire, rapture) combine to form a kind of ethos, like a magical elixir. At the time that Mauss wrote, sociologists had been thickly debating the differences between religion and magic, as well as magic and science.[1] For Mauss, however, magic was a "kind of religion" whose rites were "eminently effective": "they are creative; they *do* things," he wrote (1972 [1902]: 22, emphasis in original). It is for this reason, he noted, that magic was often associated with craftsmen, with potters and forgers—people with the power to transform materials from one form to another.[2] The Gnawa have a history of such artisan work.

There is a paradox in Mauss's equation, however. He defines affect as a generator and magical rites as performatives, yet what they produce are illusions—that is, appearances, apparitions, that have no basis in reality. In other words, for Mauss there is a difference between the creation of things "real" (clay pots, metal pans) and the creation of things that only *appear* to be real (magical illusions). While acknowledging the power of sentiment to create collective belief, Mauss stops short of analyzing how belief (what he defines as illusion, but what could also be considered imagination) creates material realities. This again tells us much about the time that Mauss wrote. Sociologists of the day had an interest in defining magic as illusory, a product of the "primitive," whereas religion, if also a result of collective belief, corresponded to a more evolved ("organic") time and people (Durkheim 1915; Weber 1963). Indeed, these distinctions not only constructed the European as more advanced, but actually created the terms of modernity itself through defining its antithesis—namely, magic (Pels 2003).[3]

In fact, illusion and imagination share many characteristics. If an illusion is something perceived but not in fact "there," the imagination is often conceptually present, but not (always) sensually realized. What interests me here, however, are the effects of both—effects that, to repeat Mauss, are "eminently effective," that "*do* things." In this chapter I explore the "mixture of sentiments" and the *mixture of senses* that exist in the discursive world of the Gnawa. These mixtures generate discourses on sexuality, trauma, and healing, while producing the affective states of intoxication, grief, and bliss. Much of the sentiment and semantics that surround the Gnawa concern illusion—that is, they have an ambiguous relation to what many in Morocco, and especially more orthodox Muslims, would call "truth"; but it is this ambiguity that gives these discourses their power. Indeed, ambiguity surrounds the Gnawa like the thick incense that envelopes their ritual ceremonies. And like this incense, it intoxicates and sometimes obfuscates.

Discourses on magic have not disappeared from either popular or scholarly texts. As Pels notes, "if modern discourse reconstructs magic in terms that distinguish it from the modern, this at the same time creates the correspondences and nostalgias by which magic can come to haunt modernity" (Pels 2003: 5).[4] The popularity of the Gnawa and of Gnawa trance and music represent one such haunting.

MAGIC AND ALCHEMY

Alchemy is better than gold, but real alchemists are very rare, and so are real Sufis.
—al-Ghazzali (1997: 7–8)

The possessed in Morocco may be said to inhabit a culture of trance, one with a particular relation to the senses and their expression. This culture of trance is not limited to Gnawa practitioners but permeates Moroccan society at many levels. Many of the Sufi sects in Morocco, such as the 'Aissawa and the Tijaniyya, are known for their trance practices, though not all would attribute possession as a cause (Brunel 1926; Rouget 1985: 264).[5] Nonetheless the forms of trance in Morocco across both Sufi ṭuruq (literally "paths") like the 'Aissawa and possession ṭawa'if (or groups) such as the Gnawa are remarkably similar, even if the histories of such groups are radically different.[6] There is a similarity at the level of the body, "techniques" that are learned and applied in various contexts (Mauss 1979 [1935]). Those who participate in trance ceremonies are linked by a somatic repertoire that distinguishes them from the nontrance community. They trance to similar "beats," are affected by the same musical lines, and breathe in the same incense—musk, ambergris, sandalwood, and benzoin. Their sense world is permeated with a distinctive aesthetic. In the case of possession, their dream life is inhabited by the same pantheon of spirits. In witnessing the performances of each other's spirits while experiencing their own, propitiants authorize and validate a plurality of subjectivities. They also sanction what many of them refer to as an addiction or intoxication—al-blia—an inebriation with the music, the incense, and in short, the ḥal or state of ecstasy in movement, the pain and bliss of being other.[7] People who share this somatic repertoire in Morocco are sometimes called ṣḥab al-ḥal, the friends of the ḥal. A ḥal is a state of heightened emotion and often mentation, a state of transcendence. ṣḥab al-ḥal are those who, in one form or another, are called to trance.

The history of Islam in Morocco has had profound effects on subcultures like the Gnawa. The predominant influence of Sufism and saint worship that characterizes Moroccan Islam has become part of Gnawa ritual, evident in ways of honoring the ancestors (Eickelman 1976; Cornell 1998). The Gnawa pay yearly visits to the sanctuary (zawiya) of Mulay Brahim in the High Atlas mountains outside Marrakech, for example, and to Sidi Abdellah Ben Hussein in the town of Tamesloht. Although they do not consider themselves Sufis, nor are they considered Sufis by others, their rituals are nonetheless imbued with Sufi influence, including the "ravissement" of the ḥal and the propitiation and adoration of Sufi saints like Abdelqadr al-Jilani. Likewise, the influx of more orthodox notions of Islam and wahhabism after independence and the subsequent reactionism to saint worship and spirit possession has caused the Gnawa to be disdained as magicians. Bertrand Hell notes that the Gnawa have used the cover of therapy to continue their rituals and belief system and that all the Sufi ṭuruq and healing ṭa'ifat in Morocco (such as the 'Aissawa, the Darqawa, and others) consider the Gnawa to be the most knowledgeable group, the experts, with regard to the jnun (1999a). Despite this acknowledgment, the Gnawa do not fit in easy categories. Knowledge of their cosmology, even within the ṭa'ifa, has diminished (Pâques 1991; Hell

2002b). They are ambivalent persons, able to enter many worlds, but belonging easily to none but their own:

> The Gnawa call themselves the people of the khla, the hidden part of creation where the genies reign. They are in fact and in essence marginals playing the game of the strange stranger (in the double sense that is contained in the Arabic term gharib). Gatekeepers of a counter world, the Gnawa move in the night and on the limits of the licit. Marked by a fundamental ambiguity, they are transgressors who can handle blood with impunity and can control the most dangerous of forces. Embodying a "troubling strangeness," these descendants of black slaves see themselves as invested with the most powerful supernatural powers. (Hell 1999a: 160)[8]

For Pâques, a student of Marcel Griaule who carries forth his interest in cosmology, the Gnawa are alchemists: "La nuit, c'est toute la forge et les Gnawas sont des forgerons-alchimistes," she says. "The night is the forge and the Gnawa are the blacksmith-alchemists" (1991: 90, translation mine).[9] For Pâques, the ritual "night" (lila) or derdeba (as it is also called) is an enactment of the principles of the universe. The Gnawa cosmology is an ontological reality and not an intellectual ideology. It must be performed to be known. "To enact the derdeba is to 'learn the trade,'" notes Pâques, "to learn how the soul goes from life to death to come back to life, passing through the seven colors of the Universe. These colors are stages of the year and of human life, as well as stages of the barley that, like man, enters raw into death and emerges cooked to serve as food for the demiurge-cherif. The derdeba helps the adept attain these stages" (1991: 255, translation and italics mine).[10] For Pâques, the Gnawa not only experience the transmutation of matter in their bodies as the transmigration of souls, but they facilitate this understanding—which is somatic and rarely conscious—for others. This is why she considers them alchemists.[11]

It is widely acknowledged that when medieval writers spoke of attempts to change base metals into gold, this concept was symbolic of another: namely the quest to purify the human spirit of its drosser elements, to approach a more rarified and spiritual state, and "to reach the intellect via the senses" (Maier quoted in Roob 2001: 11)[12] The alchemists did not adhere to the mind-body split, but considered the spirit and the material inseparably linked. "The alchemists had a general principle, which appears to have summed up perfectly their theoretical reflections," notes Mauss in his General Theory of Magic. "They always prefixed it to their schemes: 'Each one is the whole and the whole is in each one'" (1972 [1902]: 90). In their preoccupation with the materialization of subtle principles, the alchemists had much in common with what religious scholar Henry Corbin has termed the "imaginal world" of Sufi thought, the *mundus imaginalis*, "the realm where invisible realities become visible and corporeal things are spiritualized" (Chittick 1989: ix).[13] The imaginal world is a cornerstone of Sufi philosophy—the esoteric strand of Islamic theology.[14] For Sufi writer Ibn al-'Arabi, for example, the imagination is not a realm of fantasy, but rather the subtle level that mediates between spirit and materiality and is inseparable from both.[15] The imagination is active and agentive since it is the force of imagination that causes the invisible to take form.[16]

THE TASTE OF ADDICTION

Hnaya mrad b-jawi

Allah y-šafu-nah

We have the sickness of incense

May God heal us

—m'allem *Abdellah El Gourd*

Gnawa blitu-nah, a blitu-nah

Gnawa you've intoxicated us, addicted us

—*The late m'allem Sam (Mohammed Zourbat),*

1993, recorded by Antonio Baldassare

We are in the driveway in a middle-class neighborhood in Rabat. Above us green tarp provides a makeshift ceiling, the high cement walls surrounding us are draped with green and red velour cloth. The glint of dawn reflects on the clouds, visible between the top of the walls and the tarp. Inside this interior we are many, huddled together on sunken mattresses, or on the floor shoulder-to-shoulder, women scarved against the night in long silky robes. Sidi Mimun is invoked, the gatekeeper, patron spirit of the Gnawa. His color is black. A woman throws herself violently down before the musicians, then rises up energetically, throwing head and shoulders back and forward, stamping the floor with her feet. She gets down on hands and knees, swaying heavily over the incense, so close her hair might catch on fire. She rises again into deep pelvic contractions, pushing her elbows backward stridently. A red cloth is draped over her shoulders. She seems to be barely conscious of it. The Gnawa master nods his head in time with her movements. "*Khadam 'ali-ha,*" he tells her, "work for it." The sexual innuendo, I believe, is intended. His fingers and her limbs move in tandem. When the song is over she collapses on the floor and is pulled to the side by another woman who caresses her and sprinkles her brow with flower water. The lights are turned off. Another song begins. The Gnawa are playing loudly, clacking their heavy cymbals together, calling Aisha Qandisha, the genie of threshold and danger. Two women trance madly before us in the din. Yet calm reigns. We are all drunk on fatigue and incense and sound.

Mbliyin. Intoxicated.

The force of Eros is, itself, a kind of spirit inhabiting these ceremonies. The sensuality of gyrating bodies, the thick smells of incense and sweat, the attention that is proffered on those who have just fallen, the moment of ravissement, when eyes roll backward and the body and spirit both find release—all invoke an ambiance of emotional and bodily intimacy. Women attend carefully to other women in these ceremonies. Women who have fallen are perfumed with rose water, stroked, and kissed until they return to their senses. Csordas defines such somatic modes of attention as "culturally elaborated ways of attending to and with one's body in surroundings that include the embodied presence of others" (1993: 138). The somaticism of these ceremonies is particular. Experienced trancers seem to have proprioceptive facility even when deep in trance. Although less-experienced trancers may bump into others or fall over the incense brazier, such incidents are rare. Rather, once they rise up the spirits are aware of each other in space, aware of the body hexis of their host and other hosts. The possessed sometimes remember their possessions and sometimes do not.[17]

Sexual energy is also present in the ceremonies. The prowess of different Gnawa masters is a topic of clandestine gossip. Some women are rumored to have had affairs with the masters. Some masters are sexually aligned with their mqaddemat. Although there is no general rule regarding such practices—no ritual sex of any kind proscribed—the promiscuity of at least some of the male Gnawi is well known and does not tarnish, indeed only augments, their ritual status. As one scholar of the Gnawa put it, "m'allem M, m'aruf, Master M, he's well known [for his sexual escapades]. They say that he even does it between nubas [spirit propitiation 'numbers'] in the back room. He's known for having had more women than all the others." Whether sexually consummated or not, the master always has an intimate relationship with the possessed, and the discourse of sexual performance is present in the community. He divines their spirits, knows details about their personal lives, and is the conduit for their emotional and spiritual healing. Eroticism is not necessarily sexual practice, but a sexualized imaginary that tinges experiences with a certain hue and energy. As Georges Bataille notes, "The whole business of eroticism is to destroy the self-contained character of the participators as they are in their normal lives" (1986: 17). Not only do the *spirits* challenge the "self-contained character" of propitiants then, but the relations between the inhabited (*maskunin*) and the Gnawa, also break open a space of Eros not found in normative experience.

MUSICAL MAGIC IN HISTORY

Music, magic, and Eros; these forces form a trilogy that is almost a cliché. Nonetheless it is worth noting the historical precedents for such matrices. Citing medieval theologians has become commonplace for those discussing Sufism and traditions such as the Gnawa's that developed in a Sufi-imbued milieu.[18] This has several effects: (1) it elucidates a theological tradition that is also very much a philosophical one, thereby revealing a non-Western metaphysical tradition usually unknown to anyone other than specialists; (2) it brings attention to a metaphysics that does not necessarily privilege the visual, and thus exhibits a different hierarchy of the senses than that in Western tradition (Gouk 2004), and (3) it connects contemporary practices to a past that seems to presage the present, thus creating a historical link, a continuity that may or *may not* be recognized by the present practitioners. Invoking the medieval texts, then, involves the scholar in a process of historiography. Through the linking together of stories, influences are created and the meaning of contemporary tradition "reinvented" (Hobsbawm and Ranger 1983).

This said, scholars frequently remark on the correspondences between medieval theology and contemporary musical practices. In the European Renaissance, for example, music was endowed with the power to actively create harmony at all levels of existence, from the body to the stars. In particular, "harmony created from dissimilarity" (*discordia concors*) was thought to balance the dualities of sympathy and antipathy, sameness and difference, in the cosmos (Tomlinson 1993: 50).[19] As Gary Tomlinson's study of music and magic in the Italian Renaissance makes clear, both music and magic employ sounds (incantation) to effect a transformation—magic seeking to control supernatural powers, and music manipulating the emotions.[20] He cites the texts of sixteenth-century magician/philosopher Agrippa (*De Occulta Philosophia*) on the power of music as a form of celestial magic that included "ecstatic trances and frenzied possessions" (Tomlinson 1993: 59–60).[21] Through its powers of mimesis, music magic was thought to affect bodies, manipulate the energies of the stars, and induce gnosis in ecstatic and possessed states.[22]

The European metaphysical tradition surrounding music and magic has some relevance for contemporary enactments of possession as well. As Erlmann notes, "sound not only figured prominently in the thinking of Renaissance theorists and early modern Englishman but was the chief medium for enacting transitions from one realm to another" (2004: 6; Gouk 2004, 1999). Indeed, following Pâques's work on the Gnawa, there are close correspondences between their cosmology and Agrippa's theory of musical magic (1991; Hell 2002a, 2002b). The correspondence is not completely fortuitous. While music was an undeniably magical force in the European Renaissance, beliefs about the power of sound were inextricable from beliefs about the imagination, and both were indebted to earlier texts of Islamic philosophy, astrology, and mysticism.[23] The ancient Greek philosophers, it should be said, were as influential for Muslim thinkers like Ibn Rushd (1126–1198), Ibn Sina (980–1037), and al-Farabi (c. 870–950) as they were for Agrippa.[24] Nonetheless, without entering into debates about when the Renaissance began and with whom, it is clear that Arab thought played an important part in European Renaissance thinking about magic and music, particularly for tenth-century Arab philosopher and astrologer al-Kindi, for whom objects or beings in the universe possessed radiations that affected all other beings (Couliano 1987: 14; Hourani 1991, 1992). Following al-Kindi, humans not only emit and receive these radiations (and their accompanying emotions), but can actually induce them through mental imagery, gesture, and most importantly, sound (Couliano 1987: 120–121).[25]

The relation of music and magic, then, has historical basis, but so does music's relation to Eros. Building upon the work of al-Kindi, Italian magician Marcilio Ficino (1433–1499) asserted that "the whole power of Magic is founded on Eros" (Ficino quoted in Couliano 1987: 87, 119).[26] In the trilogy of body, soul, and spirit that he thought comprised the human being, Ficino advanced the theory that spirit (*pneuma*) was the substance that conveyed "the animating force of the soul to the body and the stimuli received by the corporeal senses back to the soul" (Tomlinson 1993: 106). In other words, spirit was a translator of sorts, an aspect of the imaginal world, a kind of *barzakh* between the body and the soul (Corbin 1998).[27] More relevant for this discussion, Ficino equated this spirit with music; both were composed of air, and both relied on movement. Ficino invested music with the power to possess:

Musical sound moreover moves the body by the movement of the air; by purified air it excites the airy spirit, which is the bond of body and soul; by emotion it affects the senses and at the same time the soul; by meaning it works on the mind; finally, by the very movement of its subtle air it penetrates strongly; by its temperament it flows smoothly; by its consonant quality it floods us with a wonderful pleasure; by its nature, both spiritual and material, it at once seizes and claims as its own man in his entirety. (Ficino quoted in Tomlinson 1993: 111)[28]

The spiritual and material power of music to "seize" and "claim" the human being is related to Ficino's belief that music had great mimetic ability. He asserted that song "imitates and enacts everything so forcefully that it immediately provokes both the singer and hearers to imitate and enact the same thing" (Ficino quoted in Tomlinson 1993: 112). Such mimesis found application in the conjuring of demons as well. For if music could mimetically evoke and harness celestial radiations, it could also provoke, indeed create, demons—beings thought to inhabit the air, ether, and watery vapors. Indeed, for magicians of the Renaissance, the creative power of the imagination was itself a kind of demon or genie, and both music and demons acquired "true existence" via the imagination (Tomlinson 1993: 124–125).[29] Sixteenth-century philosopher Giordano Bruno also made a clear connection between Eros, affect, and power: "[H]e who wishes to bind [i.e., the magician] is obliged to develop the same emotions as he who must be bound," he noted, with the exception that the binder must not be possessed by these emotions, but must learn to cultivate and control them. "He must, indeed, cultivate assiduously the same passion he wishes to arouse in his victims, taking care, however, not to be possessed by his own phantasms and never to aspire to the assuagement of desire, else the strength of the bond disappears" (quoted in Couliano 1987: 101). As Mauss asserts, the magician controls his possessions, while the entranced does not (1972 [1902]: 49).

The philosophies of the Arab East certainly filtered through those of Europe, but also traveled to Africa with Islam. Nor have these beliefs disappeared, in Europe, in the United States, or in Morocco. They are part and parcel of the commemorative rituals of the Gnawa and are also couched in discourses surrounding African American avant-garde music as it intersected with the history of the Afro-futurist movement, the interest in ancient Egypt, and the ideas of Hermes Trismegistus (Szwed 1997, 2005; see chapter nine). Insofar as magic is a "science of the imaginary," it has given rise to many strands of history, including that of the social sciences and humanities. As religious scholar Ioan P. Couliano notes, both "magic and science . . . represent needs of the imagination, and the transition from a society dominated by magic to a predominantly scientific society is explicable primarily by a change in the imaginary (1987: xviii–xix). The discourses about music and magic in the Renaissance come back to haunt the musical imagination in the twentieth and twenty-first centuries as well.

THE DESIRE FOR ENTRANCEMENT

Trance is called *jadba* in Moroccan Arabic, from the classical Arabic verb *ja-dha-ba*, to attract. The entranced are *majdhūbīn*, attracted and attractive (to God, to the spirits). Attraction, of course, cannot be separated from desire. Indeed desire plays an important role in Sufism, where the metaphor of the longed-for "beloved" is used to talk about one's relationship with God. "Between lover and beloved the pleasure (*ladhdha*) of encounter (*liqa'*) is greater than the pleasure of unceasing companionship," notes Ibn al-'Arabi (Chittick 1989: 106). Estranged from the beloved, the desire for meeting is increased— the desire for approaching the divine through experiencing a state or *ḥal* of spiritual communion. In Sufism, it is the intensity of desire for God that brings one near to him. And although this desire is a spiritual one, the metaphors used to elicit it are corporeal. In the case of trance, however, the desire is also acknowledged as a sexual one. Indeed, the possessed often refer to their possessors in sexual terms. Tuhami, the main interlocutor in Vincent Crapanzano's book of the same name, feels himself to be married to the *jinniya* Aisha Qandisha, for example (1980). The relationship between the possessed and their *malk* is not that different than that between lover and beloved. There are conflicts and disagreements but there are also ecstatic experiences, as well as moments when the body may be transcended altogether. Indeed it is common to see Gnawi run sharp knives over their tongues or candle flames and hot wax over their chests without wincing and without injury. Such mortification practices also exist in Sufism. An early Sufi named Sarraj, for example, was said to have "put his face on the fireplace and prostrated himself before God in the midst of the fire without being hurt" (Schimmel 1975: 84). Such feats, which seem to defy nature, are signs of being in a state of grace, *baraka*. In such states spirit is not embodied so much as the body takes on the attributes of the spirit—it becomes invulnerable and protected. Acts such as slashing oneself with knives, exposing the skin to flames, cutting off one's oxygen by pulling a scarf tightly around the neck, and eating glass are common elements of Gnawa ritual and testify to what we might call the "alchemical transformation" of the body as it supercedes itself in altered states of consciousness. The realization of such states is a primary experience of ritual life for the Gnawa; however achieving these states is less dependent upon the desire of the practitioner to extinguish herself in divine than upon mastering communication with the *spirits* who enter the body and induce trance (Fuson 2001; Hell 2000).[30] Such experiences, especially when they are known in youth, mark one's subjectivity; they are what Jean Françios Lyotard would refer to as initiatory events: "[W]hat makes an encounter with a word, smell, place, book, or face into an event," notes Lyotard, "is not its newness when compared to other 'events.' It is its very value as initiation. You only learn this later. It cut open a wound in the sensibility. You know this because it has reopened since and will reopen again, marking out the rhythm of a secret and perhaps unnoticed temporality" (1992: 106).

The notion of a secret temporality entered through the wound is very Sufic in nature and one that applies to Gnawa ritual, where the initial encounter with the possessing *jinn* is lived first as an affliction, but which then has the potential of turning into a vehicle of empowerment. What is the nature of this temporal and sacred wound?

SOMATIC MEMORY AND ENSLAVEMENT

It is no accident that initiates into the Gnawa *ṭa'ifa* become symbolic slaves (Pâques 1991).[31] Cathy Caruth asserts that "[w]hat causes trauma . . . is a shock that appears to work very much like a bodily threat but is in fact a break in the mind's experience of time" (1996: 61). A temporal rift is not void however; other temporalities flood in like spirits to occupy the traumatized subject. The temporality of the wound inhabits history as a repetition, like a record that skips, repeating the same phrase over and over. Henceforth the temporality of the wound may even be invoked by this "other" rhythm.

The temporal and spatial displacements of slavery and the somatic memory of slavery in the body and in ritual are evoked in the Gnawa ceremony. The wound returns in ritual guise, this time as a point of distinction. The ceremony gives the wound a voice and yet also repeats the scene of the wounding metaphorically, as literal wounds are inflicted on the body with fire, blades, and other mortification practices (Caruth 1996: 2–3). This time, however, the body is invulnerable, the wound thereby symbolically healed—at least temporarily, for the wound never fully disappears. Spirits cannot be exorcised. The necessity to repeat the ceremony is perennial. If the propitiation ceremony is not enacted regularly, the propitiant falls ill again. This is, in part, because the initial wound was indelible, incurring a "breach in the mind's experience of time, self, and the world—[which] is not, like the wound of the body, a simple and healable event . . . but rather . . . returns to haunt the survivor later on" (Caruth 1996: 4). Because the experience of the first wound was not assimilated (be it slavery or spirit possession) it remains "unclaimed," and thus is destined to repeat itself symbolically in the future.

Certainly not all the participants in Gnawa lilas remember pasts in slavery. Indeed, there are very few who do. There is evidence to suggest, however, that trauma is passed on intergenerationally (Caruth 1995; Young 2002b; L. Brown 1995). Katharine Young asserts that trauma and other affective states are passed on through somatic memories embedded and embodied in gestures. Fear, anxiety, and other effects of oppression are learned unconsciously in the techniques of the body passed on through family members and other caretakers.[32] These physical and emotional gestures embody attitudes toward the social world, ones that may not be recognized by their carriers at all. It is in such a context that the Gnawa may be said to keep alive the memory of slavery in their pasts (as well as in more conscious evocations of this history in the lyrics of their songs). They are "commemorative rituals," ceremonies that carry social memory in the body and its gestures (Connerton 1989). These ceremonies attract those whose wounds are bound up with oppression, whether racial or sexual (Boddy 1989). Indeed, the ceremonies born of the wounds of slavery go on to cure wounds originating in other forms of domination. The wound defines the community. With trauma, "[I]t is always the story of the wound that cries out, that addresses us in the attempt to tell us of a reality or truth that is not otherwise available. This truth, in its delayed appearance and its belated address, cannot be linked only to what is known, but also to what remains unknown in our very actions and our language" (Caruth 1996: 4). It is thus not surprising that throughout the ceremony a call is made to God and to the saints for healing: allah y-'afu. allah y-šafi. May God forgive. May God heal.

The nature of the wound in the case of Gnawa spirit possession is both personal and social. Moroccan sociologist Abdelhai Diouri suggests that possession is (must be) the result of a transgression, an act against nature, sometime in the past (1979). For Diouri, the event of possession must have an initiatory moment, something to blame. The wound is a result of this transgression. In the case of the Gnawa, it is not a self-inflicted wound so much as the wound of slavery and, if we are to believe Diouri, the wound of deferred jouissance; that is, in the case of women (who comprise a majority of the possessed), the wound of patriarchy itself (Lewis 1989 [1971], 1986). There is a clear relation between sexuality and spirit possession. Not only do most future adepts "fall" (become possessed) at puberty, but the relationship with the spirits is discussed in sexual terms.

Despite very real expressions of past trauma, however, it is wrong to collapse the categories of slavery and the Gnawa, especially today when a large number of Gnawa musicians do not come from a sub-Saharan lineage but rather apprentice themselves to masters (some who trace their lineage back to sub-Saharan Africa, others who cannot). The fetishization of blackness that is present in Euro-American expressive culture is not absent in Morocco. Just as the slave song became an emblem of and a means to healing after the Civil War in America, the music of the Gnawa plays a symbolic role "as a primordial cure for the ills of a civilized and increasingly mechanized [and postcolonial] modern society," both in Morocco and in the African diaspora more generally (Radano 2000: 460).

HEALING

If the wound (of slavery and other forms of hegemony) is always present in the Gnawa ceremonies, so is the availability for healing. These ceremonies are, after all, rituals that intend to heal the wound through the music and incense that permeate the body and bring through the spirits and through sacred words that resonate within the body. In the invocation to Sidi Mimun Seryamu, for example, we find these solicitations:

> l-'afu mulana / a mimun l'afu mulana
> w r-rja f-llah al-'ali / w r-rja f-llah al-'ali
> a sidi dawi ḥal-i / mimun seryamu
> rabbi dawi-ni / a mimun rabbi dawi-ni
> llah y-dawi a sidi / w llah y-šafi

> Forgiveness oh my God / oh mimun, forgiveness oh God
> Hope is with God the Highest / Hope is with God the Highest
> Oh sir heal my state / Mimun Seryamu
> My Lord heal me / oh Mimun, Lord heal me
> May God cure oh sir / and may God heal[33]

Hope—rja—may also be translated here as "expectation" or "anticipation." People come to the ceremonies with the hope but also with the intention to be healed. Healing also comes through forgiveness, as in the song of the same name, "al-'afu":

l-'afu ya mulana l-'afu / ṣ-ṣla 'ala nabina l-'afu
l-'afu rijal-llah l-'afu / hurmati Muḥammad l-'afu
ṣ-ṣla 'ala nabina l-'afu / barakat- Muḥammad l-'afu
llah llah l-'afu / l-'afu ḍif-llah l-'afu
y-henn llah l-'afu / llah y-šafi l-'afu
ṣ-ṣla 'ala nabina l-'afu / l-'afu mulay driss l-'afu
l-'afu syadi llah l-'afu / la illaha illa llah l-'afu
l-'afu ya mulana l-'afu

Forgiveness, oh my Owner / prayers on our Prophet, forgiveness
Forgiveness, men of God, forgiveness / my holiness Mohammed, forgiveness
Prayers on our Prophet, forgiveness / the blessings of Mohammed, forgiveness
God God, forgiveness / forgiveness, guests of God, forgiveness
May God provide ease, forgiveness / May God heal, forgiveness
Prayers on our Prophet, forgiveness / forgiveness, Mulay Idriss, forgiveness
Forgiveness, sirs of God, forgiveness / there is no God but God, forgiveness
Forgiveness, oh my Owner, forgiveness (Welte and Aguadé 1996: 55, translation mine)

In this song the word "forgiveness" functions to create parallelism between all the lines. It is repeated after each phrase, after each invocation and prayer. Mulana, "my owner,"[34] is not a reference to the possessing spirit, but is a synonym for God. There are three verbs of healing that recur frequently in the ceremonies, all as implorations to God and the spirits: dawa, šafa, and 'afa. Dawa means to treat or cure a patient, but etymologically it has a relation to sound. Indeed, in one form of the Arabic verb,[35] dawa means to cure, but another form,[36] dawwa, is to sound, to resound, to drone, echo or reverberate. šafa means to heal or cure; 'afa means to forgive, to excuse, or to relieve. While these words are chanted repeatedly over the course of hours, their effects come not only through their referential meaning (though that plays a part) but also from their performative efficacy. That is, the repetition of sacred words has a healing effect on the body—both because the sacred names of God and the Prophet are considered to contain healing power, and because, like trance, the rhythmic repetitions of the words connect them to a sensorium in which the body opens to healing forces (see chapters three and four).

As in many such healing rituals, effectiveness is tied to the ability of ritual to restructure the hierarchy of the senses and to bring the senses and often the environment into alignment through sound and other aesthetic means.[37] Healing rituals help "fuse" different sensory phenomena into a sense of health and wholeness (Stoller 1989a). As Charles L. Briggs notes, "[T]he performance of ritual induces some degree of fusion among signaling modalities and a condensation of their function" (1996: 189). Briggs demonstrates the complex interplay that creates the work of healing among the Warao of Venezuela by examining the parallelism of the chanted words, the structure of the melodic line, and other dimensions of the poetics of healing. He focuses particularly on the metapragmatic functions of words in the healing context. Pragmatic linguistic forms tie the narrative act to the context of their enunciation, but metapragmatic forms make interlocutors *aware* of this linking function; in other words, metapragmatics create reflexivity (Briggs 1996; Silverstein 1976, 1996). Briggs cites the use of meaningless vocables in the Warao healing ritual as signs that draw attention to both the presence of the spirits and to the performance of healing that they affect. The sounds of words alert the healer and the person being healed that transformation is taking place. The double process whereby referential and poetic functions of language are deployed to effect healing will be explored in greater depth in chapter four. It is worth noting here that the components of healing in the Gnawa ceremony correspond in many ways to those delineated by anthropologist Thomas Csordas in his analysis of the healing ceremonies of Catholic charismatics in the United States (Csordas 1996: 96; 1994b):

1. The rituals are *public*; they are thus performance events in which the healers—whether spirits, Gnawa musicians, or female *mqaddemat*—assume responsibility to an audience for a display of communicative competence (Bauman 1977).
2. The rituals are enacted by *performance genres*, in the form of musical suites (*nubat*) divided into cuts or numbers (*qiṭ'a*) devoted to a particular spirit. Each suite has its corresponding color and a subpantheon of spirits that manifest within it.
3. Within these performance genres, verbal incantations, and invocations, codified gestures and trance ensue (chapter three). These acts in part

create the healing, thus *the ritual language itself is performative* (Austin 1962).

4. The rituals have a *rhetoric*, a terminology, largely metaphorical, that defines the community of trance. Concepts like *tagnawit* (authentic Gnawa identity); being inhabited (*maskun*), falling to the spirits, having the spirits rise up within you, and what I will turn to now: "working the spirits."

WORKING THE SPIRITS

It is a remarkable fact that a magician, to a certain extent, can control his possession:
he brings it on by appropriate practices, such as dancing, monotonous music or intoxication.
To sum up, one of the magician's professional qualifications, which is not only mythical
but practical, is the power of being possessed and it is a skill at which they have
long been expert. . . . The liaison between a magician and his spirit often
develops into a complete identity one with the other.
—Marcel Mauss (1972 [1902]: 49).

According to Mauss's definition above, Si Mohammed is, indeed, a magician insofar as he controls his own possession. The ability to go into trance at will is called "working the spirits." It denotes a mastery of the possession state and an ability to serve others in the capacity of an adept. There are many recognized stages of initiation in the Gnawa *ṭa'ifa*, some of which correspond with chronological age. Children of all ages attend the ritual lilas (see figure 4).

Possession, especially when one belongs to a family whose members fall to the spirits, often occurs at puberty. At this time, however, the spirits control the propitiant, demanding sacrifice, incense, and acknowledgement. Over the next several years it is common for more spirits to inhabit the host, though one (usually the first to arrive) "rules" over the head. These years of perpetual accommodation are often fraught with drama and tension as spirits are divined, ceremonies held, dreams dreamed, and stories recounted.

The *mqaddema* Malika explained it this way, when I asked her about the obligations of the possessed vis-à-vis their spirits: The possessed woman, she said, "must follow the conditions [they impose] from year to year, or if she receives a lot of people, if a lot of people are visiting, she does what they need done (*kat-dir li-hum dak-shi dyal-hum*). And each time you work, you also have Gnawa working at your home. They [the spirits] don't do anything to you. To the contrary. They're good. They give her good luck (*rzaq*), and they give her

FIGURE 4: Children at a possession ceremony. Photograph, Joel Sherzer

health, and they stand by her (kay-waqfu ma'-ha). They don't do anything to her, they don't hurt her. To the contrary."[38]

"But they don't leave?"

"No. They stay. And they protect her. She doesn't have a reason to fear. In any circumstances, if she's walking down the street or someplace where she's going to be uncomfortable, if there's someone there or something, they're there surrounding her. They're surrounding her. She's in the middle, and they're all around her. She doesn't need to be afraid of anything! Anything that wants to hurt her, no one can hurt her."

"Sometimes I wonder how a woman who is possessed by many spirits feels—as if she has many selves?" I said.

"Many . . . no. You don't feel them. Only at the times when you're working, like during a Gnawa lila. That's all, the mluk are all standing there (waqfin), they're all encircling [you]. But in normal [life] you don't feel anything [different]."

"But they say that the jwad rule over her. Does she rule herself? Who rules over her?" I asked.

"They rule. The one who is reasonable (ma'qol) in her rules over her. The one in her who is designated. He's the one who rules. He's the one who rules.

There's one who inhabited her first. The one who got there first, he's the one that is meant for her. *ahuh.*

"If they see that there's something not quite right, you didn't fix something well, they oppose you. They'll start appearing to you always, until you do it right. But if you fix it for them again, real good, as they want, then they'll leave you alone, they won't bother you. That's it; you vow your submission to them [*kat-tlubi min-hum tslim*] and then they leave you alone."

As the possessed woman becomes accustomed to her spirits, she slowly learns to understand and cater to their whims. Her trances become more controlled. Instead of being thrown to the floor by the spirits, she may calmly get up to trance when the music of her spirit is played. As she ages, marries, has children, and perhaps divorces, people will call her *sherifa*, a title of respect for a middle-aged woman.[39] At this time she may learn to "work the spirits," to divine them in others, to "see" as a clairvoyant, to help younger and less experienced women (and men) manage their possessions. In other words there is a movement from being possessed by the spirits to a self-possession where one is in control of the possession experience. As ethnomusicologist Deborah Wong astutely notes, when "performing bodies . . . enact historical memories of subjectivization and injury. . . those memories [may be rescued] by refashioning their labor as cultural work" (2000: 67). The metaphor of "working in spirits" has resonance on many levels: not only is agency given to the possessed who work them, but also the labor performed in slavery is symbolically "rescued."

The social nature of trance is well known. Trance effected in solitude is unavailable for mimetic reproduction as a technique of the body. Gilbert Rouget calls these solitary states "ecstatic"; they are characterized, he says, by immobility, sensory deprivation, and recollection. Trance on the other hand, to continue following Rouget, is accompanied by noise, sensory overstimulation, movement, company, and amnesia (1985: 11). Such categories always have their exceptions. There are people in Morocco who do remember their trance possessions, for example, and others who do not. Lewis distinguishes between trance as a psychophysiological state and possession as *a cultural-specific theory* that explains trance (Lewis 1989: 9).[40] Indeed, in Morocco there are those who experience possession trance and those who experience other kinds of trance (self-induced, music-induced). Rather than debate the categories and their authenticity and applicability, I rely on the testimonies of the possessed, as well as my own phenomenological descriptions (Merleau-Ponty 1962), using the vocabulary that is current among *shab al-hal*. It is within this community that trance takes on its meaning, as spirits are divined, visions recounted, experiences interpreted, and desires cultivated.

THE ALCHEMY OF PLEASURE AND PERCEPTION

Women talk about possession trance as a kind of addiction or intoxication (al-blia). Even the songs of the ceremony make use of this metaphor. In the opening of the lila, in a song called "yubadi," for example, the Gnawa sing,

> yubadi ya yubadi / yubadi ya llah llah
> yubadi mša l-s-sudan / yubadi jab l-luban
> yubadi ya llah llah / yubadi rijal llah
> llah y-bli-k b-ḥubb llah / ḥetta ta-lbas d-derbala

> Yubadi oh Yubadi / Yubadi oh God God
> Yubadi went to Sudan / Yubadi brought back amber
> Yubadi oh God God / Yubadi oh men of God
> [May] God intoxicate you with the love of God / until you wear the rags
>   [of bu-derbala]. (Welte and Aguadé 1996: 37)

If the wound or transgression defines initiation, pleasure is also a large part of the experiences that open to the adept. Al-ḥubb llah, the love of God, is a spiritual force that transforms. It is a state, or ḥal, that is so powerful that people become mendicants and wanderers, dressed in rags (as the figure of bu-derbala in the Gnawa pantheon). Yubadi is an African spirit, and the "men of God" is a euphemism for the spirits in general. The Gnawa are invoking the spirits, and Yubadi in particular, but also God and his love. "Llah y-bli-k b-ḥubb llah, May God intoxicate you with His love," is a ḍa'wa, an oath that may also be a prayer (Kapchan 1996, as well as chapter nine).

In the Sufi worldview, a ḥal is a state in which one may be either "present" to the senses and to the body or "absent," unconscious of one's bodily state, transported out of the body, so to speak. Al-ḥaḍra (presence) is a synonym for a kind of ecstatic trance and evokes the presence of God, while al-gha'ib (absence) is a synonym for the exile of the Sufi whose life goal is to return "home." The pain of exile is alleviated only in the presence of God. For Sufis, al-ḥal is a state of oneness (tawḥid) with God. In daily parlance, al-ḥal refers to an altered state of consciousness, one that is often spontaneous: it comes from God (min 'and-llah) and not from the ego (nafs) and thus brings grace to its bearer. Whereas imitation of gestures associated with ecstasy can bring on such a state of communion, listening is another way to induce these states. It is the music that calls the spirits to manifest, and the ear of the propitiant that senses them.

Listening has a special status among Islamic mystics. The act of *sama'* (literally "listening") is active and transformative. It is the key to the door of the subtle and higher emotions. Listening is a way of perceiving the world that then changes the things perceived for the perceiver and consequently for the intersubjective world that the perceiver inhabits. The Sufi path utilizes the senses, bringing the initiate to God not through the obliteration of feeling (though *al-fna'* [extinction] is a Sufi metaphor for those who die to the world and are born in the spirit), but through a heightening and refining of the senses and the emotions. The role of imagination here is patent. Imitating the gestures of devotion brings image, body, and emotion into a recognizable (because historical) correspondence. This is not unlike the process of "ethical listening" described by anthropologist Charles Hirshkind in his study of a community of Muslims in contemporary Egypt who listen to audiocassette sermons in order to create a more perfect moral character. For Hirshkind, the practice of ethical listening itself hones the perception and brings the world to which those practices aspire into being: "[P]roper sermon audition," he says, "demands a particular affective-volitional responsiveness from the listener—what I will call an ethical performance—as a condition for understanding sermonic speech, while simultaneously deepening an individual's capacity to hear in this manner. To 'hear with the heart,' as those I worked with described this activity, is not strictly something cognitive but involves the body in its entirety, as a complex synthesis of disciplined moral reflexes" (2001: 624). The metaphor of "hearing with the heart" is grounded in the Sufi notion that active listening is related to and may transform the moral being.[41] Such practices are imbued with "sensory histories," that is, they involve a particular configuration of the senses, as well as a repertoire of emotions—a sensibility—associated with them: "[T]o listen properly . . . is to engage in a performance, the articulated gestures of a dance (Hirshkind 2001: 624, 626).[42]

Perception is an active power. In order for it to be a pleasure an "inward sense" is required; beyond audition, this sense is not found in the ear (at least not for the Sufis), but in the heart: According to al-Ghazzali,

The cause of those States befalling the heart through listening to music is the secret of God Most High, and consists in a relationship of measured tones to souls and in the subjection of souls to them and their receiving impressions by them—longing and joy and sorrow and elation and depression. The knowledge of the cause why souls receive impressions through sounds belongs to the most subtle of the sciences of the Revelations which Sufis are granted, and the foolish, the frozen, the hard of heart, who are shut off from the pleasure of music and poetry, marvels how he that listens takes pleasure and at his ecstasy and state of emotion and change of colour. . . . And for all that there is one cause, and it is that pleasure is a kind of perception and perception demands a thing perceived and a power of perceiving. Then, in the case of him whose power of perception is imperfect, that he should have pleasure through it is not to be imagined. How can he perceive the pleasure of things to eat who lacks the sense of taste, and how can he perceive the pleasure of melodies who lacks ear, and the pleasure that lies in the conclusion of the reason who lacks reason? Even thus is the tasting of music and singing in the heart. After the sound has reached the ear it is perceived by an inward sense in the heart, and he who lacks that lacks inevitably the pleasure that goes with it. (al-Ghazzali as translated by MacDonald 1901: 230)

It is a subtle sense that translates the senses one to another such that music is not just heard but "tasted." In Sufism, taste is an important and central sense. Dhawq, taste, is a kind of initiation—knowledge, whether of the divine or of the profane, is not truly possessed until it is tasted, blending with the perceiver, ingested, inundating the individual. Ibn al-'Arabi, for example, is concerned with the tasting (dhawq) of Being, which is both to perceive and to be that which truly is (Chittick 1989: 3). Thus is music also tasted, not with the tongue, but with the heart. The awakening of this inward sense is a maqam, or level of initiation that has as a consequence the transformation of perception itself into pleasure.[43] Al-Ghazzali is describing the eidetic (and metapragmatic) moment when one is aware of oneself perceiving the world and such perception becomes wondrous. It is as if the emotional tenor of the phenomenal world changes, accompanied by a change of color as well. For al-Ghazzali emotions have a hue, while for the Gnawa, each spirit has a color.

The translation of the senses is present in other aspects of Gnawa ritual life. Incense, which is essential to the manifestation of the spirits, at times becomes food. There are those who say that they actually bring up jawi, or benzoin, from their inner organs: "kan-rudd aj-jawi," several women told me over the course of my research, "I bring up (or vomit) benzoin." As jawi is a food of the spirits, those who can actually produce jawi become, themselves, food for the jnun. Others eat *jawi*. A resinous rocklike substance, it has a soapy taste that is not easily forgotten and that stays in one's taste buds long after it is spit out. Whether eating or spitting up *jawi*, the incorporation of what is usually smelled is a way of translating the senses one to another—synaesthesia, yes, but also an embodiment of purifying and powerful substances, ones that are sacrilized and sacrilizing. The power of olfaction is married to the mystical agency of taste.[44] Pleasure is the result of the union.

But one can become accustomed to pleasure, used to "tasting the music and singing in the heart." Indeed al-Ghazzali acknowledges that "Custom is the Fifth Humour," by which he means that imitation—even of the Glorious States—forms habits that are then naturalized and thereafter hard to break. Once learned, passion—whether for a love object or for music—may be impossible to shake. This is what Moroccans refer to as being *mbli*, addicted to or afflicted with something. Addictions to alcohol, to cannabis, and to wantonness are all considered misfortunes, maledictions to be overcome; they are also "states" (*aḥwal*, pl.), but ones that are pitiable, especially since they are not usually volitional. But the verb *ba la a* in Moroccan Arabic has many finely nuanced meanings that are not all pejorative. It refers to intoxications of all sorts, including the intoxication with the divine. "And of those who fall into ecstasy there are some whom a state overcomes which is like that drunkenness which confounds the reason," warns al-Ghazzali (1997: 710).[45]

As Janice Boddy illustrates in her analysis of the *zar* ceremonies in Sudan, even practices such as female genital excision are so embedded in systems of aesthetics that it is almost impossible to opt out of the system without great social stigma. For Boddy such overdetermination is one of the factors contributing to the practice of spirit possession in the Sudanese community in which she worked, where the smooth, the closed, the pure, the fecund, and the beautiful are equated, and the excised woman becomes a embodiment of these qualities. Women who cannot conform to the ideal of womanhood (mothering sons, for example), often find themselves possessed, entering a repertoire of feeling and experience outside the sanctioned norms (Boddy 1989). The culture of possession in Morocco also has a complex system of aesthetic meaning and value (though one totally unrelated to circumcision practices). When I asked the Tangier *m'allem* Abdellah El Gourd about the significance of incense in the ritual ceremonies, for example, he scoffed and said, "We have the sickness of *jawi*. May God heal us." His remarks index the detrimental, even addictive aspects of the aesthetic complex of spirit possession. The culture of possession is compelling to the point of compunction precisely because it involves the subject in a sensory domain that joins smell and sound to movement and trance, the energy of Eros to the propitiation of spirits, and this amalgam takes one outside the bounds of normative experience. The possessed person is implicated in a lifelong relationship with the spirits that requires propitiation in the form of animal sacrifice, incense, and music. The emotion created in these performances is dramatic and begs to be reproduced. And indeed, control over the emotions and the particular sensory configurations with which they co-occur is a key to trance activity. "Control of the autonomic bodily responses of emotion and the ability to affect the intensity of those physiological responses is one definition of a trancer," Becker notes. "They are profoundly in control of themselves," paradoxically controlling what is often defined as the uncontrollable (2004: 68). "Working the spirits" is the Moroccan idiom for this control, while intoxication/addiction qualifies the experience.

"Mbliya bi-hum, I'm addicted to them," Sukayna told me about her relation to the Gnawa. "I need to hear the music. I need to smell the incense. I need to trance."

One common complaint about the Gnawa is that they use their powers to addict people to their music and to their placation ceremonies, which do not come free of charge.

"Les Gnaouas sont rapaces," a Moroccan scholar of the Gnawa told me in the beginning phase of my research, "the Gnawa are rapacious." It was a strong warning. "Kay-ḥalbu-k," he said, "they milk you."

Tasting such pleasure as the music brings has its price.

◆ 3 ◆
"A GESTURE NARROWLY DIVIDES US FROM CHAOS" GESTURE AND WORD IN TRANCE TIME

◆ ◆ ◆

All these games, these sacrifices, these dances that everyone may attend are, of course, destined to hide the secret knowledge of the initiates, but they also constitute the processes of memory that allow them to find in the slightest detail all the alchemy of the human soul, which is that of the world and of God. —Viviana Pâques (1991: 24)[1]

Incense swirls around me in thick clouds: *jawi, musk, lambre*. The names themselves are intoxicating. Frankincense, musk, myrrh, black and white benzoin, ambergris; the resinous rocks melt on the hot coals of the earthen brazier. Not like wax melts, but first sizzling, the pieces of incense bubble up like hot glass, then drip down the sides of the charcoal as if to envelope and snuff it out. Instead they turn into a yellowish liquid on the reddened coals and almost as quickly the liquid burns and evaporates into a gray-white smoke. This smoke I inhale. From melted stone into gas I inhale its essence, again transmuting substance into substance, the smoke meeting the liquid in my lungs, dissolving into the blood in my veins. And then my brain waves change, electric. The limbs move; the body sways. *Trisitay,* as Moroccans call someone who moves energetically: electricity. This is the alchemy of magic.

Suykayna, the woman sitting to my left is in the Boutshishi ṭariqa. The Boutshishi are in the lineage of the Qadiri Sufis, a mystical form of Islam that originates with the teachings of Abdelqadr Jilani in Persia and follows the chain of lineage through Sidi Boumadyane Ben al-Mnawwaral Qadiri al-Boutshish, to Shaykh Sidi Hajj Abbas and finally to Shaykh Sidi Hamza al-Boutshishi (Ben Driss 2002; Zouanat 1998). For many of the Boutshishis in Morocco, the last in this chain, Shaykh al-Hamza, is the quṭb, the living axis of the faith in this generation. He has a huge following in Morocco, including people from the most elite and powerful sectors of society. Sukayna says that she is a direct descendant of the shaykh. She is about fifty, with thick bones and regular features. There is a Boutshishi pilgrimage site (zawiya) here in Rabat, she informs me. Shaykh Hamza, she says, is her grandfather. Early on in the night she gets up and trances to Jilani, the only saint of her lineage that is honored in the Gnawa lila. He is one of the saints in the "white" pantheon—al-ṣalaḥin, the saints of Islam. Her movements are awkward, jerky. She tells me later that she began to trance to Jilani after her father died. One day the family was gathered together for a ceremony to propitiate the spirits, and she went into trance, totally unconscious until she woke up in the middle of the floor. Despite her unconsciousness, she was aware that her trancing made the entire family cry and also trance. She was the catalyst for a heated session (ḥal).

It is not unusual for death to provoke a possession trance (Diouri 1990). Crying is thought to attract the spirits. The spirits live and thrive around bodies of water—oceans, rivers, creaks, pipes, even tear ducts—places of passage and of transport. The passing of life into death and the grief that it evokes are events that stir the spirit world. Tears, the passage of water from inside to outside the body, leave the body open for passage in the other direction as well. Grieving invites spirit possession, and spirit possession induces grief. Loss (the death of a loved one, divorce) may be accompanied by acquisition (possession by a spirit).

Crying is also an act that triggers social memory (Stoller 1995: 7). Like lamentation, the sentiment that glues a community of trancers (majdubat, fem. pl.) together is the expression of public sentiment (Feld 1982).[2] Indeed, anthropologist and scholar of the Gnawa, Abdelhai Diouri, finds the comportment of grief to be prevalent in Gnawa ceremonies, enacting losses both physical and metaphysical (1990). In Morocco public grieving is signaled by the rising of the voice, scratching and renting of the face, touching (women embrace each other), rocking of the body, and tears. Crying evokes the memories of such embodied performances that, in Morocco, are socially marked as feminine. That spirits enter the body at moments of grief ties the performance of spirit possession to a feminine aesthetic. In grieving, as in possession trance, the body is open to other (affective and spiritual) forces while performing a fairly codified choreography of gesture. While the gestural economy of keening and spirit possession overlap only in part,[3] the indexical links between possession and collective keening are clear: both enact a form of sociability, a community of affect, that is marked as feminine and is created in aesthetic and embodied performance (Urban 1988).[4] Possession trance is "a phenomenological arena in which cultural memory is fashioned and refashioned" (Stoller 1995: 21).

The woman to my right is twenty-nine. Fatna already has three children (the oldest is twelve). She married at seventeen. Her husband just came back from the pilgrimage to Mecca. He is forty-eight.

"Does he object to you having trancing ceremonies?"

"No. He sees me having a crisis, *une crise*," she says, switching momentarily into French from Arabic, "and what can he do?"

She first tranced only four years ago. She heard Gnawa music on television, dropped everything, and started trancing. Since then she has been attending *lilas* and holding one of her own every year during the week of the Prophet's birthday. She says she is possessed (*maskuna*). With whom? I ask.

"*Bzaf*," she says, "Many." Lalla Aisha, Lalla Malika, Lalla Mira, and others. "Every time a new one shows up." She had a *crise* just yesterday, she told me, and then leaves my side in order to trance to the spirits in black.

Fatna's use of the French word *crise* is telling. Literally a "crisis," it is generally used to refer to an episode of hysteria, a condition that early European analysts often attributed to the possessed (Rouget 1985). Indeed, Moroccan women are conscious of the different forms of therapy available to them. A few will even seek help with a psychoanalyst for some of their ailments.[5] Fatna's code-switching indexes the degree to which foreign discourses of spirit possession have entered the local semantic domain, but also her cognizance of competing systems of interpretation. She is able to find herself in the two systems at once, without contradiction (though she doesn't see a therapist herself). But if Fatna recognizes the European attitude toward these practices, she is also aware that she needs to be at a Gnawa *lila* and not on a psychoanalyst's couch. Being inhabited (*maskuna*) may have a symptomology that a European may confuse with hysteria (paralysis, lethargy, unexplainable and recurrent illness), but its treatment is of quite a different order.

The man who hosts the *lila* trances all through the night. He knows all the songs. His wife also just returned from Mecca, though he himself has never made the pilgrimage. Nonetheless he is called al-Hajj (one who has made the pilgrimage) in deference to his age and to his wife, the actual Hajja. He likes chewing tobacco and always asks me to procure him some so his wife, who controls the money, won't know. Despite his age, he is very involved with the Gnawa, going to a lot of their *lilas*. Tonight we are assembled in his tented driveway. Although he trances to many of the pieces, his most moving and pathetic performance is with Sidi Musa, or Moses, the *jinn* of water. He becomes infantlike, wanting to make a run for it to the beach. He has to be restrained, then submits to restraint, screaming bleakly, a desperate empty look in his eyes. He trances and sways, crying out to God for forgiveness (llah y-smaḥ 'ali-nah); he is bathed with water, finally falling down, his small feet and hands yellow, his mouth ajar.

At Sidi Mimun's song I get up to trance, not finding my rhythm right away.[6] The floor beneath my feet is littered with crumbs and under the carpet I feel the uneven rough cement. Closing my eyes, I initially lose my balance and have to slow my movements down to a steadier rhythm in order to keep from falling backwards. Someone covers me with a black scarf, grabbing me by the back of my belt (I later learn that it is the "daughter of Boutshishiyya," bant al-butšišiyya). Then my body is free to counterbalance its movements to her support, my head swaying back and forth. When the music is over, I return to my seat next to her and she tends to me. Later in the evening I can't find a seat, and she pulls me down on the floor in front of her, resting me between her thighs, resting her chin on the top of my head. Her large toenails, painted red, catch my peripheral vision on both sides.

After trancing, women wish each other good health: "b-saḥt-ak," they say.

"The jnun rose up in you last night, eh?" the m'allem Si Mohammed says to me the next morning as we are drinking our breakfast soup in the chill of the coastal morning air.

"I was just moving around," I reply, smiling coyly.

"They rose up in you," he repeats, this time much more somber, ignoring my flippant tone, and goes back to drinking his soup.

As soon as I enacted a trance, Si Mohammed immediately put me in the category of the possessed. Having spent months attending ceremonies (and attending to the bodies in the ceremonies), one night I felt moved to get up and participate. It was a night where many women were present. The floor was packed with bodies. My heart sped up, as it does before a performance, and in an instant I was on the floor, eyes closed, swaying my body as I had watched so many others do. Having grown up with a mother who was a dancer (and having taken lessons myself), I was attuned to the small gestures that make up a "combination"—the tension in the fingertips, the placement of the head in relation to the neck and the rib cage. I had observed how experienced trancers transited from a seated position to join the entranced. I knew the way they held their arms behind their backs, their hands sometimes clasped together, the tilt of their torsos, the rhythmic motion of their chins moving left and right through space. The music was compelling. I could no longer hold back. I got up. At that point, I didn't know what jinn was being propitiated, but someone covered me with a black scarf, and I later realized it was Sidi Mimun.

That night was a turning point in my research. Henceforth I was accepted into the community in a more profound way. I never felt possessed and never asserted that I was. Nonetheless, my bodily participation corresponded with a different level of awareness and imagination. I had visions, lucid dreams in which I felt I was completely conscious. I heard voices. My dream life was populated with the *jnun* of the Gnawa pantheon. I was involved in my own narrations of trance.[7]

ENTRANCING EMOTIONS

My research among the Gnawa began with an emotion of awe. Observing modalities of being-in-the-world that I had never witnessed before, states wherein people cut and burned themselves without evident injury, talked in prophetic voices not their own, and generally evinced emotions of either rapture or total abjection, my initial reaction was to understand not "why" (this had been postulated in numerous studies, with the answer being "therapy," "healing," "resistance," "over-determination," "epilepsy," as well as spirit possession), but rather *how*. How did these women put themselves in altered states of being with such relative ease? How were they able to transition from a state of despondency to one of ecstasy in a matter of seconds without recourse to the cannabis that the male musicians used so freely? How was the performance of trance "keyed" (Bauman 1977; Hymes 1974)?

I spent months studying these transitions—the moments when women moved themselves (or were moved by other beings) to the floor in front of the musicians where the trancing occurs. I found several different genres of transition. There were those who seemed to be forcibly thrown to the floor by a power within, their limbs flailing, their heads whipped violently from left to right, their eyes rolling back in their heads, gasps and gags emitting from their throats. (It is problematic to speak in the second person active voice when discussing these movements, as the impetus and agency of these actions are open to question. Human? Jinn? Unconscious?) In their movements, these women resembled the ritual animals—goats, cows, sheep—that were sacrificed for the propitiation of their spirits, animals in their final moments before expiration, desperately lurching out into a reality fast escaping them. *Al-fna'* (extinction) is a term from Islamic mysticism, evoking a rapturous self-obliteration in the divine, the goal of many mortification rituals.

The women whose gestures were this dramatic were often young, and were either experiencing possession for the first time or were fairly new to the experience. It is frequently the case that once a woman is possessed by one *jinn*, others progressively take up residence within her as well. It is thus not uncommon for women to experience violent possessions for several years, as new spirits "show up" at each ceremony.

More experienced women had other ways of going into trance. Many simply bowed their heads down into their hands, closing their eyes. Dropping the head is a small act of falling; the head, which is often a metonym for the self in Moroccan Arabic, falls before the spirit who then rises up. Lowering the head (often into the hands) is an "iconic" and a conventional (or ritualized) gesture that denotes the transition into possession trance. This was the signal for the mqaddem (the male Gnawa overseer) to hold a brazier of incense under their noses, on which cue the women would get up from their seated position, almost float up out of their seats, and start to go into trance, swaying their bodies back and forth. These women were more in possession of their possession; they had learned how to "work" the spirits or at least how to accommodate them graciously.

There is a finely nuanced notion of subjectivity among women who are multiply possessed. While all experience is authentic and real for the experiencer, judgments about who is truly possessed ("the poor thing") and who is working out stress in an emotional catharsis ("to her health," they say afterwards) are common in the discursive world of trancers.[8] I do not enter into debates about the reality or authenticity of possession here; rather my interests lie in understanding (1) how metaphors of possession inhabit and find their basis in body and gesture, (2) how ritualized gestures effect shifts of temporality (perception, subjectivity), and (3) how women (and men) interpret these new subjectivities to themselves and others. In other words, I will move from an analysis of embodied poesis to one of narrative and poetics, delimiting the connections between these realms.

EMBODIED POESIS

Viviana Pâques asserts that it is neither race nor genealogy per se that defines a Gnawi but the ability to enter into a certain kind of trance. In Pâques' words, this "explains why all blacks are not necessarily Gnawa and why we find whites and mulattos in the [Gnawa] sect. *It is the possibility to go into a certain kind of trance that makes one belong to the 'true race of slavery,'*" she says, "becoming [thus] the slave of God, 'Abdellah'" (1976: 176, emphasis in original). *'abid allah* in Arabic means both worshipper of God and slave or servant of God. Pâques plays on this linguistic ambiguity making the true race of slavery synonymous with the true race of worshippers. Trance becomes a means of worship in this system, one that creates bonds of community among practitioners regardless of race. The "certain kind of trance" to which she refers is intricately related to the experience of spirit possession, to being "owned" by one spirit or many. Following Pâques, trance is the link between slave and master and between human and spirit. What is it about the embodied performance of trance that brings the Gnawa as well as their analysts to define it as this central and symbolic link?

Women in Morocco who are "inhabited" by spirits themselves possess a repertoire of movements that are recognized as preludes to possession-trance. Bowing one's head with closed eyes, for example, signals a focus on the inner world and elicits response from the ritual overseer who witnesses the gesture and comes to aid the propitiant in her movement into trance. Extending the limbs forcibly out, as if electrified, while seemingly being thrown to the ground is another example of a choreography of gestures that facilitates a change of state. These are what I call *gestures of transit*—gestures that bring the subject from one realm of subjective experience to another. In Henri Lefebvre's words these gestures "allow passage from one code or subcode to another, interrupting the one so as to open the way to the other" (1991: 215–216).

Lefebvre is interested in how gestural systems create social space and affect. He asserts, for example, that "organized gestures, which is to say ritualized and codified gestures, are not simply performed in 'physical' space, in the space of bodies. Bodies themselves generate spaces, which are produced by and for their gestures" (1991: 216). He gives the example of the cloister, whose space is determined and created by both the microgestural realm of prayer, walking, eating, and contemplation and the macrogestural realm of communion and sermon. All "gestural systems embody ideology and bind it to practice" notes Lefebvre. "Through gestures, ideology escapes from pure abstraction and performs actions" (Lefebvre 1991: 215). This is not only to say that meaning and power are encoded in the body's gestural repertoires—in "techniques of the body" (Mauss 1979 [1935])—but that these codes are produced as well as transformed at the site of the body and its movement (Bourdieu 1977; Butler 1999).

The ritualized gestures of trance also create a sacred space, but this space is not one of stone, vault, or corridor. Rather the gestures transform existent and usually interior spaces of domesticity into places of sacred play or ritual drama (indeed the introductory part of the ceremony is called *al-la'ba*, "play").

The transformation and sacrilization of space is created in self-conscious gestures at the beginning of the ceremonies, as milk—a pure and purifying substance—is taken from the ceremonial bowl with a ladle and lightly spilled in strategic places: in the four corners of the room, in the four cardinal directions, on the instruments of the Gnawa, and finally, again from the same ladle, into the mouths of the Gnawa themselves, offered also by the mqaddem to all those present at the ceremony. Space is created in commensality and in gesture—in intercorporeal and extracorporeal movements. Such spatial transformations also serve to change the experience of time, of course, from quotidian time to ritual or sacred time.[9]

How do conventional and ritualized gestures enact bodily-based metaphors and perform memories that signal the subject's transition into other states of being, notably possession-trance? To what extent are gestures themselves performatives, creating the reality that they iconically and metaphorically project?[10] The gestures that I examine co-occur with—and, I argue, help effect—a change in being, a dissolution of one socially recognized self and the emergence of another socially recognized self or set of selves whose intentionality is quite different than the initial self. The gestures of trance are embedded in a performance context, of course, but not one in which spoken language is dominant.[11] Rather, the gestures co-occur with music and incense, audition and olfaction, finding their significance in a multisensory matrix.

METAPHORS OF POSSESSION: FALLING/RISING/STANDING

In Morocco, one "falls" into trance (kat-ṭaḥ). Falling is the primary metaphor for the act of possession trance. At the beginning of ceremonies, I was often asked, "Do you fall? wesh kat-ṭaḥi?" It is another way of asking, "are you possessed?" Falling is a relinquishment, a capitulation to the experience, a submission. Once this happens, however, the spirits "rise up" in the body (al-jnun kay-ṭlaw fi-k). It is a downward sensation—women fall to the spirits, who then rise up within them. Falling and rising, which signal the transition into otherness, are also accompanied by strong physical sensations—tears, quaking, as well as smell, movement, and sound. All of these factors are co-occurent with the experience of possession, though they are specific to each jinn: Lalla Mira rises up to the smell of musk, emanating the color of yellow, producing laughter and emotions of gaiety. Sidi Mimun rises up to his music, to the odor of black benzoin, and sometimes obliges the propitiant to slash her body with knives.

The experience of falling is foundational. We fall down as children repeatedly and learn about directionality, balance, and control thereby. We make a game of falling so as to bring under our volition what is usually out of our control: "Ashes, ashes, we all fall down." To fall intentionally is counterintuitive, which is why it evokes laughter in children and in slapstick comedy. Falling is relinquishing to gravity, letting go, releasing. To fall down before someone is to submit, whether in English or in Arabic. As Michelle Dent and M. J. Thompson note, "falling is . . . that last desperate act of agency we are left with when faced with the terror and tragic beauty associated with loss and grief—or even, the frisson and anticipation of illicit or new love. It is in this dropping into the blaze of the unknown that we suddenly find ourselves no longer in control of the determining events that shape our lives" (2004: 8).

Rising up, on the other hand, takes volition; it is the spirits who rise: *kay tlaw f-ik*. Spirits rise up in a body that has ceded them place by falling. When the spirits rise up, they use the bodies of their hosts—animating their limbs, using their vocal chords. By contrast, when a spirit appears *outside* the body, in a vision or a dream, they are said to "stand up before you." "Aisha appeared [or stood up] before me, *waqaf ʿali-ya aiša*," I often heard. Spirits stand before you to deliver messages, to give warning or counsel, and generally to make their presence known. There is a recognition implied in the idiom, as well as a confrontation. *Waqaf* also means to stop. A spirit who appears before you, whether in a sleeping or a waking vision, stops you in your tracks. It is a rupture in one's experience of time, the entrance of one reality into another, the lifting of the veil that separates worlds and perpetuates the belief that human time is the only time. This collision of realms is also a transgression of sorts. It is the initiatory event of which Jean Françios Lyotard speaks, scarring one's sensibility like a wound and "marking out the rhythm of a secret and perhaps unnoticed temporality" (1992: 106).

GESTURE, SUBJECTIVITY, AND TEMPORALITY

We experience time by witnessing the differential effects of time on objects and beings that surround us—the growth of children, the withering of age, the wakes and ripples of movement through space. Maurice Merleau-Ponty compares time to a "gesture . . . that includes all the muscular contractions necessary for its execution" (1962: 419).[12] While one is aware of the gesture, one is usually unaware of the multiplicity of other factors that comprise and determine it—the bones, the musculature, even the intention to move—and yet they are all interconnected and interdependent. Becoming *aware* of the way time is unconsciously constituted, like a gesture and in a gesture, creates a break in our experience of temporality, transforming the habitual and ordinary into the extraordinary and reflexive (Abrahams 1986). The perceiver does not step *out* of time (this is an impossibility for Merleau-Ponty), but steps *into* another rhythm and another viewpoint on the naturalized world. This experience of a different rhythm is an "initiation" in Lyotard's words. And like many forms of initiation, he envisions it as a "wound" (Lyotard 1992: 106).

The ritual of the Gnawa *lila* is also a rhythm marked off from other temporal experiences. While the psychic wounds of slavery are publicly commemorated in the ceremony,[13] they are also symbolically re-experienced in the particular body of the practitioner, both in the mortification practices of the ritual (burning, cutting, eating sharp objects like glass) and in the afflictions brought on by the spirits themselves in the bodies of the practitioners. The wounds of the present body, in other words, evoke historical wounds of slavery, serving to anchor the subject to an environment and to connect what Emile Durkheim called "personal time" to historical memory (1915: 441; Merleau-Ponty 1962: 416). Gestures of mortification allow the propitiant to symbolically repossess the body from the historical wounds of ownership. The wounds inflicted by the spirits are not painful (as the body transcends them), and may even be pleasurable as they stimulate what Sufis consider the higher emotions.[14] They are wounds that empower.

Miriam recounts that she was sick when she was an eight-year-old child. Her mother took her to the hospital, but without result. The needle, she said, wouldn't enter her skin ("*al-briya ma-bghaš y-dkhul li-ya fi-jaldi-i*"). Miriam remained impermeable to allopathic cures and to Western medicine. Her body resisted the introduction of a foreign object, an object—the hypodermic needle—that also symbolizes the foreign. Indeed, her spirit would not permit the entrance of anything other than itself. Needles are often synonymous with effective cures in Moroccan folk belief, a result of the French protectorate and the way the French colonialists "drew upon medical icons and practices to impose their domination upon subjects and collectivities" (Comaroff and Comaroff 1993: 216). While the hegemony of the Western system of medicine has been countered by a resurgence in traditional healing methods in Morocco (Akhmisse 2000), ailing people often wait for hours to see a doctor in a state dispensary and are not satisfied if they don't get *al-briya* (a needle) before they leave. The inability of Miriam to be pierced or entered by a "Western" system of medicine signals that she belongs to the *jnun* and must be cured by them alone. It locates her in a Moroccan system of traditional healing, one that neither acknowledges nor reifies the West. It also has resonance in the sexual domain, however, as Miriam may be said to be *mtaqaf*, "closed." To be closed is to be ensorcelled; such magic often occurs during rites of passage like marriage (Kapchan 1996). A closed man is impotent, while a closed woman is impenetrable. And indeed, Miriam, while in her mid-forties, is unmarried and has always been so. She has never been "entered." Her life is devoted to the spirits and to her clientele and has been since she was a child, despite the interdictions of her older sister who to this day does not approve of Miriam's life with the spirits.

Once as a child she ran away to a sanctuary (*zawiya*) after her sister had beat her, she told me. She heard Gnawa on the street and began to follow them. "I fell, I was sick, and kept repeating 'I want Gnawa, I want Gnawa.'"

"Another time I was at our neighbor's place, on the fourth floor," she recounted. "Gnawa passed by and the neighbors wouldn't let me go out and see them. I fell from the roof, from the top to the bottom, and went with them."

"You fell?"

"Nothing happened to me. *ma tra li-ya walu.*"

Like the possessed woman in chapter two, Miriam also fell from the roof and was unharmed due to the protection of the spirits.

At about the age of ten she began to be clairvoyant. She would dream things and they would come to pass: "Whatever I saw by night came to pass by day." Her reputation spread, and now she makes her living as a clairvoyant (*shuwwafa*) and Gnawa ritual overseer (*mqaddema*), "seeing" for people, guiding them and arranging propitiation ceremonies. People come to her for counsel, and she consults with the spirits in her dreams. Her clients give her money (referred to euphemistically as *al-baraka*, blessing) and she puts it under her pillow: "*kat-bat 'ali-ha*, you sleep on it" she told me, "and the spirit answers your questions in your dreams." Here the symbolic sacrifice of money is placed under the sleeping body in order that clairvoyance be facilitated.

Spirits often communicate via dreams, especially what are called "lucid dreams" in the West, where the somatic body is asleep but the dreamer is aware of herself dreaming and can sometimes control the course of the dream. This place of not-sleep/not-waking is a particularly fecund and traveled place among the possessed. It marks what Vincent Crapanzano describes as "a change in ontological register," a place of *barzakh* where the material realm (here the money that is sacrificed) becomes a spiritualized propitiation and the spiritual takes form in images, voices, and sometimes smells (Crapanzano 2004: 14).[15] The spirit Aisha Qandisha appeared to Miriam in a dream and told her that she was to relieve people who were ensorcelled. "Now it's been twenty-four years and no one has ever come to me with reproaches. But after the afternoon prayer and on Fridays I don't work. Twenty-four years, I have what to eat and drink, praise and thanks be to God." As in the Gnawa ceremonies, money that is offered to the spirits (by way of a clairvoyant) has a special status, the profane rendered sacred via the intention of its giver. A sacrifice (here monetary) is offered, entering the propitiant into contract with the spirits (via the mqaddema) who relieve the possessed of affliction and may even bestow blessings and grace in return for the sacrifice offered.

"Several times a year I still get sick. I get dizzy. I get nervous. I cry. I don't want anyone to talk to me. When that time comes I have to have the Gnawa; I have to trance; I have to smell incense. I have to see blood, and that's it. In my dreams I feel people pulling me, saying, jdab, jdab, trance, trance."

Miriam falls twice in this narrative—once into trance, the next time from a roof. That her body was not injured in the fall is another sign that she has the protection of the spirits, protection that defies logic. She fell from the roof and followed the Gnawa, unhurt. There is an equation here between falling physically and falling into possession trance. The corporeal fall signals the first (incorporeal) fall—that is, the submission to the spirits, who then inhabit the body, making it more than itself, more than human. It is only the fall that allows the spirits to rise up and only that arising that gives the subject access to powers of clairvoyance. Signs and wonders; such narratives are common among shab al-ḥal, the friends of trance. Women who are destined to be mqaddemat (pl.) learn to control their possessions. They "work" the jinn. The grace exhibited by their unimpeded and inconsequential falls is a sign that they are favored by the spirits, that they are not simply possessed by them but are able to enter their ranks, so to speak, to "work" them instead of being worked over by them (see figure 5).

EMBODIED METAPHORS

One of the symptoms of being "struck" by the spirits (maḍrub) is the inability to move. Either paralysis or complete muscular lethargy is common.[16] Trance, by contrast, moves the body, loosens and frees it, transforming it from a stiff or heavy entity to a loose, fluid, and most importantly, mobile one. It is a process of opening up to flow. Mihaly Csikszentmihalyi defines flow as an autotelic experience—an end in itself (1990). Far from a complete letting go (as

FIGURE 5: *Mqaddema*. Photograph, Jamila Bargach

the metaphor of "falling" implies), the experience of flow, he says, involves asserting control in a difficult situation.[17] While control is usually not thought of
in regard to trance, the metaphor of "working the spirits"—attaining mastery
over them—makes us rethink concepts of intentionality and volition in regard
to trance activity. Indeed, the tension between control and loss of control is
endemic to trance experience generally. As mentioned in chapter two, trancers
often have a somatic awareness of their bodies and the bodies of others (proprioception), even when deep in trance. Judith Becker refers to this as "controlling the uncontrollable" (Becker 2004: 67). The possessing spirit is beyond

the volition of the possessed, but the body, insofar as it has memorized the gestures and dispositions of the spirit, is able to assume and corporealize the intentions of its specter, much as a dancer assumes the moves and effects of the choreographer. There is, indeed, a choreography of trance (Browning 1995; Deren 1983). As dance and performance studies scholar André Lepecki notes, "Choreography demands a yielding to commanding voices of masters (living and dead), it demands submitting body and desire to disciplining regimes (anatomical, dietary, gender, racial), all for the perfect fulfillment of a transcendental and preordained set of steps, postures, and gestures that nevertheless must appear 'spontaneous'" (Lepecki 2006: 9; Althusser 1994: 136). In the choreography of trance, the spirits determine the steps, but the body assumes them.

Possession implies not a lack of control, but a (volitional or nonvolitional) transfer of control to another entity. Of women in trance it is said: y-fajaw m 'a ras-hum, they find release, catharsis, sublimation. The transitive verb fa ja a, means "to open" (the noun fajwa means "opening, aperture, breach, gap [or] interstice").[18] The notion of space inheres in the word. To say kay-fuwwaj 'ala qalb-i (literally "he makes my heart open") implies that one was in a tight space and that someone created an opening or aperture which gave breathing room and alleviated pain. Thus fuwwajat 'ali-ya aj-jadba means "the trance gave me space" or "the trance relieved me." The verb is also used when talking about travel: ghadi n-mši n-fuwwaj 'ala ras-i, literally "I'm going to make some space for my head," is a common way of saying "I'm going to travel."[19] The relation between trance, gesture and travel is not fortuitous. Changing states and moving towards new spaces is what trance facilitates.

Trances are gestures towards flow in the sense implied by this verb, employing codified movements to literally create the space of flow. Enacting the ritualized gesture of falling or the movements of trance itself are also ways of moving into other experiences of time (Csikszentmihalyi 1990).[20] These gestures co-occur with music of course; indeed, music is a medium for transitions of ontological register. "By enveloping the trancer in a soundscape that suggests, invokes, or represents other times and distant spaces, the transition out of quotidian time and space comes easier. Imagination becomes experience. One is moved from the mundane to the supra-normal: another realm, another time, with other kinds of knowing" (Becker 2004: 27). When women "fall" into trance in Morocco, it is both a literal and a metaphoric fall. Certainly a change of mind occurs as one subjectivity cedes place to another, but more aptly, there is a change of bodily state. The muscles of the body all of a sudden no longer hold up the skeletal self. As the body swoons, so it changes key; there is a re-

FIGURE 6: Entranced woman with a knife. Photograph by Ariane Smolderen

linquishment of will to the possessing spirit. "I no longer have power over my-self," says Aisha: literally, "*ma kan-ḥkamš fi-ras-i*, I no longer rule over my head" (the head being synonymous with the "self" in the Moroccan idiom). But "working the spirits" is a deliberate invocation of this "unruliness," an act that exposes the paradox at the root of trance phenomena—namely that there is a (largely unconscious) somatic awareness of an enactment keyed as an entrance to the nonvolitional. Through imitation and repetition the trancer becomes not a victim of possession so much as the performer of a complex script, a ritual drama (Becker 2004; Schechner 1988; Turner 1974).[21]

The idiom of falling into trance is not restricted to Gnawa performance. Indeed, in his work with charismatic Catholics in the United States, Thomas J. Csordas notes that "the divine and demonic falling of Charismatics . . . has become . . . a prominent feature of the contemporary cultural landscape" (1994b: 230). Falling, whether swooning into a state of grace or stumbling into a kind of tortured affliction, is what sociologist Marcel Mauss has called a "technique of the body" (1979 [1935]), a corporeal attitude, gesture, or habit learned in a cultural environment that is often unconscious but that is a site of subjective and intersubjective meaning. By extension, "falling" may be called a "sacred technique of the body" and is found in many trance repertoires, whether it be the "going down" of Catholic Charismatics (Csordas 1994b), the "falling out" of fundamentalist Christians (Schechner 2002: 164) or the falling of the possessed in Gnawa ceremonies. All of these movements imply a relationship of self mastery vis-à-vis both nature and gravity, and are implicated in relations of distance and encounter between human beings, who confront each other face to face while standing but whose relationships change radically once they are no longer vertical (Csordas 1994b: 228).[22]

PRESENCE AND ABSENCE

Don't call up my person. I am absent.
Live in my absence as if in a house.
Absence is a house so vast
That inside you will pass through its walls
And hang pictures on the air.
—Pablo Neruda (Poirot 1990: 14)

"Falling," "rising," and "standing" are part of a sacred vocabulary related to healing trance (trance that occurs to propitiate a possessing spirit) in Morocco, forming part of a larger semantic domain of esoteric concepts related to the body—what in Moroccan Arabic are called "presence" (al-ḥaḍra) and "absence" (al-gha'ib). "Presence" is the term used to describe a state of transcendence that nonetheless is accompanied by a heightening of the senses—one is present to the body and what inspires it, whether that be God or a possessing spirit or jinn. Presence is a term from Islamic mysticism defining a state of communion with divinity. "Absence," on the other hand, is the term applied to those who leave their bodies in order to cede place to a possessing spirit or to travel as prophets and visionaries travel to "sites" where they may receive revelations. North African psychoanalyst Malek Chebel translates absence (al-gha'ib) as "le mystère" and "l'irreprésentable" (2002: 61). Being possessed, one is absent to the intentions of the self. Trancing without being possessed, on the other hand, is more akin to the Sufi ceremony of al-ḥaḍra (literally "presence") wherein a state of heightened mentation is brought on voluntarily through chanting and repetitious bodily movements.

Subjects in trance, whether possession trance or self-induced trance, have similar gestural economies. One frequent gesture is the index finger extended as if pointing. It is also commonly understood as a gesture meaning "There is no God but God," the first phrase of the Muslim testimony of faith and a founding concept of tawḥid (unity) the notion that everything is from God and returns to God and that, in fact, there is nothing but God.[23] God, however, is an imponderable for humans. Pointing towards God is also signaling what cannot be known, absence, al-gha'ib. It is an acknowledgement of the presence of another realm insofar as the volitional body points towards the nonvolitional body, indexing the unknown and unknowable.[24]

THE PARADOX OF TRANCE

The premise of possession is that the subject loses control of her volition and is inhabited by a foreign presence. The subject's intentionality becomes absent and is replaced by an "other" intentionality. When working the spirits, however—deliberately going into a possession trance—there is a volitional invocation of the nonvolitional body. The body is absorbed in its projects, often to the exclusion of any awareness of itself, and the absorption is experienced as not theirs. How does possession become resistant to the interference that returns us to our self-awareness, our conscious intentionality, in which we can think about our acts as well as or instead of being absorbed in them?

Soumaya gives us this account:

I'd just scratch myself or turn around, and I'd start to fall. I'd fall and begin to quake, to quake; and they'd bring me *jawi* [incense] and I'd be okay. Benzoin and sandalwood and orange blossoms, and I'd be okay. Just the odor, the odor. If I just smell that odor, it relieves me. I become okay. That's it. I stayed like that. But the day my mother had a *lila*, like the time comes around for Fatima to have her [annual] ceremony, they start going into trance. They just start playing a line of, one line of [the song for] 'Abd al-Qadr, they say: "I'm imploring you, my burden has fallen in your hands, oh mulay 'Abd al-Qadr." When they said this, I could no longer see anything. All of me starts working, working until I see myself, that's it, I've fallen. [*šift ras-i safi, ṭaḥat*]

Here it is a line of music that triggers body memory and response. The word for a musical line in Moroccan colloquial Arabic is l-*iyd*, hand. It is as if a part of the body was speaking to the whole or the musical body speaking to the cells. Indeed, while music is a catalyst for trance in this instance, it is inseparable from an aesthetic complex that includes gesture, olfaction, and memory.[25]

It is clear from this account that Soumaya experiences falling into trance as a loss of control, triggered by audition, soothed by olfaction. The trance itself, however, is indexed by "falling," in which the body actually drops to the floor, followed by writhing, twitching, rolling, and other repetitive movements—the body "working, working." The spirits have their own gestural economy. The possessed are often "caught" by attendants surrounding them so as to prevent injury and are helped up to their feet as the spirits "rise up" within them. The loss of control is brought on by gestures that are highly conventional, repeated and recognized by all participants in the possession-trance community. In other words, the reported feeling of loss of control is publicly signaled by gestures that are codified and repeated. This irony inhabits the phenomenon of spirit possession.

In her analysis of gestures in a session of somatic psychology, Katharine Galloway Young asserts that gestures are not visual cues for others so much as they are "expressive acts directed to the self," ways that the imagination inhabits the self (2002a: 46). This process contains its own reversibility—postures concretize the imagination and the imagination manifests and is known (and knows itself) in the gesturing body. The same may be said for the gestures that accompany the transition into trance—they concretize, or make real, the possession by another entity (both for the self and for others) while the spirit enacts its own being in the gestures of the possessed.

While gestures may be kinesthetic ways of inhabiting metaphor, ways that the subject knows herself, clearly the visual aspect of gesture also plays a role in the way trance is performed collectively. Observing trance—as well as feeling and smelling and hearing the trances of others—contributes to intersubjective performances. Possession ceremonies that propitiate the spirits with music, incense, and, most importantly, ecstatic trance are festive events in Morocco, and children are often present. Indeed, it may be posited that the bodily techniques of possession-trance are learned from an early age, incorporated into the individual body by corporeal mimesis (through sight, tactile, and instrumental participation).[26] Imprinting is a significant part of Gnawa trance culture. Growing up in an environment where ceremonies are held regularly, children observe their parents, their aunts and uncles, and siblings "fall." They witness the way the possessed move. They also observe the onset of possession—the headaches, the swollen legs, the fatigue and depression-like symptoms of lethargy. And they see the modalities of cure—the way the body moves to the music, the ritual gesture of inhaling the incense and propitiating the spirits. Observation is undeniably important in the transmission of the culture of trance, but the body learns in many modalities. Imbibing the incense is enough to make some people fall. For others, hearing the music is the catalyst. There is a different somatic repertoire at work in possession ceremonies. Even while young, children feel the percussive rhythms of the Gnawa deep in their bodies. They learn to move to them. Bodies learn about possessed bodies not just by seeing them but also by smelling and sensing them. Most all children who grow up in a family that holds ceremonies for a possessed family member become possessed themselves—usually around puberty.

On the other hand, these gestures are related to very basic bodily and spatial orientations—those of falling and rising. The possessed subject may be said to fall into a relation of self-disintegration, a kind of abject state of multiplicity. That the metaphors of falling and rising are employed by the trance community is not spurious. They represent an indexing of basic experiences of control and loss of control, of encounters with relinquishment and volition; these same fluctuations of absence and presence are found in the trance ceremonies.

INHABITING SOCIAL METAPHORS

Gestures mimic the root metaphors of trance, based themselves in the body: falling and rising. According to Mark Johnson,

A metaphor is not merely a linguistic expression (a form of words) used for artistic or rhetorical purposes; instead, it is a process of human understanding by which we achieve meaningful experience that we can make sense of. A metaphor, in this 'experiential' sense, is a process by which we understand and structure one domain of experience in terms of another domain of a different kind. (1987: 15)

The emblematic gestures of "falling" recall early bodily experiences with equilibrium, agency, control, and balance. In English we say that we "fall in" with a group of people, we "fall into and out of love," we "fall toward the sidewalk"—all expressions which denote relations to different kinds of force, directionality, and volition (either the absence of will or its presence). They also mediate relations between persons, denoting various degrees of intersubjectivity and control by and over others. To have a "falling out" with someone is to be outside his or her circle of influence. To "fall at someone's feet" is to volitionally subject oneself to the power of another. Likewise Moroccan Arabic has the idiomatic phrases "ṭaḥat 'ali-ya fikra," an idea "fell" on, or occurred to me; "ṭaḥat fi had shi," I fell into [those] circumstances; or "ṭaḥat fi Sidi Mimun," I fell to Sidi Mimun [in trance]." These expressions also denote differing relations to agency and nonagency. The metaphor of "falling" is clearly part of what Johnson calls the "Up-Down Orientation," related to primary experiences of verticality, of high and low; but it also participates in the schema of "force," which involves the subject interactively with relations of power. Possession-trance may, itself, be seen as a metaphor for mediating the complex relations of self and other, power and agency, in a limited and highly dramatic realm.

Falling to the spirits, one is subject to them. Working the spirits, one has achieved a certain mastery over the same forces and is thus empowered. The transition from victimization to a limited mastery is evident in the concept of work. Soumaya describes her entranced body as "working, working"; it is her body that has the agency. Unlike some others who are unaware of their possessed state, Soumaya reports seeing the action happening to her. She is a witness as her body labors, much like a slave in relation to its owner (or malk), until it becomes empowered and is able in turn to work the malk. This transition is also evident in the gestural economy as the body falls to a particular rhythm (called a duqqa) and rises in a new identity.[27]

Metaphoric gestures are those gestures that make an abstract notion concrete, interpreting one thing in the terms of another (falling to the spirits is concretized in the falling of the physical body). Iconic metaphors, on the other

FIGURE 7: Mortification with fire. Photograph by Ariane Smolderen

hand, are depictions of the concrete object, a kind of mimesis (McNeill 1992; Young 2002a, 2002b). In one section of the trance ceremony, for example, the Gnawa (and others) mimic the gestures of wild animals. This section is called *rijal al-ghaba* (the men of the forest, though "men" is a euphemism for spirits here). The possessing *jnun* oblige the possessed to enact animal movements (and often to eat raw meat and other symbolic foods). But these movements are always the same—the possessed is on the ground on his side, the upper leg bending back and forth at the knee, the arm motioning as if scratching the waist. Later the possessed gets down on his belly and eats a mixture called *zmita* (made of grilled flour and chick peas without salt), his arms back at his side, his mouth bent down to the dish. This section, associated with the color black, is often enacted by men. These iconic gestures are conventional and appear to be volitional yet they do more than represent meaning: they actually enact it. They are performative. The gestures have attendant spiritual and emotional attitudes; "acts of the mind *are* a body shape, a postural experience that forms a bodily self" (Young 2002a: 48, emphasis in original). They also contain qualities that belong to the realm of pantomime, as men become lions and other wild animals without the mediation of speech (Kendon 1993b, 1994, 1995; McNeill 1992).

INHABITED BY OLFACTION AND AUDITION

If the gestures of trance and transition are, in the Moroccan example, indicative of basic states of absence and presence, control and loss of control, they also depend on sensate realities—material conditions—that are always present: the gestures of trance co-occur with music and with olfactory stimulation provided by the thick smoke of incense. Like spirits, both music and incense invade the parameters of the body. One cannot protect oneself from their influences. They permeate experience and incite emotional response. They are intertwined with gesture as closely as gesture is with speech—more closely even, insofar as music, like gesture, is vibration and movement.[28] These are not autonomous gesture systems, in other words, but are entwined in a larger affective and sensate weave, shot through with emotions of high intensity.

The subject in trance encounters another experience of temporality, another rhythm. The subject falls to that rhythm and rises up in another identity.[29] The narrative that ensues is a recollection of what phenomenologist Edward S. Casey calls "body memory." Casey asserts that, like the mind, the body has its own way of remembering. It is a kinesthetic memory and one with a particular relation to the experience of time. When the body remembers, there is a collapsing of past and present into the now; indeed the past feels co-immanent in the present (Casey 1987). "Body memory," Casey asserts, "alludes to memory that is intrinsic to the body. . . the way the body itself, in its sinews and on its surface, remembers its own activity." Memory of the body, on the other hand, "refers to those manifold manners whereby we remember the body as the accusative object of our awareness, whether in reminiscence or recognition, in reminding or recollection" (1987: 147). Body memory is kinesic, synaesthetic; it feels as if it is embedded in the bones. Memory of the body, on the other hand, views the body as an object; in this way it is reflexive, giving rise to metadiscourses.

Body memory is by definition nonverbal. It follows that any linguistic recollection of the body, then, necessarily relies on translating somatic experiences into intellective reflection (a process that Jakobson calls "intersemiotic translation"); there are moments, however, when the body is not simply remembered in narrative but when it is actually made present through gesture. "Well, my body started to fill up. I'd be sitting there, and I'd start to cry. My heart would fill up this way [her hands expand as if around a balloon in front of her heart] and I'd start to fall. I fall and I become absent [kan gha'ib]." Soumaya's gesture is a metaphoric enactment of a bodily memory. Young asserts such gestures are not ways of making the narrative real, but are rather ways of entering the body into the narrative and the imagined world it conjures (what she calls the "taleworld"). "Gestures," she notes, "are ways of being engaged bodily in the constitution of the taleworld. The captivation of the body by the narrative is not a matter of how narrators confer reality-status on a narrative world . . . but of how narrative worlds confer reality status on the body of the narrator" (2002b: 46). Understood this way, Soumaya's body becomes a container—"my heart would fill up"—into whose depths she falls, ultimately losing consciousness and becoming "absent."

Music has a privileged relation to the body and to memory. It is prior to syntax in language acquisition, for example.[30] As vibration, music is inseparable from movement. Intonation carries meanings that we recognize before we understand much else. This is as true of laughter as it is of expressions of anguish. Indeed, the intimate relation between sound and subjectivity is acknowledged in native exegesis: the spirits are thought to dwell in the sound, just as they dwell in the body. "You have to know how to listen to the hajhuj," one possessed woman told me. "You listen and the spirits pass through [the hajhuj] and rise up within you." The relation of sound to possession is clear. It is the ability to give passage through the senses that allows the subject to be inhabited. Incense has a similar effect. Fatna notes that the Gnawa need only put the incense on the brazier, and she falls into trance: "it's like, I've been dressed," she says, "it's like, I become all numb and tingly. My whole body starts to work. It's like that that I fall."

To be dressed or clothed (*malbus*) is to be possessed, seized by an inhabiting spirit. This expression arises from the fact that when in trance the possessed are literally clothed in the garments and colors of their possessors. One of the first things an initiated *mqaddema* does is to assemble the cloths—veils, *jellabas*—of the *mluk*, so that they may be used to cover those who fall into trance (Chlyeh 1998). The color of one's spirit is linked to the color of one's dress. Being clothed is a metaphor for being possessed, and being clothed in a particular *color* indicates which spirit inhabits the body. This is another example of the way metaphors spread out into many dimensions of aesthetic experience—from gesture to clothing to color (Feld 1995b: 129–131). For Fatna, it is incense that causes this change of state. "My body is pins and needles from my head to my toes (*det-i kat-t-šuwwak-ni min ar-ras ḥetṭa r-rjlin*)," she elaborated. The horripilation (goose-bumps) that Becker describes as characterizing states of deep listening, is here attributed to olfaction (2004). Incense was the catalyst and Fatna's body then reacted. What music and incense have in common is their ability to invade the parameters of the body, to move the body, just as metaphor moves identity (Fernandez 1986). But where in the case of metaphor there is a posited, though arbitrary, isomorphism between form and image, sign and signifier, in body memory sign and signifier are co-immanent, fused, as it were. "In body memories the past is a direct constituent of the present, a constituent mediated neither by image nor by word" (E. Casey 1987: 168). In other words, the infusion of incense in the body causes the body itself to remember, as past experiences of falling arise anew.[31]

NARRATING EMOTION, NARRATING THE ABJECT

The "fall" into trance is also a fall into an emotional state. Like genres that, following M. M. Bakhtin (1982; 1986), contain their own worldview, their own relation to time and space, so emotions have their own spatio-temporal orientation (think of frenzy, awe, nostalgia, regret). Dread is oriented towards the future, melancholy towards the past. Emotions inhere in a historically determined sensorium, co-occurring with a vast array of material artifacts and physical postures.

Spirit possession is a way of experiencing a repertoire of emotions in a context that is set apart from normative life. C. Nadia Serematakis calls such ritual contexts "sensational" (as opposed to merely "sensory"); they are zones of public memory that are narrativized, entering history through the repetitions of the habit body (1994: 20; Merleau-Ponty 1962). All phenomena are emotionally inflected, but rituals carry and create emotional repertoires in marked ways. In the case of the Moroccan Gnawa, spirit possession ceremonies instantiate repertoires of emotion in the edifice of the social, not only through words or images but through gesture, the body, and its senses. Although inseparable from the possessing spirits, the range of emotion experienced in the ritual ceremony is marked, codified, and set apart from the emotional repertoires of quotidian life.

Not surprisingly, the emotion that characterizes "falling" is often abjection. According to the *Oxford English Dictionary*, to be abject is to be "cast off, cast out, rejected." And indeed, the possessing spirit does just that, as the person's usual subjectivity is cast aside to make room for that of the possessing *jinn*. The word abject comes from the Latin *abjectus* "to cast off, throw away." To be abject is literally to be "Cast down, downcast, brought low in position, condition or estate, low-lying" (OED). It has both a physical and an emotional component. It is to be brought low in both realms, "brought low in position" and "down in spirit or hope" (OED).

The abject has a dual status. It is precisely that which is not homologous with the subject and yet it is inseparable from the subject.[32] Like spirits that possess, abjection is something that haunts—it inhabits the self, but is not the self. The abject both summons and repulses with equal force. As performance studies scholar, Karen Shimakawa notes in her discussion of national abjection and the Asian-American body in performance, the abject is defined in the tension between being "not absolutely or permanently excluded from . . . [an] identity and yet not quite representative of it" (2002: 3). It is this perpetual turning, this in-between, that defines the possessed body:

◆ ◆ ◆

Soumaya is sitting on a low sponge mattress, leaning against unevenly stuffed pillows, when suddenly her body jerks; she throws her arms up over her head, flailing in the direction of her neighbors. She arches her back, sending her legs out towards the center of the floor, her body almost melting onto the floor. Women help her to turn over; she gets on hands and knees and crawls towards the musicians, bending her head over the clay brazier where smoking incense rises up into the cool air. She bathes her face in the fragrance of burning sandalwood, turning her head from side to side, opening her jaw and waving the smoke into her mouth. Only then is she up on her feet, arms extended out to the sides, her head thrown violently back and forth as if her neck were loose. She stamps the ground with the heel and ball of her left foot, then the right; she jumps up with both feet, her torso quaking from impact with the hard ceramic floor tiles.

When the music stops, the possessed woman once again falls, this time backward into the arms of the mqaddema, who begins to speak with the possessing jinn. "What do you want?" she asks the spirit several times. No answer. "Do you want a sacrifice?" The girl's head nods a barely perceptible "yes." "Who are you?" the mqaddema continues, "Who are you? Are you Aisha [Qandisha]?" Another affirmative nod from a head with glazed eyes, vision unfixed, her curly long hair strewn across a forehead running with orange-blossom water, used to revive those who are taken.

Soumaya's experience of trance begins in the body when her limbs contort and she loses control to the other presence that occupies her. Forthwith she falls down and seeks out the smell appropriate to this particular jinn and imbibes it.

Only then is she able to rise up; or rather the spirit rises up within her. Soumaya may be said to be experiencing a state of abjection, not only literally in her fall and despondency, but in the sense that psychoanalyst Julia Kristeva employs the term, as that which "does not respect borders, positions, rules" (1982: 4). For Kristeva, the subject experiences abjection when boundaries dissolve and the codified sense of self disintegrates. In these terms, the possessed are always engaged in a relationship with the abject—with what "disturbs identity, system, [and] order" (Kristeva 1982: 4.) Indeed the emotion of abjection is pervasive at the ceremonies as women give themselves up (or are given up by their malk) to a perpetual turning between self and otherness. Abjection inhabits these ceremonies as a kind of collective spirit. For Kristeva abjection also represents a return to what she calls the "semiotic body," a place of coexistence and continuity with the mother and with sensation, both pain and pleasure. This place of unity (which is the imaginary) precedes the subject's entrance into language and subjectivity, but it is sacrificed when one enters the symbolic phase of development where one is able to use signs and substitute one sign for another. Being inhabited by spirits is also a substitution of sorts—the substitution of one identity for another. But in the case of spirit possession, there is an inversion at work. Instead of sacrificing the semiotic body to enter the realm of the symbolic, the possessed initially sacrifices language and self-hood and returns to a place of coexistence—not with the mother per se, but with the possessing spirit. This fall into abjection is what, for Kristeva, accompanies—and indeed is responsible for—all forms of artistic creation, poetry, and even religion.

Once the possessing *jinn* is divined—given a name—only then is it born into language, becoming a permanent inhabitant of the body. There is henceforth a relation between the self that is inhabited and the inhabited or possessed self. This relation is a sensate one—the body of the possessed is engaged in the corporealized experience of the spirit. Sometimes this consists in a sharing of memory.[33] Unlike schizophrenia, whose borders do not permit entry or overlap, the inhabited self may remember its other states, if not as a recollection, then as an embodied emotion, a "feeling" of having been other. If, as anthropologist Katherine P. Ewing notes, "we constitute the self as a string of memories," then it follows that the constitution of multiple selves relies on discrete sets of memories, domains of memory (sensate, intellective)[34] that come with their own co-occurence rules, their own relation to the sensate world and to narrative form (Ewing 1990). And, indeed, each spirit has its own characteristics, its own histories within and without the body of the possessed. As will become evident, these histories have a narrative life within the community.

Sacrifice is an important aspect of this relationship. As in many religions, in Islam sacrifice is a central ritual, symbolic of man's covenant with God and drawing on the substitution of a lamb for Abraham's son.[35] In Morocco, sacrifice may be a way to propitiate God, or a way to placate a spirit (Rachik 1990). While the interpretation of sacrifice in universal terms is debated (Evans-Pritchard 1965; de Heusch 1986; Girard 1972), there are two evident meanings of sacrifice in the context of Gnawa ritual. Sacrifice of a chicken, a goat, or even a cow initiates the ritual, and is (1) "a means of communication between the sacred and the profane worlds through the mediation of a victim, that is, of a thing that in the course of the ceremony is destroyed" and (2) a means of commensality—that is, the sacrificed animal is eaten, and thus the propitiants at the ceremony ingest a common meal and incorporate a common blessing (Hubert and Mauss 1964: 97). For the Gnawa, sacrifice is central to all propitiation ceremonies, an offering to the spirits and an initiation of a lifelong relationship with them. It both appeases the spirit and nourishes the community.

Sacrifice is also a means of substitution. Following Kristeva, it is a metaphor for the entrance into the Symbolic itself: in sacrificing unity with the mother, the subject becomes Other: it receives a name and can now assign them. In the Gnawa worldview, giving a name to the possessing spirit means entering into a verbal economy where subjectivities are redefined. (The fact that it is often the mqaddema, another woman, who elicits the "name" reinforces the collective and feminine enterprise of this rite of return.) Thus does the trance experience enact a return to the semiotic body and then, once the physical sacrifice of the animal has been substituted for the body of the possessed, reenacts the separation, the abject loss of the mother, the ability to substitute one sign for another—in short, the entrance into language. For the possessed, the discourse of possession is a language that only initiates speak.

TRANCE AND COMMENSALITY

Falling into trance, or having the spirits rise up in the body, usually transpires in an environment where the afflicted or entranced person can be attended to, cared for, and perhaps most importantly observed. In a ritual situation such as a lila, a person in trance may need to be brought "center stage," before the musicians and the incense. Or she may need to be caught when the trance is over, and she falls into semiconsciousness on the floor. These transitions are critical in the ceremony and rely upon the attention of others in the ritual milieu to the entranced body itself. There is thus a heightened degree of intersubjective awareness, an acute somatic attention that is always in play.

There are very specific bodily comportments that co-occur with trance states. When they are adopted publicly in a ritual context these postures are a means of "commensality," which C. Nadia Serematakis defines as the "exchange of sensory memories and emotions, and of substances and objects incarnating remembrance and feeling" (1994: 37). Commensality is a key concept in understanding performance and trance phenomena in particular. Etymologically, it refers to the experience of eating together at the same table; it also evokes a tenant/host relationship where the tenant and host share food (as opposed to one being food for another, as in a parasitic relationship). To be commensal with another is to be nourished by the same substances. (The notion of commensality assumes that a community is what it eats!)

In the aesthetic realm, commensality is a particular configuration of the senses and the body with individual and public memory and emotion. Steven Feld gets at this when he talks about musical experience as containing "crossmodal homologies"—formal correspondences between music and other aesthetic dimensions, such as verbal or visual styles and other sensate and imaginative cues (Feld 1995b: 131). Implied in this notion is a necessary inter-dependence, a mutual sustenance between emotions and gestures, between sensate experiences like olfaction and audition, and between all these things and particular social memories and meanings. All these aesthetic forms co-occur and contribute to an experience of the subject and of intersubjectivity or the collective.

While Serematakis employs the term commensality as a trope for aesthetic exchange, it has quite literal implications for the rituals of the Gnawa, where food for the spirits as well as food for the participants is a primary focus. Indeed almost all the spirits have a particular food that is ingested by the possessed while in trance, and subsequently distributed to the others at the ceremony (see table 1). These foods are always made without salt and with benzoin—the essential condiment of the jnun.[36] Both these ingredients are symbolically charged.

As Diouri notes in his brilliant analysis of laḥlou, the meat dish made for Sidi Hamu and the red spirits, salt both preserves and conserves and thus mediates between the raw and the rotten. It is the equivalent of culture and the cooked. To be without salt is to be basl, tasteless (often said of personalities), but it is also to be savage. The spirits embody this symbolic savagery. On the other hand, historically salt was introduced to Africa by the Moors in the twelfth cen-tury and quickly became one of the commodities traded for slaves. Indeed, slaves were later employed in excavating salt in the Sahara. That the food for ge-nies is without salt, then, also ties this food to a preslave past in Africa, making the equation between saltlessness and the spirits one of honor (Diouri 1990).

The addition of jawi (the word comes from "Java," its origin) to the ritual food of the jnun is also significant. Jawi is a resinous substance that gives off an odor when burned. It is not food, however. Thus, when eaten, there is a kind of synaesthesia involved: it is smelled through taste. What is usually burned and turned into smoke is instead eaten. There is a transgression of categories (nonfood is eaten)—a signpost of the jnun, who also eat raw meat and drink blood. Diouri remarks on the presence of jawi in funerary meals in sub-Saharan Africa, where the substance symbolizes the body of the deceased, furthering underscoring the centrality of lamentation and grief in the cere-monies of the Gnawa (Diouri 1990: 198). In Morocco, jawi is still burned in sanctuaries and at funerals.

The spirits ingest foods, but they are not the salty, delicious foods of the human realm. Indeed, by eating what is usually burned and inhaled (incense), the spirits demonstrate the transmutability of all substances—both physical

TABLE 1. *The Foods of the Spirits*

Color	Mhalla, Group of Spirits	Ritual Foods
White	The opening, *ftuḥ ar-raḥba*	Milk, dates, orange-flower water
Seven colors	Buhala	Bread, dates, dried figs
Black	Sidi Mimun/Lalla Mimuna	—
Light blue	Sidi Musa, *al-musawiyyin* (or sea spirits, *al-baḥriyyin*)	Bowl of water with coriander seeds, benzoin
Dark blue	Sky spirits, *as-samawiyyin*	—
Red	Sidi Hamu	Sacrificed meat, usually chicken (made with water, olive oil, cinnamon, sugar, saffron, coriander, benzoin, and gum arabic), raison juice. Sometimes walnuts, almond paste, and dates
Green	*šorfa* (plural of *šarif*, the noble ones)	—
Black	"The men of the forest," *rijal agh-ghaba, al-ghabawiyyin:*	
	a. Briandu	a. *Dughnu* (milk, cinnamon, sesame seeds, gum arabic, benzoin)
	b. Ulad sorgho	b. *Zammita* (barley, corn, watermelon seeds, anis, sesame seeds, sugar)
	c. Ju-ju nnama	c. Raw meat (chicken, pigeon)
	d. Bala dimma	d. Raw eggs
Yellow and multicolors	Al-layilat, the women:	
a. Green	a. Malika	a. Malika's soup, or the drink of Malika (fresh or dried raisin juice, or other fruit drinks), *nefqa* (a tray with cloves, dried wild roses, orange-flower water, lavender, myrrh, senbel, fragrant woods, *zuwwaq* [traditional lipstick], mirror)

b. Yellow	b. Arbiya, Mira	b. henna
c. Black	c. Aicha (x4)	c. olives, olive oil, milk, dried figs, honey, day-old bread without salt, *nefqa*
The colors of the *mqaddema*	*Khruj al-mida* (taking out the "table")	Buttermilk, walnuts, almonds, dates, raisins, olive oil, honey, *zammita, illane, doghnu*

Adapted from Diouri 1990: 208.

and spiritual. Spirits and humans eat together at the ceremonies. They eat the sacrificed animal (without salt and with *jawi*), yet all the foods eaten at the ceremony become sacrificial, symbols of what is offered to the spirits. Food, in its ability to transmute, becomes a medium of exchange par excellence, uniting interior and exterior, material and immaterial, human and spirit. In the act of commensality, memory joins the sensory and produces emotions of grief and of communion.

MEMORIES OF THE BODY

Iconic associations between postures and states are learned in infancy such that certain physical stances always co-occur with certain emotions. The emotions that are effected by trance co-occur with the presence of incense, the pentatonic melodies of the *hajhuj*, the rhythms of the *qraqab*, or castanets, the colors of cloths draped over the head and body. To say that someone is possessed by Lalla Mira (literally *fi-ha Lalla Mira* or Lalla Mira is in her), for example, is to map the attributes of this *jinniyya*—her frivolity, humor and vanity—onto the possessed. This is more than a simple metaphoric overlay. The possessed woman embodies these qualities, approximating, if not fully becoming, Lalla Mira. It is a relationship based on resemblance—as the body of the possessed woman becomes an icon of the *jinniya*, laughing her laughter, demanding her beat, and delighting in it.

The *jnun* need to move through the body unimpeded, and the possessed is relieved or "opened" (*mufaja*) by the unobstructed passage of the *jnun*, the smooth invasion. It is when the body presents obstacles, resistance, that possession becomes ṣaʿb: hard or difficult. Falling into possession-trance is regarded as an affliction by spirits. Particularly vulnerable are women who succumb to frequent crying. "A young woman has to be courageous," said a wrinkled old woman, turning to me. "If you cry all the time, they will strike you. Spirits are everywhere. If you cry all the time and are unhappy, they'll possess you. In the bathroom, in the kitchen; wherever there is water. You have to be courageous." Linking tears and spirit possession reinforces the belief that jinn are attracted to water. It also elucidates, however, the role of possession in a largely feminine economy of affect based on excess. Water is boundless, and tears cross the boundaries of the body, in effect, challenging those limits. The body's porosity, its ability not only to be closed and solid but to be open and fluid, makes it available to possession. People become vulnerable to spirit possession because of tears—the expression of negative emotion—but also during transitional moments in the life cycle when new emotional solutions have to be found. Poet and literary critic Susan Stewart notes that we are in the "immeasurable flow" when we are weeping. A new temporality inhabits the mourner. Like a person in trance, the "weeper has no measure and is in fact the vessel of the agency of his or her tears." Tears, and the emotions that accompany them, take possession of the subject.

This is true of sound as well. As Soumaya recounted:

> I fall and go. And I'm contorted [maʿuja]. My whole self is contorted [kul-i maʿuja]. And they rise up inside me. Each one of them speaks in me, with my voice; she talks in me: Mira, Mimun, Aisha; they all . . . speak in me. Each one asks for something . . .
>
> I remember, but I no longer control myself [ma kan-ḥakemš f-ras-i]. I don't know what I'm saying and I'm not in control of myself. But I know that I have fallen, the fit [crises] has taken hold of me. But I'm no longer. . . . Like now, Mira takes hold of me I start laughing, laughing, laughing, laughing; until I no longer feel myself [ma kan-ḥass b-ras-i]. I can laugh for a whole hour. I can't control myself. I can't control myself. I can't control myself.

Crying and laughter are both eruptions that break through the surface of the self, inhabiting by their very nature other spaces and other beings and permitting entry to the same. Through both audition and olfaction the body is open to being inhabited. It is not the senses that allow entrance, per se, but the sounds and smells that act to stimulate the senses, and that pass through.

The repetition of key phrases gives emphasis to Aisha's narrative—she is not in control. Literally she doesn't "rule" (ḥakama) over herself, her intentionality and volition have been usurped by the possessing spirit. She is present, however, and she *does* remember. There is an observing "I." But the repetition in her discourse also enacts a desire at the level of the senses. It provides a musical cadence to her speech. As she notes, the spirits speak in her voice, creating a counterpoint between her sound and their message, between form and content, subject and other.

> Now I only have to hear that beat of his and my heart starts to beat, beat, beat, beat, beat. It's like a mortar and pestle beating in my heart. I have to fall and that's it. I fall for Moulay Abdelqadr, or for Lalla Malika, or for Lalla Mira. They just put that musk [on the brazier], and I close my nostrils, I can't smell, it's like I've been clothed [talbist], it's like, I become all numb and tingly. My whole body starts to work. It's like that that I fall.

Aisha's relation to odor is itself confounding. She is relieved by the scent of *jawi* (benzoin), but the odor of musk makes her nostrils "close," her body repelling the scent as she is transforming into another. Like music, incense also invades the parameters of the body. The music makes her heart beat, beat, beat. It is a prelude to possession, a warning before the fall.

Possessed women lament their condition and are lamentable; but as with all collective keening, a powerful beauty emerges in the sharing of misfortune. Indeed once women have become acquainted with the spirits that reside within them, they may go on to embrace and access their spirits' powers and clairvoyance at will. The narration of this process is also a narration of feminine empowerment. Music, movement, and odor become primary metaphors for the transmutation of subjectivity precisely because they are the senses that most challenge notions of the fixed and stable subject in time and space. Analyzing these narratives as memories of the body, we find the following:

1. Possessed women narrate the senses—particularly olfaction and audition—to describe transitions from a state of self-possession to one of inhabitation or spirit possession. Indeed, a memory of synaesthetic engagement is always present at the level of narration.
2. Narration of the sense-based experiences of possession is also accompanied by a narration of emotional response—expressed either in the form of laughing or crying, both forms of eruption that break open the boundaries of the body.

3. The language that these women use is *poetic*—that is, the form of the language dominates the meaning (Jakobson and Halle 1971: 82) thereby affecting a transformation in the linguistic hierarchy and indexing corresponding transformations in the sensorium.

"Poetic language," as Kristeva reminds us, "[is] an attempt to symbolize the 'beginning,' an attempt to name the other facet of taboo: [not incest, but] pleasure, pain." (1982: 61–62). The return to this state, or its return in the subject, is responsible for art, for religion, and for poetic language. It is also one of the main factors driving the phenomenon of trance. If, as Young notes, "narrativity shifts my attitude to life from my engagement in it toward my reflection on it," narrating sensate experience is an act with special and dual status (both engaging and reflexive) (1987: 12). There is a performative aspect to the description of sense phenomena, an enactment that takes place, at least for those who share the same sensory and sensational associations. A bodily empathy accompanies the narration, making the distinction between the narrative and narrated event porous. Borrowing from Merleau-Ponty we might say that narrating the senses is an "ecstatic" act—one that reaches out into the world with intentionality at the same time that it draws in the world for interpretation (1962). An intermingling of word and sense takes place, a melding of signifier and signified, body, and word.

What these narratives remind us is that trance performance is multisensory and interaesthetic. Understanding a phenomenon as complex as trance necessitates an analysis of many semiotic systems—gestural, musical, olfactory, and linguistic. These modalities of meaning-making are interdependent. The particular configurations of the aural and the motile, the olfactory and the emotional are ritualized and culture-specific. Furthermore, they are attached to memory as ligaments are attached to bones and muscles. Such experiences are "initiations" in the most basic of senses—providing introductions to different sensory hierarchies, different experiences of temporality and the body, even new ways of defining the parameters of the self. There is a dialogic relationship between image, word, and body such that metaphors (falling and rising) inhabit and determine the body, while also finding reverberation with memories and bodily schemata that are prelinguistic and foundational to the formation of a first experience of subjectivity. By re-enacting the subject's early experience of separation from the mother and self-hood, propitiation ceremonies draw upon profound emotional and embodied memories to elaborate the creation and accommodation of multiple and new subjectivities.

WORKING THE SPIRITS
THE ENTRANCED BODY,
THE ENTRANCED WORD

♦ ♦ ♦

Any poetry produced under conditions that suppress the recursive and patterned
dimensions of form cannot hope to move the reader or listener beyond the
expectations of speech absorbed into the time of everyday life.
—Susan Stewart (2002: 82)

After all, there is no such thing as experience outside of embodiment in signs.
—V. N. Volosinov (1972: 85)

To Berber, Arabic, and French, it is necessary to add yet another language,
"a fourth language: that of the body, with its dances, trances, suffocations."
—Mireille Rosello (2005: 80, quoting Djebar 1999: 14).

Changing rhythms of the body move the subject into other experiences of temporality. And language? How does language transit the subject out of everyday time and into "trance time"?

In her 2002 book, *Poetry and the Fate of the Senses*, poet and literary scholar Susan Stewart notes that poetry, through its reliance on rhythm, changes one's relation to time and space. She invokes poet Paul Valéry's discussion of walking to bring attention to the possessing character of rhythm itself: "I had left my house to relax from some tedious piece of work by walking and by a consequent change of scene," recounts Valéry. "As I went along the street where I live, I was suddenly *gripped* by a rhythm which took possession of me and soon gave me the impression of some force outside myself. It was as though someone else were making use of my *living-machine*. Then another rhythm overtook and combined with the first, and certain strange *transverse* relations were set up between these two principles (I am explaining myself as best I can). They combined with the movement of my walking legs and some kind of song I was murmuring, or rather which was being murmured through *me*" (Valéry 1961, quoted in S. Stewart 2002: 211–212, emphases in original). In these sentences, Valéry speaks of rhythm as having an agency of its own. It possesses him much like a spirit. Valéry's words resonate with the Platonic belief that poetry has an agency that moves through the poet seemingly without consent or volition. ("And every poet has some Muse from whom he is suspended, and by whom he is said to be possessed, which is nearly the same thing, for he is taken hold of" says Plato (1936: 289–290, quoted in Stewart 2002: 112). For Valéry, this possession begins in rhythms that inhabit and move him—both symbolically and literally.

Was Valéry possessed by the entrancing powers of rhythm (and polyrhythms) or was he possessed by a spirit with musical inclinations? Was he what Judith Becker calls a "deep listener"—someone whose emotional state changes according to their auditory practices and sensibilities? If so, where were those powerful sounds coming from?

Rhythms "take hold" of Valéry's body, and he is possessed by song. This is not surprising if, following philosopher Henri Lefebvre, we turn our attention to the way that movements in space create experiences of time. For Lefebvre space is defined by the rhythms that occupy and produce it; these are often gestural. "Rhythms in all their multiplicity interpenetrate one another. In the body and around it, as on the surface of a body of water, or within the mass of a liquid, rhythms are forever crossing and recrossing, superimposing themselves on each other, always bound to space" (1991: 205). Perhaps more pertinent to Valéry's experience, and the experience of all who are possessed, is the shared nature of these rhythms. They are like waves that pass through the body or like "ether traversed by waves." They are also intricately related to hearing. "Space is listened for," says Lefebvre, "as much as seen, and heard before it comes into view." Hearing, he continues, "plays a mediating role between the spatial body and the localization of bodies outside it" (1991: 205, 199–200). Valéry may be said to be hearing the music of space and, in aligning with it, he contributes to its production.

If the relation of poetry and possession goes back to ancient Greece, there are nonetheless few studies that actually analyze narratives of possession and the way that parallelism, rhythm, and repetition produce a sonic and somatic "alignment" between words and the world (Nuckolls 2004). In this chapter I compare the rhythm of trance activity to the rhythm of language, positing a causal, or at least a commensal, relation between the two. In the process we understand how narratives about trance become entranced and entrancing narratives.[1]

Poetics is in many ways the study of the musical dimensions of language. "Only in poetry with its regular reiteration of equivalent units is the time of the speech flow experienced as it is . . . with musical time," writes linguist, semiotician, and literary scholar Roman Jakobson (Jakobson 1987: 72). Jakobson delineated six functions of language: the emotive, the referential, the phatic, the metalingual, the conative, and the poetic. Among those, music shares at least three: the emotive (sound symbolism is an example, but so is the measure and/or volume of a word or a note—its sound shape—as it creates emotion);[2] the phatic (language and music whose purpose is not making meaning but *marking* communication);[3] and the poetic function, a "focus on the message for its own sake" (Jakobson 1987: 69).[4] Cases may also be made for music having a "metalingual" dimension—music about music. Musical citation in jazz improvisation, for example, parallels the processes of reported speech in language, a function that also is metalinguistic,[5] and some music (programmatic music, for example) may be considered referential as well (Lidov 1980). Clearly there is much overlap between musical form and the form of language (Feld and Fox 1994). My interest here is not to insist upon either the similarities or the differences between music and language, but to demonstrate that shifts in ontological and temporal register take similar form in both the embodied performance of possession trance and in narratives about that trance (Urban 1988, 1989). Music, particularly in its rhythmic aspect, plays a crucial role in this process, as the poetics of trance narratives reproduce the rhythms and repetitions of music-induced corporeal trance. This then is an analysis of music in language, emerging from a focus on ethnopoetics and an interest in the power of the voice in performance.

The form of the following narrative is indebted to trance time, to the poetics of the lived body and the music of the Gnawa. It is also unique, however, in terms of its theme and the promise it holds for restructuring relations of subjugation, transforming them into relations of domination by employing and appropriating the sense that has been absent in the previous narratives—that of sight (specularity, of course, being the modus operandus of the Symbolic). Here the referential appropriation of specularity becomes a means of controlling the images and fixing subjectivity, even in the state of multiplicity. In other words, this narrative repeats the ontological register of trance time in its poetic function, while asserting a politics of representation and control in the domain of referentiality.

◆ ◆ ◆

It had been months since I first met Fatna at a ritual *lila*. She had been sitting next to me at one of my first ceremonies, and we had had a conversation. She was an attractive woman nearing thirty, and she tranced with exceptional energy. I next saw her at Fatima Chaouni's place in a small cement-floor house in the Rabat casbah, an old section of town surrounded by stone walls on the edge of a precipice that overlooks the Atlantic ocean at the mouth of the Bou Regrag river. After that *lila* Fatna invited me to her home, and we became friends. I told her that I was writing a book about the Gnawa, and she offered to tell me her story, agreeing to be recorded. Soon after, she invited me as well as two of her closest girlfriends for lunch one Friday afternoon. Fatna lives in a spacious apartment in the Hassan area of Rabat, a fairly well-to-do neighborhood. Her husband was at work at the bank. Fatna made a big couscous with her ten- and fourteen-year-old daughters, and we all ate in the small room off the kitchen where the television was—the eating room for her family. After lunch she made mint tea, turned the television off, and I got out my Marantz recorder.

"Are you sure it's okay if I tape?" I asked her. I had already asked her, and she said she was happy to oblige, but I asked again anyway when I took it out of my bag and placed it on the table. "I can turn it off," I volunteered.

"Well now you've put it on, leave it on," she said giggling. She was clearly feeling a bit like an actress about to be interviewed. Her friends and her daughters also giggled with excitement.

"So when did you first fall?" I asked her.

"I told you, one day I had guests here," she began.

I had some guests that I had invited. There was that music. . . . I was married and had kids and all. And I felt the music, I heard the music of the Gnawa on television. You know, I was at the sink, washing the dishes, when I found myself jumping. I left the faucet open, I left everything, and I'm going and started going. . . . And the entire living room was full of people, it was full of men and women. And the people were sitting there and they hear "thump thump" with my feet; they thought I was holding a drum, and I was hitting it. And my feet were banging, banging, you know, I was about to bang into the wall, and they all came running. They came running, and they found me trancing, trancing, trancing. Right here, right in the kitchen. I left the faucet running. I didn't sense myself [*ma ša'rtš b-ras-i*]. I left the water faucet open and left that stuff and I kept trancing. That's the first time that I ever tranced.

Fatna begins her narrative with the quotative *galt-lak*, I told you. This is a rhetorical phrase that appears in almost all personal narratives and colloquial storytelling in Morocco (Kapchan1996; Pandolfo 1997). While Fatna had never recounted this story to me before, her use of the quotative verb frames the story as story, setting it apart from everyday speech. It signals her awareness of both the narrative event—the storytelling context of our afternoon in her Rabat apartment—and the narrated event—the story that she tells (Bauman 1986; Jakobson 1960). "The discourse within the frames is understood to be of a different ontological status from the discourse without. In particular, the storyrealm, the realm of narrative discourse, conjures up another realm of events, or taleworld, in which the events the story recounts are understood to transpire" (Young 1997: 33, 1987: 15–18). In this narrative Fatna moves deftly between these two realms.

Although Pâques asserts that she never saw anyone "fall" into possession by merely listening to a cassette, here is an example of a woman who experienced her first trance through the mediation of the television (Pâques 1991: 286).[6] Fatna did not see the images, but she heard the music. That the Gnawa were on television speaks to their growing popularity not as ritual healers but as folkloric performers. They have become icons of Moroccan popular music, as is evident in the Essaouira Festival, otherwise known as the Gnawa Festival, which since 1998 brings tens of thousands of people (mostly Moroccans but many foreigners) to the small port city each June. This narrative was recorded before the festival began, however. The Gnawa have been televised for many years in the role of entertainers, but their status in the popular imagination did not prevent Fatna from falling. She heard the music. Indeed she "felt" it before she heard it (*ḥsit bi-ha*). And she began trancing, trancing, trancing, in spite of (because of?) the company in the household. Her narrative emphasizes her lack of control—she left the water running, she almost banged her head into the wall. Water, as mentioned earlier, is associated with the spirits. The *jnun* are often thought to inhabit *al-qawadis*, pipes, drains, and waterways. Here the image of the water running returns us to the flow that trance often facilitates. She continued:

From the first time I ever moved into this house, I couldn't sleep. When I want to sleep, images come to me. Not imaginings. Like that, I just do this and I start to see. I see women, I see . . . I just put my head on the pillow and the light is out, I'm not sleeping. I just go like this with my eyes and those things appear to me before my eyes. Like one time, I had just gone to sleep, you know, and I see myself sitting in the middle and women are encircling me and are happy for me. And they do this to my hair, they gather it up, and they're burning incense. They're treating me like a bride. I wasn't dreaming. I just do this, and I open my eyes. Like a film that is going on near my eyes. And afterwards I open my eyes and my heart pounds, pounds, pounds. And I get afraid [kay ji-ni al-khof, fear comes to me]. It's as if they're happy with me, since, you see, in the beginning they wanted me to begin to work, to begin to see, you know, that kind of work.

"Who?"

"Me."

"But who wanted you to work?"

"They wanted me to work as a seer."

"Who?"

Aj-jnun [the spirits] Aj-jwad [the generous ones]. They come and appear to me all the time. They burned [ceremonial] incense for me and one [woman jinn] brought me a bundle [rizma], that bundle of theirs, that bundle that they bring like a tbuq [a large woven bread basket]. One of them brought me that bundle and said, "You see? These are the colors that you have to start to wear." It was mixed colors, yellow, red, green, all the colors. She said to me, "Those are the colors you're going to start to wear." They're sitting there burning incense for me, happy for me, that I entered their group.

The bundle that Fatna mentions is the assemblage of different colored cloths that an initiate puts together so that she may host a lila. Called a ḥmel, something one carries and sometimes a "burden," the ḥmel forms part of the essential material of the mqaddema. Each color corresponds to a different jinn (or repertoire of jnun, as there are several spirits in each color) and the appropriate cloth is put on those possessed by the spirit invoked. Wearing all the colors signifies being possessed by the entire pantheon of spirits. A mqaddema is often able to "work" all of them.

"Was this in your dream?" I asked her.

Not a dream. I just do this with my eyes. At night. When I do this [she blinks]. I imagine, I see it right next to me. I'm not asleep. And when that stuff is over, I open my eyes. Like a film that's turning. Like a film that I see. And afterwards I do like this with my eyes, and it goes away. I became, you know,

I couldn't sleep. To the point that one time, we were almost going to sell the house. Darkness approaches and my heart starts beating. It pounds and pounds and pounds. I just go put my head down and that [spirit] comes next to my eyes. You know, I went through a war here in the house when I moved in. I can't get up at night, in the dark, I can't stay by myself in a room, I couldn't.

For Fatna, the veil that separates the human and the spirit realm is as thin as an eyelid, that place of suture between inside and out, between what phenomenologist Drew Leder calls the "recessive body"—the interior body that recedes into its own unconscious depths—and the "ecstatic body"—that reaches like a hand into the world. Eyes, as organs of perception usually "disappear from thematic awareness precisely because it is that *from* which I exist in the world. Directed ecstatically outward, my organs of perception and motility are themselves transparent at the moment of use" (Leder 1990: 53, emphasis in original). Yet Fatna is aware of her eyes as entries to another ontological register. She blinks, and she "imagines" [kan-khayl], she has a vision. Fatna also becomes aware of another aspect of her recessive body, the heart. It "pounds and pounds and pounds," making her aware of what is usually under the surface of consciousness—that is, her body itself, and its occupation by another entity. Leder refers to such moments as the body's "dys-appearance," that is, the body becoming aware of itself because of a kind of dysfunction (1990: 85). Fatna has a heightened sense of proprioception, an awareness of her body in time and space, as well as an awareness of its interface with other subjectivities.

"Like a film that's turning." Fatna's inner eyelids become a projection screen of sorts. She inhabits this realm as if she were in a film: she just blinks and the scene changes. With the cinematographic vocabulary that Fatna employs, it is not surprising that the person she seeks out for consultation and relief is himself a television director, an expert in celluloid images and in the construction of an imaginal world, a world between physicality and spirituality:

And afterwards I went to see one *fqih*—a director of television, a big director. I went to him, and he said, "You have Aisha, you have Mimun." I would dream that a tall black man was running after me, black, completely naked. He's running after me. I run and he runs, I run and he runs, I run and he runs after me. When I went to him, and he said to me "You have Aisha, you have Mimun." And he began to wrestle with me, and he began to struggle. When I used to go to him, three times I went to him, I didn't used to speak.

I was mute. I become mute when I go to him. He starts talking to me, and nobody answers him. Until they gave him a time, the day when they were going to speak to him. That's it. They gave him three weeks, until the moon is I don't know where in the sky in a certain place and then they'd . . . because he was speaking with that Mimun; he told him, "Leave this woman. She's not going to work with you; she's not going to do anything with you. Whoever wants something should come to me. But her, leave her be."

"Who? *The Fqih?*"

"The *fqih*. He's a director. But he's also possessed. He has Aisha l-Baḥariya, because he's addicted to fishing. And Aisha al-Baḥariyya possessed him. And he too got into this. He too became a *fqih* [who] writes [charms]. Those fisherman, all of them are possessed by Aisha."

It is important to remember that Fatna lives in Rabat, the capital of Morocco and home to its most important television and radio-broadcasting stations. Rabat is also a coastal city, a place where the salt water meets the fresh at the mouth of the Bou Regrag River. Many people fish in this estuary. The title *fqih* is a designation for a cleric, but here the term is used loosely to refer to someone who has a certain authority vis-à-vis the spirit world. For among the jobs of an *fqih*, especially in the Moroccan countryside, is the divining of spirits and the writing of Qur'anic verses as charms and amulets to ward against them (Wagner 1993). This *fqih* has a day job as a television director, and he is able to divine Fatna's spirits as Sidi Mimun and Aisha Qandisha. (He himself is possessed by one aspect of this spirit—*aiša al-baḥariyya*, Aisha of the Sea.) Fatna envisions Sidi Mimun as a tall, black man who pursues her relentlessly. His nakedness underscores the fact that there is a sexual dimension to possession. As Hell notes, blackness, like the blackness of the Gnawa, has stereotypical connotations of being "hot" (Hell 2002a). There is a dimension of desire in this narrative—Mimun clearly desires Fatna, and she is aware of this desire, and of her status as an object to be possessed by the spirit.

Finally a date is given for a verbal exchange.

I was mute when I went to see him. You know, he said, "if there had been a camera there, we would have videoed you." My husband was there. So was Amrouch. . . . He's the guy that took me to him. He said if there had been a camera, when he started to read [the Qur'an] to me I was straining and straining and straining. He said, when I let go, I screamed as if a ball came out of my mouth. A scream: waaaaaaaaaaa. He said, "if there had been a camera to film you, it would have been amazing."

In this semiprivate divination, Fatna is mute, her voice forcibly contained and silenced by the spirits. The *fqih* speaks to the possessing *jnun*, offering himself as a substitute for Fatna, but at first there is no response. As we saw in chapter three, the senses that are most invoked in narrations about the transition into another state are those of olfaction and audition. Fatna however lost her voice three times when faced with the *fqih*, who in this case is also a master of images and, by extension, a symbol of representation and objectification. Her silence has many ramifications. It is not uncommon for the possessed initially to lose their voice to a spirit. Before the proper channels of mediation are established (in sacrifices, incense, and musical ceremonies), the voice is arrested; it does not flow. Interestingly, the word *gnawa* in the Tamazight language means the "mute ones" and was the designation for those who, coming from parts unknown, were not able to communicate with those in their new environment. Being mute thus symbolizes being a foreigner and, to a certain extent, a captive. And in fact Fatna is a captive of her possessing spirit who renders her mute. Taking away her voice is equivalent to taking away her agency and her subjectivity. Spirits strike their subjects dumb. Most importantly her silence—and the silence of the spirit—is a defense, a refusal to be objectified and to communicate. She narrates her silent body as if it were a container that, if opened, would let out the spirits within, much like the tap of water that Fatna narrates as running in the faucet—unimpeded and excessive. While Fatna is rendered mute by the spirits, there is nonetheless a soundtrack playing in the narrated event: it is the voice of the *fqih* reciting verses of the Qur'an. The implication is that the power of those sacred words will have an effect on the spirit. And indeed, when Fatna "let go," as she said, she screamed "as if a ball came out of [her] mouth: waaaaaaaaaaa." The scream is a kind of transit from the voice of Fatna to the voices of her possessing spirits. It is not a gentle transition, however, but one that seemingly explodes from the inside out. After the symbolic scream, the muteness disappears and not only does Fatna speak, but her possessing spirits speak as well.

> At that point, I kept talking to him. She [Aisha] kept talking to him, negotiating. . . . Mimun was talking to him. He said to him, "I need a sacrifice. I need a he-goat. She has to slaughter for me, then . . ." And that was it. From that point on, he didn't appear to me again. I trance to him, but he doesn't come to me, he doesn't come close to me, or anything. From the time I did the first sacrifice for him—because he demanded his sacrifice—he said, "I want a he-goat"—a sacrifice of a goat. That's it. But Aisha, Aisha

is another story. Aisha, he said to her, "As long as you don't harm her, or go near her . . . but if you want her to work, she can't work for you. Her children are still young and so forth. The woman is not going to work for you; she won't do anything for her. Just don't harass her this way."

And that's how it was. We invited the *ṭolba*. We brought the goat that week. And we brought *ṭolba*. At that point I wasn't even falling. The fits hadn't begun to take hold. The day that I slaughtered the goat here, that day I fell, at the sacrifice I fell. They just slaughtered, and I fell. I stood with them myself, when they slaughtered it at eleven at night. We slaughtered late. As soon as they slaughtered the goat, I passed out [fell]. At night when I slept, what did I see? They came to me, and said, "You just got up and slaughtered for us? You didn't clean for us." Not you didn't clean, [she corrected herself] but "you didn't burn incense, you didn't follow our rituals of sacrifice. You just got up and slaughtered for us."

The next day we did the *ṭolba* [again]. And that *fqih* came to our place. I told him, "this is what happened last night, they appeared at night, and he said and said . . ."

He said, "that's true. You should have burned incense before you sacrificed." We sacrificed without burning incense or anything. His sacrifice needed incense.

The botched sacrifice and her chastisement by the spirits for not conducting it correctly is significant. Fatna did not burn the incense before sacrificing the animal to her spirits, and thus did not facilitate their entry. Incense of course does not respect boundaries, but permeates the air, as it is inhaled and exhaled from the body. By not burning incense, Fatna kept the boundaries closed and the spirits noticed.

We may well ask why Fatna first quoted (or misquoted) the spirits as reproaching her for not cleaning. Whose voice, in fact, are we listening to when she reports the words "you didn't clean for us"? Does Fatna often receive (and report on) such reproaches from others? Is this, in other words, a quote from another narration, a strip of discourse from what Voloshinov calls "inner speech" that has slipped into this narrative?[7] Her self-correction indicates not only the habitual weight of the quoted words (which spilled spontaneously out of her mouth), but her ability to step out of and correct her quotations. The misquoted words (and the spatio-temporal context they index) do not fit here, and so she breaks into the narrated event with a reflection upon her own narration.

Fatna did not initially go to a clairvoyant or a *mqaddema* in the Gnawa tradition. Rather, she went to a *fqih*—that is someone who is learned in the Qu'ran and has the ability to divine spirits. His response, however, was to try to get the spirits to leave Fatna of their own accord (an impossibility in the world of the Gnawa, for whom spirits are permanent residents of the body.) To that end, the *fqih* recited from the Qu'ran and counseled her to bring the *ṭolba* to the house. *ṭolba* (literally, students, though they are often aged or blind) are professionals who recite the Qu'ran in unison (Waugh 2005). They are often brought at moments of passage—births, deaths, and returns from the *ḥajj*. The recitation of the Qur'an, the actual material vibration of the words, endows the house with *baraka* (grace or blessing). As ethnomusicologist Kristina Nelson notes, the "transmission of the Qur'an and its social existence are essentially oral. Qur'anic rhythm and assonance alone confirm that it is meant to be heard. But the oral nature of the Qur'an goes beyond euphony: the significance of the revelation is carried as much by the sound as by its semantic information. In other words, the Qur'an is not the Qur'an unless it is heard" (1985: xiv). The performativity of the Qur'an is thought to reside, in large part, in its sound—that is, in its poetic function. Infusing the space with sacred and transformative sound, the *fqih* hoped to placate the spirits and prevent their permanent habitation in Fatna. A sacrifice was still necessary, however. While Fatna did sacrifice a black he-goat as Sidi Mimun requested, she did not do it with the ritual ceremony of the Gnawa or with incense. Thus her sacrifice was not accepted (*maqbul*), at least not completely. The spirits came to her that evening and reprimanded her. Still, when the blood of the animal began to spill, Fatna went into trance, she "fell." Indeed, she lost consciousness. She became "absent." Henceforth, Fatna was not mute; the spilled blood opened the channels and the words began to flow.

In spirit possession and propitiation there is a relation between internal substances that flow out of the body (blood, tears, laughter) and substances that flow in (music, words, incense). Blood, however, stands both with and apart from these substances. While blood (*dam*) is a primary symbol of identity in the Islamic world (L. Abu-Lughod 1986), the substance of blood as it overflows the bounds of the body (in animal sacrifice as in menstruation) is polluting (Combs-Schilling 1989). Only the first spurts of blood from a sacrificed animal are thought to contain *baraka*. After that, it quickly becomes a contaminant. The possessed, especially those experienced at "working the spirits," often throw themselves upon the sacrificed animal to drink those first ebullitions; but part of the power of the Gnawa resides in their ability to touch and imbibe blood in all its stages. They are able to handle ritual pollutants with immunity. For this they are both feared and respected in Moroccan society (Hell 1999a).

After the sacrifice Fatna went into trance, ceding her voice to the possessing spirit, who began to talk. Fatna uses the verb *na ṭa qa*, to utter, as well as *ha ḍa ra*, which in Moroccan colloquial Arabic means "to speak." Propitiating her spirits with sacrifice, naming and acknowledging them, loosened not only her body, but her vocal chords as well. The spirits used her voice to express their wishes as well as their clairvoyance. The ability to give voice to the spirits signifies their presence: they speak. Fatna is also able to *revoice* or narrate their voiced desires in the narrative event, repossessing her voice in the act of reported speech:

1. At that point, I kept talking to him.
2. She [Aisha] kept talking to him, [she] negotiating . . .
3. Mimun was talking to him.
4. He said to him, "I need a sacrifice. I need a he-goat. She has to slaughter for me, then . . ." And that was it.

In the above discourse, the personal pronoun "I" is an index with multiple referents. The pronoun literally shifts the subject between identities (M. Silverstein 1976). On the first line it is Fatna who is indexed: "I" kept talking to him (the *fqih*). The pronoun "she" on the next line indexes the spirit Aisha Qandisha, and the spirit Sidi Mimun is mentioned on line three. It is important to remember, however, that both spirits use Fatna's voice in the taleworld, which Fatna is able to objectify and report to me in the storyrealm. On line four Fatna uses direct reported speech, further multiplying the referent of the personal pronoun: "He [Sidi Mimun] said to him [the *fqih*], "I [Sidi Mimun] need a sacrifice. I need a he-goat. She [Fatna] has to slaughter for me [Sidi Mimun], then . . .""

To slaughter to is make a sacrifice for the propitiation of the spirit. There are in fact two symbolic sacrifices indexed here—the sacrifice of a he-goat, as well as the sacrifice of Fatna's voice to the spirit. Revoicing these words as reported speech gives Fatna a way to control what, at the moment of possession, was beyond her control—namely, her voice. As the speaker, Fatna's voice "infiltrates" all these pronouns (Voloshinov 1972: 120–121). She is the person reporting about Sidi Mimun; she is the "I" inside the quotation marks who is voicing the desires of Sidi Mimun; she is the object of Sidi Mimun's directive—"She has to slaughter for me." As Voloshinov asserts, reported speech is both "speech within speech, utterance within utterance, as well as *speech about speech, utterance about utterance*" (1972: 115, emphasis in original). In other words, reported speech has a metalinguistic function; it reports not just the past utterances of others, but it *reports on* their manner of reception by the speaker (Urban 1984b).[8] The quotation marks set the speech apart from Fatna, making it autonomous; and yet they cannot hold out the grain of her voice, the weight and tenor of her past actions and utterances, the texture and timbre of her acoustic being, infused with the experiences that make up a life (Barthes 1985). Unlike other examples of direct and indirect reported speech, the utterances of possessing spirits have only ever existed in the vocal apparatus of their hosts. Reporting the speech of spirits is a kind of double ventriloquism: the voices of spirits are always already revoiced in the bodies of the possessed, and their later quotation expresses not only "an active relation of one message to another," but a relation of one subject to another: "Orientation of the word toward the addressee has an extremely high significance," notes Voloshinov.

> In point of fact, word is a two-sided act. It is determined equally by whose word it is and for whom it is meant. . . . I give myself verbal shape from another's point of view, ultimately from the point of view of the community to which I belong. A word is a bridge thrown between myself and another. If one end of the bridge depends on me, then the other depends on my addressee. A word is a territory shared by both addresser and addressee, by the speaker and his interlocutor. (Voloshinov 1972: 86)

In the context of trance narratives, however, there are more bridges and territories than in usual dialogue. Fatna clearly remembers what the spirits said and revoices their utterances to me and the other women present. But the first bridge is that between Fatna and her spirits. The words uttered by Fatna are only sometimes her own. When the spirits are speaking, she acts as both addresser and addressee. To elaborate on Voloshinov, each and every word in narratives of possession trance expresses the "one" in relation to the "many."

Greg Urban provides the terms to analyze the different "I"s employed in this kind of discourse. Urban draws on the work of Emile Benveniste (1971 [1956], 1971 [1958]), who brought attention to the particular "nonreferential" status of pronouns in language (the pronoun "I," for example, indexes different persons depending on the speaker; its interpretation is thus tied to its *pragmatic context of enunciation* and not a referential meaning). Urban focuses on the relation between the pronoun "I" and reported speech. When the pronoun "I" is used in quotation marks it no longer refers to the subject who is speaking (as in "He said, 'I am going'"). It is this relationship that interests Urban and that interests us here, as the use of the pronoun also indexes the way the social self is constructed (Benveniste 1971 [1956], 1971 [1958]; Singer 1984). Urban delineates several pragmatic contexts of the pronoun "I," beginning with the indexical referential "I" that stands for the speaker (what he calls the "everyday self") and moving progressively in the direction of "I"s that index a self other than the everyday. The further one travels from the everyday self, the more reliant the pronoun's meaning is on extralinguistic pragmatic cues. Employing what Urban calls the "theatrical I," for example, an actor identifies with a self in a cultural script to such an extent that the everyday self is hidden. The acting is nonetheless understood. Finally, what Urban calls a "projective I" is enacted when "the actor . . . become[s] so immersed in another 'I' that the other 'I' becomes once again virtually indexical referential" (Benveniste 1971 [1956], 1971 [1958]: 38). Possession is such an example. When Fatna reports "He said to him, 'I need a sacrifice. I need a he-goat. She has to slaughter for me, then . . .'" she is reporting a moment in the past when she (Fatna) was He, Sidi Mimun, and she/he used the projective pronoun "I" to refer to herself (which was himself). "And that was it!" she exclaims. Urban notes that certain forms of narrative, such as myth-telling, employ the projective "I" and that "the trance-like quality that is involved [in such uses] suggests a possible comparison with *actual* trance behavior and possession," going on to say that if "the present suggestions should be borne out by empirical research, it will be possible to link together trance and theater, as well as other phenomena, such as the Shokleng origin myth-telling, in a single scheme, in which the discourse 'I' of these forms grows out of the basic anaphoric [substitutive] 'I' of direct quotation" (Urban 1989: 41, emphasis in original). The discourse above provides one such example of empirical research.[9]

If pronouns in Fatna's discourse are anaphoric (substituting one identity for another) in the referential domain, the sonority of her voice always remains in some way her own. The voice is usually equated with the body and with its specificity: beginning in the muscles of the diaphragm, rising up with and through the breath, resonating the vocal chords—it is an expression as physical as gesture, only auditory instead of visual, a mark of personal identity. We recognize language groups through phonemic systems and regional groups through intonation patterns. The voice of an intimate is immediately known, evoking emotional and physiological responses. Marcel Proust, upon hearing his grandmother's voice on the telephone for the first time, could immediately identify not just his grandmother, but the suffering that she has endured and that is encoded in her voice (Proust 1993; S. Stewart 2002: 107–108).

In Islamic theology, the voice is primary. On receiving the revelation of the Qur'an, the Prophet Mohammed was told to recite it aloud, and it is still chanted, the rules for its enunciation highly codified. To voice something is to body it forth, to possess and own it. But the voice, like music and incense, inhabits the listener. Indeed, it cannot be kept out. As writer Wayne Kostenbaum notes in regard to opera, "a singer doesn't expose her own throat, she exposes the listener's interior. Her voice enters me, makes me a 'me,' an interior, by virtue of the fact that I have been entered. The singer, through osmosis, passes through the self's porous membrane, and discredits the fiction that bodies are separate, boundaried packages" (1993: 43). This is certainly true in the case of possession, where the voice of the spirit resounds through the body of its host and its environs. But it is also true of the music (some of it vocal) that propitiates the spirit and causes the possessed subject to trance. The rhythms of the qraqab inhabit the listener long after the ceremony is over.

That the voice of Mimun or Aisha comes through Fatna's body is proof of her possession. It is an expression of intimacy with the spirits. Quoting them is also a repossession (by Fatna) of her subjectivity vis-à-vis the spirits. And, like spiritual utterances in other traditions (speaking in tongues, for example), the voice of the spirit carries with it baraka: blessing and grace.

> And from that point on I [Fatna] began to fall all the time. I fall and I start uttering [nṭaq], always I fall and I start speaking [kan-bda kan-hder]. Like now, like now me, I, the fits [crises] take hold of me. I become absent [kan-ghaib] and start to talk. Like now, if I'm nervous, I fall. And if I laugh a lot, I fall also. The two. Just like that, I start to laugh, to laugh, to laugh and then I go.
>
> Take for example, Aisha, she takes hold of me and contorts me completely. You know, I've been through a lot.

Like the scream that came barreling out of Fatna's mouth "like a ball: waaaaaaaaaa," laughing is an outburst of emotion. The opposite of being mute, both laughter and crying symbolize a loss of control of the voice through an excessive performance of that voice. In a sense, the voice overcomes the subject. Laughter, like crying, is also accompanied by tears, the emissions of the body outpouring. Flow. And, in this narrative it is poetry, or at least the poetic function that "organizes [laughing and] weeping into intelligible expression." (S. Stewart 2002: 206).

Nerves, on the other hand, are unvoiced bodily reactions, but they are no less overpowering. Laughter, crying, and nervous agitation are all connected to emotional states triggered by external circumstances. Fatna uses the French word *crise*; she also transforms the French word *nerveux/euse* (nervousness, tension, or depression) and makes it into a Moroccan Arabic reflexive construction, *ila kan-t-nervvas*, "if I get nervous." Why the introduction of foreign terms here? Why the code switching? Is it because she was talking to me, a foreigner? Perhaps. But her close friends and her two adolescent daughters were also present, and understood her completely. Moroccan Arabic is replete with formal code switching as well as with less formal (more creative) renderings of French words into Arabic grammar (Moha Ennaji 1985, 2005; Heath 1989; Sadiqi 2003).[10] Using the French-derived words indexes a condition that is recognized as pathological in the West. Fatna does not say that she is neurotic or depressed, but she does acknowledge the role of "nerves" (and by extension, neurosis) in spirit possession. She does this again by using the French word *crise* as a synonym for falling into possession trance. Before Fatna falls, she experiences an excess of emotion—either in the form of hilarity and laughter or extreme nervous agitation.

Fatna has a case of nerves. As anthropologist Nancy Scheper-Hughes has noted, to talk about "nerves" is often to corporealize and medicalize states that are social in nature; rather than blame the high rate of children's mortality among Brazil's poor on malnutrition or the sickness of workers on "chronic deprivation," for example, the people of the Alto de Cruzeiro in Northeast Brazil instead speak of having a case of nerves or suffering from nervous crises (1992). And although *nervios* is not related to spirit possession per se, the symptoms that sufferers of this ailment describe are remarkably similar to those reported in cases of spirit possession in Morocco—trembling, shaking, heat and cold seeming to "enter" the body, fatigue, dissociation, temporary paralysis, and loss of control (Low 1994: 140, 157). While spirit possession cannot be equated with *nervios*, similar metaphorical processes are at work nonetheless. Both *nervios*, a cross-cultural symptom for embodied distress, as well as *falling* (to the spirits), are bodily metaphors that have social ramifications. There is in both cases "an exchange of meanings, images, representations, between the body personal and the collective and social body social" (Scheper-Hughes 1992: 169). Both enactments may sometimes be considered forms of resistance to dominant expectations,[11] and both may arise from "bodily experiences [that] are metaphors of self/society relations, with the body acting as the mediating symbolic device" (Low 1994: 157).

Fatna does not suffer from malnutrition or disease, at least not noticeably.

She lives in a comfortable apartment in one of the capital's more affluent quarters.[12] The case of nerves that Fatna evokes, while not indicative of poverty, may nonetheless be related to gender, (Bourguignon 1976; Lewis 1989 [1971], 1986) and what Janice Boddy in her work on spirit possession in the Sudan calls the "overdetermination" of women (1989). While Fatna has fulfilled her social function as a mother of three, she began her reproductive life at the precocious age of fourteen, and her relationship with her older husband was a source of anxiety for her. The falling body is also the body subjected—to spirits, to humans. It is a body that is not under one's control. And, like *nervios*, it is possible to interpret the performance of spirit possession as a resistance to other forms of hegemony, a way of talking back, both in the realm of gender (Boddy 1989) and in the realm of politics and colonialism (Stoller 1995).

Fatna acknowledges that for her, nerves are a catalyst or at least an accompaniment to spirit possession. They are a symptom, and symptoms call for cures, or at least responses. It is not surprising then that people often become vulnerable to spirit possession at transitional moments in the life cycle when new emotional solutions have to be found. Possession is a way of "working through" from the emotional status quo that no longer "works for" the propitiator to a new state of emotional readiness or workability (Reddy 2001). Possession trance enables the possessed to enact an expanded emotional repertoire. It is a way of breakthrough both into the performance of another identity and into a social realm wherein different norms apply. Fatna, for example, eventually left her husband (or created the conditions for divorce), explored her sexuality, and traveled abroad after becoming multiply possessed. The trance ceremony is a performance of repertoires of emotion—forlornness, regret, anger, abjection, beatitude, and rapture. Novices are controlled by them, while experienced trancers learn to control the trance, the spirit, and the emotion.

THE ENTRANCED EYE/I

There are similarities between the virtual world of technology and the virtual worlds of spirits and the way the power of the imagination works through both. Spirits, when they are envisioned, materialize like images on a screen. And film conjures a world that possesses and inhabits the viewer. This irony was not lost on the ethnographer and filmmaker, Jean Rouch, who filmed trance ceremonies among the Songhay in Niger. Rouch called his method of documenting trance "*ciné-transe*"—that is, an entering of trance in order to film trance. He did not presuppose that his cinematic trance was in any way the same as the trances he was filming. Nonetheless, it was the process of changing states that interested him, that is, the methodology—what might be called the "technology of trance." As someone who studied the methods of world-making through images, Rouch the filmmaker was like a magician who, following Mauss, "is capable of being possessed . . . is conscious of it and generally knows the spirit that possesses him" (Mauss 1972 [1902]: 48–49).

In ciné-transe Rouch transposed the techniques of trance performance from one medium (the body possessed by a spirit) to another (the filmmaker's body possessed by documentation), creating a third performance, contained in the celluloid itself. Like possession trance, filmmaking requires an audience, people to witness the fabrication of worlds and, more importantly, to enter into them. Rouch himself enacted what performance theorist Richard Schechner has called "restored behavior" wherein a performance is "treated as a film director treats a strip of film. These strips," notes Schechner, "can be rearranged or reconstructed; they are independent of the causal systems (social, psychological, technological) that brought them into existence." Like spirits, "they have a life of their own" (1985: 35). Restored behaviors are the building blocks not only of theater, but also of all performances. They are like morphemes in linguistics, mythemes in Lévi-Strauss's structural analysis of myth, or phrases in music. "Restored behavior can be put on the way a mask or a costume is. Its shape can be seen from the outside, and changed. That's what theater directors, councils of bishops, master performers, and great shamans do: change performance scores. . . . Put in personal terms, restored behavior is 'me behaving as if I am someone else' or 'as if I am beside myself,' or 'not myself,' as when in trance" (Schechner 1985: 37). For Schechner, the link between trance and theater is self-evident. Rouch made similar innovations into film; the restoration of ciné-transe has yet another life when new audiences receive it. Rouch's work presaged and influenced other French scholarship that viewed spirit possession through the lens of theatrical performance (Stoller 1995: 20).[13]

Film is a medium whose power resides in the seeing eye. In Fatna's narrative the "eye" is a recurring symbol: It's "not a dream," she says. "I just do this with my eyes. . . . [she blinks.] . . . I open my eyes. Like a film that's turning. Like a film that I see. And afterwards I do like this with my eyes, and it goes away." Fatna begins to have visions that she compares to film. And she becomes the main character in this film. She becomes an object to herself, an actor in a script. The script belongs to the jnun. They are the authors, yet their script—which contains the reflexivity that mediation fosters—allows Fatna to see herself as if from outside, from the perspective of "they"—in effect, cinemato-graphically. Like an actor, she is possessed by her role, but is also aware that she is in it. The medium of film—even the idea of it—allows Fatna to come to terms with her possession, to extract herself from the embodied state of being *maskun*, or inhabited, to the objectified state of seeing. Fatna's ability to imag-ine her possession experiences as film imagery allows her to fix and thus con-trol what is inherently mutable and moving. Just as the female viewers of Egypt-ian melodrama analyzed by Lila Abu-Lughod, Fatna narrates her life as if it were a movie—and a modern and mediated one at that (2005). Choosing to fix her experiences in visual images is a way to stay time, to arrest the ephemeral, and capture states of otherness that can only be recounted in a certain chronology (though they may be experienced differently). This act, which is evidenced in Fatna's narrative, is one of empowerment and control. While Fatna's narrative may or may not be an example of what Freud calls a "screen memory"—that is, a projection of a select memory that acts as a gateway to other, less-accessible memories, a memory that both screens out and stands in for another—it is cer-tainly a *screened* memory: Fatna "screens" her possession—seeing it as a projec-tion, but also translating it to herself and others.[14]

Remembering, narrating, and re-enacting relations of submission and domination—whether subjugation to spirit owners or actual flesh-and-blood oppressors—always contains a part of desire, however mechanical or per-verse. Narrating those memories is a second-order representation, one that al-lows the speaking subject to express desire, to create it, and, most importantly, to redefine it. Reading the phenomenon of possession as a metaphor for larger historically determined relations of power, we see that the power to restruc-ture the relations of the past depends, in part, upon the ability of the subject to rewrite history in the present. "In the structure of desire that animates ac-tion, the present condition becomes a means for achieving future goals," notes Leder (1990: 18). Judging from Fatna's narrative, technology provides one avenue of promise in our ability to reimagine relations between owners and their possessions.

Attending to the embodied poetics of narrative, however, is at least equally important.

REVOLUTION IN SENSORY LANGUAGE

The production of desire in narrative is not only expressive, it is also creative. Fatna's narrative has the power to involve the listener on many levels. It is a form of entrancement. It is precisely the intersubjectivity that these narratives perform that makes the somatic aspects of language worthy of attention. As Antonin Artaud reminds us, "A gesture narrowly divides us from chaos" (1958). But gestures can also catapult us into chaos. The somatic indexes in language act as gestures in this regard—they are the flesh of narrative, actively possessing the listener through the performance of sound-symbolism, repetition, and rhythmic alterations—all aspects that create the hypnomantic states described in the narratives of possession themselves, fabricating worlds that both speakers and listeners inhabit together.

Repetition

It is significant that Fatna's first trance experience was evoked by a mediated event—she heard Gnawa music on television—the "medium" par excellence for the mechanical repetition of images. As elsewhere in the Arab-speaking world, the last twenty years have seen a radical change in the daily viewing habits of Moroccans (L. Abu-Lughod 2005). In 1982 when I first went to Morocco, there was only one state-run channel with restricted hours. A few years later, a second cable channel was introduced. Now, however, a vast majority of Moroccans have satellite dishes—regardless of income level. The roofs of every city are dotted with dishes that seem to look, like eyes, into the sky. Even the remotest of Saharan villages has access to an array of national and international images. The diversity of information available to the average Moroccan has increased exponentially. There are sitcoms that feature the tribulations of people in different regions of Morocco, to say nothing of the portrayal of life dramas in Egypt, Syria, Latin America, and the United States. There are plays and music videos and, during Ramadan, serials about the life of the Prophet. What's more, the repetition of images that television facilitates helps to fashion consumer habits and modern subjectivities (L. Abu-Lughod 2005).

As Roland Barthes notes, the visual image repeats "mechanically what could never be repeated existentially" (1980: 15). When Fatna went into trance she was not watching the screen, however. She heard the music from the other room; she felt it in the rhythms emitted from the screen. And she found herself trancing, as if she were an observer to her own performance, without volition. Her narrative uses repetition and intonation: "And my feet were banging, banging, you know, I was about to bang into the wall, and they all came running. They came running, and they found me trancing, trancing, trancing. Right here, right in the kitchen. I left the faucet running. I didn't sense myself [ma ša'rtš b-ras-i]. I left the water faucet open and left that stuff, and I kept trancing." And afterwards, "I open my eyes, and my heart pounds, pounds, pounds" and "[d]arkness approaches, and my heart starts beating. It pounds and pounds and pounds," and once again, "Just like that, I start to laugh, to laugh, to laugh and then I go."

All the words that Fatna reiterates have to do with rhythm—she "bangs" her feet, making repetitive and percussive noise; she "trances" (also involving regular rhythmic bodily gestures), and her heart "pounds," also recalling drum beats. Her body becomes a drum: "And the people were sitting there and they hear 'thump thump' with my feet; they thought I was holding a drum, and I was hitting it." Indeed the same verb is used for her feet and her heart: ḍa ra ba: to beat, pound, or bang. It is hard not to invoke Rodney Needham's work here on the dependable presence of rhythm in states involving transition (1967), but George Steiner's work on narrative and temporality also comes to mind: "The mind," Steiner says, "has as many chronometries as it has hopes and fears. During states of temporal distortion, linguistic operations may or may not exhibit a normal rhythm" (1998: 137). Fatna has no recourse to actual instruments (like those used in the trance ceremonies), but she makes her body and words percussive, a link to the "spiritual world" (Steiner 1998: 608). The same rhythmic changes that accompany the possessed subject into the different temporal dimension of trance are repeated here in parallel repetitions:

Erjli-ya kanu kay-ḍrub, kay-ḍrub, kay-ḍrub
My feet were banging, banging, banging
Kunt ghadi n-ḍrub ras-i f-al-ḥaiṭ
I was going to bang my head against the wall

Wa jauw kay-jriu
And they came running
U lqauw-ni kan-jdab, kan-jdab, kan-jdab
And they found me trancing, trancing, trancing

ma ša'rtš b-ras-i
I didn't sense myself
khalit l-rubinay mḥlu:l u khalit dak ši u bqit kan-jdab
I left the faucet open and starting trancing

ghir y-uṣl ẓalma wa qalb-i kay-bqa kay-ḍrub
When darkness approaches my heart starts to bang
kay-ḍrub, kay-ḍrub, kay-ḍrub
It bangs and bangs and bangs

bḥal haka
Just like that
kan-dḥak, kan-dḥak, kan-dḥak
I laugh and laugh and laugh

The italicized words all share an assonance that is striking. Like much repetition in poetry, the narrative has a haunting quality, one that "gets under the skin." This is another example of how, in the words of Katharine Galloway Young, "narrative inveigles the body into entering into its reality, into being embodied by the narrative" (2002a: 46). But what, in fact, is inveigling what or whom? Adam Kendon has noted that physical gesture often corresponds with the rhythmic patterns of language. "Gesture phrases pattern with the stress and intonational structure of the speech they co-occur with in such a way as to have a visual rhythmic character that seems to mark out the rhythmic organization of the utterance. There is, thus, a dimension of discourse structure marking to be observed in all co-speech gestures" (Kendon 1995). For Kendon, language leads, and gesture follows. In the example above, however, the bodily rhythms and repetitions of possession trance imprint language. Traces of the body are found in all the words; or rather, the body and its words are indivisible. There is what linguist Janice B. Nuckolls calls a "sound alignment" between the bodily experience of trance and the narrative that recounts it; but instead of a purely "sonically driven disposition" creating the alignment, there is a somatic impetus to the words; the body is also present therein (2004: 65).

Sound Symbolism

Derrida notes that "As soon as a sign emerges, it begins by repeating itself." (1978). Repetition, in fact, becomes one of the ways that desire is embodied in language and that a narrative about trance becomes an entranced narrative. Although the repetition of key phrases in Fatna's narrative is not devoid of actual content meaning, the assonance, intonation, and parallelism of the words she uses forefronts their form more than their meaning. As Stewart notes,

> sound patterns teach us to listen and not merely hear. A volition that is intersubjective and active is required. Indeed, patterns or orders in time differ from randomness and disorder in part because they *are* memorizable. Experiments in memory show that of all the information borne by a melody, the temporal relationships internal to the work are the most central to our capacity to retain it. Variations in pitch, loudness, and timbre can all be completely changed and the melody is still recognizable, but if the internal

temporal relationships are changed, even without any other changes, the melody is unintelligible. (S. Stewart 2002: 205–206)

Fatna employs words for their sound symbolic value—onomatopoetically. Indeed their very excess makes their "sense" less important than their sound. It is the density of sound symbolism that creates the effect. The words that Fatna uses are overfull in that they mean in several dimensions—content-wise, to be sure, but also in their capacity as melodic phrases and percussive interjections. In this they may be considered ideophonic—that is, they not only refer to a meaning, but they *perform* meaning with their sound shapes: intonation, drawn-out vowels, and staccato phoneme repetitions. These sounds are also imitative of other nonverbal sounds found in the ritual ceremony: the hollow metal bell of the *qraqab*, the softer clap of hollowed palms, and the low vibration of the *hajhuj* strings thrumming. "Through ideophones' performativity, speakers enact their alignments with the world by means of sound" (Nuckolls 2004: 67). The alignment performed here links music to body to word in a context that engages the listeners and draws us in.

Temporal Acceleration

Acceleration in tempo is often the indicator of trance in possession ceremonies. Indeed, the possessed dancer is in synch with the ritual musician, who gradually speeds up the tempo of the song until the propitiant actually falls to the ground, signaling the end of the session. This musical acceleration is found in other Sufi-influenced rituals in Morocco as well. Sufis in the Qadiriyya order, for example, will chant the names of God, moving their bodies in time with the incantation, which gradually gets faster and faster. Such acceleration in regular and rhythmic increments leads to ecstasy for the Sufis and trance for those who are possessed by spirits.

Such acceleration is also present in the music of the narrative. A crescendo accompanies Fatna's increasing involvement with her story. More noticeable still is her change of tempo, which gets faster and faster, just as her words get more rhythmic and repetitive. Clearly there is a mimetic faculty at work in this narrative that is transferring the embodied experiences of trance into the narrated world. There is an isomorphism at the level of form that changes the quality and tenor of the expression, making a narrative about trance into an entranced narrative. But this change of "key" (S. K. K. Langer 1957)—which is also a modulation from narrating memories of the body to performing bodily memory—also changes the "chronotopic" dimensions of the genre. That is, the spatio-temporal relations that predominate in narrations about the body change dramatically when the narrator begins to perform a somatic repertoire, appropriating icons and gestures from another realm into the text. An entranced narrative is also entrancing, actively involving the interlocutor in an intersubjective and sense-based experience.

SENSE AND SIGHT

In Fatna's narrative, a tension emerges between the poetic voice of sound and the objectifying voice of sight, the filmmaker. In recounting her experiences, Fatna watches herself being watched. Her eye becomes the objective eye: whether open or closed, she sees herself as if she were another. It is this ability that allows her to accept her multiplicity, but also to subjugate it to her own will. She turns the gaze back upon her spirits—in other words, making them objects in her scenario. In the end, she is not only inhabited by the spirits but she possesses *them* in the idea of objectification. The invocation of cinematic metaphors facilitates this. The incorporeal is exteriorized, the spirits inhabiting not just her body, but also an image that she herself can see. If possession is an expression of power relations, Fatna's narrative recounts her desire for the spirits, her acceptance of them, and ultimately her ability to control them. Through her narration, she becomes, in effect, the owner of the owners (*malika al-mluk*), the master (*m'allema*).

Yet Fatna's narrative is also a poetic text that reiterates, through formal imitation, the bodily experiences of trance. Jakobson might insist that one of these functions—either the referential or the poetic—must be dominant (Jakobson and Halle 1971), though it is difficult to assess which one that would be. Rather, the power of this narrative resides in its multifunctionality as well as its ability to align speaker and listeners (human and nonhuman) with the world of *jinn* and trance through music and rhythm. Just as the voice of the narrator shifts to many identities, so the intersubjective realities created by her words are different for each pair of ears that hear them. This narrative of trance attests to:

1. The (often abject) desire that underlies the relation of the possessed subject with her spirits.
2. The connection between the body and language in the production of this desire, particularly by means of sound alignment.
3. The ability of the possessed subject to become an object to herself and

for others, not only in the dissociation of the trance state, but also in her ability to narrate her own multiplicity as if cinematographically, to objectify and thereby control her desire.

Inhabiting the sensorium of the spirits, possessed women are inhabited by sensate worlds and hierarchies otherwise unavailable to them. As Carol Laderman and Maria Roseman remind us, "if healing is to be successful, the senses must be engaged" (1996: 4). The alignment between sound and world heals the disalignment between spirit and host. Engaging her listeners thus, Fatna inveigles them into her narrative so that auditors are likewise able to both possess a different relation to the senses than the habitual and to approach—analogically and perhaps even physiologically—a world where multiplicity is not exotic but embraced.

ON THE THRESHOLD
OF A DREAM

♦ ♦ ♦

*Everyone knew very well back then that words and what they described were so close that on
mornings when the fog descended on the phantom villages in the mountains, the words and what
they described were intermingled. People who woke from their sleep on foggy mornings could not
tell their dreams from reality, poems from life, and names from human beings. Back then, stories
and lives were so real that nobody even conceived of asking which was the original life or which
was the original story. Dreams were lived through and lives were thoroughly interpreted.*
—Orhan Pamuk (1990: 263)

*Dreams are interpreted, but that which is perceived by sense perception is not interpreted.
However, when man ascends in the degrees of gnosis, he will come to know through
both faith and unveiling, that he is a dreamer in the state of ordinary wakefulness
and that the situation in which he dwells is a dream.*
—William C. Chittick (1989: II 379.24, attributed to Ibn al-'Arabi)

*[I]n the end the only events in my life worth telling are those when the imperishable world
erupted into this transitory one. That is why I speak chiefly of inner experiences, amongst which
I include my dreams and visions. . . . They were the fiery magma out of which the stone that
had to be worked was crystallized. . . . All other memories of travel, people and my
surroundings have paled beside these interior happenings.*
—Carl Jung (1963: 4–5)

In February 1995 I woke to find myself in ascent, as if my soul were detaching
from my body and rising up. Instead of fighting this sensation and trying to
remain in my body, I let myself go. Almost immediately I was in the clouds.
Standing close to me was a woman of immense stature. She was a giant
dressed in white robes. There were other robed beings in the vicinity, like angels but of human scale. Only this woman was gigantic. Although no words
were spoken, I knew she was benevolent and that she was welcoming me.
When I woke to my body I felt that I had been visited by a grace that would con-

tinue to protect me. When I later recounted my dream to the Moroccan professor who had first introduced me to the Gnawa, he pulled the car he was driving over to the curb, looked at me squarely in the eyes and pronounced: "That was Lalla Malika."

What is the relation between dreams and sensation, between the senses and narrative? We usually think of the senses as a component of our waking life, while images are the domain of dreams. In fact, the senses play an important role in dreaming and dream interpretation, as they do in narratives about trance. "Dreams, like other acts of the imagination, offer us alternative embodiments" (Young 2002a: 47). The relation between senses and the unconscious, though tacit, is also intimate.

With Freud, the focus of oneiric studies shifted from the importance of the dream to collective and social life to the importance of the dream in the inner life of the modern subject. And although the interpretation of the dream is considered subjective and often veiled in symbols, there is a faith that its truth exists "somewhere" in the dream narrative. But this is not representative of much philosophical and intellectual thought in the West. Anthropologist Greg Urban notes that in

> modern Europe and America, the dream is of little or no public interest. It is not thought to pertain to anything outside the individual. It is inconceivable, for example, that a dream narrative from an American president should become the focus of national interest. The interpretive or metadiscursive patterns associated with dream narratives define them as irrelevant to the empirical project. Although dreams are experiences, they are not the kind of experiences capable of revealing anything fundamental about the universe or about the inner working of things. (Urban 1996: 8)

Yet, as both Urban and anthropologist Laura Graham demonstrate, in some cultures dreams—and particularly dream narratives—may be essential ways that individuals perform their identity vis-à-vis the community as well as ways that the community itself is defined from within (Graham 1995). In discussing dreams, it is important to keep in mind that dream narratives are not dreams per se; rather, "the dream-text, however distorting, is itself evocative of the dream-experience, perhaps even formative of it. It is appellative. It evokes our experience of the dream, and presumably those of our interlocutors" (Crapanzano 2004: 22).

The dreams of kings—in Morocco or elsewhere in the Arab world—do not make the news. However the importance of dreams in the Arab-Islamic tradition, as well as their place in contemporary society, is quite different than that in the Western tradition. In the Islamic world the tradition dates back to the Prophet himself, whose interpreted dreams are recorded in the Hadith (the "sayings" of the Prophet). The literature on dream symbolism, recollections, and interpretation in Arabic is substantial. Islamic Studies and Arabic Literature scholar Toufy Fahd notes that "oneirocritic literature represents for Islam the most authentic cultural history of its Semitic past" (1966: 351). Indeed for Fahd, reading manuscripts that describe dream scenarios is like reading history; "the dream is like a screen on which is projected the daily life of every class in the society" (1966: 360).

In Morocco many believe that the soul leaves the body during sleep, traveling to visit other places and other souls. (When I recounted to a Sufi leader in the Boutshishi order, for example, that I often travel to places—houses, apartments, dwellings—in my dreams and that I can remember those places even in waking life, he explained to me that my soul was visiting other souls, and that the dwellings were symbolic of other beings). Sleep is also compared to death. The soul leaves the body temporarily during sleep, but permanently at death. "It is this factor of death," anthropologist Stefania Pandolfo notes,

> that determines the truth value, the authority, and the effectiveness of dreams—a *parole* coming from elsewhere; dreams can resolve conflicts, deliver a person from illness, and determine decisions that change the direction of one's life. Their course can be influenced by prophylactic actions and utterances, and in some contexts they can be ritually induced, as when a person who is ill, paralyzed or possessed goes to a saint's tomb to dream, and sleeps there—sometimes for months or years—waiting for the dream that will bring release. The symbolic economy of certain sanctuaries where the sick and possessed go to seek recovery is rhythmed and regulated by the *parole* of dreams, a *parole* that is law." (1997: 184)

Recollections of dreams, visions, and experiences of trance provide the discursive fabric of a collective imaginary among a community loosely called *shab l-hal* or the friends of trance in Morocco. As mentioned, a "state"—*al-hal* in Moroccan colloquial Arabic—is a phenomenological condition that, in Sufi usage, originates from God, bestowing grace or *baraka* on its recipient. It is often related to mystical states of communion with the divine.[1] (Sufis are said to enter *al-hal* frequently in their *dhikr* or "remembrance of God" ceremonies. And music can often induce it [During 2001: 92]).[2] Revelations come when one is in a particular *hal*, as do visions. Some dreams may also be interpreted as altered states in which humans receive messages from the nonhuman world. These dreams are events that call for interpretation and sometimes action. A visitation from a dead parent or ancestor, for example, is usually auspicious, though it may require the dreamer to give an offering (ṣdaqa), often to the poor.

DREAMS

Another dream: On a cool March night I awoke suddenly. To my immediate left a huge dark head was looking straight at mine. Ugly, it reminded me of a gargoyle, with exaggerated and aggressive features. I knew intuitively that this was Sidi Mimun. In the Gnawa ceremony Sidi Mimun wears the color black, and black benzoin is burned for him. He often impels those he possesses to cut themselves with knives, though they are rarely wounded. I wanted to wake my husband who was sleeping peacefully beside me, but I could not move, locked as I was in an encounter with the symbolic. Paralyzed, I felt terror.

"Henaya n-subqu," the head said to me in Arabic. "We will win out."

"La t-sabaqu-š, you won't win out," I heard myself respond with great difficulty. He then disappeared, and I woke a second time—this time to my body. I felt my heart beating quickly; the blood rushing through my veins was loud in my ears. My husband did not stir, and I did not wake him. What would I tell him? Of a visitation? He would not believe me or would simply send me back to sleep in the comfort of his arms. I listened to the sounds of night. Down the street at the big mosque the chanting that precedes the dawn prayer (al-ibtihalat) had begun, mournful and low; the sounds moved through the still dark air, seeming to rustle the palm fronds that were lined up like a path between the mosque and the balcony outside my bedroom. As my heart slowed I drifted back to sleep until the morning.

Where did this voice come from? My unconscious? The spirit realm? I heard it clearly and it remained in my memory. On the subject of hearing, al-Ghazzali notes,

> And, therefore, did al-Khadir, when he was asked in the dream concerning Hearing, say, "It is pure slipperiness, there stand not fast upon it save the feet of the learned." This is because it moves the secret parts and the hidden places of the heart, and it disturbs it as that drunkenness which confounds the reason, disturbs it, and almost loosens the knot of fair behavior from the secret thoughts, except in those whom God Most High protects by light of His guidance and the benevolence of His protection. ((1907: 711–712)

Hearing is different than listening, or sama', the Sufi ritual wherein the initiate approaches unity with God through active audition in a musical context. Hearing, a less volitional act, "is pure slipperiness"; voices may come from anywhere—the angels, the jnun, or the unconscious. In the imaginal realm, which has a separate ontological status than that of rationality, distinguishing "dreams from reality, poems from life, and names from human beings" is not always easy (Pamuk 1990).

Knowing nothing of my auditory and visual visitation (hallucination?), Fatima Chaouni, a well-respected mqaddema now deceased, would later tell me that Sidi Mimun was my malk, and having had this vision, her words would take root in my disposition. Hadn't I first tranced to his music and his color before I even knew about the pantheon of jnun? "He is powerful," she would tell me, "he will strike you and strike you. But when you submit to him, you will partake in his power. You will belong to him, and he will not forget you."

There are two words for dream states in Arabic. ḥulm describes an ordinary dream, one that combines the details and personages of our daily life into a hodgepodge of disconnected images flavored with fears and desires, both sexual and other. Ru'ya (coming from the word ra'a, to see) is a dream of another order. Also translated as "vision," it is a direct message from the spirit realm to the human realm. Ibn al-'Arabi considers it an apprehension of the divine through the intermediate realm of barzakh, a realm wherein the divine communicates with the human through the mediation of highly charged, but highly subjective, symbols. For Ibn al-'Arabi the human being vibrates at a much slower and denser frequency than God, and thus our ontological experience of God must occur through symbols. Symbols, however, are not illusions. For the Sufi, God is not a theoretical construct but an experienced reality (ḥaqq). Because God's manifestations are myriad, however, God's self-revelation to human beings in symbols is also myriad. No one's symbolic repertoire is another's. This is why dream interpretation is such a developed art in the Islamic world. Not unlike a process of psychoanalysis, the dreamer must learn to recognize the primary and recurrent symbols in her dream life. Unlike psychoanalysis, however, these symbols do not explain waking neuroses stemming from early childhood sexuality; rather they educate the dreamer in other realms of existence. Dreams may be a portal to initiation. They are a private university of the soul. Chittick notes that "dreams are in fact a God-given key to unlock the mystery of cosmic ambiguity and the constant transmutation of existence" (1989: 118).

This does not mean that dreams and visions are always blissful or even inspirational. In the Islamic worldview espoused by Ibn al-ʿArabi, God is compassionate (raḥman) but also encompasses all that is: terror, might, and power. Because of this inclusivity, critics of Ibn al-ʿArabi accuse him of pantheism. Yet the mystery of Ibn al-ʿArabi's teachings is found in his response: God is everything, but he is One (tawḥid). He is found in the contradiction, in the enigma of paradox (he is/he is not huwa laysa huwa). It is only when the seeker is able to embrace paradox that he or she may be said to have attained a certain maqam, or station, of gnosis—not rational knowing, but knowledge of the imaginal realm.[3]

As noted, in the Sufi worldview sleep is often compared to death and life to dreams: "When we wake up and want to understand our dreams," Chittick notes, "we try to interpret them or go to an interpreter to do this for us. So also, when we die and thereby 'wake up' to the cosmic dream of God, we will find the interpretation of our dream (even though that 'waking up' is itself another stage in the cosmic dream)" (1989: 113). Thus, for many Moroccans, dreaming of death or of the dead speaks of new beginnings. As Si Mohammed recounted,

waqfat ʿali-ya mui l-bereḥ. šḥal hadi ma ḥalimtš bi-ha. min l-waqt faš matat . . .

My mother appeared to me last night. It's been a long time since I've dreamt of her. Since the time of her death . . .

I saw her, was with her. She took me to a place, to a woman who was possessed by Aisha Qandisha. We went to her house, and they sat there in the middle of the room talking. I left them there, and when I came back my mother was dead.

"You brought her here to die, here at my place," the possessed woman cried out. I began to cry. I cried, and I cried.

"Crying means laughter," Si Mohammed interjected, the logic of opposites. He went on:

I saw a guy I used to know. He was a gravedigger. He worked digging graves until he died one day digging a grave. I had my mother in a cart, like the kind pulled by horses or by donkeys, hašak (you should pardon the expression). I was crying and crying. I had no money to bury her. He took me to a place where there were lots of the dead. They were everywhere. Just skeletons. I said, "No, I won't bury my mother here." I had to bury her in the cemetery by the Chellah gardens. "Okay, don't worry. I'll give you the money to do it," this poor gravedigger told me. And he did. So we went . . . Then all of a sudden I woke up.

"Crying is happiness," he repeated to me. "It's been a long time since my mother appeared to me like that. It's a blessing."

"How do you interpret that?" I asked.

"As a good omen," he replied. "Before my mother died she told me that blessings would follow me after her death, that she would protect me."

◆ ◆ ◆

Si Mohammed told this dream to me on the seventh floor of a Paris apartment where he and his family lodged when they had a three-month contract to perform at a nightclub near Place Pigalle. At the time, Si Mohammed saw the possibility of living in France and of becoming a French national as part of the blessing coming from his mother, symbolized in his dream. He told me that his agent was working on getting him French working papers so that he would have the right to come and go as he pleased, without a visa. He held up his CD. "I already have this recording," he said. "It was made in France."

When Si Mohammed was younger he was struck by Aisha Qandisha. Indeed, she continues to visit him. His mother knew what to do when that happened: she brought him to a mqaddema, a clairvoyant and Gnawa healer. Si Mohammed's Gnawa lineage is direct.[4] His paternal grandmother was a Gnawa mqaddema, a dada (a term of respect for female elders in the Gnawa tradition) and a healer from Timbuktou. "Twaret fi-nah had-ši; she passed this heritage to us," Si Mohammed told me. Her name was Mbaraka bant Bilal Samba bant Malika al-Guinea.[5] She was also a slave who was bought by a local governor in Ouarzazate (in Southern Morocco), al-Qaid Ahmed al-Ouarzazu, and freed. She eventually went to the coastal city of Safi, where Si Mohammed's father was born. From 1914 onward, Si Mohammed's father was in the Royal Guard; he served in France in the French army in World War II, and when he retired he became a makhazni, a guard in the Royal Palace. This is where Si Mohammed was born—in twarga, the place of residence for the guards and servants of the palace. The King's own "Gnawa" lived there.

It is not surprising that in his dream Si Mohammed brought his mother to Aisha (that is, to a woman possessed by Aisha) before the moment of her death. Insofar as both death and possession signal new beginnings, there is a logical synchronicity here. On the other hand, there is also a correlation between Aisha, the attractive and dangerous she-demon and the figure of the mother. As we will see, Si Mohammed is not the only one to conflate the categories of mother and female *jinniyya*.

Tears are bodily emissions and an opening of the body. Tears are produced in the body, yet they are between ether and material. Flowing out of the inside, they connect the subject to the outer world. Tears flow, then evaporate, disappearing like *jinn* but also attracting the *jinn* who are drawn to water. They emerge at the thresholds of the body and provide a passage across them. But tears in this self-interpreted narrative symbolize laughter. As in the narrative in chapter three, tears and laughter are both associated with spirit possession and act as substitutes for one another.

Ru'ya (visions or "lucid dreams") such as this one are not necessarily uncommon. They are nonetheless distinguishable from the majority of dream states by their intensity—one is aware of having awoken from one state and entered another. Like an author who develops a second self that watches the human drama unfold and yet remains impassive, observant, and aware, the lucid dreamer watches him or herself dreaming; it is a state of being double.

One afternoon, while sitting in a café overlooking Jma al-Fna, the performance square in Marrakech, Si Mohammed told this dream narrative to me and Mustapha Baqbou, a Marrakshi Gnawa who has become most known for being a member of the vastly popular music group Jil Jilala (see chapter seven).

"That day I was with the Gnawa in Jma al-Fna," Si Mohammed told us. "At night I had a dream that I was playing at a *lila* with Jews. The next day, I was in the Jma al-Fna again, with twelve other Gnawis. And I saw two guys approaching me. They came straight to me, not the others. One was a Jew."

"How did you know?" I asked.

"Because he was wearing a cap (*tegiya*)."

"You wear a *tegiya* too," I laughed.

"Yes, but he was wearing that hat of theirs, that kind that they wear. Anyway, he came straight towards me and told me that he wanted me to do a *lila*. And I told him, 'I'll go right away.' And so, I went, and I played. There were a lot of people there, a lot of men with long white beards. It was exactly as I dreamed it."

"You see, the power [he has]?" Baqbou said, turning to me.

"It was a lila for Lalla Mimuna," Si Mohammed continued. *lalla mimuna dyal-hum, ḥetta huma 'and-hum lalla mimuna.* Their Lalla Mimuna. They also have Lalla Mimuna."[6]

In this narrative, the power of dreams is clearly attached to the power of clairvoyance. Si Mohammed is not only a master musician, but in many ways he is an acknowledged visionary as well. It is not accidental that he states that there were twelve other Gnawi with him when the Jew sought him out. In Islamic law, twelve witnesses are needed to constitute a fact.

VISIONS

The Gnawa arrive at Malika's place. The have come by bus from Yousseffia. The sons arrive first—Younis and Muṣbaḥ—carrying the large drums. Hassan follows in his green *jellaba*. Polite and fine-featured, Hassan is the most discreet of the Chaouqi brothers. He plays the *ṭbal* in the beginning of the ceremony and the *qraqab* other times. He sings, but never trances or gets up to solicit offerings and give blessings. Hassan is a worker; he does his job as a member of the family.

I am sitting with Malika in her small room when they arrive. Malika runs to the top of the narrow stairwell when she hears them coming.

"*Marḥaba, marḥaba;* welcome, welcome," she tells them, ushering them into the small living room on the second floor of the house.

This dwelling belongs to her father, a large and forbidding man who nonetheless tolerates the presence of the Gnawa, as if he had no choice but to let them into his house and cure the maledictions that his daughter sustains and also helps to cure. She is divorced, with a child. Her clairvoyance is a source of income for her and her family. The young Gnawa remove their *balgha* as they step over the second-floor entryway, lowering their heads as they shake hands with the father and Malika's oldest brother before being ushered into the "salon" by Malika. On this second floor there are four rooms, all small: a living room furnished with foam rubber banquettes covered with thin flowered material, Malika's room, her father's bedroom, and a hallway where the family of eight watch television and eat. It is a narrow building with a steep staircase of uneven concrete leading from the ground-floor kitchen up to the second main floor and ultimately up to an open flat roof on the third floor where the ceremonies are held. Malika's sister, her new husband, and their baby live in one corner on the roof level, where a small room has recently been built for them. There is a water closet there and on the ground floor.

A few minutes later Si Mohammed arrives with Khadir and old Mbarak (also known as *al-Briyq*), a wizen little man no more than four feet and ten inches tall who used to be a *mqaddem* and who now simply attends the ceremonies with the m'allem. Mbarak carries a hand-carved staff that helps him to walk. The cane seems to be the only thing keeping him connected to the earth; he is almost as light as air.

When I hear that all the Gnawa have settled in, I get up from Malika's room and venture to the salon where I greet all the Gnawa, shaking hands with the sons and brothers, but embracing the m'allem on both cheeks. "Glassi ma'-nah" the m'allem instructs me when I do not sit down right away. "Sit with us." I do not hesitate, despite the fact that a Moroccan woman might have deferred and stayed with the women in Malika's room, which is also bayt al-jwad—literally the room of the generous ones or spirits, where she conducts her divination. My history with the Gnawa is close and follows different rules. Still, I wait for the invitation.

Malika has gone downstairs. I stay with the Gnawa. The discussion turns to dreams. Si Mohamed turns to Mbaraka, another mqaddema, and says,

> al-bereh fi lil waqaf 'ali-ya aiša. hiya galsa f-erjli wa ana f-l-fraš. ma-qder-š n-tharag. qult li-ha, "tlaq-ni" wa-allah ma bghetš. ma qderš n-teharag u hiya galsa foq erjliya habsat-ni wa ana khufan. bghit n-tharaq erjliya walakin ma khalat-niš. šwiya man ba'd, mšet f-hal-ha.

> Last night Aisha visited me. She was sitting on my legs when I was in bed, and I couldn't move. I told her, "let me go," but she wouldn't. I couldn't move, and she was sitting on my legs stopping me [from moving], and I was afraid. I wanted to move, but she wouldn't release me. Then finally she went away."

Si Mohammed recounted this story to Mbaraka, the mqaddema. She, as well as my friend, anthropologist Jamila Bargach, and I were the only women there. Malika, her sisters and a few other gnawiyyat were preparing the ceremony on the roof, as well as preparing tea for the Gnawa. Si Mohammed was both narrating a vision and implicitly asking for an interpretation from the mqaddema.

"Bghat dbiha; she wants a sacrifice," was all Mbaraka told him. The month of š'aban was approaching and with it, the m'allem's annual lila.

In this ru'ya Si Mohammed's body becomes stiff, as if dead, but only temporarily. The "small death" of sleep manifests in the physical inability to move (Pandolfo 1997: 184). Nonetheless, the sense of feeling (touch, proprioception) is quite active in the dream—Si Mohammed can feel Aisha's weight on his legs and the spirit's force. His words—"habsat-ni; she stopped me"—attest to the ability of the jinn to inhabit multiple domains—spiritual, psychological, and physical. The inability to move is a result of the jinniyya's deliberate encumbering of the body, a state that placation and trance will heal. A relation of force exists with the *jinn*, even at more advanced stages of possession.

VISIONS OF DESIRE

The possessed are engaged in a relationship of desire with their spirits, one that is often overtly spoken about using sexualized metaphors. Fatna recounts, for example, how she was visited at night by Sidi Mimun, who came to her in the form of an animal: "I felt him enter the room where I was lying next to my daughter," she told me. "I was wide awake, not sleeping. I felt him come towards me. Then, I felt a tongue lick my neck, all over my neck. It was the tongue of an animal, not a human being. It was Mimun. I started reciting the *fatiḥa* [prayer] and calling out for God. *allah, allah!* He finally went away."

Again, we have a narration of proprioception: "I felt him come towards me." Fatna is aware of a physical presence: her own and another. She also feels the sensation of a tongue on her neck. It touches her. It caresses her. It is not a human tongue, but an animal tongue. How is an animal's tongue different than a human tongue? Is it bigger? Rougher? Wetter? And why would a spirit manifest as an animal? Sidi Mimun is an African *jinn* in the black pantheon. He thus represents a pre-Islamic or animist spirit. He is also the "keeper of the gate," a patron spirit of the Gnawa who holds the keys to knowledge and initiation. "Baba Mimun," notes Bertrand Hell, "is the patron of the brotherhood. He is the *Moul al Sieff* (the "Master of the swords"): he demands blood from those he possesses" (2002b: 173). Those possessed by Mimun (especially in his incarnation as Ghumami, "the storm") often "take up the knives"; that is, they engage in dramatic mortification practices with sharp implements (not unlike those used for sacrificing an animal), drawing blood. The flowing of blood, like tears, passes over the thresholds of the body, turning interiors out and making them visible, a spectacle, and a proof of grace or *baraka*.[7]

While Fatna has not taken up the knives at this point, she is at a threshold—that of accepting the spirits' world into her own and of acknowledging their continuity. What's more, her narration brings the listener to a threshold as well. Narrating the feeling of Mimun's tongue on her neck as she is laying next to her daughter in bed (and is thus in a mother role) places the listener in a sympathetic sensory domain. The viscerality of sense-talk, like the power of poetic language, blurs the threshold between the taleworld and the storyrealm. Conjuring the senses functions much like deixis in language: it grounds the listener in the here and now or the there and then of sensory experience (Hanks

1990). The senses create a place for the listener in the imaginal world of the speaker. Fatna's narrative bleeds frame into frame making the narration an active producer of desire. Indeed, because it draws upon body memory, it blurs the line between then and now.

There are other thresholds crossed. Fatna dreams of Aisha Qandisha, the powerful female *jinn* of threshold and danger, often referred to simply as Lalla Aisha. She used to be afraid of her. But then Lalla Aisha appeared to her in a dream wrapped in a black sheet and beat her, saying "Why are you always afraid of me? You're our daughter. Take care of us and we'll take care of you." She then took off her black sheet and was wearing ordinary clothes underneath.

"Every time she comes looking differently," Fatna tells me. "Sometimes she's heavy and is dressed like my mother. Sometimes she's tall and thin and is dressed all in white. Every time, it's something different." Like the different-colored cloths draped on the possessed, the *jinniyya*'s shape and demeanor change according to her dress and its color and according to her aspect and attitude.

Once Lalla Aisha asked Fatna if she wanted her to continue to visit in dreams or if she wanted her to appear as a real person in flesh and blood. Fatna was still afraid of her then and told her to remain in her dream life, wanting to keep the spirit and the human realms separate. Fatna gets tired of always burning incense for her, however. Yet whenever she stops the weekly rituals, her life becomes problematic. In one of these instances a friend—a Moroccan visiting from Switzerland—sat across from Fatna on her couch and became possessed by Lalla Aisha. She began screaming at Fatna: "Why don't you burn incense for us anymore? Why don't you give us our way? We haven't been in this house for fifteen days." Then Fatna herself became possessed by *aiša al-baḥariya*, Aisha of the Sea; she began throwing water around the house, went into the bathroom, and told her friend to pour milk over her head. Then Aisha left, and Sidi Mimun manifested in Fatna "Don't you have any black benzoin [incense]," he asked her? "Where's the black benzoin?" After this experience, Fatna began placating her spirits once again.

The abject relation between the possessing spirit Aisha Qandisha and the image of the mother is explicit. Sometimes she is the good mother, dressed in white—the color of purity, of mourning, of the pilgrimage—and sometimes she is dressed in black and is aggressive, hitting Fatna into obedience. In either scenario she is the more powerful, requiring Fatna's submission. To placate her spirits, Fatna must fumigate the house with their preferred incense weekly, an act that has an effect on all the members of her household—including her banker husband, her three children, and her maid. Failure to fill the house with the heady smoke subjects her to unexpected visitations that impel her to wash down the apartment with water and her head with milk. The jnun want to be remembered, to be made present in the material realm.

Repercussions of trance activity always involve the practitioner in a domain whose *sensory hierarchy is different from that present in the quotidian*.[8] Narrating the entranced body is thus always a narration of the senses, and it is this relation of sense and word that both expresses and produces the desire between spirit and propitiant. As Michel de Certeau has noted, both psychoanalysis and mysticism acknowledge that the body is "itself a symbolic language and that it is the body that is responsible for a truth (of which it is unaware)" (1992: 8). Al-Ghazzali notes in "The Knowledge of Self" that the five senses are

> like five doors opening on the external world; but, more wonderful than this, his heart has a window which opens on the unseen world and sometimes foreshadowings of the future. His heart is then like a mirror which reflects what is pictured in the Tablet of Fate. But, even in sleep, thoughts of worldly things dull this mirror, so that the impressions it receives are not clear. After death, however, such thoughts vanish and things are seen in their naked reality, and the saying in the Koran is fulfilled: "We have stripped the veil from off thee and thy sight today is keen." (1997: 5)

Al-Ghazzali notes that the five senses play a role in dream as in waking, as does the "sixth sense," that of the heart.

In Fatna's narrative, *she* not only becomes possessed, but her friend does as well. In principle there are two women together and at least two jinn in communication as well. The Swiss-Moroccan was present enough in her body to comply with Fatna's request that milk be poured over her head. Fatna is anointed with a substance thought to possess *baraka*, for milk (along with dates) is a food offered to guests and people of honor, especially at moments of transition, whether crossing a literal threshold—as in the case of an honored guest entering a home—or a symbolic one, as when dates and milk are served to wedding guests, for example, or presented at the outset of a Gnawa *lila*. Although the above possessions took place outside the ritual context of the *lila*, the two women participate in the same system of representation. It is unlikely that Fatna would become possessed while just she and I were having coffee in her living room. The inhabitation took place within Fatna and within her friend, but also *between* them. Merleau-Ponty notes that "Truth does not 'inhabit' only 'the inner man,' or more accurately, there is no inner man, man is in the world, and only in the world does he know himself" (1962: xi). This holds true for *jnun* as well who know themselves and are known in the bodies of their subjects.

Fatna's friend became possessed and began to chastise her in the voice of Aisha. This, in turn, provoked Fatna's possession. She began to throw water around the house—an emblem of the sea, since *aiša al-baḥariya*, Aisha of the Sea, was making herself present. Like Fatna, who changes disposition and dress according to the spirit that rises up within her, the *jinniya*, Aisha Qandisha, may take many forms. There is one Aisha, but many incarnations. "Aisha," one Marrakshi *m'allem* told me, "is present in all the colors."

The spirit asks Fatna if she wants the line between dreams and visions to be erased. Fatna says no. She is not ready to confront the dissolution of categories and boundaries. She is not ready to acknowledge the continuity between her conscious and unconscious selves. The ability of Aisha to take form in dream as well as in corporeal existence attests to the belief in the transmutation of forms. The *jnun* inhabit multiple realms of experience.

◆ ◆ ◆

Before leaving Morocco in August of 1995 I had a *ru'ya*. I was looking down on the coastal city of Essaouira, inhabited by Jews for hundreds of years and now abandoned by them, an old Portuguese port, a stop in the slave trade, and the only place in Morocco where there is a *zawiya* for the Gnawa. Indeed, the Gnawa in Essaouira are renown for their artistry and their power, so much so that there is now an annual Gnawa festival there each year. Their music and culture have become icons of the city itself. In 1995, however, the festival had not yet begun and Essaouira, though known worldwide as a pilgrimage center for Jews, sub-Saharans, and Arabs as well, was still a sleepy little whitewashed town that I had only visited once as a tourist in 1982.[9] In my dream, my vision of the city was panoramic, as if I, myself, were boundless, a spirit sailing above the city, a *samawiyya* or sky-spirit. Below, I saw a large mound of sand on the beach and a sacrificed goat lying on top of it. I heard the words, *al-m'allem matet*, the master has died, spoken as clearly as if they were said to me in a waking state. (Death signals new beginnings.) A feeling of peace filled the scene, permeating the ether and my being. I began speaking words to my mother, who, though not present bodily, was there, a presence in the ether as surely as I was. "Take care of Hannah," I said. Hannah is my daughter, born to a Moroccan father from the Ben Izznasan tribe in the north. "Take care of Hannah.

I am going away to France for four years." In my dream I knew that my daughter would be safe in her grandmother's care and that I was about to experience an important life change.

That was 1995. I went back to the States and to my job at the university, to the tenure process and teaching. Little did I know then that I would find myself in Essaouira in 1999 and that the conditions of my life would, by then, be drastically different.

◆ PART 2 ◆
POSSESSING
CULTURE

◆ ◆ ◆

THE CHELLAH GARDENS

I walk the long pathway to the Chellah gardens in Rabat, a large, walled fortress dating from the Roman era, containing sumptuous gardens overlooking the Bou Regrag River. Although a few Roman columns and ruins remain within its walls, it is most known for being the cemetery of the Marinids who ruled Morocco from the thirteenth to the fifteenth centuries. It is, as historian Janet L. Abu-Lughod notes, "a setting of spectacular serenity that still attracts Moroccans and tourists alike who seek a temporary withdrawal from the urgencies of urban life" (1980: 59).

This is where the Gnawa "sit" during the day, when they are not recovering from an all-night ceremony. When the tour buses circle the *rondpoint* outside the city gates and turn down this dirt and gravel road, the fine yellow dirt rises up so thick that it touches the windows of the high Volvo carriers; the tourists, who are hermetically sealed inside, approach the walls of the casbah through a Plexiglas barrier and a veil of dust outside. But they do descend. I watch them emerge in their shorts, white socks, and athletic shoes. They all have expensive cameras hanging around their necks. Most of them are over fifty and wear hats. They are in a good mood. It feels good to get off the bus and stretch their legs. And look at the orange clay walls! Yes, they must be centuries old. The tour guide, who wears a white cotton *jellaba* with an official metal badge on it, tells them that this *qaṣbah* dates from the fourteenth century but also contains Roman ruins from when this was the main Roman outpost in North Africa. The group saunters toward the gate. The Gnawa have already gotten up. Two are beating their *ṭbal*, a third clacks the heavy iron cymbals together. All of them wear hats with pompoms that they circle in the air by moving their heads as if to draw large circles of light around them with a laser beam emitting from the tops of their skulls. The tourists seem not to notice the air and energy whirling about the Gnawa. They regard them as if these men were salaried by the tourist bureau, paid to entertain them on their tour of the world. But they are not. They simply have permission to perform for the tourists for tips.

"You should put up a sign on the wall," I venture, "YOUR GENEROSITY IS APPRECIATED, Merci pour votre generosité."

"The tour guides tell them to give us money," Khadir assures me. Yet only a rare few offer them some coins after their promenade in the gardens.

The Gnawa have a different relation to the Chellah gardens. "This place is full of jnun," Si Mohammed told me once. "One time we were having dinner here after dark. We were sitting on the ground eating chicken when we saw Aisha [Qandisha] approaching. She was angry, and we fled. Later when we returned, the food was still there. It was amazing. The place is full of dogs, but they didn't touch our dinner. The [other] spirits protected it for us."

I have walked through these gardens many times. Once inside of the thick portals, you find yourself on a hill overlooking the Bou Regrag River that separates the city of Rabat from the city of Salé. The sounds of turtledoves cooing and swallows chirping fill the ears. There are two paths the you can take. Both descend down the hill. One path passes by the Roman ruins. Bougainvillea is abundant, and the white fragrant bells of Bella Donna (Datura) trees line the path. The other path bends down to the right, past a small, closed tomb, and right through another ruin where the graves of the Marinid Sultan and his English wife—renamed Shams ad-Doh, the Sun of Dawn—lie unprotected from the elements. Shams ad-Doh converted to Islam in the fourteenth century in order to marry. A guide of the gardens will show you the mosque and school, the baths where Qur'anic students bathed, and the pool where they washed their dead. A bit further down there is a zawiya, a small, white saint's mausoleum. Its one room is calm and cool; lined with woven raffia, the cement-encased coffin of the saint Amor el-Mesnaoui stands steady and unchanging inside. Women kiss both ends of the velvet-draped tomb and say the fatiḥa, the opening prayer of Islam, hoping to be cured of sterility. Outside this zawiya a woman sits selling candles—offerings for the saint. Beside her, there is a manmade pool where eels live. It is a haunted pool; the eels are charged with a certain power. For a few coins the mistress of the zawiya, who is also the guardian of the pool, throws some hard-boiled eggs into the black waters and you can watch the eels emerge from their dark corners to eat. They swim slowly into the patches of sunlight, and the visitor or pilgrim solicits their favor, calling on their blessing and power.

The tourists leave. The buses pull away. The eels abandon the vestiges of eggs floating in the pool and seek cover of darkness in their watery caves. I sit with the Gnawa outside the garden walls. They offer me the only stool they have and themselves sit on scraps of cardboard on the ground. We pull ourselves as close to the ramparts as possible to take advantage of a few inches of shade. Si Mohammed walks over to a lean-to that he has set up about a hundred meters away against the wall of a twentieth-century cemetery that faces the *qaṣbah*. There he has a small bottle of cooking gas and a metal teapot. He opens the bottle, lights a match, and sets the small pot on the flame. A few minutes later he is back, carrying a tin tray with the teapot and four small glasses that are filmy with sugar. He pours the tea and offers me a sticky glass, which I accept and sip. It is strong and very sweet. We all sit, our backs to the wall and drink our tea.

"*aywa? labas 'al-ik?* So how are you?"

"*aywa. šwiya. labas. Kan-adiyu. wa antah?* I'm okay. We're getting by. And you?"

"*labas barakalluhu fi-k.* Okay, may God bless you."

kan-adiyu: "We're getting by." To say that one is getting by is to acknowledge the difficulties of daily life and that one is not immune to their impact. On the other hand, to use the first person plural is to include oneself in a larger group. We are all just getting by. No one is immune; common plights are easier to bear.

"Last night I went to bed and I was fine," I continue, "but this morning I woke, and I can hardly move because of the pain in my lower back. *Dayr li-ya trrrung!* It went trrrung. This muscle here," I motion to my lower back, "just snapped. Then I went to plug my computer into the wall, and there was an explosion. *ḍo';* the electricity jumped out at me like lightening, and then all the lights in the house went out. All the fuses blew at once."

"That's Aisha," the *m'allem* interjected. "It's Aisha that is responsible for all that. That's what she does."

"Well, I knew I had to get dressed and go see Si Mohammed," I continued.

"It's good that you came," he said.

"I want to have a small ceremony, just an afternoon thing. Nothing big. I didn't come with a lot of money this year."

"It's better at night," Si Mohammed said. "The *jnun* come out at night, not during the day. A *lila* is better."

"I know. But Mbaraka has 'afternoons'; they go well."

"Mbaraka's sister won't let her have the ceremonies at night," Si Mohammed says, insistent.

"I know. I know," I concede. "Do you think a chicken would be an acceptable sacrifice instead of a goat?"

"That's between you and your possessors," he answered. "That's between you and the *mluk*."

Then Younis squats down next to me. He is still young, the m'allem's young-est son, but he got married last autumn and now has a new baby. This is news.

"Šhal fi-'amr-ik? But how old are you?" I ask, surprised.

"Twenty-one," he says. "ash ghadi t-dir? benadam khus y-juwwaj. What are ya gonna do? People have to get married," he tells me, laughing. I notice that he has knife scars on his forearms, keloids where he has sliced himself with blades during the ceremonies.

◆ ◆ ◆

One winter day I go to see Si Mohammed at 5:00 in the afternoon at his home. I have my recorder with me to tape the next series of ritual songs and tran-scribe the words. I tell the taxi driver to take me to Youssoufia, near the new mosque, past the ḥammam, up the hill. Si Mohammed's house is among many cinder-block domiciles that look over the Bou Regrag river to Salé beyond—a shanty-town turned into cement when the government gave land rights to the squatters with the condition that they build. Walking down the incline to-wards his narrow street, his son Younis calls my name. I turn around and find him beside me. He tells me that his father has gone to his uncle's house. There is a lila tonight, and he has taken the hajhuj, the drums, and the qraqab with him. His father will come back later to get me, meanwhile I am to have tea with Fatima, Si Mohammed's wife, Younis's mother.

"Mothers of twins have baraka," Fatima tells me, referring to herself. "They can heal broken bones by massaging them. But against spirits they have no power." A baby dead at eight months—"Aisha," she tells me, "struck her." They brought her to the hospital. "Ma 'and-ha walu, nothing was the matter with her," the doctors told her, "but leave her here, and we'll examine her more closely." In the afternoon she was dead. "Aisha struck her down."

Her little twins run around, one bare-bottomed, both barefooted, hair un-kempt and strewn with pieces of lint. The floor is cold. Si Mohammed's wife sets down a tray with tea and glasses and accidentally knocks over the tea pot. Steaming-hot water splatters on the cement floor, flicked with tea leaves; it al-most reaches our feet. An omen I wonder?

Again, another child, at two years old—or was it at eighteen months?—her limbs limp, her eyes wandering. "I wrapped her in a blanket and put her on a mat in the middle of the floor, lit some incense—jawi—and left her there. If she lives, she lives. If she dies, she dies, I said." This child lived. "We hold a ceremony for Aisha every year now, so she won't be struck down again. She's eight years old. So far she's been okay."

Si Mohammed comes back and we leave shortly afterward, taking a cab to the medina. On the way he tells me that his *aṣl* or origin is in Sudan and that he used to work in the palace. Was his father a Gnawi? No. As a young man he was apprenticed to a master who gave him his vocation. His grandmother was the *gnawiyya*. Tall and thin, she played the *qraqab* and was a *mqaddema*. He plays the *hajhuj*, the drums, he sings. People followed.

We get out of the taxi. We see Si Mohammed's brother waiting for us on the main street; he knows the house. They wait for me to buy a sugar cone, an offering to the hostess and a way to make change so that I will have money to offer during the ceremony in exchange for blessing and clairvoyance. We follow his brother down a narrow street, knocking on a door towards the end of the passageway. Entering, we pass a large metal pot simmering on top of a gas-bottle stove in the hall. We are seated on mattresses in a courtyard covered over by a tarp to provide privacy from the view of the upstairs neighbors. There are a few women sitting in an adjacent room. They are watching *Manuela*, a Mexican soap opera dubbed in Lebanese Arabic. In the courtyard, the other Gnawi are already there—five in all. They smoke *kif* (Moroccan cannabis) nonchalantly, waiting for lunch.

After a meal of chicken, olives, and pickled lemons that I share with the musicians, I am ushered into the women's room by the only daughter of the hostess. They want to know who I am, and I tell them: an American doing research on the Gnawa. In the room are six other women: three young, two over sixty, and the hostess. I learn that the woman of the house has been visited by Aisha most of her life; she sees her in waking visions, even conversing with her. She tells a woman dressed all in white about a vision she had recently when she was at the beach. Aisha appeared right next to her. The most dignified guest—al-Hajja—consoles the hostess and tells her that all will soon be well. But the woman of the house has been inviting the Gnawa for more than twenty years to propitiate her spirit. She knows what to expect.

The men in the courtyard stand, picking up two large drums, and removing two pairs of bent sticks and their large hand cymbals from a velour bag. They leave the house. The women bring another mattress into the main courtyard, and the hostess goes to change her clothes. I wait inside, but hear the music from way down the street. The Gnawa are alerting the neighbors of their arrival. They are calling the *jnun* to manifest.

Twenty minutes pass. When the musicians finally re-enter the house, the hostess is seated in the middle of the floor, her eyes closed. They encircle her, moving in light steps to the rhythm of the cymbals. Slowly she gets up. She sways. The Hajja holds her by the sleeve so she will not lose her balance. The Gnawa sing. The music is loud; so loud, in fact, that I feel the beat permeate my bones; the skin of my skull tingles like the curve of the cymbals, the timbre of clacking iron reverberating in my body. The hostess is moving more briskly. She bobs her head up and down. She beats the carpeted floor with her bare feet. Now her scarf falls off and her thinning blackened hair is thrown up and covers her eyes as she throws her head violently on her chest and then from side to side, as if her neck were made of rubber, the sweat of her forehead glistening against the cool air of February. This fifty-something woman collapses on the floor and the Hajja attends to her, coaxing her to the side of the room where she sits her down, wiping the sweat from her brow and sprinkling her hands and face with cool flower water. The Gnawa set their large drums aside and sit on cushions against the far wall.

Before us, a Gnawi flails his arms and his head, salivating profusely, his few teeth evident in his open mouth. The sound of the *hajhuj* resounds like a contrabass, the resonance of the cymbals, the steady beat of hands cupped and clapping, and the smell of cannabis as the smoke floats out of the musicians' lungs and is taken into my own.

After a period of trancing, the hostess stands motionless in the middle of the room. A young girl approaches to give her money and to receive her blessing in return. The hostess is alert, her eyes wide. She is possessed by Sidi Chamharouch, the king of all the *jinn* whose tomb is in the High Atlas Mountains. (The Gnawa make a yearly pilgrimage there.) She holds the girl's hand and looks directly into her eyes. "Don't worry about what the others say. Go in through the door; it's a narrow door, not a wide door. *al-ma'qol ṣa'ib*. What's right is difficult. Don't be afraid. Go in through the door." The girl nods. The allusions seem to be understood. The hostess gives her some anise bread and sugar cubes from a large scarf that she has slung around her side, the food of the spirit, containing blessing, *al-baraka*. She proceeds around the room, speaking to each of her guests and giving them advice. She is in a state of grace and can therefore "see." To me she says, "your health has to come first, only then knowledge [*ṣḥa hiya l-uwla, 'ad l-'ulum*]." This chills me, as I am worried about my health, feeling pains where I usually don't feel them pretty consistently.

A few nights later I wake up hearing the beat of the Gnawa. For what seems like a good five or ten minutes I sit up in bed, listening, expecting the sound to diminish as I eventually come out of a sound sleep. But it does not. I sit up, turn on the light, and listen as the beat continues . . .

◆ 7 ◆
MONEY AND
THE SPIRIT
◆ ◆ ◆

The spiritual energy and sheer force and power of African traditional music has been mostly
forgotten, lost to dreams of long ago or simply ignored. Randy Weston, pianist/composer and
cultural ambassador decided to explore this most powerful layer of African culture many years
ago. He decided to recapture this spiritual energy and force on this recording, The Splendid
Gnawa Masters. He has spent nearly four decades on this exploration and rediscovery of the
journey of the spirits of our ancestors. You will rediscover, as I did, as Randy did, the divine
elements missing from much modern day music, as well as a rediscovery of our true connection
with God, because in its true form, untainted, what is music but the voice of God? What are
musicians but God's instruments? Perhaps this recording will remind us all that we have
to get back to listening to the voice of God, that we may quiet the noise of man.
—Liner notes from The Splendid Master Gnawa Musicians of Morocco,
author unattributed (The Splendid Master Gnawa Musicians
of Morocco and Randy Weston 1994)

Traditional music is often the emblem of a return to a spiritual source, and ritual musics are often portrayed as pure traditions, uncontaminated by the
effects of the marketplace. This is sometimes the case with African and African American music, which many scholars, writers, and musicians themselves
have considered sacred (Monson 2003a [2000]: 9). Musicologist Travis A. Jackson, for example, calls attention to music's role in achieving transcendence,
asserting the importance of the blues aesthetic and of "performance as a sacred, ritual act" in jazz and other African American music genres (2003: 25).
Jackson documents the ritual function of the blues, drawing upon the work of
African American writers (Amiri Baraka and Ralph Ellison) as well as scholars
of African American music for whom music is a performance ritual and musicians are symbolic shamans (Jackson 2003: 32).[1] Musicologist Samuel A.
Floyd notes that the "similarity of the jazz improvisation event to the African
dance possession event [is] too striking and provocative to dismiss, but in the
absence of a provable connection, it can only be viewed as the realization of an

aspect of ritual and of cultural memory" (1995: 140–141). While for Ronald Michael Radano and Philip Vilas Bohlman, that "certain traits of African-American music are fundamentally African is fundamental to claims of authenticity in the African diaspora" (Radano and Bohlman 2000a: 29).

African American music is portrayed as having a sacred aspect stemming from its origin in Africa. In summarizing some ways that African music is represented, musicologist V. Kofi Agawu asks (not without irony): "What is the secret of African music? Some say that it is communal and inviting, drawing in a range of consumers young and old, skilled and unskilled. It allows for the spontaneous and authentic expression of emotion. It is integrated with social life rather than set apart, natural rather than artificial, and deeply human in its material significance" (2003: xi). The reification of a certain kind of preshizo-phonic African music arises from both a postcolonial nostalgia within Africa (and the diaspora) and an "imperialist nostalgia" in the West that longs for (and perceives itself as lacking) such emotionally-galvanizing music (Rosaldo 1989). "It is as if the faint traces of Africa's ancient musical history," Agawu continues, "point to a magnificent era now permanently inaccessible, an era to be desired, invented, and reinvented as often as is necessary" (2003: 22).

This "era" is invoked in the liner notes of Randy Weston's *The Splendid Master Gnawa Musicians of Morocco*, a 1994 compact disc that brought together several of the older Gnawa masters in Morocco in an unprecedented co-performance (usually only one master is featured at a ceremony or on a recording), with Randy Weston's piano blending in with subtlety. The tension created (we might say "invented") between the "noise of man" and the "voice of God" mirrors other tensions—between the centripetal forces of homogenization and the centrifugal forces of differentiation, for example, or between essentialism and hybridization. I do not wish to reify these categories or to imply that all discourses on African music draw upon tropes of the sacred. Certainly many scholars writing on African music in Africa and the diaspora do not.[2] Rather my intention here is to understand the complex schismogenetic choreography that such tropes of the sacred inspire. Dichotomies like that of the sacred and the secular (marketplace) are not, in the words of Erlmann "mutually exclusive features of musical globalization . . . but . . . integral constituents of musical aesthetics under late capitalism"; indeed, he notes that "the contradictory experience of the universal marketplace alongside proliferating neotraditional codes and new ethnic schisms, is the key signature of the postmodern era" (Erlmann 1996: 469).[3] While the appropriation of Gnawa music is seldom done in the service of creating ethnic or racial schism (Radano and

Bohlman 2000a: 32), nonetheless the Gnawa as ritual healers and musicians do become symbols of authenticity, purity, and the sacred in discursive representations in the West.

Not surprisingly, discourses about Gnawa identity within Morocco are quite different, mainly due to their necessary alliances with market forces. They are sometimes characterized as magicians who addict people to their music for the profit it brings. Representations of Gnawa music and musicians evince what Paul Gilroy calls a doubleness, an "unsteady location simultaneously inside and outside convention" (1993: 73). Hell refers to the Gnawa as embodying a deep symbolic ambiguity (1999a).

Moroccan Gnawa music is indisputably sacred (if we understand the sacred to mean music that praises or worships a deity or deities), and the impact of the marketplace on its ritual life is subtle and complex, part of the repercussive spiraling between money and the spirit. If these two values seem oppositional on the surface, however, on closer examination they are, in fact, seen to be convertible—both money and the spirit being privileged symbols, universal equivalents of sorts, by which other values are measured (Goux 1990). Their analysis uncovers the deep entanglement of sacred music and the world music market. But first the story . . .

LIFTING OFF FROM THE SOURCE: MARRAKECH

In March of 1995 I went on a pilgrimage to Marrakech. With me were Si Mohammed and Paco. At the time I met Paco (Pierre Alain Claisse) he was a young European (twenty-eight) who had grown up in the capital of Rabat. The son of a French "cooperante," a schoolteacher under post-Protectorate contract with the French government to teach in Morocco, Paco had attended French schools in Morocco with the local bourgeoisie, socializing with Moroccan schoolmates. Although his mother still kept a beach house in the suburbs of Rabat, he had moved to France ten years earlier in order to go to college there and was now back in Morocco to do research for his Master's degree in Anthropology. He was studying at the Sorbonne and writing on the Gnawa. Paco had spent years with the Gnawa and knew Si Mohammed and his family well. In 1996 he wrote his Master's thesis about Si Mohammed and the experiences that he had with him in Rabat, and this thesis eventually became a book, *Les Gnawa Marocains de Tradition Loyaliste* (Claisse 2003). At the time, however, Paco, like myself, was very much a student of the Gnawa and of Si Mohammed in particular.

My husband and I left our apartment early and jumped in a taxi. We met Si Mohammed and Paco at the Rabat train station—"Rabat Ville." It was bustling as usual. Si Mohammed was not dressed in his ritual garb of robes and turban, but in traveling clothes: synthetic pants, a used jacket that fit him poorly, and a *casquette*, a cap that he wore pulled down over his brow. He was not chic, but rather looked a bit awkward in his ill-fitting clothes, his nobility somehow swallowed up by his evident poverty. Yahya stood and talked to the two men as I went off to purchase my ticket. When I returned it was time to walk down the stairs to the *quai*. Yahya kissed me modestly and sweetly on both cheeks and confided us all to God's care. Then the three of us—a black Gnawi, a blond, blue-eyed, young European male, and a woman in her thirties who passed for Moroccan—descended the stairway and began our journey. In the train, Si Mohammed would talk of the honor that Yahya had bestowed upon him by entrusting his wife (me) to go on a trip with him (Si Mohammed). It had never occurred to me that Si Mohammed ever thought about me as anything but a researcher. But I was clearly wrong. In this scenario, I was the wife of a Moroccan professor, a woman, and thus a being who did not always lead with her 'aql (intelligence), a woman whose *nafs* (desires), might lead her astray when not under the jurisdiction of a male guardian. Clearly Si Mohammed felt a responsibility for me on this trip.

Marrakech is a city of markets and performance, a city of sales spiels, tourism, charlatanism, mendicantism—a city of tricksters. I had already lived in this city of ebullient light ten years earlier from 1984 to 1985. It was the first year of my marriage, and we had a house in the old medina in "*derb al-gnaiz*"— the quarter of the corpses. Not an auspicious neighborhood for newlyweds, perhaps, but Marrakech had many such gruesome-named quarters. The famous square—jma' al-fna—(which some translate as "the square of the dead" from *fna'*, "extinction") was the scene of a brutal battle during the reign of the Saadians, which ended with the heads of the vanquished hoisted up onto the city's walled ramparts as emblems of victory and warnings of retribution, or at least oral folklore holds as much. (Others say it is from jm' al-fann, "the square of art.") But Marrakech's bloody past was not evident in its present climate. The red clay walls of its buildings shown golden in the cool spring air. The snow-capped mountains to the south glistened above us, seen through the palm groves that surrounded the city. Marrakech always welcomed me home. It felt like my city—its smells, its colors. It was, it is, the gateway to Africa in Morocco. The road to Timbuktu begins there. It was the northern destination for the caravan trade and is still populated by Saharans who come to Marrakech to do business for several months a year but return to the Sahara to build their houses and see their women and children. Protected by the seven saints enshrined there (including Sidi Mimun, who is said to have been a gatekeeper for one of the city gates) Marrakech was, for me, a beatific city where I was always happy just to be alive and where I was visited by an inexplicable grace *min and-llah*, sent by God. Magic happened in Marrakech, good magic. There was power there coming up from the red clay.

We were not on a pilgrimage to visit the seven saints, although I would make that pilgrimage several years later under very different circumstances. We were on a pilgrimage to see a legendary giant, a sort of musical *jinn*, who was revered not only in Morocco but also worldwide. We were on a pilgrimage to see jazz pianist Randy Weston. Paco had somehow learned that Mr. Weston was playing a concert there. He was taking Si Mohammed to see him so that Si Mohammed might play for him, so that Si Mohammed might play *with* him in the future. I was simply along for the ride.

Weston was born in 1926 in Brooklyn and grew up listening to Ellington, Monk, and others. Although originally oriented toward athletics (Weston is almost seven feet tall), he began playing the piano at the age of fourteen and never stopped after that. He developed a syncretic style of playing, mixing African rhythms and instrumentation with jazz harmonies. "I couldn't play like Monk or Duke," he later explained to me, "and so I had to create my own style."

Weston went to several African nations in 1967, including Morocco, on a tour sponsored by the State Department, which sent African American musicians to Africa to foster musical and cultural exchange. It was on this tour that Weston discovered the Gnawa. But it was the response of the audience as much as Weston's own fascination with Morocco that determined his future path: the Moroccans so loved Weston's playing that when Weston returned to the States, he immediately received an invitation to return to Morocco. He went back soon afterwards, finally settling in Tangier for several years. "I knew I wanted to live in Africa," Weston explained to me years later, "and the hospitality of the Moroccan people was overwhelming. I had to go back." Weston opened a club in Tangier called African Rhythms. It was a private club—one needed to belong in order to get in. Evelyn Waugh was the first member, but Paul Bowles and other literary and artistic figures were also frequent attendees.

By 1973 the African Rhythms club was quite popular and plans for the first Tangier Jazz Festival—a festival that continues today—were underway. The ambience of Tangier and of Weston's club is evoked in an article by Robert Palmer in the May 1973 issue of *Rolling Stone*:

TANGIER, Morocco—

American Randy Weston's African Rhythms Club is an opulent upstairs den, above the Mauritania Cinema and across the Avenue du Prince Heritier from another notable Tangier nightspot, the Parade Bar. Each serves an overlapping community of international expatriates and affluent, upwardly mobile Moroccans.

The Parade's garden exudes the scent of honeysuckle and the aural elegance of records by Marlene Dietrich and Billie Holiday. Its ageless proprietress, reputedly a former lion tamer, presides over a clientele that may on any given night include a Tennessee Williams or a Truman Capote—people expect to see and be seen.

Weston's club is dark and smoky, many of its habitués all but invisible. To reach it you climb a winding orange staircase decorated with indistinct black faces fading into abstract tribal designs. The club operates between 11 P.M. and the hours before dawn, [and] depending on the time of night, the floor will be filled with couples dancing to the latest James Brown records or cleared while Weston, a dashiki-clad apparition nearly seven feet tall, plays his patented brand of jazz, which owes as much to the rhythms of Moroccan folklore as to the bristling angularity of Thelonious Monk and Duke Ellington.

Even in 1973, Weston's club, like a Gnawa *derdeba* lila, operated all night long.

Weston left Tangiers and returned to Brooklyn in the mid-seventies, but he has returned yearly since then sometimes to play in the Tangier Jazz Festival or to do performances in other cities in Morocco and sometimes just to visit. This time he was playing in Marrakech, and we were traveling there to see this jazz great, a man who Moroccans had accepted and claimed as their own.

It was spring, and there had been some rain. The fields lining the coastline were light green with wheat, the earthen road that followed the train tracks bore the imprint of muddy donkey hooves on their way to market. As the train veered away from the coast and into the interior, Paco began to talk me of his studies in Paris and of his interests in tracing the Gnawa culture back to Niger and the Songhay Empire, back also to Mali. There were similar possession cults in many countries south of the Sahara, he said, the Bori in Niger, the Hauka in Nigeria. Understanding the syncretism of Moroccan Gnawa rituals depended on knowing the influences that helped create them.

"Many of the people who came up from Africa were already Islamicized," Paco explained. "But they had their own beliefs about spirits and about magic.

In fact, they had very sophisticated understandings of psychic power. These ideas were not as prominent in the Islam of the Middle East of the time. But the Gnawa came up from Africa. They live in a world where agency is not confined to people's physical forms, but extends to the invisible world. *L'esprit chez eux c'est très puissant et très sophistiqué*, the spirit for them is very powerful and very sophisticated."

Paco already had an alliance with the famous ethnographic filmmaker, Jean Rouch, who had documented the possession ceremonies of the Songhay people in the 1950s and 1960s. Rouch was based in Paris at the Musée de l'Homme, the most prominent and active center for ethnographic study in France. (Many years later, Paco would introduce me to Rouch, who would regale me with his stories for hours.)

All of Rouch's more than one hundred films were archived there, including *Les Maîtres Fou*, the Crazy Masters, a startling film that depicts a group of initiates, possessed by the Hauka pantheon of spirits, in trance. In this film, however, the initiates take on the identities of their British colonizers—becoming "captains" and "generals" of the English army and, in some interpretations, parodying them. The film was criticized for being sensationalist. Its scenes are lurid with people foaming at the mouth and thus can be interpreted as portraying the "natives" as primitive and feral. Rouch was less interested in disproving the European prejudice against Africans, however, than in proving the ingenuity of the African and human spirit, especially as it responded to the restrictions of colonialism. Heavily influenced by both the Griaulian school of ethnographic documentation and the surrealist movement, Rouch's aim was not to represent "reality," but to capture a truth among truths (Rouch 2003; Stoller 1992).

Rouch had been a student of Marcel Griaule, a French anthropologist working in West Africa whose extremely thorough methods of documentation left their impression upon generations of ethnologists. Griaule was the teacher of many renowned scholars and artists, including Léopold Sédar Senghor, poet, founder of the Négritude movement in Paris (with Aimé Cesaire), and the first president of Senegal, but also Viviana Pâques, one of the most prolific writers on the Gnawa. In a preface to a *festschrift* for Griaule, Senghor writes "Too often . . . [scholars] had borrowed the technical procedures more than the values: more than the soul. It's Marcel Griaule and his School that had learned, beyond words, beyond the style of symbolic images, melodies, and rhythms, to penetrate to the Heart, to the very soul of Négritude" (1987: vii, translation mine).[4] Griaule was the director of the famous Dakar-Djibouti Expedition that crossed fifteen African countries between 1931 and 1933; with him were Germaine Dieterlen and Michel Leiris, among others (Dieterlen 1988 [1951], 1999; Leiris 1934). Jean Rouch credits this trip with having produced the first ethnographic films in Africa (Rouch 2003: 52), particularly among the Dogon, the people to whom Griaule would subsequently devote most of his life's work (Griaule 1938, 1947; Griaule and Dieterlen 1965). Griaule believed that ethnographic analysis must combine linguistic analysis with photography, music, material culture, dance, and perhaps most importantly, knowledge of cosmology. "The hallmark of Griaule's method," notes Paul Stoller, "is intense documentation and long-term field research. For him ethnography is nothing less that a long apprenticeship during which the ethnographer collects material objects and rudimentary facts, 'during ten years if necessary' (Griaule 1957: 36). It takes time, Griaule writes, to gain access to the more ontological aspects of culture" (Stoller 1992: 19). The methodological imprint of Griaule on French ethnography was profound. At the time of our trip to Marrakech, Griaule's student, Viviana Pâques, had just published her third book on the religious practices of populations in North and West Africa, this one dedicated entirely to the Gnawa. La Religion des Esclaves, was in the window of Kalila et Dimna, one of the oldest French language bookstores in Rabat. I had just bought it, but hadn't read it yet.

"What do you think of Pâques's book?" I asked Paco.

"It's a very in-depth study," he answered. "She lived with the Gnawa for many years. She even bought a house in Tamesloht where one of the annual pilgrimages takes place. She's is a student of Griaule just like Rouch. She lived in sub-Saharan Africa for many years before coming to Morocco. Her book bears the imprint of Griaule. For Pâques, the lila ceremony is an entire cosmology lived in one night. Every aspect of the ceremony is symbolic of the soul's journey from life to death and back to life. She is interested in finding links between the cosmology of African populations, particularly the caste of metallurgists there, and the Gnawa."

"And what do you think? Are there links?"

"Most definitely there are links. But since she says that the Gnawa don't have a discourse about this, and since she also says that most of the Gnawa have already forgotten the philosophy behind the ceremony, it is hard to evaluate. Have you read her first book, L'Arbre Cosmique? Her argument begins there. She tracks how ritual cosmologies and practices traveled with the slaves from Niger to Algeria, and ultimately to Morocco."[5]

"I'll have to get to it," I said.

We were pulling into Marrakech train station.

"*Yalla*," said Si Mohammed, pulling down his suitcase from the rack above our heads, a bit impatient with all the talk about books in French. "*Ha waṣl-nah*, we're here."

We took a taxi to Jma al-Fna, then continued by foot to the home of an old friend of Si Mohammed, a Gnawi who lived in the Mouassine area of the Marrakech medina in a very small apartment with his wife and seven-year-old daughter. Despite a rather pronounced physical disability, the man had a normal family life. We ate a lunch of chicken and olives and lay down on the banquettes for a nap. In the afternoon we thanked our hosts for their hospitality and went off to buy a pair of *qraqab*, the iron (now metal) castanets that the Gnawa clack for hours on end during their ceremonies.

The location of the smithies is deep in the belly of the medina. Here the cobbled streets are black with metal chips and burned soil, lined with rusting metalwork—lamps, large filigree room dividers, decorative statues, and finally, in a small side-street, *qraqab*. Paco and I followed Si Mohammed down the narrow corridor where the smithies were welding, bending, and pounding metal into various shapes. After Si Mohammed had found his friend and introduced us, they began a long conversation punctuated by tokes of the *šqofa*, the kif pipe. Paco and I found a few bricks to sit on nearby and waited. Choosing and negotiating the price of the *qraqab* was a ritual process that would clearly take a while.

When Si Mohammed had finally procured the deal, he once again led us through the labyrinthine streets of the medina and back to Jma al-Fna. Night had fallen by then, and we went to a small restaurant off the square for a bowl of *bissara*: pea soup with olive oil. Dinner finished, I said good night and checked into a nearby hotel while Si Mohammed and Paco returned to our lunchtime hosts.

We met up again the next afternoon. Paco had already gone in search of Weston at his hotel. He was in town to play for a conference sponsored by IBM, and the concert was by invitation only. There were no tickets available and no way to see Weston. We were all disappointed but Si Mohammed simply said, *ma ktabš*, it wasn't written.

Since the evening was free, Si Mohammed suggested we visit Mustapha Baqbou, the Gnawi who had made himself renowned by playing with the popular group Jil Jilala. Not only did this group enjoy an enormous popularity with the majority of Moroccans, but Baqbou also now had a solo career, traveling to Europe and making many recordings. I thought I had noticed Baqbou's face in a recent film about the Gnawa, *Rainbow Trance*, by the Iranian filmmaker Hamid Farjahad, which documented a *lila* in Marrakech. The *m'allem* in that film was the late *m'allem* Sam, a Casablanci *m'allem* known for his expertise and kindness.

Baqbou lived in modest dwellings in the heart of the medina. We were escorted into the living room and seated on banquettes. His attractive wife brought in tea, but then left the room. A few younger Gnawis arrived. The discussion turned to music. Baqbu showed us his newest compact disc, a solo effort produced by a Canadian recording company. Indeed, he was about to leave Marrakech and go on tour in Canada. "And listen to this," he said excitedly. He brought out a compact disc by a Malian performer, bought on his last concert tour in France. "It's Gnawa," he said, "listen, listen."

We listened and drank tea. There were indeed many similarities in the two musics. Si Mohammed brought out the kif pipe. The men passed it around. It was the first time that Si Mohammed had ever offered me a toke. I didn't take it, feeling a bit out of place in the role of symbolic male. When the wine appeared, I knew the men would be more comfortable alone, and I asked one of the younger Gnawi in the room to escort me to my hotel. He agreed and descended the narrow stairs with me to the street, then asked me to sit on the bar of his bicycle and proceeded to ride me home. We passed through Jma al-Fna, still awake even at midnight, a few Gnawa musicians sitting on the asphalt, clapping and singing softly, and other performers lingering near small gas-bottle lamps. A bit farther on I got off the bike and said good night, happy to be back in my little *ryaḍ* hotel in the medina by myself.

The next day we got on the train and went back to Rabat. We hadn't seen Randy Weston, but Si Mohammed had returned with a pair of new *qraqab*, having renewed his ties to some of his friends in Marrakech.

MONEY AND RITUAL

Money is baraka is mana—a substance with power,
that is power-endowing, that is active, contagious.
—Marcel Mauss (1972 [1902]: 135)

While at Baqbou's house, I had asked him if he knew Hassan Hakmoun, the Gnawi that had migrated to the United States and become well known as a performer and recording artist. "Of course," was his reply, "*huwa wald ad-derb*, he's a local boy."

"*Maši Gnawi huwa*," said another person in the room. "He's not a [real] Gnawi."

"He's not?" I said.

"*Ma 'and-uš tagnawit*," the young man replied, "he doesn't have Gnawa-ness," or, more aptly, he's not an authentic Gnawa.

Hakmoun left Morocco as a young adolescent, knowing the repertoire of the Gnawa, but not having attained the status of *m'allem*. His mother was a clairvoyant with ties to the Gnawa community. My suspicion was that his in-authenticity in the eyes of this Marrakshi was due to his success in the marketplace more than his lack of experience. Hakmoun, perhaps more than any other Gnawi, has marketed Gnawa music to the West, combining Gnawa music with jazz and American pop. His compact disc, *The Fire Within*, is an example of world music that combines many of the ritual songs of the Gnawa with what might be called a "blues aesthetic": the *hajhuj* as lead instrument and his voice as the main vocal. Today when he returns to Morocco, he is celebrated as both a cultural pop icon and a Gnawi. At the 2004 Gnawa festival, he was one of the most popular performers.

Hassan Hakmoun came to the United States from Marrakech in the 1980s. He credits his mother with passing on to him his Gnawa heritage. She was a *shuwwafa*, literally a "seer" or clairvoyant, with ties to the Gnawa community (Hakmoun 2004). Although versed in the ritual music of the Gnawa, Hak-moun has gone on to do quite eclectic things. When he married the American pop singer Paula Cole, they produced an album together, *The Gift*. Hakmoun has also explored other musics. In an August 11, 2002 article in the *New York Times* entitled "Marrying a Moroccan Sound to the World's Music," journalist Ben Sisario quotes Hakmoun as saying, "Michael Jackson was my hero. He was only four or five years older than me, and I saw the opportunities he had with his family. I grew up with the same kind of family in Morocco, and that showed me that there is opportunity in America as an artist."

Clearly Hakmoun is creating his own links and lines of association. Indeed, he continues to create and expand them. Going to Brazil in 2000, "he found himself jamming with some of the players from Olodum, the famous samba group from Salvador da Bahia," Sisario notes.

Once they began playing, all the musicians were struck by the rhythmic similarities between samba and Moroccan music. "They were freaking out when they heard Gnawa music," [Hakmoun] said of the Brazilians. "And to me the Brazilian style sounds like African music. It was like uniting a family with music." Next on the agenda is a trip to West Africa, to explore the source of Gnawa music. "I know that's where my roots came from originally," he said. "In Mali and Senegal, and all over West Africa, they play the same kind of music I play. It's like searching for a lost family. I want to find my origin." (2002)

Hakmoun began his nomadic journey with the example of Michael Jackson, an African American who has achieved superstar (and now infamous) status. He left Morocco seeking what he could not get as a ritual musician in the Marrakech medina: money, recognition, and artistic freedom. Hakmoun exhibits what Erlmann calls a "global imagination": "beginning in the late nineteenth century," Erlmann notes, "in the West and Africa, a complex play of absences and presences inscribes itself in the very syntax of all kinds of discourses of racial, ethnic, national and sexual identity (1999). Autobiographies, Christian hymns, travel diaries, colonial shows, Michael Jackson concerts, and music videos—all in one way or another register the strange situation in which a person's understanding of himself or herself and their sense of the social world no longer coincide with the place in which they take place and are increasingly being shaped by other people's understandings elsewhere" (Erlmann 2003: 84). It is the "elsewhere" of postcolonial discontent that impelled Hakmoun to leave Morocco. Nonetheless, he left still seeking his "origin," as he said. Schizophonia seems to imply nostalgia, even for things one has willingly renounced. His home is not so much in the Marrakech medina and its ritual life as it is in the music of trance in the African diaspora—in Brazil, in West Africa. Hakmoun finds his home in the artistic and stylistic links he forges with his African ancestors and his present-day collaborators in the world music market. He is not a ritual healer, as are many Gnawa in Morocco, but a cosmopolitan nomad. As Rosi Braidoti notes, "Nomadism consists not so much in being homeless, as in being capable of recreating your home everywhere. The nomad carries her/his essential belongings with her/him wherever s/he goes and can recreate a home base anywhere" (1994: 16; Deleuze and Guattari 1977). Clearly the postmodern moment gives rise to different forms of belonging (Kapchan 2006).

Taking issue with theories that hold the "specular" as the identifying trope of modernity and the modern subject, Erlmann asks,

If the auditory is deeply caught up in the modern project—rather than standing apart from it—and if therefore the ear joins the eye in consolidating the fragile modern self, we must nevertheless ask the reverse question:

How are these modern identities constantly being sonically haunted and . . . troubled by a return of the repressed? What do we really know about vocal knowledges that are being forced underground, silenced, or ridiculed as superstitious?" (Erlmann 2004: 5)

How would Hakmoun answer these questions? Clearly there are things he has relinquished in order to live as an expatriate in New York and to perform around the globe, but since he was never an actual m'allem in Morocco, he might not miss the functions of a ritual specialist and musical healer. And yet the sacred vocal knowledges of the Gnawa are in some sense being silenced—or rather, they are being forgotten, as fewer and fewer youth learn the ritual repertoire and the healing arts, interested only in taking the "beat" to the "world." The very style that makes Hakmoun attractive (what some have called the "jadba beat," the trance beat) is being emptied of its ritual significance and its healing power in order to be circulated on the world music market. This is the irony of the commodity fetish. To ask the reverse question, however: How does the rapid commodification of the genre of ritual trance music affect Gnawa musicians living in Morocco, especially in their traditional roles as healers of the possessed? How do processes of the marketplace infiltrate and change musical/ritual life? In the remainder of this chapter I analyze the symbolic role of money in the ritual lives of the Gnawa and their participation in a world music market. Gnawa musicians participate deftly in several symbolic and material economies, but as the young man's response to Hakmoun demonstrates, their worth as "authentic" healers has transformed in the discourse of those who employ their services. At stake are the claims of who possesses tagnawit.

Money for Blessing

The exchange of money for blessing is an integral part of the rituals of healing and trance among Moroccan Gnawa musicians and their followers in Morocco. During an all-night ceremony (lila)—usually intended to divine and/or propitiate the possessing spirit(s) of an afflicted woman—money is used as a symbol that will "open the door" (ftaḥ l-bab) both to the spirits and to the curative faculties of the Gnawa. In addition, the gift of money to the musicians at several intervals during the evening invokes a "fatḥa" (literally an "opening"), a formulaic prayer of blessing recited by one of the Gnawa. Indeed, all the blessings bestowed upon the attendants at the ceremony are predicated upon the exchange of their capital for the words, music, and spiritual state (ḥal) created by the Gnawa. This is referred to as an exchange of baraka (literally meaning "blessing"). Baraka is also the euphemistic term used to refer to the money given to the Gnawa in exchange for their more literal conference of blessing. That this sacrifice is monetary should not surprise. Apart from its value as currency, money often plays a symbolic role in possession rituals; indeed as Lambek notes, "sanctity uses money to its own ends" (Lambek 2001: 758; Masquelier 2001: 184–185; Schechner 1985: 15). Money becomes not just a currency, a means to an end (buying power), but an actual material symbol in its own right. It is worn, displayed, and proffered. Unlike the Bori cult described by Besmer (1982: 25), however, the money at the Gnawa ceremony flows only one way—from the host/hostess and his or her guests to the Gnawa. The guests do receive food from the spirits as well as from the host, implicating them in a system of long-term reciprocity (the trance community is well-knit through such gifts and invitations); money, however, is reserved for the Gnawa.

Mauss made the equation between money and *baraka* in 1902. For Mauss, money is *baraka* is mana—a substance with power, that is power-endowing, that is active and contagious. Mana "enjoys the same role as the copula plays in a grammatical clause," he says, "it is "heterogeneous and ever immanent" (1972 [1902]: 151, 137). To extend Mauss's metaphor, it is a link, something that serves to connect people with things, people with other people, and people with spirits. The presence of money in a sacred musical ceremony is not anomalous in this cult of trance; however the lilat (pl.) of the Gnawa take on a more commodified aura when they become not only healing ceremonies, but also celebrations of status and performances of personal and spiritual power. That is, spirit propitiations, considered obligatory by those who are possessed, are becoming more and more expensive; and the reputation of Gnawa musicians as rapacious money-seekers who take advantage of those unfortunate enough to be possessed is becoming more widespread. In such a climate, it is not surprising that money becomes a symbol of contamination; practitioners are becoming nostalgic about the days when the Gnawa worked all night for only their meals. Discourses about "authentic" (meaning noncapitalistic) Gnawaness (*tagnawit*) are prominent in narrations between practitioners.

Symbolically, money and the spirit represent two systems of value in Morocco and historically have often defined each other by their dialectical relation. Given the historically vast differences between the *ša'b*, or popular class, and the aristocracy in Morocco, money (at least from the perspective of the _ *ša'b*) is associated with corruption and decadence, and spiritual purity is associated with the poor. These are imagined categories, of course, and with the emergence of an educated middle class and access to credit in the last thirty years or so, they do not hold (Kapchan 1996). Indeed, the gradual hegemony of materialism and market capitalism over the spiritual in Moroccan quotidian life changes the relation of these general equivalents, such that the economic accedes to a place of privilege over the spiritual. Thus does the exchange of Gnawa music for capital on the international market produce a mirror effect: in the Moroccan context, transglobal processes instantiate *money* as a privileged symbol in ritual life, as Gnawa musicians participate in their own commodification and fetishization. In representations of the Gnawa for European and American markets, by contrast, these values are reversed, and it is the *spirit* that becomes the privileged symbol (as exemplified in the opening quote). This inversion is a result of a defined "lack" in each of these markets. Money and the spirit come to substitute for each other, albeit in different contexts. Furthermore, both these substitutions imply different constructions of the consuming self and its identity vis-à-vis local and global "symbolic economies" (Goux 1990).

Money and Exchange in Gnawa Ritual Life
Exchange is a primary function of Gnawa ceremonies. Not only do the Gnawa facilitate the exchange of one identity for another (or several others) for those possessed, but the hostess also provides meals and monetary offerings for the Gnawa in return for their expertise and time. This exchange of money is not considered a fee, as overt payment for spiritual services is inappropriate in ritual contexts; however, it is generally acknowledged that a sum of several hundred dirham should be placed on the ritual tray with the incense and other sacred objects used in the ceremony (this is in addition to the money they will receive from the guests throughout the night). Money is displayed as an object.

"Who will open the door?" one of the Gnawa shouts out, waiting for one of the attendees to offer him a ten or twenty or fifty dirham note. Upon receiving this money—which is referred to euphemistically as *baraka* or blessing—the Gnawa confer a verbal blessing on the offerant, such as: "God bless our sister, Fatima. May she come and go with health. May she receive all that she is wanting. Bless her son in college. Bless all her relatives both near and far. God make her achieve her goal." Such blessings are said throughout the night after the completion of each musical piece. If the music inspired a particularly heated trance session—one that made many people fall into and get up to trance—offerings and blessings are abundant; which is to say that the musicians are appreciated and financially compensated for their ability to induce trance states. Often after a charged trance session the hostess or *mqaddema* will remain in trance and become clairvoyant. When this happens, the guests wait their turn and approach her, stuffing bills discreetly in her closed palm in exchange for a reading of their future or for counsel about a particular problem. The money is later placed on the tray of incense that sits before the musicians. Spirit propitiations, considered obligatory by the possessed, are also venues for distinction-making and identity-building—the abundance of food served, for example, equaling the symbolic capital of the hostess or host of the ceremony. The success of a lila is judged in later narratives primarily by how many people went into trance, but also by the beauty of the ambience and hospitality.

In practice, of course, capitalist exchange and religious ideology are of necessity interdependent, especially in a sacred society such as Morocco's (Kapchan 1996). Yet mirroring the changing consumption patterns, the role of money has changed in the context of Gnawa ceremony in recent memory: now women often complain that the Gnawa seek only to "milk you" (y-ḥalbu-k), saying that when one's money runs out, so do their blessings.[6] Some go so far as to say that the Gnawa use magic in order to addict practicants to their music, thus assuring themselves of a steady livelihood. The fact that some Gnawa roam the streets, clacking their cymbals and soliciting donations (majdub style) adds another layer to this reputation.

The reputation of Gnawa musicians as profiteers taking advantage of those unfortunate enough to be possessed is not spurious. As class divisions have become sharper in Moroccan urban centers, the symbolic capital of traditional healers has diminished in favor of more "modern" practices. What's more, the ceremonies, which many refer to as an addiction or inebriation (l-blia) with the ḥal (the aesthetic and spiritual state often attained in these rites) has given way to addictions of other sorts: huge supermarkets, department stores, boutiques, and other forms of capitalist consumption. As with all subaltern groups that depend on the community for survival, the Gnawa have had to interact with the market. Given their historical place in class and racial hierarchies, they have found themselves at a disadvantage. It is not surprising, then, that they would capitalize on the skills that the market does appreciate; namely, their mastery of music. Yet their success in making recordings with Western jazz artists has introduced yet other criteria for evaluation and identity-construction; namely, debates about authenticity. Among the Gnawa themselves, there are distinctions between those who still have tagnawit (ritual knowledge) and those who no longer answer the true Gnawa calling to be healers in the service of the community. Those who consider themselves "true" Gnawa are harsh in their criticism of those who work as entertainers,

FIGURE 8: Si Mohammed invoking the spirits; money under his *šašiyya*, or hat.
Photograph, Deborah Kapchan

valuing money more than tradition. A m'allem in Rabat recalled times in history, for example, when the pantheon of spirits was more expansive; "now," he said, "many of the spirits have been forgotten and there are fewer and fewer apprentices interested in learning the actual rites." Many of the younger Gnawa hire themselves out for weddings and other celebrations—l-frajat, spectacles. Although people often go into trance on these occasions, they are intended as entertainments and not as healing rituals, the market determining the performance repertoire. What's more, other Sufi groups now market themselves as doing all-night ceremonies. "We, too, play the nubas (the suites in the Pantheon of spirits)," one Aissawa musician told me. "We too will stay all night long." In the vocabulary of this Aissawa musician, spirit placation was an item on their list of ritual services.

The Gnawa ritual lila has no doubt changed radically as it has moved from places like Timbuktu to Casablanca. As there is no record of these early ceremonies, however, we only have oral testimony that the pantheon has diminished (the Jewish spirits rarely or no longer manifesting). The transformation of the ritual in the last ten years in Morocco, however, is measurable. Ritual lilas have become theatricalized as they are performed in contexts like nightclubs and university concert halls. Whereas lilas to propitiate spirits in Morocco are often held in humble households whose rooms hold a limited number of people, the Gnawa know that their earnings, which come largely through the offerings made by the guests in exchange for blessings, are increased in more bourgeois contexts, especially those where foreigners are present. Not surprisingly, the changes that are created by performing in new contexts—changes such as a shortening of the ritual songs, as well as alterations in the progression of a ceremony that was once sacred—are circling back to influence the ritual practices in Morocco. The Gnawa have become professionalized and are aware that their very identity is a commodity. At the same time, the power of trance as a cultural symbol has become salient. Whereas sex and rock and roll dominated the search for authenticity by Western artists in Morocco in the 1960s (Schuyler 2000), trance now holds a similar status. This is true for the Western consumers of Moroccan "trance music" as well as the Moroccan bourgeois consumers who are fetishizing their own traditions, inviting the Gnawa to the chicest of hoi poloi gatherings.

Representing the Spirit in Discourses for the West
Not surprisingly, the prevalence of money as a symbol of either blessing or contamination in Gnawa ceremonies is not recognized in the representations of

the Gnawa to Western audiences. Nor is mention made of their ambivalent reputation as magicians and tricksters within the hierarchy of Sufi-influenced ṭariqat and ṭai'fat. Rather, in the retranslation of ritual sound, only part of the symbolic economy is appropriated—the part that corresponds to the lack in the Western market, namely spirituality, particularly as it pertains to ecstatic rituals of trance. There is an inversion of signs at work. In the representations of Gnawa for Euro-American audiences it is their sub-Saharan and pre-Islamic (pagan) roots that are stressed. This, despite the fact that the Gnawa have been Muslims for centuries, and many of them were Muslims before slavery ever brought them to Morocco. Contemporary history is repressed, while ancient history is revived as the Gnawa become icons of changelessness. Speaking of a ceremony they attended in Marrakech, for example, music producers Randall Barnwell and Bill Lawrence write: "The energy and power of the music appeared in everyone's faces, in their eyes and expressions, filling the senses with an ageless, timeless music that reaches into the heart of Africa, into the history of life itself" (1995: 41). That music is the aesthetic medium most inextricable from time is ignored. The theme of timelessness is echoed again on the first page of the same booklet accompanying their 1995 release entitled *Trance*:

> Since time immemorial, some fortunate individuals have known how to penetrate the veil that separates ordinary awareness from the extraordinary. In trance, some enter a deeply relaxed state where the mundane self lets go, opening to alternate realities; others vacate their mindbodies, allowing spirits, deities, and protectors to manifest through them. Many of the world's great spiritual traditions use music to effect this opening. (Barnwell and Lawrence 1995)

Bill Lawrence is well aware that these words are addressed to an audience of nonspecialists interested in trance music, and not in Morocco or the Gnawa per se (Lawrence 1999). Nonetheless it is worth noting, following anthropologist Johannes Fabian (2002), that the invocation of "time immemorial" to describe exotic cultures makes them appear as if they do not change, when in fact, so-called traditional cultures are as likely and as quick to change as others. Fabian exhorts the analyst to write of the coevality of cultures rather than portray them as somehow outside of modernity. Here it is not "culture" that is constructed as timeless, however, but trance as a physiological and spiritual state. Trance becomes the means for entering timelessness. It functions as an emblem of return to an earlier but more holistic mode of being. This is not particular to Gnawa-influenced music but characterizes world music generally: "What is of concern to listeners," notes ethnomusicologist Timothy Taylor, "is that the world music . . . they consume has some discernable connection to the timeless, the ancient, the primal, the pure, the chthonic; that is what they want to buy, since their own world is often conceived of as ephemeral, new, artificial, and corrupt." (1997: 26).[7]

Representations of the other-worldliness of Gnawa trance music abound in world beat. Musician Patrick Jabbar El Shaheed is a lead musician in a group called Aisha Kandisha's Jarring Effects (AKJE). AKJE describes itself as a "crossover" group "influenced by . . . Gnawa, Reggae, Ragga, HipHop, Ambient, Trance, House, and experimental noises." Their website states that the band "is named after a spirit from the Moroccan mythology [sic]. Aisha Kandisha is a figure in the form of a woman. Legion. Manifold. A Mass Psychosis. Paul Bowles said that she was married 25 years ago to 35,000 men in Morocco. A lot of the people in Ber Rechid—the psychiatric Hospital—are married to her" (El Shaheed 1993). Not only does this discourse pathologize spirit possession, it considers the spirit pantheon to be "mythology." As Aisha Qandisha is one of the most powerful and dangerous of female *jinn*, to invoke her as the icon of this musical group is either courageous or naïve. It certainly bespeaks an outsider relation to spirit possession. El Shaheed notes, "With the record and the live shows, we want people to open themselves to AKJE and let themselves be free to forget everything in their lives and trance to the music" (Aisha Kandisha's Jarring Effects 1993). While for the Sufi, trance is remembering God, for El Shaheed, it is forgetting life. AKJE markets itself as embodying what it calls the "Marrakshi Jedba Beat," the Marrakech Trance beat; it is an example of how one aspect of ritual style may be extracted from its context of origin (shizophonia) and enter an economy of signs where it lives a new life (shismogenesis), changing the overall aesthetic of the music, but drawing nonetheless upon its sacred aura—in this case, the "jedba beat" (T. Taylor 1997).

Whether we trace the popularity of Gnawa music in the United States to Hassan Hakmoun and his collaborations with the jazz trumpeter Don Cherry or to the earlier 1970s collaborations between the jazz pianist Randy Weston and the Gnawa in Tangier or that between the Gnawa and horn-players Pharoah Saunders and Archie Shepp, there is no doubt that Gnawa music is now being marketed to a much different audience in a social climate where "trance" becomes an end in itself and very much a commodity as Americans reenact rituals that, for many, exist only as images on dust jackets and interpretive descriptions by trance authorities cited in liner notes, including both Western scholars and Moroccan ritual specialists. (Indeed, the role of the scholar in these discourses is pervasive.) Focusing on the African origins of the Gnawa allows another link to be made: that between African American traditions and those of North Africa. Gnawa master Ahmed Boussou is quoted as saying that "Randy Weston's music is related to Gnawa music, by virtue of its African roots; the exodus of Black people during the age of slavery transported Gnawa ritual both to America and to the North African Maghreb. Such ritual, after its development in America, was lost in concentration on sheer rhythm, while the influence of the Church gave rise to the 'Negro Spiritual'" (Weston 1994: 8). The same liner notes quote African American author Mildred Pitts Walters as saying that the Gnawa lila recalled to her "the ring games and circle dances of my childhood; the music and dance in the Pentecostal Church; the dancing to drum beats in Haiti, in Nigeria, in the Gambia and Senegal, and I knew that the mysteries of that music were connected to what I had just heard and seen there, in Morocco" (Weston 1994: 8). Whereas I appreciate the sentiment of these associations, they participate in a flattening of difference. What is to be gained by comparing children's circle games with possession by the powerful genie Aisha Qandisha? The answer is, of course, a connection to Africa and, by extension, to the sacred.

In critiquing the representations of trance for the West, I am not underestimating its importance in ritual and devotional life. I concur with Charles Keil about the transforming and healing potential of music, as one possibility among others "for fusing with primary reality" (1995: 4). Keil would no doubt consider the seemingly transglobal interest in musically induced trance states as an example of "how global feelings are catharsed through music" (1995: 5). While it is important to pay attention to large-scale waves of interest—"structures of feelings" (R. Williams 1977) like the re-emergence of trance practices—it is important to recognize who is inducing what and by what means.

CONCLUSION

Feld uses Murray Schafer's concept of schizophonia to describe the processes and consequences of sounds being removed from their original performance contexts and recontextualized in others, giving rise to new trajectories of social interaction and formation—schismogenesis, or what might be called imaginal realms of dialogue and contestation (1995). It is important to realize that what appear to be contradictory forces are in fact completely interdependent and coproducing, each side being obliged to represent what the other side lacks. Sacred music and money are not two poles but two of many interlocking forces in the creation of politically charged expressive culture. Indeed, it is helpful to think of M. M. Bakhtin's concept of inner and outer orientation of genre in this regard—the inner orientation being the aesthetic relations internal to the genre, and the outer orientation being the life that genre lives in the world and its political economy (1985). Changes are certainly happening in the internal realm of Gnawa music—in the aesthetics of the ceremony, in the presence or absence of techniques of healing—and these changes transform the relations of the outer genre—the way sacred music is taken up and circulated as a fetishized commodity in the world music market and the power it has or doesn't have for its community of origin. And vice-versa.

As Talal Asad reminds us, in "an interdependent world, 'traditional cultures' do not spontaneously grow or develop into 'modern cultures.' People are pushed, seduced, coerced, or persuaded into trying to change themselves into something else, something that allows them to be redeemed" (Asad 2003: 154). This works for both sides of the traditional/modern divide: as the Gnawa see redemption in capitalist gain and the Western artists who work with them (as well as others who "consume" them) find the promise of redemption in the return of the sacred in its aesthetic guise.

In the appropriation of sound and meaning it is not surprising that signs are emptied of some of their associations and infused with others. What is noteworthy is which meanings are repressed and which are taken up as metonyms of cultural identity. In their ritual lives, Moroccan Gnawa practitioners incorporate the marketplace into the very heart of their ritual, dancing with the ambivalence that money and commodification import to a tradition struggling to survive. But where Moroccan Gnawa musicians must commodify their spirituality in order to participate in both local and global economies, Euro-American musicians must spiritualize their commodifications, suppressing a large part of the history and politics of trance. In fact, what the Gnawa repress in the commodification of their music (its spiritual aspect and its ability to heal) returns as the main icon of Gnawa identity in Western appropriations of the music, while the exchange relations that are misrecognized in the West return to haunt the ritual life of the Gnawa. As Moroccan Gnawa musicians debate what counts as "real" Gnawa music among the spiralings of sound, money, and fetishization, Euro-American audiences naively consume beats that may hinder as well as help the healing they purport to effect, confusing in the process the "voice of God" with the "noise of man."[8]

IN FRANCE
WITH THE GNAWA

◆ ◆ ◆

In June 1999, the late King Hassan of Morocco went to Paris to inaugurate a
year-long series of concerts, performances, and festivals celebrating Moroccan culture in France. After Algerians, Moroccans are the largest minority in
France, and their birthrate in 1999 exceeded the birthrate of the European
French, a fact that worried some conservatives. King Hassan II, himself educated in Bordeaux and known to be as comfortable in French as in Arabic, had
excellent relations with the president of the French republic, Jacques Chirac.
Nonetheless the far right had made strides in the previous decade. The politics
of LePen had taken hold, and hate crimes against North Africans made front-
page news several times. In order to heal these wounds and cultivate an appreciation for Moroccan culture in France, 1999 began with an official visit by
King Hassan to Paris, parades, fanfare, and speeches. Before the year ended,
however, King Hassan had died, and the public in both Morocco and France
mourned his passing with eulogies in the press and the media.

Before the King's death, Si Mohammed and his brothers went to Paris to
perform a three-month gig at the Divan du Monde, a nightclub in the eighteenth *arrondissment* near Place Pigalle. It was not the first time they had been
in Paris. In fact, they had traveled to France for several consecutive summers
playing festivals in Montpelier, Marseille and elsewhere. This was the first
time that they had stayed so long, however. They had a new agent now, someone who was not a musician himself, but a young producer of Moroccan descent. (Their previous agent, a French percussionist who, for a time, was married to a prominent Moroccan chanteuse, was also featured on their first CD
and thus had different interests). Si Mohammed had faith in this person, if
only because they were making a little money, signing contracts, and had
promises of French working papers.

That summer I had an apartment in the fifth *arrondissement*, between Rue
Mouffetard and the Grand Mosque. Situated on the Left Bank, it was a second-
floor flat from the nineteenth century with hardwood floors. Sparsely but

tastefully furnished and adorned with abstract colorist paintings done by my friend Susan Ossman, the owner of the place, the apartment was flooded with the light of the sun during the day and the light of the animated street below by night. The tall, insulated windows kept most of the noise out. And the bedroom, which looked over a courtyard in the back, was as tranquil a room as I have ever slept in. On Fridays I would sit by the living-room window and watch as North Africans emerged one after another from the "Monge" metro stop and head towards the mosque; some men in *jellabas* and skullcaps, more in street clothes, but many women scarved and robed and walking briskly towards the minaret a few blocks away. The mosque itself dates from 1926, and its architecture is reminiscent of the mosques in North Africa. There is an "Arab café" open to the public on one side of this mosque, where sweet mint tea is served in small glasses and a variety of sweets—mostly from the Middle East—are available. Through the doors and to the left of this café is a *ḥammam*, a steam bath, also open to the public, where women and men spend hours sweating and scrubbing, albeit during different hours of the day. Not unlike a similar scene in Morocco, poor women sit along the outside walls of the mosque asking for alms. Unlike Morocco, inside the walls a beautiful garden is open to tourists on days of nonworship. The large carpeted halls for prayer are reserved for the faithful.

Si Mohammed and his brothers never went to the mosque, however. Apart from a few excursions to the Tour Eiffel and Notre Dame, they confined themselves to their neighborhood, a *quartier* populated mostly by North African and sub-Saharan African immigrants. During the day they drank their tea in outdoor cafés, smoked, and bought items in the street markets that lined Boulevard de Rouchechouart, near Barbès. Occasionally they walked up the hill to Montmartre and once took in the view from the Sacrée Coeur de Paris. They were lodged in a seventh-floor walk-up around the corner from the nightclub. Walking up the winding wood staircase was training for amateur athletes.

Si Mohammed's apartment was a strange configuration of small rooms, as if it had been converted into a place for visiting artists long ago. Entering, there were three small bedrooms and a bathroom off a narrow and long hallway. One of the bedrooms had a small kitchenette built into the wall. There, Zaynab, Si Mohammed's third wife (whom he divorced shortly after their marriage) and his twenty-year-old daughter Hasna cooked lunches for themselves and the men—mostly *duaz*: vegetable stews made from a base of tomatoes, ginger, cumin, turmeric, cilantro, and parsley. Sometimes it was *duaz* with green beans, sometimes potatoes, sometimes with some chicken, sometimes some beef. In this area of town you could find the round loaves of spongy bread that Moroccans preferred to sop up the murqa, the sauce that defined the cuisine. Most of the time, however, they simply bought baguettes, called comir in Moroccan Arabic.

The first time I visited them I went to the club where they were rehearsing in the afternoon. The lobby was set up with a small spice stand. Indeed the show was billed as a North African marketplace. It was meant to be an experience, entertainment for the five senses. There was a bar to the left of the stage where people could buy sweet mint tea before the show. There were sweets for sale as well. And the balcony was set up with couches where people could lounge while looking down over the stage. When I entered, the chairs that would surround the stage on the ground level were folded up against the back wall. A group of young North African hip-hop artists were rehearsing. The music was canned, but the dancing was first-rate: handstands spinning down to the floor, twirling on the back, then the body snapping up again, rubber spines, North African rap in French.

I stood and watched for five minutes and then, when they paused, I spoke up.

"Est-ce que Si Mohammed est là?" I asked. "Is Si Mohammed around?"

"He's in the back," one of the dancers said. "Come, I'll show you." And he led me backstage to the dressing rooms.

"Si Mohammed," the dancer called out in a French accent as we entered a corridor behind the stage. The dancer was North African but had been born in France and didn't speak any Arabic. Si Mohammed appeared in a doorway.

"ahlan! ahlan lalla najma!" Si Mohammed said, embracing me on both cheeks in French fashion and hugging me warmly. "When do you get here?"

"Oh, about a week ago," I answered.

Just then his son Younis came out of the dressing room.

"najma! la bas? b-khir? Najma, how are you? Are you doing well?"

Si Mohammed's brother Khadir appeared, then Hassan, and finally Zaynab and Hasna. I greeted everyone with kisses and inquiries into their health and happiness. We were all crowded in this small hallway. Finally Si Mohammed took me by the arm.

"Come," he said. "I'll show you where we're living. Did you see the spice market in the entry? That was our idea."

"And I paint the patron's hands with henna before the show," volunteered Zaynab. They were delighted that the response to their performance was so favorable.

"You work every night?" I asked as we walked through the theater.

"Wednesday through Saturday," Si Mohammed replied.

"Do a lot of people come?"

"It's packed, 'amr. I'll leave you some tickets here at the box office for tonight's show. You'll see. The place is packed."

"I don't think I can come tonight," I said, "but tomorrow."

"Okay, tomorrow."

"Is it mostly North Africans that come?"

"North Africans, Africans, French. Everyone comes. They're crazy about us, kay-ḥamqu 'ali-nah."

"It's all wonderful," I told them, as they scooted me through the lobby and out the front door. A left on Rue Rouchechouart, a few doors down, and we were there.

"It's here," Si Mohammed said, pushing through a heavy street door and into a dingy hallway. We began walking up the winding staircase. The stairs were wooden and old, worn in the middle, and they squeaked and moaned under our feet as we ascended. There were graffiti tags on the walls. At the completion of each full circle of steps was a landing with a door to an apartment floor. We continued up.

"Where is this place?" I finally asked, as we mounted the fifth set of steep steps, my quadriceps burning.

"Just a few more," Si Mohammed assured me. "We're on the seventh floor."

The top. Si Mohammed ushered me into a small room on the right with a bed, a tiny kitchenette, and a table. The windows were small dormer windows looking out over Place Pigalle, the XXX movie theaters, and the rooftops of Paris beyond.

"Sit down," he told me, motioning to the mattress.

"Ara haduk qrai d-monada," Si Mohammad instructed his daughter. "Bring over those bottles of soda. Do you want Coke or Orangina?" He asked.

"Either is fine," I said. "Just water is fine."

"No water!" Si Mohammed insisted, pouring me a glass of Coke. Although mint tea was served as the authentic Moroccan drink at the Divan du Monde, soda has largely replaced mint tea as the beverage of choice for guests in Morocco, especially during the summer months. It means that you can afford to be extravagant with your guests. Soda in returnable glass bottles only hit the local grocers there in the 1980s, and in the 1990s they were replaced with plastic. Since then, the Moroccan countryside is not only littered with the black plastic bags that greengrocers use to pack up their produce, but with plastic bottles and tin cans. Coca-Cola has opened a bottling plant in Morocco, marketing not just Coke, but Hawaii, Sprite, and now, water itself. But we were in Paris.

"Drink!" Si Mohammed said, lifting the bottle to pour more. I waved my index finger back and forth in the air, indicating that I wanted no more.

After I had quenched the thirst acquired by the walk up the steps, Si Mohammed got out his *cartable*, his vinyl briefcase, and pulled out some papers, handing them to me. Si Mohammed kept all his official documents and pictures in his cartable. I had already read one of his previous contracts while in Morocco—the one he signed to make the compact disc in 1994 and had admonished him to be careful.

"It seems like six thousand dirhams is a lot," I told him then, "but the agent is probably getting a lot more than that." I talked like an authority, though I didn't realize at the time that even producers don't make a lot on the marketing of compact discs. I just assumed that musicians from the developing world were exploited, a liberal prejudice.

Si Mohammed handed me this year's contract, silently asking me for my opinion by raising his eyebrows and looking me in the eye. Si Mohammed doesn't read. This time the deal was much more generous. The musicians were making twenty thousand francs each for the three months in addition to free housing and travel expenses. Si Mohammed, as leader of the group, was making about twice that amount. The problem was that the money was not all given upfront, and so they had to be very careful about what they ate and how much money they spent everyday. They were responsible for their food.

"Who are you working with now?" I asked.

"He's a young Maghrebi," answered Si Mohammed, "He is straight, *nishan*. He's trying to get us green cards so that we can live here. Even if we didn't live here, if we had green cards we wouldn't need to go up and down (*ṭla u ḥabaṭ*) trying to get visas every time we come."

"That's great. But how can he get you green cards if you aren't French?"

"We've got a CD We contribute to the *patrimoine*," Si Mohammed said, code-switching into the French. "The CD was recorded here in France, so we've already worked here. Hasna, my daughter, doesn't want to go back to Morocco. She's already had a marriage proposal here."

"Really? Who?"

"A Moroccan who's been living here for a long time. But I don't know. She wants him, but he doesn't have a job."

"You don't want to be poor in Paris," I say to Hasna who was sitting to my right. "Do you want to marry him?"

"I don't know," she said blushing.

"I don't know," Si Mohammed repeated, shaking his head.

"Well, I better get going. I'll see you all tomorrow night."

Si Mohammed put on his cap and escorted me down the stairs to the street where I headed towards the metro.

"*b-slama 'ali-k*," he said. "Go with God.

THE PERFORMANCE

I arrived late to the performance. The Algerian woman comic was just finishing, to applause and laughter. She was a *beur*, a second-generation daughter of immigrant parents, and spoke fluent French. She was riffing off life as a French youth who was not quite accepted as French and who was caught between two worlds: the traditional world of her parents, who thought a girl should be at home and marriage should be arranged, and the world she encountered in Paris among the French. She clearly had sympathizers in the audience. There seemed to be quite a few people of North African descent in the crowd. The Arab hip-hop artists were next. They got the audience moving and clapping. Then there was a short intermission. The audience was encouraged to go out into the lobby and peruse the Moroccan *suq* (marketplace) that had been set up. There were stands set up with mounds of spices—cumin, cinnamon, ginger, turmeric—as well as piles of henna leaves. Each pile was labeled. There were steaming cups of sweet Moroccan mint tea for sale, as well as sweets made with rosewater and almond paste.

The lights blinked on and off, and people sauntered back to their seats. The lights went out. From the back of the theater we heard the beat of the *ṭbal*, the big snare drums used at the beginning of the Gnawa *lila* to invoke the spirits. The Gnawa filed in—Khadir, Hassan, and Younis first, then Hasna and Zaynab, then the *m'allem* Si Mohammed. They circled around, beating the two drums and singing. Then the *m'allem* sat down on the stage, while the others sat on the same level with the audience. Much to my surprise, the *m'allem* launched into the invocations in the ceremony. They played some *qiṭ'a*, or cuts, from the green spirits, and then began the black. There were some people in the audience who were on their feet, swaying with their eyes closed. When they played Sidi Mimun's song, Hasna and Zaynab got up and started trancing. Soon after, they took off their scarves, letting their long hair flow freely as they threw their heads from side to side, throwing their hair over the front of their faces. They women fell to the floor and remained there for a few minutes as they waited for the music to stop. Then they got up and went to sit with the Gnawa. The next song was Sidi Hamu. Khadir got up and started trancing. He took off his shirt and gave it to Hassan, seated in the ground with his qraqab. Hassan then handed Khadir two bundles of candles, which Khadir lit himself with a lighter. He continued trancing, his bare chest exposed, the candles licking the hairs under his forearms as he held the bundles first under the left arm, then under the right. Then he set the candles down on the floor and bent backwards over them so that the flames touched his back. The crowd was enrapt, as they were witnessing what some intuited to be behavior from a serious ritual. Others were simply agape at the performance of such a mortification rite. The Gnawa ended by invoking Lalla Mira, the mirthful *jinniyya* who loves perfume, henna, beauty, and dance. Zayneb and Hasna tranced, danced, and pulled members of the audience up to the floor to dance with them. When the music ended, the Gnawa paraded off the stage to great applause, but then canned music was put on, and the crowd continued dancing for a good two hours while Zaynab circulated among the patrons with a cup of henna paste and a syringe and offered to henna their hands.

I was rather shocked at the performance the Gnawa gave. I had never seen the Gnawa—any Gnawa anywhere—perform anything but songs from the beginning of the ceremony (the 'ada), in public. But Si Mohammed and his group actually performed the invocations to the spirits, complete with trancing (though there was no incense used). They did not adhere to the order of the colors, nor did they complete the qit'a; however they did enact aspects of the ceremony that are usually not performed outside a ritual context. What's more, Khadir bared his chest—something that I'd never seen him or any Gnawa do before. Was this a way to perform North African savagery and exoticism for a foreign public? And the women tranced among an audience of strange men and women. Surely this could only happen in France!

The recontextualization of the lila in a French theater was just the first such performance I was to see. I saw others later, given by other Gnawi in other cities that were equally shocking. Why was I shocked? Because I had been told that the music had such power that it would be dangerous to play it outside its ritual context, at least those songs that invoked the jnun.

"Aren't the jnun going to be angry?" I asked Si Mohammed eventually. (I had already congratulated him on a wonderful performance).

"It's all *niya*," was his reply. "It's in the intention. They *mluk* know our *niya*."

The recontextualization of the sacred in the space of the secular does have its dangers. Co-occurrence rules change, license reigns. Ethnomusicologist

FIGURE 9: Trancing at the Divan du Monde. Photograph, Deborah Kapchan

Jean During says the sacred does not disappear, it just changes form (1988). If so, what forms are the Gnawa ceremonies taking now? How is the sacred transmitted across boundaries of religion, ethnicity, and gender?

2000

The next summer I was back in Paris, in the same apartment. This time the Gnawa were on a three-month tour in Brittany, however. They were collaborating with a group of traditional Breton musicians based near the port city of Brest. I was due in Brittany in a week. Before that, however, there was other work to do in Paris. African American jazz pianist Randy Weston was in town and playing at a club in the tenth *arrondissment*. For Weston, the Gnawa were a link to a spiritual path through music, a healing force emanating from "mother Africa." He had promised me an in-depth interview, and I was determined to get it.

Our adventures began almost immediately. I called Mr. Weston's agent in Paris as instructed to and found out that he was playing the next night at the New Morning. After that gig, he and his New York–based band were traveling south with the Gnawa (arriving from Tangier the next day) to play a jazz festival there. I had twenty-four hours to recover from jet leg and get into documentary mode.

My first day in Paris was uneventful. I walked up to Place de la Contrescarpe and had an *apertif* in one of the cafés that surrounded the square. The air was warm but not hot. The square was packed with local youth and tourists. I watched the people pass on foot and on their scooters, motorcycles, and in their miniscule cars.

I knew the metro system, and the next night I ventured out to the nightclub. I got off at Strasbourg Saint Denis in the tenth arrondissement. I didn't know this area, but my friends equated it immediately with Harlem. There were only people of color: Africans, North Africans, and Indians. The graffitied buildings were clearly less well maintained than those in the fifth *arrondissment*. There were more gates on the windows.

I found the club about three blocks away and went in. The first set had already started, and the place was packed. I had to stand. Despite the neighborhood, 75 percent of the audience was white. Mr. Weston was on stage, seated at the piano, his large aura reverberating with the harmonies he was sending out. With him were bassist James Lewis, saxophonist and flutist Talib Kibwe (T. K. Blue), and African percussionist Neil Clark. Everyone except Lewis was based in New York. Lewis lived in Paris and played with Weston when he toured in Europe and Africa.

The music was entrancing. Kibwe's flute playing was haunting. Weston took his solos, but also passed them around to the rest of the band members. They closed the first set with the piece that Weston always closes with: "Blue Moses," the song Weston wrote in the 1970s based on the chord progression and rhythm of the Gnawa melody used to invoke the spirit of Sidi Musa, or Master Moses, in their possession ceremonies. Weston had attended these healing rituals to placate spirits when he lived in Tangiers. Each of the spirits in the Moroccan pantheon has a corresponding color, incense, and melody. Weston discovered an affinity to the "blue spirit" Sidi Musa and pays homage to him at every performance. After the first set, the audience thinned out a bit, and I was able to sit down. I went to the stage door and asked to see Weston. Instead his European manager took him a message from me. He was visiting with Archie Shepp right now, he returned to say, but had been expecting me. I was to come see him after the show.

The second set was equally inspiring, and they closed, once again, with "Blue Moses." Afterward I waited until most of the French fans had left, then went back to see Weston. He stands almost seven feet tall, and his generosity of spirit is equal to his stature. His fans adore him both for his music and for the love that infuses it. A magnificent Senegalese woman was there with her sister who lives in Paris and her little niece. The other musicians were also there, the soundman, and Weston's manager.

"Well hello!" he intoned, recognizing me and bending down a bit to give me a hug. He introduced me to his friend, who I had actually met in Fes when she and Weston were there for the Sacred Music Festival the previous summer. After exchanging some remarks about his music, he said, "We're going to Souillac tomorrow on the train. Are you coming?"

"Where is Souillac?" I asked.

"About an hour outside of Toulouse. We're playing a jazz festival there. It's beautiful. You really should come."

"Will we have the opportunity to talk there?" I asked. Weston knew that I was writing a book about the Gnawa and that I had come for an interview.

"We'll talk on the way back in the train," he promised. "We'll have five hours on the train."

That was it. I went home and packed that night.

Weston and the Gnawa left early the next day, but I waited for a later train to leave. The train for Souillac departed from the Gare d'Austerlitz, the very station from which I had departed year after year on my way to see my "French family" in the Massif Central. France for me was full of memories. I had spent my seventeenth summer there on an informal exchange, then come back again for three summers in a row when I was living in Morocco between 1982 and 1985. I had brought my Moroccan husband to meet my French family in 1984 and then had brought my daughter when she was nine months old, when she was two, and again when she was three. We had all spent Christmas there one year. I had spent summers in Paris and Montpelier as a divorced woman while visiting some friends, and I had visited my dearest friend in Paris and then in Nimes for weeks at a time. I had gone through many of the passages of my life in France. As the train pulled out of Paris, through the stucco-roofed suburbs and eventually through the rolling farmland and hillsides of "la France profonde," I saw the French countryside once again *de nouveau*, as if for the first time.

When I arrived in Souillac five hours later, there was little indication of a festival of any kind. The train station was on a hill, and, after asking directions in an empty bistro, I began walking, suitcases in hand, to the center of town. It was indeed a long walk, but well worth it. When I finally found the hotel, Weston and his musicians were just finishing a late lunch in the dining room. I greeted them, then went upstairs to a large room with French windows that overlooked the patio. I could watch all the activity in the street from my room.

Souillac dates from the eleventh century, and the concert that evening was held in a cobblestone square in front of an old abbey from that century. When I arrived, the sun still hadn't set. Weston had already reserved a front-row seat for me, next to the mayor. I set up my tape recorder, and I watched the square fill up with hundreds of people as night fell. When Weston and his band appeared on stage, the applause was clearly from an audience familiar with their music, and for two hours we were taken up by the trance-like rhythms of the Gnawa and the open harmonies of Weston's piano-playing.

After the concert I was invited to a private party thrown by the town dignitaries for the musicians. It was on a back street in the old quarter of town, with winding, narrow alleys. Apart from the streetlights, we could have been in the Middle Ages. At midnight, there were still a few people in a local café, but otherwise the streets were dark and quiet. I wandered for a good twenty minutes, then ran into Neil Clark, the percussionist, and followed him to the party.

Once inside I ran into the bassist, James Lewis.

"Hey, how are you doing?" he asked.

"Great," I answered. "I loved the music." Lewis often plays with Weston when he tours in Europe.

"How long have you lived in Paris?" I asked him.

"Seven years. I've got two kids now, two sons."

"You're lucky," I said.

"Yeah, but it's not easy supporting them as a musician in Paris," he replied. "Not anymore."

"I'm writing a book on the Gnawa," I volunteered, "and their collaboration with Randy. Have you ever been to Morocco?"

"Sure, we went. I was in Tangier and Marrakech."

"Did you attend a lila?" I asked.

"No, we never got around to that. We were always too busy playing. But I'd like to. Before coming to Paris, I used to play with Pharoah Saunders. I played with him for six years."

"That's great. Pharoah played with the Gnawa too."

"I know. I know."

"I'm going to go talk with them a bit," I said, excusing myself. I walked toward the corner of the room where three Gnawa were standing and eating some of the hors d'oeuvres.

It is always a delight to speak Arabic with Moroccans outside of Morocco. The Moroccan dialect is one of the dialects that is furthest from standard or classical Arabic, containing Berber syntax and many borrowings from French and Spanish. The vowels in Moroccan Arabic almost disappear. To speakers of other dialects, it is sometimes incomprehensible. It's like a secret language.

The m'allem, Abdellah El Gourd, spoke slowly and with consideration. He had been playing with Weston for thirty years. Although younger than Weston, he had a white beard and the polish of someone used to dealing with foreigners. Still, I could see that my level of Moroccan Arabic impressed him. And although he answered my questions with only the most perfunctory answers (answers, I was soon to discover, that were an almost a direct translation of Weston's answers, except in Arabic), his eyes twinkled with warmth.

The m'allem maintained his reserve, but the two younger Gnawi began to engage me in conversation. At first they thought I was a Moroccan who had migrated to France. But I corrected them, giving them my "rap": I had lived in Morocco for five years, married a Berber, had a child, divorced, still do research there, etc. Unfortunately before we could get to their histories, we were being led out of the reception hall and towards a jazz club several blocks away. The club was called Le Black Club. No joke.

The place was tiny, and it was packed, but when one of the festival organizers saw us at the door she went immediately to the French sitting in the front booths and removed them from their seats. They seemed to get up graciously to make way for the Moroccans. The organizer then beckoned to us, and we squeezed our way through the crowd of bodies to the small stage and the front booth—me, the two young Gnawi, and Neil Clark.

James Lewis was already on stage jamming on his bass with a young French horn player, a French pianist, and a drummer. Then Kibwe took over the horn part. The tune was Bird's "Anthropology"—a fitting number from my perspective—and Kibwe played it so sweetly, making the changes and the patterns sound incredibly easy. Then he stepped down and encouraged a young French girl with a tenor sax to take over. About twenty with a beautiful complexion and auburn hair, she stepped onto stage and began to blow, tenuously at first, then with more confidence. Kibwe kept encouraging her with verbal remarks. He had clearly been a musical mentor for a long time, despite his less-than-middle age. It was very generous of the American musicians, I thought, to invigorate the community not just with a concert, but also with an active involvement in the local scene with aspiring young artists.

The next day we all met at the train station. I exchanged my second-class tickets for first-class, hoping that I would be able to find a seat in the same compartment as Weston and his group. I saw them across the quai and approached. The morning sky was still overcast and there was a slight chill to the summer air. Neil Clark, the percussionist, began to talk to me.

"Randy tells me you're an anthropologist," he said. "You work in Morocco?"

"Yes," I answered. "I've been doing research in Morocco since 1982. Now I'm writing a book on the Gnawa."

"Cool, cool. I'd like to talk to you about that," he said. "About their worldview. Do you know Mbiti's book on the history of African religions?"

"I haven't gotten to that book yet," I said. "Though I've heard of it."

"You have to read it," Neil insisted. I got out my notebook and wrote down the title.

We felt a faint rumbling that shook the pavement and entered our bones. We both looked down the tracks at the same time, glimpsing the headlights of the approaching train.

"We'll talk more on the train," I said, as Neil began to gather his bags.

French trains have reserved seating, and I did not have a reserved seat. I followed Weston and his band into the first-class compartment. Weston found his seat and sat down while the younger members of the band and the two agents brought in the instruments and the bags. I was a bit forlorn, as all the

FIGURE 10: *From the left, standing:* Abdellah El Gourd, Neil Clark, a local producer, Randy Weston, James Lewis, Talib Kibwe; *squatting:* Road Manager Jaap Harlaar, and another local producer at the Souillac train station. Photograph, Deborah Kapchan

seats in the car were technically "*reservé.*" I sat down close to the band anyway, and hoped that I would not be displaced. In fact, I wasn't. I sat down next to Weston with my tape recorder and, once the train began moving, began my interview, which lasted about forty minutes. I tried to draw Weston into conversation that was more than just a public relations spiel, and at times we did have a real dialogue. The breakthrough was when I told Weston that I also went into trance to the Gnawa music.

"So you're possessed too!" he laughed. "A Gnawiya, like the rest of us."

After forty minutes I had asked all the questions I could think of. Weston looked at me. "Do you have enough propaganda?" he asked, a trickster grin on his face.

I turned the recorder off, thanked him, and got up, complicit, or somewhat.

Weston wanted to rest. I went to look for another seat. I spotted a seat across from Neil Clark. He was sitting in the seats that face each other—the kind with a table in the middle. Kibwe was catty-cornered from him, next to me, and had his feet up on the seat next to Clark.

"You mind if I sit down?" I asked. The seats actually belonged to the agents, but they were in the cafeteria car having lunch.

"Not at all," was Clark's reply, gesturing for me to sit.

"The concert last night was wonderful," I began. "And when the Gnawa came on stage, the energy really changed. Did you feel it?"

"Yeah. When the Gnawa start playing it's a whole other thing. The minute that they start playing, I'm functioning in a different capacity than I'm functioning in the ensemble, cause Abdellah is the model. So I have to fall into where that is and . . . and . . . They have given me the freedom to interpret on my instrument yet still, there's a consciousness, an awareness of the structure of Gnawa music that I have to conform to. Yeah, or else it's not real, it's disrespectful."

"Have you been to Morocco? Have you attended Gnawa ceremonies there?" I asked.

"I've been to Morocco several times," said Neil, "but I haven't attended a ceremony yet. I would like to do that. But you know, it's a lot like Santeria ceremonies. I've been playing percussion in Santeria ceremonies for twenty years now."

"Where?" I asked.

"In Brooklyn," he replied. "And it's the same gig. You gotta stay inside the structure. And there's freedom there."

"Do you think the spirits are real?" I asked somewhat naively. "Have you had visions? Do you get possessed?"

"You know, God is an imponderable. We can't grasp it as humans. And so we give God the form that we understand. Some people see God as Exu or one of the Orishas, others see God as Sidi Mimun or Vishnu or Buddha. The form changes according to the culture."

Neil was an anthropologist. Or a Buddhist. He understood about the one and the ten thousand things; he understood what Ibn al-ʿArabi, the thirteenth-century Sufi mystic, meant when he said that God was both God and Not God, negative and positive, absence and presence, white and black.

The train pulled into the Austerlitz station at around 7 P.M. Kibwe and Clark started unloading the equipment with the others. There were many bags. On the *quai* I went over to Weston to hug him—no easy feat for a 5′3″ woman and a 6′7″ man. I thanked him. I said I'd be in touch. I said my good-byes to the others and proceeded down the *quai* and out into the anonymity of Paris.

I found the bus stop that said "Place d'Italie," boarded the bus, then got off at "Gobelins" and walked the rest of the way back. Past the café-restaurants where the specialties were oysters, past the little open-windowed bistros where the locals were eating their steak and *frites*, past the *tabacs*, past the LOTO kiosks, past the closed boutiques, I made my way down the blocks, up the hill, to Rue Monge, my temporary dwelling-place in Paris. I punched in the code that residents use to open the heavy wooden doors to the apartment buildings, I walked up the curving wooden staircase, worn with more than a hundred years of footsteps, turned the key, entered the apartment, opened the shutters to the light of the Paris evening, and poured myself a glass of wine. Home.

◆ ◆ ◆

The next day I spoke to Si Mohammed, the Gnawa master, on the phone. He called me Najma, my Moroccan name. I took this name for the memory of my grandmother, Stella, a Hungarian immigrant with special powers. Like Stella, Najma means "star."

"*najma? ki dayra? labas? aywa. foqash n-šuf-ak?* Najma, how are you? Are you well? Well, when are we going to see you?"

"I'm coming on Tuesday," I said. "In order to attend your performance on Wednesday. I arrive on the 6 P.M. train."

"We'll be at the station," he assured me, then passed the phone to his French collaborator, Geneviève, who told me she was anxious to meet me.

After three days I went to the Gare du Nord and boarded a train for Brest, a coastal city and the capital of Brittany, the region of the furthest west coast of France, known for its Celtic culture and language—le *Breton*.

I had never been to this part of France before, though my French friends had told me it was beautiful as the British isles were beautiful—with jagged coastlines, fog, and fairies. Indeed, it was the fairies that were responsible for me being there at all, for the Breton musicians that I was about to meet were convinced that there were important similarities between the local fairy lore and the Gnawa (indeed, Islamic) belief in genies (or *jnun*). Both traditions, they asserted, assumed that invisible creatures populated the earth, causing mischief for the humans among whom they lived. Both traditions had night-long musical rituals that placated the spirits and soothed the suffering of humans. Both traditions were Dionysian—the Bretons dancing with abandon until dawn to the high pitch and fast rhythms of the bagpipes, the Moroccans trancing all night to the piercing clacks of large iron castanets and the base-line melodies of the three-stringed *hajhuj*.

I arrived at the Brest station around six, which, during the French summer, is still midafternoon. I looked around for Si Mohammed and their French hosts, but they had not yet arrived, so I went outside the station to wait. There were some cumulus clouds floating high above the bay, but the sun was brilliant. The air was cool.

Suddenly a van pulled up to the curb before me, and I recognized Si Mohammed's face peering out at me from the passenger seat. His brothers Khadir and Hassan were in the back. He opened the door and, both of us smiling from ear to ear, got out of the van, his white cotton robe flowing, his colorful skullcap as brilliant as the Breton sky. We embraced—going back and forth from left cheek to right cheek several times before we stopped to look at each other.

"*aywa? la bas? la bas 'ali-k? ki dayra?* Well, well, Najma . . ." he laughed and grasped my shoulders. By then, Geneviève, the woman responsible for the Gnawa being in France this summer, was at my side.

"*Je suis Geneviève,*" she said. I took her hand and kissed her on both cheeks as if she was related to Si Mohammed.

"Deborah," I responded, saying my name with the three syllables that it should have in English but doesn't.

"*Enchantée,*" she replied. "*Montez,* get in," she told me, opening the passenger-seat door. I deferred to Si Mohammed who had been sitting there, but he refused to resume his place, getting in the back seat, and motioning to his brothers to follow him. The two European ladies were put together, the Africans in the back.

I kept turning around, uncomfortable with the seating arrangement, to ask about the health of the Si Mohammad, Khadir, and Hassan, about the health of their wives and children back home in Morocco, about the way things were going here in France.

"I'll tell you everything later," Si Mohammed said to me in Arabic, lowering his chin and raising his eyebrows as he spoke to me with his eyes.

Geneviève's house was in a little town in the suburbs of Brest. It had been built of stone in 1897and had three stories. We were escorted into the kitchen, which took up the left side of the house and were invited to sit on benches surrounding a huge dining-room table made of rough-hewn wood. The floor was also made of square stone slabs, and a large wooden hutch took up most of one wall. It was about 7:00. The air was warm, and the sun was still relatively high. Khadir started rolling a joint. Geneviève set down several bottles of red wine. Glasses were distributed, and Si Mohammed let loose, telling me in Arabic about the crazy times they had been having all summer and how he and the rest of the Gnawa felt trapped in the Brest apartment where they were lodged between gigs. Si Mohammed had been fighting with his brother Khadir, and they weren't speaking. The youngest brother Hassan had taken Khadir's side, and both had threatened to return to Morocco prematurely. Meanwhile, Si Mohammed's son Younis had shaved his head like a punk rocker and was hanging with Geneviève's adolescent daughter despite his recent marriage back in Morocco.

Geneviève and her husband Robert had seven children. When we arrived, the youngest two greeted the Gnawa warmly, jumping up into their arms. They were little seven-year-old twin boys, blond and blue-eyed with long hair cut like a bowl around their foreheads. One of the twins was a little taller than the other, who had been born with a congenital heart condition, and the smaller boy had his left ear pierced and was wearing a little gold cross. They both had on overalls, and their skin seemed translucent, especially against the blackness of the Gnawa. They kissed us all, and the smallest sat on Si Mohammed's lap, obviously used to being lavished with attention. There was an extremely precocious girl of fourteen (she played the accordion) and a boy of sixteen with long, light-brown hair. The next-to-oldest daughter had a child—an absolutely beautiful little girl of five. She, her boyfriend, and their little girl were planning on going to Andalucia to work in a grape orchard for a while. They were applying themselves to Spanish, and a language text was open on the table. The oldest girl was twenty-two. Also a traditional musician, she had already left home and was living in Brest with her boyfriend and their two-year-old child. All of the siblings had golden complexions and silky hair. All these children, their friends, and boyfriends, and children, circulated around the house, greeting us, sitting down for a while, making conversation, getting up, bidding us good-bye. It was a carnival.

Geneviève made us a delicious dinner: fish and potato casserole, with tomato salad, bread, and wine. I had brought Geneviève some Randy Weston compact discs so that she could hear another version of a Gnawa/Western mix. After we ate, we listened to those songs together, talked about the overlap she saw between the Breton rituals and the Moroccan ones, and discussed the difficulties of intercultural communication. She was disappointed that two members of her band were not interested in anything but a musical exchange. "The bass player and the percussionist haven't done anything to get to know the Gnawa," she said. "Only Robert and I have spent time with them. We saw this as a cultural exchange, not just a musical one, but they haven't been interested." Still, when Si Mohammed was distracted, she lowered her voice and confided that she had had no idea when she invited them that some of them were such heavy drinkers. "Several liters a day!" she exclaimed. "And they get positively cantankerous," she went on. Geneviève indeed had gotten more than she had bargained for.

"Musically, however, it's working," she said. "We are actually creating something. You'll hear it tomorrow."

By this time I could hardly keep my eyes open. Geneviève offered to take me upstairs.

The next evening well before sunset, Robert, Geneviève's husband, picked me up at the hotel and drove me to a park on a promontory looking out over the ocean. There was a band shell there, and the musicians were conducting the sound check. A tent had been set up for the musicians, and I helped myself to a chicken sandwich. When Si Mohammed found me I noticed that he had a gash on his cheek near his eye.

"What happened?" I asked.

"Khadir," he replied. "He scratched me."

The brothers' quarrel had taken physical form. Their conflict was accelerating.

I took a walk along the coastline with Robert and one of the twins while a small crowd from the local community gathered.

The concert was interesting. The Bretons played a few of their own compositions first, which were already fusions of traditional motifs and rock, with a bassist, a percussionist, Geneviève on flute, and Robert on *cornemeuse*, a double-reed wind instrument from the region. The Gnawa played two solo pieces as well. Then they all played together for the finale, a Celtic melody with African rhythms. The crowd liked it. It was not often that they got to hear the native airs of Brittany enlivened by the pulse of Africa. The Gnawa were dressed in their ritual garb. They danced on stage.

After the performance I congratulated the Gnawa. They were beaming, performance for foreign audiences being relatively new to them. They forgot their quarrel and soaked up the energy of their small part of fame.

The next day was spent in rehearsal, though not of the music, but of the theater piece that the Bretons were creating, animated by the Moroccans. I spread a blanket on the lawn, turned on my tape recorder and became a silent observer. The storyteller, Chantal, a talented young woman from the region who had done theater studies in Paris, was telling the story of Lankou, the powerful spirit of death in Breton folklore, and a poor fisherman who implores his mercy in order to feed his large and hungry family. Very quickly, however, this Breton tale turned into a Middle Eastern adventure, as the fisherman finds a bottle in the ocean and a genie appears out of it. The Gnawa came in with musical numbers at appropriate breaks in the story, sometimes dancing. The storyteller, who was really an excellent actor and comedian, was

FIGURE 11: Rehearsing for a performance in a Breton backyard: Si Mohammed Chaouqi and Geneviève. Photograph, Deborah Kapchan

quite nervous about her new performance piece and kept eliciting assurances, which I gave, of course. Her acting was indeed wonderful.

The next day we all piled in a large Peugeot van and took the show on the road to Saint Brieuc, a small medieval town about ninety minutes away. They were to perform the musical storytelling as part of a cultural arts festival. They did a sound check early and then we sat around the main square listening to a Reggae band do their sound check and drinking *menthe à l'eau*. I took the opportunity to interview Si Mohammed on tape about his beliefs in the *jinn*— who each one was and their order in the ritual ceremony.

After a while, we went to another establishment. There was a back room there and the owner of the bar had volunteered the space to the performers. The storyteller put on her make-up and the Gnawa put on their performance clothes while I sat in front having an aperitif and eating nuts (see figure 12).

At the appointed time we all walked up the cobble-stoned hill to a small square where the performance began. There were probably a hundred people seated on the ground, many of them children. Chantal began to enchant the audience, casting a spell on the children, and delighting the adults with comic lines that broke the frame and commented on her own performance. For their part, the Gnawa were like minstrels animating a theater piece, providing musical and exotic relief. I kept my critique to myself, of course. Anyway, I was too

FIGURE 12: Khadir Chaouqi, Younis Chaouqi, and the late Hassan Chaouqi,
waiting to perform in St. Brieuc. Photograph, Deborah Kapchan

busy taking pictures. At the very end of the performance, as if on cue, there
was a loud clap of thunder, then a huge downpour of rain, a deluge. The audience dispersed, running for cover under lintels and awnings. The musicians
scurried to protect their instruments. We eventually made it back to the bar
where we had left our belongings, soaking wet and laughing. Then we all went
out for a meal.

That was Friday. There was one more performance scheduled before my return to Paris. It was on Sunday and was in a village a good two hours away
by car. At 10 A.M. on Sunday the van pulled up in front of my hotel. Si Mohammed, Khadir, Hassan, and Younis were in the back seats. Geneviève, Chantal, and Robert were in the front and middle of the van. We got in beside Robert
and began the trip. For my benefit, Geneviève insisted we stop in Quimper, another medieval town, though much larger that Saint Brieuc. Its cathedral, the
Cathedral of Saint-Corentin, which has been completely cleaned and restored,
is among the most beautiful examples of Gothic architecture that I've seen. We
toured the cathedral with the Gnawa, then walked through the narrow streets
of the Celtic town, window-shopping, and admiring the buildings that were
almost a thousand years old. This was a different France than I had ever seen.
In fact, this was not France; it was Brittany.

We piled in the van again and continued driving in the direction of Rennes,

Geneviève at the wheel. Robert was scanning the newspaper for reviews of the festivals and announcements of the upcoming concert. He found a small story about Lila-Noz. He read it aloud: "Si Mohammed Chaouqi, who has played with such greats as Jimmy Hendrix . . ."

"You played with Jimmy Hendrix?" I asked, surprised.

"ma'lum; of course. Jimmy Hendrix, and so many more. Bizaf min-hum. He loved to smoke kif. He was always high (metkiyyaf)."

By the time we got to the small town outside of Rennes it was almost 3:00. We hadn't had lunch and were hungry, but there was nowhere to get food. The performance was set to take place on church grounds well outside anything re-sembling a "centre-ville." Despite the growls of our stomachs, the place was idyllic. The church dated from the eleventh century and was made of heavy gray stone with a spire extending to the heavens. Surrounding the church were large oaks, a few even taller than the spire, and down a slope from the church was a natural spring that had been channeled into a baptismal pool centuries ago. The weather was warm. I lolled about on the grass while the Bretons and the Gnawa did the sound check on a stage that had been built on the church lawn. About two hundred chairs faced the stage in a semicircle. This place clearly hosted performances all summer long.

I eventually fell asleep, as much to forget my hunger as to rest. Nonetheless, when I woke from my nap the afternoon still seemed endless. I wondered why I hadn't returned to Paris. I had already seen the theater piece, after all. I had recorded the script. But it is often when the body is pushed to levels of dis-comfort and the mind skirts the edges of boredom that we are forced to new levels of awareness.

At about 7 P.M. the congregation began to arrive. This was a performance for the churchgoers. Some of them set up a table for the musicians. The parishioners had brought us a meal of roast chicken and peas. While we ate, they opened the huge doors of the church. The inside was luminous with the light of sunset as it streamed through the blue and green stained-glass win-dows. Once all together, the congregation walked down the hill to the spring and began mass in the open air of approaching dusk. They then walked slowly up the hill again and circled the church, intoning the notes of a French hymn as they took their places in the pews. I was tempted to go into the church my-self, but remained at the table with the Gnawa where they were enacting their own sacrament of the bread and the wine. The church doors were closed. We finished our meal and prepared for the performance.

When the service was over the parishioners filed out of the church and mingled on the lawn. It was about 9:00 P.M. The sun was just starting to set in the Breton countryside. The people took their seats in front of the stage, the sun slipped down under the horizon, and the storyteller began to work her magic on the crowd.

It was the same plot as two nights previously in Saint Brieuc—poor Breton fisherman encounters powerful genie from the east—this time with a few of the kinks worked out. Unlike Saint Breiuc, however, the performers were elevated on a stage, separated from the audience. It was night. The stage was lit. When the Gnawa danced, it was in a circle all together, as they do in the opening ceremony of their possession rituals. They were dressed in red overgowns—the color of Sidi Hamu, the spirit of the slaughter house who demands blood sacrifice. The audience didn't know this, of course, nor did the Breton musicians. For them, the Africans were simply colorful. As the Gnawa danced, the lights of the stage cast their shadows in huge dimension on the surrounding oaks. The genies themselves, many of who are assumed to be giants, were encircling the unsuspecting congregation. How those shadows were cast—as big as the oaks themselves—is a mystery to me. I tried to capture them in a photograph, but the batteries of my camera went suddenly dead. The genies delight in mischief. I have a few slides of the Gnawa and the storyteller on stage from that evening, and then nothing else is documented.

The Bretons and the Gnawa were extremely satisfied with themselves that night. The crowd loved the performance. And although I heard one French father ask his adolescent son skeptically, "tu aimes ça? You like this?" most of the audience members were taken up in the magic. It was 11:30 by the time the audience began to disperse, and I was anxious to get in the van and take the two-hour trip home.

I was to have no such luck, however. Geneviève knew some people in the region—two retired professors—and they insisted that we stop by their country home. I groaned. It was almost midnight, but I had no say in the matter. The Bretons were being generous by inviting me into their world. We all piled in the van, sleepy and cold.

When we pulled up to their home, we could see nothing. The night was so dark, we couldn't find our way to the house entrance. We held on to each other, led by the son of the professors, who was himself a musician and had played traditional Breton music with Geneviève and Robert in the past. Before reaching the house, however, we all stopped to gaze at the stars above us. They were myriad. There were no city lights nearby to detract from their luminosity. The last time I had seen stars like this I was in the Moroccan desert. The darkness blotted out our bodies, and we seemed to melt into the lights above us.

The spell was broken when the professors opened the door and invited us in. The house was modest. We were ushered into the dining room where we sat around the table. Bowls of snacks were set out—*amuse-guelles*, face-amusers, they are called in French—and we all drank good red wine from their "cave." The husband in the professorial couple was himself from Brittany, and Breton had been his first language growing up. He was a retired history professor and told us about his part in the resistance during the Vichy government. The wife was a retired professor of German. Originally from the Bourdeaux region, she told us how when she married her husband and moved to Brittany she had to learn Breton just to do her shopping. "The locals," she said, "didn't even speak French at the time. It was like moving to a foreign country." They were happy in their retirement, though clearly they craved social visits, as they had insisted on our coming even at this unorthodox time. Hosting musicians from Africa in the middle of the night was no imposition.

When they learned that I was also a professor, they began to ask me questions about my research: where I worked, what exactly I was doing in Brittany. They thought it rather ironic that an American professor of anthropology who was doing research on North African ritual music would find herself in a remote region of Brittany. I agreed. It was a comment on our times, I said. The world was becoming smaller and smaller. Cultures that were once radically different were now in close contact one with another. "Just look at this group here, for example."

"Yes, tell us about the performance," the wife said, turning to Chantal, the storyteller.

This was all Chantal needed. She began to talk about her "spectacle"—how she had combined Breton folklore with Moroccan folklore to create a hybrid text that incorporated two cultural traditions into one performance.

Unable to restrain myself, I interjected, "But there's a confusion of categories here. You mixed Breton folklore with Moroccan beliefs. The Moroccans *believe* in the spirits that you are invoking in your production."

This made the group fall silent for a brief moment. Chantal and the others, it seemed, could not encompass the possibility of a belief in the palpability of spirits. For them, it was all "folklore."

The Gnawa, who were not following this conversation fully because of their lack of fluency in French, took notice of this change in tenor in the conversation. I translated for them.

"I told them that the jnun are real," I said.

"Of course they are real," said Khadir in Arabic, suddenly excited. "I still re-member one night when Hassan and I were coming home from the movies, there was a beautiful woman following us. No matter where we went, she was there. We knew it was Aisha Qandisha. She was waving for us to follow her. We started running and didn't stop until we got home."

"You think it was Aisha? Why?"

"That's what she does. She's beautiful, and she entrances you, and then you're hers."

"And then there's aiša al-bahariyya," interjected Si Mohammed. "Aisha of the Sea. She strikes fishermen and people who are by the water. Once when I was fishing when I was just young—maybe eighteen—I saw a woman on the water. She was on the water! And her eyes were lit up like a cigar: red and burn-ing. I lost my voice; I was so frightened. And I was in bed for a week! She struck me. Luckily my mother knew someone, a woman, who prepared herbs for me. For a week I was in bed. Then I got well."

As we saw with Fatna in chapter four, Si Mohammed also was struck dumb by a spirit. In his case, however, the implication is that he lost his voice just as much to the emotion of fear as to the spirit of Aisha. Without a voice, he was disempowered and remained bedridden for a week, healed eventually by the herbs of a mqaddema.

While Si Mohammed and his brothers were talking, the French had begun another conversation among themselves about the challenges of intercultural communication. Geneviève was telling our hosts that the other people in her group were not interested in anything but a musical exchange and how disap-pointing that had been to her and Robert. She also mentioned that there were great difficulties involved in such exchanges. "Il sont très difficile à vivre, très difficile à gerer," she said, "they are very difficult to live with, very difficult to manage."

One of the Gnawa started yawning, and soon we all reacted in kind. It was nearly two in the morning. Our hosts got their flashlights and escorted us to the van. We all piled in, Robert driving and Geneviève in the front with him. While the driver smoked more hashish than I ever saw anyone imbibe, the rest of us faded in and out of sleep during the two-hour drive home, me praying that five thick hashish cigars wouldn't affect his faculties in a way that would jeopardize our safety. We arrived in Brest around four in the morning and said our sleepy good-byes in front of the hotel. I thanked Geneviève and the rest for their hospitality. I was leaving the next day for Paris.

◆ 9 ◆
NARRATIVES OF
EPIPHANY
INDEXING GLOBAL LINKS
◆ ◆ ◆

Touring ritual performances around the world—and thereby converting them into
entertainments—is nothing new. The Romans were fond of importing exotics; and the records
of many courts—non-western as well as western—show the same imperial curiosity. Colonial
and/or conquering powers everywhere have done the same. Modern times—from the period of
the great international expositions and circuses to our own day—transform this aristocratic
privilege into a commercial venture. The enterprise is often cloaked in the rhetoric of respect.
—Richard Schechner (1988: 150)

Nombre de chants gnaouas . . . scandent, nostalgiques, la condition
d'esclaves . . . de manière semblable à celle qu'on trouve dans les premiers blues
nord-américains. [*A number of Gnawa songs . . . chant, nostalgically, about the condition*
of slaves . . . in a manner similar to that found in the first North American blues.]
—Abdelhai Diouri (1990: 199)

The joy of music is, then, the soul's delight in being invited, for once, to recognize itself
in the body. —Claude Lévi-Strauss (1969a: 657)

Hybrid cultural imaginations are spawned through what historian and cultural studies scholar Robin D. G. Kelley refers to as both the "physical and
imaginary links" forged in the African diaspora on both sides of the Atlantic
(1998: 50). The performance and marketing of trance is one forum for new
linkages. To speak of links, however, is also to speak of indexical associations—"the real linkage of language to culture" (M. Silverstein 1976: 12). In
semiotician Charles Peirce's delineation, an index is a particular kind of sign
that functions to connect words to their pragmatic context of enunciation
(Peirce 1982; Morris 1964; Silverstein 1976; Caton 1987). An indexical sign re-
lates word to object/event/idea by virtue of being spatially or temporally con-

tiguous with it. Thus, a blue cloth thrown over a woman in trance indexes that she is possessed by Sidi Musa. Tracking the changes in indexical relations—in the way signs are linked to the world they reference—is one way to understand cultural transformation.

How does public ritual change in transit and how do these changes transform cultural imaginations? What does the analysis of heightened ritual states like possession trance contribute to the way we understand historical constructions of race?

Janice Boddy, who has written astutely about possession in Sudan, defines spirit possession as follows: "Possession," she says, "is a broad term referring to the integration of spirit and matter, force or power and corporeal reality, in a cosmos where the boundaries between an individual and her environment are acknowledged to be permeable, flexibly drawn, or at least negotiable" (Boddy 1994: 407). Possession is a state of embodied power, but in a very specific context—one in which the demarcation between self and other, speaker and auditor, cannot be taken for granted. In possession trance, rules for interpersonal kinesthetic response, gesture, verbal expression, and dialogue, are different from those in everyday life, if only because the locus of intentionality is ever-shifting and indeterminate. In a state of possession, who speaks? Who moves? Who desires? Indeed, Boddy goes on to say that "spirit possession rests on epistemic premises quite different from the infinitely differentiating, rationalizing, and reifying thrust of global materialism and its attendant scholarly traditions" (1994: 407).

Boddy's insights into the way embodied rituals like possession trance resist commodification apply to many contexts of cross-cultural possession, where market forces, gender, and political hegemonies are not only rejected, but challenged (Boddy 1989; Masquelier 2001; Stoller 1995). Historically this has been the case with the Gnawa as well, but no longer—or rather, not exclusively. Although the rituals of the Gnawa resemble many other forms of trance possession in the Islamic world (Boddy 1989; Stoller 1995), the Gnawa are unique in their position in the world music market. Unlike many possession-trance practices, the Gnawa do not "interrupt the extension of Western hegemonies by refusing to endorse the naturalization of the commodity form" (Boddy 1989);[1] rather the Gnawa manipulate the conditions of late capitalism self-consciously and often to their perceived advantage. Their mobilization in different venues across the globe makes their performance of trance as much a commodity as a healing force.

The multiplicity of subjectivities present in spirit possession becomes an apt metaphor for the transformation of Gnawa music as it comes to reside in different contexts and traditions. In the remainder of this chapter, I explore spirit possession, music, and trance, questioning their relationship to, and indeed their interpolation in, global materialism. The "material" I examine is auditory and linguistic. I begin by analyzing different ways the music of trance is performed and interpreted through the lens of one song—the invocation of Sidi Musa, the spirit of the seas. This song was performed on three continents and in three contexts. Its context of origin is the ritual ceremony of spirit possession and placation in Morocco, the lila, though the same m'allem played this song in Paris at the Divan du Monde nightclub. My focus here, however, is on two collaborative performances: one, a performance by the Gnawa with composer and pianist Randy Weston in Alice Tully Hall in New York City (see figures 15, 16, and 17), the other, a festival performance in Brittany advertised as a "rencontre de transe," a "meeting of trance [traditions]" that combined traditional Celtic music with the music of the North African Gnawa. In both cases, the music provides the link between a spiritual world and an aesthetic performance of identity. It is the resultant performed narrative, however, that makes sense and meaning of these encounters and goes on to live a public life

FIGURE 13: Randy Weston backstage at Alice Tully Hall in New York City;
Road Manager Jaap Harlaar to his left, trombonist Benny Powell to his right;
in the background: Tangier Gnawi, Nour Eddine Touati, and Abdelkader
El Khlyfy. Photograph, Deborah Kapchan

FIGURE 14: A sound check in Alice Tully Hall: Abdelkadr El Khlyfy, Abdellah El Gourd, Nour Eddine Touati, unidentified Gnawi, Abbass Baska Larfaoui; *standing*: Jaap Haarlar. Photograph, Deborah Kapchan

FIGURE 15: A sound check in Alice Tully Hall: bassist Alex Blake, flutist and saxophonist T. K. Blue, trombonist Benny Powell, African percussionist Neil Clark, and his son. Photograph, Deborah Kapchan

Narratives of Epiphany | 179

of its own. Delineating the way musical style constitutes identity (Erlmann 2003; Stokes 1994), I go on to analyze what I call *narratives of epiphany*, narratives that translate these musical experiences into discourses of identity. As E. Ochs and L. Capps note, "narrative and self are inseparable"; what's more, "narratives are versions of reality," and they actively produce lived experience (1996: 20). "An important challenge to humanity," they remind us, "is to recognize that lives are the past we tell ourselves" (Ochs and Capps 1996: 21).

GLOBAL LINKS IN THE TRANSNATIONAL IMAGINATION

The possessed are said to be tied or linked to their spirits (Hell 2001: 252–253). According to Pâques, these links may be passed on through the sperm of the father or the milk of the mother, but they may also manifest independently when neither father nor mother have ties to the spirit world (Pâques 1991). From the root *ra-ba-ṭa*—to bind, connect, or unite—a *rabiṭa* is a connection, bond, or link.[2] It is also a confederation. Someone who is inhabited goes from the state of being afflicted by the spirits to submitting to them and ultimately learning to "work" and master them. Gnawa possession is, in part, a metaphor for the passage from captivity to freedom. Randy Weston, for example, is linked to the spirit Sidi Musa. Links may also be ties of bondage, however; and indeed being "tied" or linked to a spirit also indexes historical experiences of slavery, as these words from the song "The Sons of Bambara" attest:

> Tied in sacks they brought us, in the camel bags
> And they sold us in the wool market.
> May God pardon them.
> They took us from our country.
> They parted us from our parents.
> They brought us, alas, to the wool suq.
> And they sold us, children far from our country.[3]

The enslaved past is spoken about in many of the words of the ritual songs, as Tim Abedellah Fuson notes in his transcription of the song "Oh Sudan, Oh Mother":

Ah Sudan ya Sudan	Oh Sudan, Oh Sudan
Ah jabuni jabuni	They brought me, they brought me
Ah jabuna min as-Sudan	They brought me from the Sudan
Ah duwzuni 'ala Bambara	They brought me by way of Bambara

Ah duwzuni 'ala Timbuktu   They brought me by way of Timbuktu
Wa min Sudan l-Fes l-Bali   From Sudan to Old Fez
(Fuson 2001)

In the song "Sowiye," they recall the loved ones from whom their forbears were separated:

Wo feenkum ya Uled s-Sudan   Where are you, Children of the Sudan?
Wo feenkum ya Uledi 'ammi   Where are you, Children of my uncle?
(Fuson 2001).

And in the black pantheon of Sidi Mimun, the Gnawa sing:

Oh sirs they went they went / oh sirs they went to Sudan
They brought back Gnawa workers / eating raw meat
Eating raw eggplant / oh friend of God of friend of God
Friend of God Sidi Mimun / oh friend of God of friend of God
I spent the night at the mouth of the river / with rain and cold upon me
Oh sirs open the doors of God / oh sirs Men of God
Oh Gnawi father Mimun / oh Gnawa Sir Mimun
Oh Sirs the Gnawa have come / here they've come from Sudan
The Gnawa oh Mimun / the Gnawa oh Sir Mimun[4]

The Gnawa in these lyrics are referred to as *khaddem*, "workers," but this a euphemism for slaves. They are brought to Morocco "eating raw meat," an allusion to their ability, when possessed, to break taboos with immunity, a fact that underscores their power in the spiritual realm. It also indexes the symbolic savagery of these particular spirits, who consume what is uncooked (Lévi-Strauss 1969b; Hell 1999a). The verses above make explicit reference to their forced journey from Sudan as slaves. The address to "Sirs" is a reference to the spirits: "Oh [my] Sirs the Gnawa have come / here they've come from Sudan."

As ethnologist Abdelghani Maghnia has noted (1996), many of the names of the spirits in the Gnawa ceremonies have a West African provenance, especially in the black pantheon. Within that suite of songs and series of spirits, there is the invocation to *ulad hawsa*, the Sons of Hausa. Names such as Hawsa Ka, Barî, Sandî, and Gbanî bu Ganga, are common.[5] Indeed, it is almost exclusively the proper names that index the African origins of these songs, proper names being resistant to translation (Derrida 1985, 1978).[6] Ethnic monikers are also frequent; invocations to *ulad as-sudan*, the sons of Sudan, the *fulani*, the spirits of the Fulani, and the *hawsawi* or Hausa spirits are invoked repeatedly throughout the ceremony—indeed, hundreds of times (Welte and Aguadé 1996). While names of spirits and places/people are the most common foreign words in the ceremonies, Maghnia finds further linguistic links between the secret language of the Gnawa and the Peul language of the Fulani. The development of a secret or code language, of course, is a result of the hegemony of slavery and colonialism. Like all specialty languages, it defines in-group from out-group, often through speech play (Kirshenblatt-Gimblett and Backhouse 1976; Sherzer 2002). Indeed, one of the phrases that Maghnia mentions as a derivation of Peul is the Gnawa expression *Bucamnani yana*, which in Peul means "my colonist has fallen" (Maghnia 1996: 127). But if the links between the African diaspora are traceable through names and phrases that have survived in ritual, it is nonetheless difficult to map the exact routes of the cultural diaspora. As a Gnawa master in Fes (Ahmed Sadgui) told Maghnia, the Gnawa belong to three African groups: the Hausa, the Bambara, and the Fulani (Peul) (Maghnia 1996: 128). The Gnawa rituals reflect some aspects of all of these cultures to which they are linked by history, religion, and song. The foreign phrases index a past home in Africa as well as an emotional state of nostalgia for a home that has been forgotten in living memory.

SIDI MUSA IN THE GNAWA IMAGINARY

Sidi Musa is one of the saints in the Gnawa pantheon of spirit possession, and as all the sprits, he is acknowledged in the invocations.[7] He was [and is] a living saint of the thirteenth century, whose sanctuary exists in Salé on the coast and whose powers are thought to heal sterility and other feminine complaints. He is also the patron saint of travel. Reputed to have been able to transport himself great distances and to have been two places at the same time, he was observed for twelve consecutive years both with his family at the time of the sacrifice of the sheep ('aid al-kbir), and, miraculously, in Mecca doing the pilgrimage (Tharaud 1921: 144). The "man from Salé" and all the other avatars of the *musawwiyyin* (the spirits of Musa), however, are subject to the most significant Sidi Musa—the Prophet Moses of the Old Testament, who was set upon the waters as a child and who parted them for the Israelites as an adult (Hell 2002b: 206). "Be careful not to confuse Sidi Musa of Salé with Sidi Musa, the prophet," the *m'allem* Si Mohammed Chaouqi told Pierre-Alain Claisse. "The prophet Moses remains the chief of all Musa spirits, even if some of them are sometimes more important for us, the Gnawa" (Claisse 2003: 145). Unlike some other spirits—mischievous and afflicting *jinn*—the prophet Sidi

Musa is one of the ṣaliḥin, a holy saint who does not afflict but who blesses. He nonetheless is considered one of the mluk—literally an "owner" of the person who is moved to trance to his music and his color. Avatars of Sidi Musa are found in the rituals of ex-slaves throughout North Africa (Hell 2002b: 206). Sidi Musa is associated with the color blue—for the sea—and his incense is white benzoin (al-jawi al-baiḍ). Libations of water are often poured in his honor. He protects fishermen but also represents the source, the wellspring of life (Pâques 1991). In the lila, the invocation to Sidi Musa is done with a bowl of water, which is first placed on the ground, and then lifted by the possessed onto his or her head.[8] Balancing this bowl, the possessed person makes swimming motions with his or her arms while in three positions: standing up, on the knees, and then again on the floor, demonstrating a yogic concentration and balance (El-Belkani 2000: 98). After this performance of mastery (who other than a spirit could move so forcefully and not spill water from the bowl?), the possessed passes the bowl to those present at the ceremony, who lift the bowl to their lips and drink a small sip of the blessed water (often containing fragrant anise seeds), thereby imbibing baraka or blessing. In return, the communicants give money to the spirit, who eventually returns it to the Gnawa, the musicians who facilitated the spirit's arrival in the first place. Sidi Musa is intricately involved in the cycle of life, death, and rebirth, but particularly life. There is no doubt that Sidi Musa has given life to many creations, including musical ones.

"Sidi Musa is a prophet of God," the Tangier Gnawa master Abdellah El Gourd told me. "He freed a lot of people who asked to go with him; they went with him through the sea to escape the Pharaoh. The Israelites, as slaves, went with him. Sidi Musa in Africa is known, in Mali, in Chad."

The Israelites were slaves when Moses parted the seas and led them to freedom, and it is the link between the sea and liberation that becomes symbolic in Abdellah's discourse. "Our link is with the sea," Abdellah reminded me, speaking of the African diaspora of which he is a part. "Many of us came over on the sea; many of us died on the sea. Randy came [across the Atlantic,] all the way from Brooklyn linked to Sidi Musa (murṭabet ʿala Sidi Musa), to the color blue."

Abdellah El Gourd makes reference to what social theorist Paul Gilroy defines as the "black Atlantic," the parameters of the African diaspora as created by the slave trade. But the word "diaspora" itself, notes Gilroy, originates in Jewish thought. "The themes of escape and suffering, tradition, temporality, and the social organization of memory have a special significance in the history of Jewish responses to modernity," he notes, adding that these themes were taken up by generations of Jewish thinkers who analyzed their relationship to anti-Semitism and racism (1993: 205). Indeed, the link between the Exodus story of the Jews and the African experience of slavery has a long precedent in African American theology and political mythology, as does the idea of return—to Israel in the case of the Jews, to Africa in the case of Africans (Gilroy 1993: 205–223). While it is problematic to simplify the complex histories of both these groups into a convenient overlay (Shohat 1988), the historical precedents for these linkages, as well as their recursive appearance in popular culture is worthy of note.

In chapter two I described a ceremony hosted by a man called "the Hajj," an older man possessed by Sidi Musa. Although the suite of songs for Sidi Musa is played at every ceremony, it was particularly when we were at the Hajj's place, or when he was attending a lila with us elsewhere, that this *nuba* heated up and provoked intensive trance. This is because, in the community of Gnawi that I frequented in Rabat, he was the only one whose head was "ruled" by Sidi Musa. When the prayers to the *musawiyyin* began, he became glassy-eyed. Slowly rising from his feet, the Gnawi *mqaddem* offered him a ceramic bowl half-full with water, and the Hajj would put it on his head and begin to trance. Eventually lowering himself to the ground, he took the bowl, poured some of the water on his head and began to "swim" on the wet floor. Living so close to the sea in Rabat, one always smells the ocean air but especially smells it in the wee hours of the morning, when the fumes from cars have temporarily subsided. The Hajj lived in the neighborhood called L'Ocean (a remnant from the days of the French Protectorate). From his roof you could see the Atlantic Ocean. Not surprisingly, while possessed by Sidi Musa the Hajj tried to run outside toward the beach. He had to be held back from doing so by the Gnawa, and he ended his trance lying on the ground, asking for God's forgiveness, the Gnawa eventually moving him to one side of the room where others revived him with rose water.

As noted in the lyrics cited above, invocations and praises to Sidi Musa and all the spirits in the blue suite contain a large amount of indexical links to Africa in the way of names and phrases. For example,

> There is no God but God, *Musa* / There is no God but God
> *Sudan yarki babani Musa* / There is no God but God
> *Sudan yarki babani Musa* / There is no God but God
> *The Hausa babani Musa* / There is no God but God
> The Sea Spirits *babani Musa* / There is no God but God
> *Sudan yarki babani Musa* / There is no God but God

The words in italics are not Arabic. Although *baba* is the colloquial for father in Moroccan Arabic, and though spirits, including Sidi Musa, are often alluded to as symbolic fathers, *babani* would be a highly irregular (and ungrammatical) way of saying "my father" (technically *baba-i* in Moroccan Arabic). El-Belkani notes that over the years the Gnawa have substituted words that they know for foreign words, often relying on phonological similarities and what they think makes sense (2000). As no one is able to translate them, the preponderance of foreign words that remain in the ceremonies fulfills more of a poetic function than a referential one. The sound symbolism is highlighted, and the iconic dimension of communication becomes "the dominant" in the communicative act (Jakobson 1981: 751–756). These ideophonic words are interspersed with well-known Islamic phrases of praise. "There is no God but God," of course, is the Muslim *šahada*, or testament of faith, one of the five pillars of Islam and the phrase whose enunciation *performs* conversion. Indeed the songs of the ceremony are replete with prayers and *da'was*, or oaths, from the sacred canon (Kapchan 1996: 81–83); words such as "the blessings of Lalla Fatima / Mulay Muḥammad / Sir oh Messenger of God / Mulay Muḥammad / we'll visit Mecca and Madina / Mulay Muḥammad / God will protect us / Mulay Muḥammad."[9] Here, the Gnawa invoke Lalla Fatima, the Prophet's daughter, as well as the Prophet (Mulay Moḥammad) and exhort each other to make the pilgrimage to the cities of Mecca and Medina. In short, the lyrics in the invocations to the spirits provide indexical and iconic links to Africa, but also referential indexes to Islam and, by extension, to the Arab East. The Gnawa ceremony is a global one in its origin, a music of the diaspora that brings trance in its wake. The performance of "Sidi Musa" by the Gnawa, by Randy Weston, and by the Breton musicians furthers the reach of this diasporic music.

NARRATIVES OF EPIPHANY

By virtue of its placelessness, music of the diaspora is often concerned with home and identity (Lemelle and Kelley 1994). And as it travels, it trans(e)-forms. Trance itself is an entrance to another world or state, a transformation in transit. Why this state becomes desirable in social communities has been the subject of inquiry by many scholars. The responses are diverse: from cultural therapy, sexual sublimation, and catharsis to postcolonial identity construction and spiritual quest. Indeed, the his well-known article in which he explores the relation of filming trance to the experience of trance, Jean Rouch notes that "it appears that the phenomenon of trance (whether wild or controlled) is one of the essential features in the momentum behind great religious movements, and, perhaps, behind great movements in artistic creativity" (Rouch and Feld 2003: 88).

Certainly not all trance states are linked to music, but many studies of trance acknowledge the essential role of rhythm in producing the trance state. Although the rhythm may be created by tonal instruments such as horns, flutes, keyboards, or even voices, most often it is the repetitive fluctuation of the tones that creates trance more than the tonalities themselves (Needham 1967). What Rouget defines as "possession trance" (Rouget 1985) seems to work by aligning the subtle vibrations of the organism with vibrations produced outside the body, effecting, as stated in the dictionary definition of trance, either "a state of profound abstraction or absorption."[10]

Trance is a first-order experience, a performance based in the body. Merleau-Ponty might say that it is a prelinguistic, preobjective (though not a precultural) state (1962); Julia Kristeva might assert that it is a state of "abjection," a return to a symbolic space where there is only undifferentiated experience (1982). This is because the dominant vocabulary of trance is gestural. It resists narration.[11] In my analysis of narratives of possession trance, however, it became clear that while the poetics of the narratives had much in common with the gestural and rhythmic economies of trance, the referential meaning had another quality—one that might be called epiphanic, related to epiphany.

Webster's dictionary defines epiphany as follows:

epiphany \i-'pif-e-ne\ n, pl —nies [ME *epiphanie*, fr. MF, fr. LL *epiphania*, fr. LGk, pl., prob. alter. of Gk *epiphaneia* appearance, manifestation, fr. *epiphainein* to manifest, fr. *phainein* to show—more at FANCY] **1** *cap* : January 6 observed as a church festival in commemoration of the coming of the Magi as the first manifestation of Christ to the Gentiles or in the Eastern Church in commemoration of the baptism of Christ **2** : an appearance or manifestation esp. of a divine being **3 a** (1) : a usu. sudden manifestation or perception of the essential nature or meaning of something (2) : an intuitive grasp of reality through something (as an event) usu. simple and striking **b** : a literary representation of an epiphany.

Bracketing the specifically Christian use of this term, we can say that epiphanies make the invisible manifest, sometimes to the individual perceiver, sometimes to the community.[12] The appearance of a spirit is considered an epiphany. Epiphanies are also revelatory in that they divulge the "essential nature or meaning" of an event, providing "an intuitive grasp of reality through something . . . usu[ally] simple and striking." When epiphany occurs in a communal setting, it relies on a *shared* perception that marks the participants indelibly in a way that is *narratively comparable*. In other words, epiphanies, when they are shared, are based in the senses— very much like trance—but are then woven into an elaborate and collective narrative fabric. They rely on a second-order semiotic system—they are imbricated in representation, performing a kind of "intersemiotic translation" of perception and experience into words (Fine 1984; Jakobson 1960). It is this narrative fabric that grounds epiphany in history and gives it its agency.[13] Whereas trance may be experienced collectively, it is difficult to articulate. Epiphany, by contrast, is experienced bodily in order to be narrated verbally. Its life in words forms an essential aspect of its cycle.

This distinction is reminiscent of that made by Pierre Nora on forms of remembering. For Nora, memory lives in the body—in the gestures and ritual practices of everyday life. It is only when these practices have changed dramatically, or disappeared entirely, that history and processes of history-making become important. "Memory," he notes "takes root in the concrete, in spaces, gestures, images, and objects; [while] history binds itself strictly to temporal continuities, to progressions and to relations between things" (1989: 9). Nora distinguishes between "true memory, which has taken refuge in gestures and habits, in skills passed down by unspoken traditions, in the body's inherent self-knowledge, in unstudied reflexes and ingrained memories, and memory transformed by its passage through history, which is nearly the opposite: voluntary and deliberate, experienced as a duty, no longer spontaneous; psychological, individual, and subjective; but never social, collective, or all encompassing. How," he asks, "did we move from the first memory, which is immediate, to the second, which is indirect?" (1989: 13). Nora's answer to this question implicates forms of capitalism, postmodernism, and a disembodied mode of being in the world. Nora understands history to be a form of mediation through which experience is translated rather than an embodied phenomenon. Indeed, the popularity of forms of trance on the aesthetic market may be seen as a reaction to these disembodied ways of being, a way to return to flow and the body. Here, trance *does resist* capitalism in the very fact that it *persists*. On the other hand, like many artistic forms that facilitate what ethnomusicologist Charlie Keil refers to as an experience of "primary reality" (1995: 5), trance is quickly interpolated into history in the form of narrative—in this case, narratives of epiphany.

Randy Weston's link with Sidi Musa partakes in epiphany. An African American pianist and composer who has been playing with the Gnawa for more than thirty years, Weston has cut several compact discs with the Gnawa and often tours with them in Europe and the United States. After Weston, other artists—notably Pharoah Saunders, Archie Shepp, and Don Cherry—were introduced to and subsequently played with the Gnawa, combining the influences of jazz with the rhythms and pentatonic melodies of North Africa. Jimi Hendrix and Brian Jones came after them.

As descendants of slaves in North Africa with a vibrant musical culture, the Gnawa were a source of inspiration for Weston, symbolizing a return to African roots at a moment in African American history when such origins were avidly sought by musicians and civil rights activists. As Robin D. G. Kelley notes, in the sixties

> The Civil Rights movement, the struggle against apartheid in South Africa, the emergence of newly independent African nations, found a voice in recordings by various jazz artists, including Randy Weston's *Uhuru Afrika*, Max Roach's *We Insist: Freedom Now Suite* (featuring Abby Lincoln, Roach's wife); Art Blakey's *Message from Kenya* and *Ritual*, and John Coltrane's *Liberia*, *Dahomey Dance*, and *Africa*. Revolutionary political movements, combined with revolutionary experiments in artistic creation—the simultaneous embrace and rejection of tradition—forged the strongest *physical and imaginary links* between Africa and the Diaspora. (1998: 50, emphasis mine)

Indeed, these physical and imaginary links are key to understanding transformations effected by transnational flows of music and culture both then and now (Appadurai 1990).[14] It is precisely these links that create the political fictions that allow for the reimagination and realization of new identities.[15]

Such political fictions are often enacted by what Deleuze and Guattari have termed "nomadic subjects": migrants, diasporic populations, and other intellectual and political transients.[16] According to feminist scholar Rosi Braidoti, "nomadic consciousness consists in not taking any kind of identity as permanent. The nomad is only passing through; s/he makes those necessarily situated connections that can help her/him survive, but s/he never takes on fully the limits of one national, fixed identity. The nomad has no passport—or has too many of them" (1994: 33). Not only is expatriate Hassan Hakmoun a "nomadic subject" in this definition, so are the Gnawa in Morocco, as well as Randy Weston who has been returning there for more than thirty years to collaborate with them. (Indeed, the Fulani that the Gnawa invoke so often in their ceremonies are literally nomads, herders that occupy the sub-Saharan savannah belt from the Nile, through Sudan, Niger, Chad, Mali, and Mauritania, all the way to Senegal.) Weston considers the Gnawa an ancient culture that, through its music and beliefs, will outlive the more recent civilizations in the West. "They will be here when you and I are gone," he told me on the train from the south of France to Paris (and has reiterated many times since). For Weston, the Gnawa have retained their connection to a time and space when the powers of the spiritual world were more dominant than they are today, especially in the West. The Gnawa provide that link for Weston.

Randy Weston's engagement with Gnawa music is based upon epiphany. He recounted the following story during our conversation on the train from Souillac to Paris:

"Despite the fact that I met Abdellah in 1967, I didn't attend a lila until 1969."

"Do you remember your impressions?"

"Yes, I remember very well. I was in trance. I, ah . . . It was one of the most incredible musical experiences of my life. I had an experience really African. I heard the string instrument out front. Like having an orchestra and having a string bass as the leader. And I heard the black church, the blues, and jazz all at the same time. I really realized that we're just little leaves of the branch of mother Africa. The sound of the instrument, when I heard the sound I heard Jimmy Blanton with the Ellington orchestra, which I heard as a kid in 1937, when Duke had that bass out front. And I thought of Jimmy Blanton and later, later I looked at the photographs of Jimmy Blanton and he looks very North African, you know. . . . But that's what happened. You didn't go to many lilas. I was supposed to go back the next night. I couldn't go. It was too powerful."

"Yeah, it's very powerful stuff."

"I've been to lilas since, but nothing, nothing ever like that."

"Really?"

"Because the color blue entered my spirit. Wherever I go, I have to play 'Blue Moses,' which is Sidi Musa. I love blue. Remember that to my great masters for me—Mr. Ellington and Mr. Monk—they were master blues players. Duke even had his piano painted blue. And so I heard this particular Sidi Musa. After the ceremony I was in trance for about a week."

Weston's music has been strongly influenced by the rhythms and pentatonic melodies of the Gnawa. Indeed, Weston performs the invocation to Sidi Musa at every concert he gives. It is his ritual propitiation to Sidi Musa.

For Mr. Weston, trance is inseparable from music. It is music that immediately brought out the connections—the links—between African music from the African continent and African music from the diaspora in America. What's more, both musics are linked by and evoke a color: the color blue. It was the color blue that "entered [Mr. Weston's] spirit" and created epiphany. For Weston, however, the color blue becomes iconic of the "blues" in general. He notes that he heard in the Gnawa music "the black church, the blues, and jazz all at the same time," going so far as to note that "Duke even had his piano painted blue."

Ethnomusicologist Travis Jackson asserts that all jazz is inhabited by what he calls a "blues aesthetic."[17] For Jackson, this aesthetic is learned, a product of reflection on and engagement with performance practices in the African American tradition. He draws upon the work of Baraka (1963, 1991) and Ellison (1964) to emphasize that the blues "function not only as individual expression but as part of a ritual involving words, music, and the trappings of spirituality" (2003: 28). "African American musics and, in particular, jazz," he asserts, are concerned "both with the blues as an aesthetic or sensibility and with performance as a sacred, ritual act" (Jackson 2003: 25). Weston would concur. For Weston, Africa is nothing less than the source of humanity—its origin and its eventual place of return. African music has a sacred status in his aesthetic philosophy. Like magic, it has a power to transform. He says as much in the beginnings of most all his concert performances. The blues are an African American incarnation of that spirit power, the one that first set Weston on the path.

What did Weston hear in the Gnawa music that so reminded him of African American sacred music? The *Oxford English Dictionary* defines the blues as "melody of a mournful and haunting character, originating among the Negroes of the Southern U.S., frequently in a twelve-bar sequence using many 'blue' notes—usually the third and seventh notes, flatted or natural" (my choice of quotation is motivated). But as Charles Keil notes, other scale degrees may be flatted as well: "The flatted fifth is often referred to as the heart of 'funk,' soul, or blues feeling, and it has been said that blue notes can be found in all the cracks between the keys of the piano. The flattening or bending of thirds, sevenths, and fifths into quarter tones is part of a general defining feature . . . that may simply be called blues chromaticism" (Keil 1991 [1966]: 53).

Gnawa music is pentatonic, thus it does not contain quarter tones, per se.

Nonetheless, the pentatonic minor scale contains the flatted third and the flatted seventh—both elements of the blues scale. The call-and-response of Gnawa invocations no doubt also reminded Weston of the call-and-response in the blues form. What's more, in their singing the Gnawa often bend notes in a kind of "blues chromaticism." Rhythmically there are also similarities: the blues are characterized by "a 4/4 twelve-bar pattern, divided into three call-and-response sections," and Gnawa music also employs 4/4 patterns overlaid with triplets (Keil 1991 [1966]: 51). There is, then, a style, a kind of "blues aesthetic," that is shared by both musics. What's more, both musics have what even the OED refers to as a "haunting character"; they evoke deep emotions in those who know how to listen.

Weston does not consider himself a "jazz" musician per se (the word having a pejorative sense historically), but his music is most certainly informed by the blues. Whereas Weston's music is harmonically complex, employing many scales other than the pentatonic, he often uses a "Gnawa aesthetic"—forefronting the bass, for example, and drawing on the rhythmic structure of Gnawa music. What's more, Weston's music is a sacred and Afro-centric music. His website exhibits a map of Africa that slowly turns into a grand piano (http://www.randyweston.info), a metaphor for African music in diaspora. His musical trajectory can be read through the titles of some of his recordings (noted are the dates of the recordings, not the issuance): *Uhuru Afrika* (1960), *Highlife* (1963), *African Cookbook* (1964), *Blues* (1964–1965), *Blue Moses* (1972), *Tanjah* (1973), *Blues to Africa* (1974), *African Nite/Nuit Africain* (1975), *African Rhythms* (1975), *The Healers* (1980), *Blue* (1983), *Caravan—Portraits of Duke Ellington* (1989), *Well You Needn't—Portraits of Thelonius Monk* (1989),[18] *Spirits of Our Ancestors* (1991), *Marrakech in the Cool of the Evening* (1992), *The Splendid Master Gnawa Musicians* (1992), *Khepera* (1998), *Spirit! The Power of Music* (1999), *Ancient Future* (2001), and *Zep Tepi* (2005).

In 1959 African American poet Langston Hughes wrote this about Weston's recording, *Little Niles*:

Piano music is as old as the piano which as an instrument, in variations of its present form, dates back some 250 years. Millions of fingers have rippled the keys since then. But not until Randy Weston put the enormous hands of his six-foot-seven frame to the piano did exactly what happens in his playing emerge from that ancient instrument. Weston's pianistics have an individuality all their own.

When Randy plays, a combination of strength and gentleness, virility and velvet emerges from the keys in an ebb and flow of sound seemingly as natural as the waves of the sea. And like waves breaking against the irregularity of a craggy coastline, there is a great variety of musical sound over the steady pulse of a rhythmical tide, like the regularity of sea touching shore.

Randy Weston says that his influences are American, African and Asian. Weston was born and raised in Brooklyn, but his army service took him to Asia where during World War II he was a supply sergeant in Okinawa and the Philippines. His parentage is partly West Indian and—back a ways yet—African. His environment is urban U.S.A.

His early jazz heroes were Fats Waller, Duke Ellington, then Thelonious Monk, all giants of the piano in one way or another—all big yet delicate, strong yet gentle in their treatment of the instrument. But Weston is like none of these three when he makes his own music, often created in the playing at the keyboard. His compositions are uniquely his own, and on this record he plays entirely the music of Randy Weston.

These compositions are as much his own as are Niles and Pamela, his two children for whom and about whom this music came into being. As arranged for ensemble playing and performed now on this recording, it is music for grownups to listen to with delight, and for children to grow up to listening. All in three-quarter time, these charming little vignettes escape rigidity of beat by a fluid flow of counter-rhythms and melodies, one against another, that brings continuous delight.

Modern tone poems, impressionistic pictures, cool tantalizers of the imagination are these lyrically lovely compositions in sound created by Randy Weston. (Weston 1959, liner notes by Langston Hughes)

Hughes' prose places Weston's music not only in the African tradition, but in the watery ambience of the sea and, by extension, in the lineage of Sidi Musa. Weston's connections reach back across the "black Atlanta" (Gilroy 1993).

Weston's own words clearly portray the importance of Africa and, by extension, the blues aesthetic in the liner notes accompanying his homage to "master blues player" Duke Ellington, his 1989 recording entitled *Caravan*. For Weston, Ellington was the musician who most clearly demonstrated the fundamentality of the blues for all African American music. While I do not wish to conduct a "ethnography of liner notes," this excerpt of a conversation between Rhashidah E. McNeill and Randy Weston provides insight into Weston's regard for the blues aesthetic, and elucidates the links that led Weston to Africa in the first place. Weston recounts:

Duke's impact upon world music is simply outstanding. He named his band the "Jungle Band" in the early 20s. Duke wrote many songs about Africa and about African people. But, he also wrote about calypso, about the Caribbean, about Asia, he even wrote music for Shakespeare—"Such Sweet Thunder," based on characters from Shakespeare's plays—and he was a master blues player. That's the foundation of our music. Through music Duke Ellington wanted to show that the whole world was his.

Indeed, much of the music written and played by Duke Ellington and his Orchestra reflected, in addition to his own personal experiences or that of the Orchestra's musicians, the travel and audiences which were privileged to hear them which included the Middle East, Africa, and the Far East in 1963 at the request of the U.S. State Department, the branch of U.S. government that is responsible for America's relations with other countries. Duke's band's own tours of Europe and Japan followed. Duke traveled all over the world in the 1960s and 1970s delighting audiences everywhere. Unwittingly, he became, like Louis Armstrong, one of America's most effective ambassadors. Duke Ellington and his Orchestra, their music, gained international love and respect.

I was listening to Ellington when I was nine or ten years old. I had no idea, then, that somehow I would later be involved in playing Duke's music. It was on the radio, you know, "Take the A Train," "Perdido," songs like that and "Black, Brown, and Beige," the story of Black people. All of Duke's music had something relating to Black people in there somewhere. But, he was so sophisticated nobody quite realized what a revolutionary this man was.

For me personally, as a pianist, I discovered Ellington last, ironically. My first influence was Count Basie, master of the blues with a unique touch on the piano. Second, was Nat King Cole, a master of sheer beauty. The third piano player who influenced me was one we called "God"—that was Art Tatum. He was just simply a master piano virtuoso. His technique was flawless and he was 80% blind! Then came Monk. Monk, again, was the master of space, but mysticism and magic for me—different sounds. He created sounds that weren't even on the piano. A real mystic.

Then after Monk, I discovered Duke Ellington. I was trying to play funny things in between notes, trying to get sounds on the piano, but I hadn't heard anybody do that yet until I heard Monk. Ellington had been doing it all the while—before Monk, before me, before any of us. Duke in the 20s was already doing this but he had his full orchestra and he was so creative that it was hard to catch up to Ellington.

How I met Duke—I became very close to the Ellington family in the 70s—I played at a reception for him. His sister, Ruth, had heard me play and she wanted Duke to hear me.

Duke had done a concert at Avery Fisher Hall with the New York Philharmonic Orchestra with his trio and they had a reception for him at which I played the piano with a bass player named Peck Morrison.

We were playing. The room was crowded. I looked over and I saw Duke way in a corner, he gave me this kind of look that said, "You're okay."

I met him. He heard my compositions and my music. Then, he wanted to form a new publishing company with half of my compositions and half of his, which was a tremendous honor. The other great honor was that he asked me to do a recording for him. Eventually, this album was sold to Arista Freedom records called, "Berkshire Blues." I still have about 20 compositions with the Ellington Publishing, Co.

With Duke, I rediscovered Monk, rediscovered the piano, and rediscovered myself. From him, I learned commitment. I also learned the importance of the Blues. I learned that the world is one universe.

If we had more bandleaders today like Duke Ellington it would be a different scene entirely . . . because he took great pride in his people and he always projected that. He never left his people. (Weston 1990a)

This story is autobiographical, but it also tells (one version of) the story of the blues as an African American art form. Like Ellington, Weston also went on a State Department–sponsored tour of Africa, and, like Monk, he is a mystic. Indeed, while Weston was a visiting artist at New York University in 2003, he brought "anthrophotojournalist" Wayne B. Chandler to campus for a speaking engagement. Author of *Ancient Future: The Teachings and Prophetic Wisdom of the Seven Hermetic Laws of Ancient Egypt*, Chandler, like Weston, advances the wisdom of ancient Egypt through the teaching of Hermes Trismegistus (Tehuti, or Thoth), an ancient Ethiopian whose seven axioms provide an esoteric foundation for humanity.[19] In so doing, he traces the construction of race and racism over the centuries (Chandler 1999).[20]

Weston describes himself as a disciple of Monk: "I went to Monk's house," Weston recalls, "asked him if I could visit him. He said, 'Yes.' I went by to see him, spent nine hours in his home. He didn't speak at all, just sent vibrations like the great Sufi masters. And he refused to answer any of my questions. . . . . And at the bottom of it all is the ever-present blues. Deep!" (Weston 1989).

By recognizing the influences of his ancestors, Randy Weston has forged links into the "ancient future." Given Mr. Weston's influences and his deep concern for "his people" it is not surprising that he heard the blues and the black church in the music of the Gnawa. "Duke," as Randy told me, "even had his piano painted blue." As in the propitiation ceremonies of the Gnawa, the visual color (in this case, blue) indexes a semantic domain replete with spirits, emotions, gestures, tastes, touch, and smells. "The color blue entered [his] spirit," and the subsequent trance transformed his relation to the music and to its ritual performance. Like his mentor Duke Ellington, Weston is a master of links and epiphanies.

SIDI MUSA IN SAINT BRIEUC, BRITTANY: AN AFRO-CELTIC FUSION

The second recontextualization of Gnawa music comes from another diasporic music—that of the Celts, in this case, in Brittany. To say that the musicians who the Gnawa played with were traditional Celtic musicians is a bit of a misnomer. As Malcolm Chapman notes in his analysis of contemporary Celtic music, most inhabitants of the local villages in Brittany neither play nor listen to traditional Breton music, even those who still speak the local Celtic language. "It is not *their* music," he says, noting that most Bretons "have derived their musical tastes in much the same way as the greater British or French populations, within much the same rhythms of taste and demography" (1994: 30).[21] Those musicians who *are* interested in playing the traditional Celtic instruments and singing in the Celtic language are often a minority of local (or nonlocal) intellectuals and artists interested in reviving folklore traditions and/or involved in political movements for linguistic and cultural rights. The musicians that the Gnawa played with on the festival circuit that summer were earnest Celtic speakers, lobbying for cultural identity— their own, and others'—but they were also working musicians seeking a way to make economic ends meet. Indeed, traveling the festival circuit with the Gnawa contributed to their dossier as professional musicians, making them eligible for unemployment benefits in the off-season (Wilkinson 2003).

Their idea to collaborate with the Gnawa was not spurious. Rather it was based on perceived similarities in both musical style and, more importantly, ritual performance. In Brittany, there are all night ceremonies called *festou noz* (night festivals) where people dance to the music of bagpipes and high-pitched double-reed instruments until dawn. Although possession is not at issue in these nocturnes, the Breton musicians were intrigued by the similarities between the Gnawa *lila* and the Celtic *fest noz* (sing.) insofar as both produced states of what they considered music-induced trance. In fact, the two lead musicians in the Brittany group thought the *fest noz* ceremonies so resembled the Moroccan *lilas* that they used this perceived correspondence to construct a discourse of interculturalism. "We wanted this to be a cultural exchange, not just a musical one," the group's leader told me, a way to create "*les liens inter-culturel*," intercultural bonds or links. Trance formed the basis for the musical collaborations. Like Weston, they gravitated toward the *musawiyyin*, the "blue" spirits of Musa and the sea. Introducing the Sidi Musa song one evening, the Breton group leader said, "And here is another point that we have in common—the sea. Sidi Musa is the spirit of the sea that links us both." For the Breton musicians, an epiphany was also sought and narrated, but the epiphany found was not the one originally sought. Analyzing this collaboration sheds light on how and why some collaborations work and others do not.

Lila-Noz

The all-night ritual in Brittany of the *fest noz* was originally an intimate event limited to rural community members. The Dionysian-like ritual was "reinvented" in the late 1950s and early 1960s as a way to keep Breton traditional music and dance alive (Wilkinson 1999, 2003; Winnick 1995). The *fest noz* is no longer a small, community-based event, but a series of widely-publicized performances that bring musicians and audiences together from all over Brittany, creating, in the process, a music that can be patented as Breton traditional music. Indeed, it is the *fest noz* that, according to ethnomusicologist Desi Wilkinson, most embodies a pan-Breton identity, what he calls "pan-bretonnitude":

> The fest noz does two important things vis-à-vis identity. First, it celebrates local identity expressed in the *danse du pays*, the most meaningful and accessible way of "being Breton" for many. Second, it further activates an inclusive pan-Breton identity in both a cultural and a social sense. The fest noz is both a vehicle where localized dances and music can be celebrated—thus maintaining local social cohesion—and a melting pot where choices are made and a symbolic pan-Breton repertory in dance and music emerges. In this way, the modern fest noz event, where the round dance is performed, is the most important public expression of contemporary bretonnitude. Festoù noz are attended on a weekly basis through-

out the year by large cross-sections of the community. They operate, both symbolically and practically, in the everyday social production of breton-nitude. (2003: 223)

The Breton musicians who had arranged for the Gnawa to come to Brittany were involved in this production of local culture, but they were also convinced that the trance induced by the Moroccan three-stringed *hajhuj* and the cas-tanetlike *qraqab* was similar to the "trance" created by the Breton *bombarde* and the hurdy-gurdy. The call and response of the Gnawa, they thought, mirrored the call and response (*kan ha diskan*) of Breton song. The dancing at the *fest noz* is done in a circle, and the Gnawa also begin their ritual ceremonies by danc-ing in a circle, calling the spirits to manifest. Like much African music, the Gnawa employ a pentatonic minor in their music, setting it apart from other Moroccan music that draws upon the Arab *maqam* system of scales. Breton music also uses a pentatonic and/or modal scale, which sets it apart from much European diatonic music (Sawyers 2000: 15). Indeed, the whole tones and dotted whole tones present in pentatonic music give the Breton musicians more than ample room to bend notes, effecting a kind of blues style (Chapman 1994: 39). In these elements of style, then, the Breton musicians found simi-larities between the two traditions. Most of all, however, was the perceived change of state that resulted from both musics—the emotional effects that the Bretons (thought they) produced.

For the Breton musicians, the collaboration was an example of what Melville J. Herskovits would have called a syncretic relationship based on the attraction of like to like (1966). The Bretons wanted to create a new music of intercultural trance and to facilitate intercultural exchange by bringing the Gnawa to Brittany for three months. The Gnawa did not share these percep-tions, however. From their perspective, the collaboration had more to do with making money on the Breton summer festival circuit than it did with aesthetic iconicity. The Gnawa were in Brittany to share in the profits of that endeavor and for the adventure and repute that it promised.

The Celtic musicians had very specific ideas about cultural exchange, and they created a brochure entitled "*Lila Noz: Rencontre de Transe*" to promote their collaborations:

With "Lila-Noz, a Meeting of two Trance Musics," after having thrown some footbridges between two cultures that are both far apart and very close at the same time, we wished to consolidate these held bonds and open the field of possibilities even further.

To render the meeting between Breton and Gnawa culture more accessible, we put on display, aside from the musics, stories and dances that offer troubling similarities between Negritude and Celtitude.

Before exploring the tension between Négritude and Celtitude (or even Bretonitude) in more detail, it is important to put the Breton attraction to North African culture into a larger historical context. The Breton musicians were not the first to throw "footbridges" across the straits of Gibraltar. Irish filmmaker and writer, Bob Quinn, has advanced a theory linking the Celts and North Africans Berbers. This is quite another version of the diaspora than the one evoked by Paul Gilroy's *The Black Atlantic* (1993). In Quinn's version, the Celts are related to the Berbers, who traveled north from Africa by sea. He cites similarities in boat building, in megaliths and tomb construction, in jewelry design, in names, and even in language. Perhaps most significantly, he cites recent genetic research that finds a similar genome among populations along the Atlantic littoral, from Spain to Scandinavia (2005: 132).[22] For Quinn, the ancient maritime culture of the Atlantic links the Celts and the North Africans. "Traditionally," he asserts, "the sea did not divide peoples: it united them" (2005: 249). Footbridges were, in fact, unnecessary. Furthermore, for Quinn, today's Celts are to the French what the Berbers are to the Arabs, a people whose rich history and language has nearly been erased in the hegemony of colonization. Possible links in contemporary musical aesthetics have been noted (Laidler 1998), as have the rituals of veneration at tombs and shrines in both cultures. "History," as ethnomusicologist Caroline Bithell notes in her examination of the Celts in the Corsican imaginary, "has its fashions" (2003: 35). What is clear is that the intercultural links that the Breton musicians were hoping to forge were not without precedent in the Breton cultural imagination.

There is yet another link worth mentioning: that between the French Third Republic that colonized Algeria and the French Third Republic that suppressed the Breton language and culture within France in the name of national unity. That these "colonizing" efforts were taking place at the same time in the nineteenth century is no accident. As anthropologist Paul A. Silverstein notes, "there exists a clear correlation between the efforts at national integration within the metropole [in France] and those employed within the colonies" (2004: 60). The Breton activists explicitly related to the colonized Algerians and decolonization "became the general lens through which ethnic movements in France interpreted their struggle and refined their methods, eventually drawing directly on the FLN's [Algerian National Liberation Front's] successful use of public strikes, demonstrations, and even urban bombings" (Silverstein 2004: 73).[23] The relation between the North African colonies and the Breton ethnic struggle has a long historical precedent. With these discourses of maritime and colonial linkages in mind, the importance of Sidi Musa as a symbol is clear, and the relation between Négritude and Celtitude takes on another layer.

The Négritude movement was spawned in Paris in the 1930s as Aimé Cesaire, a Martinican poet, coined the term with fellow student Leopold Sedar Senghor. (Both would eventually become political figures, Cesaire in Martinique, Senghor in Senegal.) Négritude was an attempt by young Caribbean intellectuals, as well as thinkers from other countries in the African diaspora (Frantz Fanon, W. E. B. Dubois), philosophers, (Jean-Paul Sartre), and artists, to vindicate the pejorative term "negre" and transform it into a symbol of pride for people of African descent. As a movement, Négritude valorized the culture of Africa for Africans *outside of Africa* who, because of slavery, found themselves in very different cultural contexts. Although it has been faulted for its essentialism in positing a particularly black ontology, its force as a political and artistic tool of liberation cannot be underestimated. The Négritude movement was associated with the Harlem Renaissance and a general efflorescence of black culture on both sides of the Atlantic. Most importantly, the movement addressed itself to descendants of the atrocities of slavery, creating a way toward pride, dignity, and equality.

Celtitude, on the other hand, is a word applied to the Celtic identity as it has been redefined in the twentieth century, an identity that spans several European cultures, including France, Ireland, Scotland, and England. Tied to the revival of Breton music and sparked by the energies of musician Alan Stivell in the 1960s,[24] Celtitude is an attitude of difference, a reclamation of Breton identity within countries where the majority of the population is not of Celtic origin (Chapman 1994; Wilkinson 2003). Indeed, in a song called "Délivrance," Stivell talks about the Celtic identity as a platform for the oppressed in other parts of the world, including Africa:

Voici venu le temps de délivrance
Loin de nous toute idée de vengeance
Nous garderons notre amitié avec le peuple de France
Puis nous abattrons les murailles honteuses qui nous empêchent de
regarder la mer . . .

Nous ferons tomber la pluie sur le monde meurtri
Et nettoyer le sang graisseux dont se nourrissent les soi-disant

puissants

Et donner à boire aux assoiffés de justice

Et les feuilles repousseront de Bretagne en Espagne, du Mali au Chili,
d'Indochine en Palestine

Bretagne, centre du monde habité, tu seras un refuge pour les oiseaux
chassés pétrolés

Pour les femmes torturées en prison

Pour les vieillards bombardés

Celtie, au croisement des peuples du Nord et du Sud, aux confins du
vieux monde et du nouveau monde, aux frontières de la terre et de la
mer, à la limite du monde visible et du monde invisible?[25]

The time of deliverance has come

We are far from ideas of vengeance

We'll keep our friendship with the people of France

Then we'll break down the shameful walls that prevent us from

Looking at the sea . . .

We'll make rain fall on the murdered world

And clean the fatty blood that nourishes the so-called

Powerful

And give to drink to those thirsty for justice

And the leaves will grow again from Brittany to Spain, from Mali to Chili

From Indochina to Palestine

Brittany, center of the inhabited world, you will be a refuge for the hunted

oil-covered birds

for tortured women in prison

for old bombarded men

Celt, at the crossroads of people from the North and South, from the
    confines

Of the old world and of the new world, to the frontiers of the earth and
    of the

Sea, to the edge of the visible world and the invisible world

In this song the Celts are the center of the world, but they are also a refuge for those "others" who are suffering from different hegemonies, from ecological to racial and political. The song ends by blurring the lines between the north and the south and between the visible and the invisible.[26]

The *fest noz* that is practiced today is an invented tradition (Hobsbawm and

Ranger 1983). "Instead of the purely local dance and music tradition, the new festou noz that began in the 1960s are events where folk music and folk dance enthusiasts from all over Brittany meet to interact," notes folklorist Stephen Winick. "This has resulted in a crossing, melding, and to some degree homogenization of Breton music that does not appeal to purists" (Winick 1995: 45). The *fest noz* is an example of what Robert Cantwell calls "ethnomimesis," the imitative behaviors that give rise to new cultural formations (1993: 5–8). It is also a self-conscious creation of heritage, which, as folklorist and performance studies scholar Barbara Kirshenblatt-Gimblett notes, "is a mode of cultural production in the present that has recourse to the past. Heritage thus depends on display to give dying economies and dead sites a second life as exhibitions of themselves" (1998: 7). The reinvention of the tradition of the *fest noz* is one such exhibition. Unlike museum exhibitions, however, music performances and festivals draw the body of the onlooker into the creative act of heritage making. They are thus socially inclusive (Wilkinson 2003).

At the same time that Breton regional musics are melding into one category of Breton music—available for packaging and easy consumption by foreign audiences—however, the collaborations between Breton musicians and musicians from Africa is increasing. Both centripetal and centrifugal forces are at work. Speaking of the phenomenon of Afro-Celtic music, Winick brings attention to the historical precedents for this mix. "This particular fusion has a long and happy history," he says, and continues:

> Rock and roll is to some extent Afro-Celtic music, a product of culture contact in the seething stewpot of America. The Anglo-Celtic folk tradition, transformed by technology and commercial forces into country music, and African-American folk tradition, similarly refashioned into rhythm and blues, were the spark and the fuel that ignited rock and roll. In the old world, African and Celtic sounds have also been interacting for a long time. South African Kwela and Mbanqanga is played on European pennywhistles, and Zulus play Celtic-influenced concertina music. The banjo and bones, borrowed from African traditions by way of American minstrel shows, are now a part of Irish music.
>
> But in the 1990s the musical mixmaster has been cranked up another notch; Celtic and African musics are meeting head-on in the postmodern technoscape. (1997)

This head-on meeting is not benign, nor is it limited to purely aesthetic concerns.

Insofar as Celtitude is a movement that seeks to valorize a minority identity through arts that include music, it may be compared to Négritude and its emphasis on the unique aesthetics and philosophies of a group of people brought together through common experiences of oppression. Indeed, Franz Fanon makes the comparison in *Black Skin, White Masks* when, in talking about the political economy of language regarding dialects versus the official French, he says, "In the Antilles, as in Brittany, there is dialect and there is the French language. But this is false, for the Bretons do not consider themselves inferior to the French people. The Bretons have not been civilized by the white man" (1967: 28). Fanon acknowledges that there are surface comparisons to be made between the Bretons whose dialect has been repressed under the banner of French nationalism and the Antillean Creole speakers who use French but notes that these cases are in no way equal.

This is not the only instance where Celtic music becomes a metonym of ethnic, racial, and musical struggles. As Radano and Bohlman note in their discussion of world music and racial imaginaries, the "globalization of Celtic music . . . has resulted from far more than filiopietistic celebration in an imaginary Celtic diaspora. Politically charged in many of its local forms, Irish folk music can and does potentially resist anything from the British presence in Northern Ireland to the Palestinian struggle in the Middle East, to Spanish colonialism in the New World" (Radano and Bohlman 2000a: 33). For Celtic activists, their music becomes a political platform that extends into many domains.

The unequal comparison between Négritude and Celtitude is nonetheless troubling for several reasons. In the "Lila-Noz" brochure, the Bretons describe the Gnawa as "placed under the yoke of the Berber and Arab houses in North Africa," alluding to their past in slavery. They assert that the Gnawa "knew how to conserve under the deep pain of cultural exile a musical culture that was atypical and to save their black African identity from annihilation in the heart of Morocco." Identity is found in music in this discourse and here finds resonance in the Négritude movement, which elevated the arts as symbols of pride and authenticity. Clearly the Bretons identify with the need to conserve a minority identity in a land claimed by others. Although their history had nothing to do with being enslaved by the French, the Bretons are nonetheless involved in a struggle to assert their regional identity in a French nation. By performing with the Gnawa on the festival circuit in Brittany, they are telling a story to themselves and others, a story about their victimization and their cultural perseverance. It is also a story about music, however, and its ability to float free of local cultures, enabling associations as initially surprising as that between Négritude and Celtitude.

There are many phenomenological degrees of possession. Metaphorically, we are "possessed" by ideas, imaginations, emotions, and music, as well as other entities. Possession absorbs the attention in such a way that the difference between the agency of the possessor and the enactments of the possessed are elided. The gap between performer and performance collapses; form and meaning merge. Such "mystical" processes are closely akin to those described by Karl Marx in his analysis of the fetish. Commodity fetishism occurs when the labor that produced an object is erased and commodities themselves are thought not only to stand for but also to embody wealth, power, status, and identity. This arises from the social relations of workers, but is projected onto a social relation of things (Appadurai 1986).

In anthropology, fetishes have often been described as ritual objects— shells or scepters or holy words written in ink on paper and then worn as amulets or even ingested. A representation such as photograph may be appropriated as a fetish, either displayed or hidden away because of its magical potency. The fetish is a ritual object in which magical potency inheres. As Michael Lambek notes, "That religion is a human construction whose objects come to appear as autonomous living beings to those who worship them provided a touchstone for Marx's analysis of commodity fetishism" (2001: 735). And, discussing the magical powers of the State, Michael T. Taussig notes that fetishism "elucidates a certain quality of ghostliness in objects in the modern world and an uncertain quality of fluctuation between thinghood and spirit" (1993: 217).[27]

The power of trance to trans(e)form makes trance music attractive as a fetish. But it is clear that fetishizing the music is also fetishizing the musician: "It's been very hard," the Celtic band leader said. "The Gnawa are difficult to live with (difficile à vivre)." But, she confided, "I dream of the Gnawa every night, every night they come to me." They inhabited her subconscious much like the jinn inhabit the possessed. The Gnawa haunted her.

There is much that is haunting about Gnawa music. It literally invokes specters—apparitions that for the Gnawa have not illusory but ontological status. Indeed, we can say that the wounds and afflictions that often accompany possession trance also have a ghostly quality—like the spirits, they "stand" before you, or behind you, imploring to be recognized and healed (see chapters two and three). Trauma itself is a haunted house. Sociologist Avery Gordon describes haunting as "a seething presence, acting and often meddling with taken-for-granted realities. . . . The ghost is not simply a dead or a missing person, but a social figure, and investigating it can lead to that dense site where history and subjectivity make social life" (1997: 8). What is it that haunts the Celtic musicians? Is it the lost ritual of the Celtic past? Is it the specter of French colonialism that contributed to its disappearance? And what of the colonial specter in Africa? Is the Breton allied with France in that picture or with the African subject? The complexity of responses to these questions themselves become ghosts that haunt the imagination.

Of course the relation of Celtic culture to ghostly hauntings is renowned, providing another link, this time between ghosts and the *jnun*. "For nineteenth-century Bretons, the dead existed in a domain parallel to that occupied by the living," notes anthropologist Ellen Badone (1989a: 3). Like the *jnun* in contemporary Morocco (who are addressed every time one pours boiling water down a drain to alert the spirits to the danger), the "ubiquitous souls must be warned when the activities of the living might disturb them" (Badone 1989a: 3). Bretons are never *possessed* by ghosts, but there is a strong belief in *intersignes*, the signs that "bridge two dimensions of time, the present and the future, and two dimensions of reality, the natural and the supernatural. For those who talk about and have experienced intersignes," Badone notes, "there are no rigidly defined boundaries between these domains" (1989a: 302). Intersigns inhabit what Ibn al-'Arabi calls the world of *barzakh*, the world of in-between.

Beliefs in regard to death, religion and, revenants (or ghosts) have changed in Brittany, yet "supernatural perspectives continue to be entertained alongside scientific ones" (Badone and Roseman 2004: 285). Ironically, a main focus of tourism in Celtic countries is the de rigueur visit to the haunted house. Ghosts thus become commodities. But as noted above, commodities also have a haunting quality to them, one that Marx explicitly related to "the mist-enveloped regions of the religious world" (Marx 1977).[28]

According to Derrida: "The mystical character of the fetish, in the mark it leaves on the experience of the religious, is first of all a ghostly character" (1994: 148). If we substitute "sacred or ritual music" for "religious" in the above quote, we understand the haunting quality not only of Gnawa music but also of the Gnawa themselves in the Breton imaginary. Like the fetishistic object, the Gnawa possess an ability to a haunt the imagination.

What is it about Gnawa music that is so haunting? Why does it attract African American jazz musicians, American and European Rock musicians, and Celtic musicians, as well as techno trance enthusiasts? The music itself inhabits the body so profoundly that it resonates long after the ceremony is over, but this is only part of the answer. If we consider that trance and possession are of necessity linked for the Gnawa, we get an idea of what discourses are being repressed in these narratives in order for them to circulate in the world music market. Consider, for example, Si Mohammed's narrative of epiphany. Although he is not speaking of Sidi Musa, his words alert us to the vast differences between sign and signified in the three usages of the word "trance."

SI MOHAMMED'S EPIPHANY

For Si Mohammed, epiphany may be defined as the "appearance or manifestation of a divine being." Si Mohammed is a facilitator of epiphany. This is his function in the trance community. He inherited this role from his grandmother, a tall Sudanese mqaddema and a Gnawa priestess. As noted, the mqaddema is often clairvoyant; she sees the invisible, or essential, reality guiding and determining the events on the physical plane (Chlyeh 2000). She is "in touch" with the spirits, able to feel their presence, and in communication with them. She is a verbal conduit between realms of experience. The spirits may actually use her voice to communicate with others (in this sense she is a medium), or she may receive messages from them in dreams that she then passes on to the appropriate persons.

It is ultimately the music, however, that makes the jinn appear and that is performative. The resultant trance, or jadba, is thought to be healing and to assuage the afflicting jinn.[29] In this regard, Si Mohammed is quite literally an extension of his instrument. He is the hajhuj, the vehicle for the transmission of musical and spiritual meaning, a creator of altered states of being. But Si Mohammed not only facilitates epiphany, he has his own, attested to by his numerous narratives of intercourse with spirits. Here is another:

"Aisha Qandisha exists, she doesn't leave a single place untouched. She's even here in France. People in France have seen her," Si Mohammed told me as we were sitting in his temporary apartment in Place Pigalle, Paris.

"How does she appear to people?"

"She comes out at night just like a woman, but when you look at her feet, she has the feet of a camel. There are those who see her with a good regard and others . . . That Aisha Qandisha, she appears by rivers, or near the sea. So many fishermen have seen her! So many people who were fishing by the sea! So many people have seen her in the woods."

"And her color? She's black?"

"She's black; she's white. She changes colors."

"Really?"

Si Mohammed went on: "And then one time, here at the Divan du Monde [in Paris]. I was sleeping here, and Zaynab was there, and my daughter. We had played and eaten and drank our fill and we went to bed. All of a sudden I feel someone pulling my legs. I thought it was Zaynab or my daughter pulling me and fooling around with me. When I opened my eyes—I wasn't asleep yet— when I opened my eyes, the lights were still on; I see a woman standing above me totally undressed. She wasn't wearing anything! Naked. And her head was wild. And her eyes were like a cigar. Have you seen a cigar?"

"All lit up."

"All red. *Wayli.* I woke everyone up. I screamed. She stood, she went and stood next to the shower, and her eyes were red upon me. I screamed. They heard me. I said, 'Turn on all the lights!' They got up and turned on the lights. And she was gone. Nothing there. You know, I was soaked in my own sweat. And since then I sleep with a dagger under my pillow."

"A dagger?"

"I put it under my head. Because if she sees a knife, she runs away. Then one time we were all asleep. And that Zaynab that works with us, she got up in the middle of the night and went to the kitchen to get an apple or something. She was hungry. She gets up, and she sees a woman peering at her through the window. And we're on the seventh floor! She started trembling and came and woke me up. She found Aisha casting a spell on her. And she was struck. She came and woke me up. But Aisha had disappeared. That happened right here in France.

"We told this to some people, some Algerian women [living in Paris]. They told us, 'she always comes by this way.' There's a place nearby where they always burn candles for her. They call it 'Aisha's place.' Aisha exists and all the spirits exist."

Although Si Mohammed is not himself possessed in this discourse, the powerful *jinniyya* Aisha Qandisha does visit him and, knowing her power, he is terrified. This narrative is notable as it was recounted in France and attests to the fact that not only people, music, and trance travel, but spirits do as well. Even spirits are nomadic subjects.

That these narratives exhibit different relations to a phenomenological state of trance becomes even clearer when we see the kinds of hybridizations that take place in the performance realm. The Bretons, for example, took their musical collaborations one step further, creating a theater piece with the Gnawa. As previously recounted, Chantal, the storyteller, improvised off the famous "genie in a bottle" theme taken from the *Thousand and One Nights.* The character that finds the bottle in her production is a poor Breton fisherman; the genie that appears and eventually grants him bounty in the way of an enormous catch of fish is not the Breton spirit l'Ankou, but Sidi Musa, the Moroccan spirit.

L'Ankou in Breton folklore is the spirit of death. He—or she—is usually portrayed as a skeleton who comes with a cart, stopping in front of homes as a harbinger of death (Badone 1989a: 4–5). Sidi Musa, of course, has no such portentous associations. Nonetheless, Chantal substituted one for the other, creating a kind of syncretic folklore of Africa, the Middle East, and the Celtic world. For the Bretons, this is a self-consciously fashioned folklore with little relation to belief. For the Gnawa, however, it is precisely their belief in spirits that facilitates trance.

CONCLUSION: CREATING LINKS IN NARRATIVES OF EPIPHANY

In a very real sense, all the performances of the Gnawa—in their ritual ceremonies in Morocco, in their nightclub acts, in their collaborations with jazz artists like Randy Weston and Pharoah Saunders, and in their participation in festival fusions in France and elsewhere—are based upon epiphany, the making manifest of what is experienced as an essential reality, whether that reality be an embodied spirit or *jinn*, a color that infuses and transforms being, or an insight facilitated by trance that changes one's experience of reality henceforth. Music is the conduit for this experience of essence.

Whereas all the above contexts share the trance induced by music—the voice of God, that is invoked in Weston's liner notes (chapter eight)—the interpretations, or the "noise of man," are very different. For Si Mohammed, the manifestation is quite literal: the *jinn* exist; they visit him; they take human form, even in France. He is *marṭabit*, linked, to a presence, or presences, that speak to him and determine his movements as he reads their signs. Weston's epiphany is of a more abstract order. He also went into trance, but there was no literal being before him. Rather, he was infused with a color: "the color blue entered my spirit," he says. For Weston, the epiphany tied him to Africa, but also to a long line of African American artists—Ellington and Monk—artists that most Gnawa have never heard of or listened to until recently. And it was this experience, this "intuitive grasp of reality," that constituted the path of Weston's musical career, that led him, in fact, to be not just a superb musician, but to be a "cultural ambassador," a man with a mission: to bring the essential epiphany facilitated by the Gnawa to audiences outside Morocco. "By replicating an experience in gesture and art," notes Boddy, speaking of the role of mimesis in performances of spirit possession, "the experience becomes known and familiar, incorporated by the individual and her society. But it is also interpreted and thereby transformed" (1994: 425). Such a transformation is evident in Weston's experience and recounting of trance as well as in his musical renditions; it is another example of how repetition secretes innovation (Lefebvre 1991: 203).

In Brittany in 2000 there was also epiphany. The lead musician became possessed not with a *jinn*, but with the Gnawa themselves. A "perception of the essential" differences between cultures, of a reality quite different from the Bretons' own became all too clear. Although not the commonality that they hoped to find through the trance experience, this, too, was an important insight, an epiphany, however hard-learned.

In all cases, physical and imaginary links across geography, culture, and the body instantiate subjectivity and create public identities. These narratives recount very different experiences of trance; yet all are imbued with a common desire to return to the body and to a memory of primary reality perceived to reside therein. Indeed, it is the *desire* for entrancement that is salient and that travels from realm to realm.

Analyzing the music complicates the picture. Despite the different aesthetic styles employed, all the musics use the pentatonic minor and all rely on a rhythmic structure associated with a kind of entrancement in local cultural contexts. All are carriers of an affective repertoire that indexes, if not the sacred, the ritual—the framed performance of transformation—despite the variance in form. The instrumentation in Weston's piece "Sidi Musa" (on the *Spirit of the Ancestors* recording) resembles the Gnawa insofar as he forefronts the bass, using it like a *hajhuj* and employs the triplets found in the ritual version. He suspends the fifth, creating an open pentatonic sound. Weston employs the *hajhuj* in tandem with the bass, and Pharoah Saunders solos on the Moroccan double-reed *ghaita* to great effect. The Bretons, by contrast, while using the same scale, overlay a Celtic melody on top of the bass line of the Gnawa. The rhythms of the *qraqab* are incorporated into the music, as they are in Weston's interpretation, but there is an overall straighter feel to the composition due to its resolution on the tonic. The instrumentation is completely different, of course, as they use traditional Breton instruments such as the *cornemeuse* and sometimes the hurdy-gurdy, and the overall rhythmic and melodic structure is less complex. While it may seem strange to compare Gnawa music with Celtic music and stranger still to compare the hurdy-gurdy with jazz piano, there is a link between these musics: in all three, a style of music (whether the "blues aesthetic" or the African "Gnawa aesthetic") functions as an iconic marker of a cultural identity, and is recontextualized with another aesthetic to produce a hybrid music, a music which aims to link the two. This style is recognized by the musicians, but also by the listeners. Much like the Moroccan multilingual who is able to understand elaborate code-switching from Arabic to French to Berber to English and back, the auditor for these hybrid musics has a trained ear that is able to identify the different stylistic components of the music. World music produces a "literacy of listening," an ability to hear the components in the mix.[30]

For Weston and the Gnawa, their collaboration is an example of what Erlmann calls "endotropic performance, the sonic construction of . . . identity . . . through the shared experience of style" (Erlmann 2003: 84). As I will elaborate in chapter ten, the Gnawa and Weston share not just the entrancement of co-performance, but a discourse of style stemming from a shared African past. This kind of community-internal identification with style did not occur with the Gnawa and the Breton musicians, however. Not only did the aesthetics of the music remain separate, their narratives about the music did as well. "The idea of a unified black musical ethos," ethnomusicologist Ingrid Monson reminds us, "is partially dependent on the continuing experience of racism" (Monson 2003a [2000]: 3). A black aesthetic is unified in the cultural imagination when it is opposed to a common enemy: racism. In that process, the binaries of black and white music in these examples were upheld.

The marketing of the trance experience is a prevalent reality in artistic realms. Indeed, much world music is sold via the promise of musically induced trance, and audiences may very well become entranced in the process of audition. Analyzing the narratives of epiphany that these experiences produce, however, underscores that all trance is not the same, and that the "voice of God"—though perhaps present in all these musics—is not easily translated into the "noise of man.

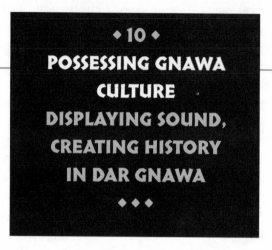

POSSESSING GNAWA CULTURE °
DISPLAYING SOUND, CREATING HISTORY
IN DAR GNAWA
♦ ♦ ♦

The implications of musicians as travelers for issues of globalization have not been sufficiently analyzed. —Ingrid Monson (2003a [2000]: 7)

[H]istory is precisely the way we are implicated in each other's traumas.
—Cathy Caruth (1996: 24)

How does one possess culture and how is one possessed by it? How do vastly different cultural imaginations travel, like spirits, and come to inhabit other hosts? And how does music facilitate this process? In this chapter I elucidate how different cultural imaginations inhabit musical forms and travel within them, and, contrariwise, how performance genres act upon and change cultural imaginations and representations of history, producing what Paul Gilroy refers to as a politics of transfiguration, "a counterculture that defiantly reconstructs its own critical, intellectual and moral genealogy in a partially hidden public sphere of its own" (1993: 37–38).[1]

In the summer of 2001 I found myself in Tangier, the northern-most Moroccan city that juts out of the African continent towards Gibraltar and Spain, separating the Atlantic from the Mediterranean Sea.[2] I was there to visit Abdellah El Gourd (also known among the Gnawa as *bu-al-khir*, the father of abundance), a master Gnawa musician. I had met Abdellah El Gourd when he was on tour in the United States with African American composer and pianist Randy Weston and his ensemble. The two of them had been collaborating for thirty years, ever since Weston visited Tangier for the first time in 1969, when El Gourd was still an electrical engineer for Voice of America radio broadcasting, then based in Tangier. As a *m'allem*, or spirit master, Abdellah El Gourd is unique in that he not only leads a ritual life in Tangier but also has an active professional relationship with Weston, who lived in Tangier for several years as well, participating in and creating a particular artistic ambience with expatriate artists as well as Moroccan musicians and literati. Although he left in 1975, Weston has continued playing with the Gnawa in international venues and with Abdellah El Gourd in particular. I was in Tangier to understand how these two men, their two musical traditions, and their histories intertwined. Further, I was interested in how both Abdellah El Gourd and Randy Weston, while each possessing their own relation to the African diaspora, music, and innovation, came to be possessed by a historical narrative that animated and defined them both.

Walking up the steep steps from the Tangier port and entering the narrow streets of the medina, I found the house quickly. It was indistinguishable from the others. It wasn't until I entered that I found the sign designating the location. "Dar Gnawa," it said, "Commemorating the Memory of God's Mercy" (dār gnāwa tuḥiyyu dhikrā at-taraḥḥum). And indeed both commemoration and memory were created and displayed here. But of what and for whom? What does it mean to commemorate memory?

El Gourd had transformed his traditional medina house into a museum of sorts, an institute for the instruction, practice, and promotion of Gnawa culture. He called it a markaz, a center or institute. After welcoming me, Abdellah El Gourd waved his arms in the direction of the photos on the walls and the instruments—an electric organ, an African djembe drum, bongos, a conga drum—all instruments that are not found in Gnawa lila. There were also Moroccan instruments, of course, including several hajhujs and two large snare drums used by the Gnawa in the opening of their ceremonies. "Hiya hadik dar gnawa," he said. "This is Dar Gnawa." Then we began immediately to climb the stairs.

On the second floor Abdellah El Gourd escorted me into his office. A sophisticated music system stood on a table in the corner, the speakers pointed out the window to the courtyard below. The plastered walls, painted a light green, were decorated with a poster from a recent Gnawa tour with Randy Weston. Other promotional materials lay on an old wooden desk. There were videos, a few books, magazine articles, compact disc and tape collections, a fax machine, and a Master's thesis that a beur, a French-born Moroccan with roots in Tangier, had written about Abdellah El Gourd in the 1990s. There were also large yellow diagrams on poster board that showed spatial choreographies for the Gnawa, maps for the movements of the dancers.

FIGURE 16: "Dar Gnawa, Commemorating the Memory of God's Mercy."
Photograph, Deborah Kapchan

"What are those?" I asked.

"They're for when we do performances," he said, using the French word *spectacles*, "so everyone knows what to do." Spectacles—or *frajat* in Arabic—are performances done for tourists at Moroccan hotels and at festivals and concerts abroad. *Lilat* (literally "nights"), on the other hand, are the ceremonial rituals of healing the possessed.

El Gourd's house is not a museum per se, but it is a public institution for the display of the musical heritage of the Gnawa. It is open to the public between 5:00 and 9:00 each evening. During these hours, El Gourd gives instruction to his apprentices, rehearsing the *qit'a* (musical numbers) with them, memorizing the *treq lila* (the "path" or progression of the ceremony). It is also a jam session and a time to listen to recorded music and to stories. It is a time for smoking *kif* and drinking tea.

Now that Abdellah has retired, his main concern is to preserve the Gnawa heritage (*turath*), which is, of course, his own. This is done through a variety of displays and performances. Exhibitions display not just objects, but the very people who create them. Dar Gnawa, as a center that is also a home, is, in the words of Barbara Kirshenblatt-Gimblett, the "ultimate exhibit of itself," presenting the cultural artifacts of the Gnawa *in situ*, as it were (1998: 4). Of course the actual rituals, while always done in a home, are rarely done in the home of the m'allem. Nonetheless, a home is the site of ritual enactments. The cultural identity displayed at Dar Gnawa is the particular vision of its curator, but it is also a socially constructed space, with influences of its Tangier locale and of the people who frequent it. Returning to Henri Lefebvre, gesture creates space. The gestures of the Tangier Gnawa as well as the Gnawi, the tourists, the scholars, and the artists who inhabit it for hours each day create a particular space of heritage. In creating Dar Gnawa, Abdellah El Gourd has come to possess the until-now purely oral cultural history of the Gnawa in sound, image, and word, but he is also possessed by these media of documentation; they inhabit and determine him in ways that both grant and deny him agency. Moreover, through his use of media, El Gourd rewrites the history of racial relations in the African diaspora, making evident the contribution of the Gnawa to African American musical traditions. Whereas African American jazz musicians tell stories of their return to Africa and African aesthetics (particularly in the 1950s, 1960s and onward), El Gourd tells the story from the other direction, a story about common ancestors who transcend time and space. In so doing, he includes himself, and the Gnawa more generally, in a racialized music history already in circulation in the world music market—that of the African diaspora (Waterman 2000: 167–168).[3] "The transnational mix has not erased race from music, but rather it has recontextualized it," Radano and Bohlman argue, and "this recontextualization has brought about an even more critical confrontation between race and music" (2000a: 37).

THE ENCOUNTER

"Gnawa always had their trades," Abdellah El Gourd was quick to tell me. "Not like now. Then you were a carpenter, a metal smith, a mason, everyone had their job. And you were also a Gnawi. Now people make being a Gnawi into a profession. It's even on their carte nationale [national identity cards]. It wasn't until 1993 when I retired that I began to go out [on tour]. . . .

"Well, I was working at Voice of America and at the same time I was playing with the Gnawa. I was at this time a muḥib, a lover of the music and trance (al-ḥal), not a master. And I knew an English teacher. And this English teacher heard Randy [Weston] play; he met Randy Weston and introduced us."

Randy Weston was on a tour of several African nations at this time, a project funded by the State Department with the intention of introducing African American artists to their roots in living African traditions. "A young Moroccan teacher brought me and Abdellah El Gourd together," Randy Weston re-counted to me later that year, speaking of the same individual. "'If you're in-terested in African traditional music, you have to hear the Gnawa,' he told me. He was like a spirit, because neither Abdellah nor I remember his name or know what happened to him."

That Abdellah El Gourd was working at Voice of America has more than just ironic import. It was his association with English speakers in this interna-tional city that opened the door to a meeting with Randy Weston, for whom Abdellah became, in a sense, the "voice of the Gnawa," a representative of a link with Africa that, although it had traveled across the Sahara, had not been broken by the Atlantic crossing. That was more than thirty years ago. It was an encounter that changed the lives of both men. Abdellah El Gourd, a ritual mu-sician, became more of an artist or *fannan*, while jazz artist Randy Weston's ca-reer veered toward ritual music. Both men found a common thread in the his-tories of slavery, for unlike other countries in Africa which were sources for the slave trade, Morocco (like the United States) was a *destination* for slave routes, particularly under the Arab and Berber sultanates who brought con-quered people from Timbuktu to Morocco between the fifteenth and sixteenth centuries, but also by the Portuguese who used Morocco as a stopover port from West Africa (Mohammed Ennaji 1994; Laroui 1982; Pâques 1991). The Gnawa culture grew up behind the palace walls and among enclaves of slaves and former slaves in the cities and villages of pre-Independence Morocco.

Randy Weston told me that it was Abdellah El Gourd's desire to educate others about Gnawa culture that led him to introduce Mr. Weston to the old masters, a privilege usually reserved for insiders and initiates. "Abdellah was wonderful," Mr. Weston remarked, "because he was always interested in doc-umenting his people when I first met him." Today, more than thirty years after this initial meeting, both Randy Weston and Abdellah El Gourd have recorded the story of their cultural encounter—Weston in more than forty-eight re-cordings, among which Abdellah El Gourd appears on two. Abdellah El Gourd has also documented the effects of this cultural alchemy by transforming his home into both into an institute of Gnawa culture and a studio/salon where local artists come everyday to listen to music, to play music, and to talk music.

Dar Gnawa is a space for the display of *tagnawit*: the lived practices of Gnawa knowledge or, one could say, the *heritage* of Gnawa. For the Gnawa, those possessing *tagnawit* experience a long initiation, until it's "in the bones" (like for El Gourd's apprentices), whereas those who do not possess *tagnawit* are the popularizers (Nass Marrakech, Orchestra de Barbès) who have adopted the Gnawa identity and music for purposes of commercialization but know little of its deeper ritual significance and its history. Discussions of who possesses *tagnawit* are common among Gnawa musicians and practitioners. It is a discourse intimately connected to notions of identity and authenticity, and there are often fierce debates around the matter. For the Gnawa, this distinction also points to a relation to place and time. For Moroccans, "real Gnawa" (*al-gnawi al-ḥaqiqi*) are located in a particular regional tradition (whether it is that of Marrakech, Casablanca, Rabat, or another city), and they have put in their time at plenty of all-night rituals. On the other hand, the practice of these local traditions varies from region to region and it is impossible to talk about a strict canon of Gnawa ceremonial practice. The practices, that is, are fluid and malleable (Pâques 1976: 177).[4]

EXHIBIT ONE: DISPLAYING SOUND

Museums of music exist, but they present quandaries. Music is not an object that can be put in a display case. In fact, music refuses to be framed. Music is performative. It is agentive. It permeates a location with both auditory and physical vibration. It also has a powerful effect on memory. Music inhabits us in a literal sense. It invades the parameters of the body and takes root, almost systemically, even when we would rather have silence. It is why we refer to "haunting melodies." Music, like spirits, is attributed with an agency of its own. Like a commanding performance, it can possess us.

Music can also transport us. This is certainly true of music that is associated, iconically, with different cultures, climates, places, and times (Feld 1996). Music captures our imaginations, possessing us and taking us to a different place. Music then is mobilizing. Not only does it affect the movement of our bodies and our sympathetic nervous system but it also can also move our imaginations into spaces that are not limited by geography. Such transport is common at Dar Gnawa, where the visitor is bathed in a wide array of international music. For despite Abdellah El Gourd's concern with preserving *tagnawit*, the soundtrack at Dar Gnawa is not what you might anticipate.

Evenings at Dar Gnawa in the summer of 2001 were always interesting. Sometimes I would enter and be overwhelmed with the sounds of Weston's music. This was not the music he recorded with the Gnawa, but his later works recorded with Talib Kibwe, Neil Clark, Benny Powell, and Alex Blake—pieces like "Creation" from his compact disc *Khepera* that were abstract and sometimes disharmonious as well as other works featuring a broad range of instrumentation, including the Chinese *pipa*, African drums, and the searing sound of Pharoah Saunders on the Moroccan double-reed *ghaita*. The *m'allem* played this music at high volume, eclipsing the possibility of conversation and obliging the visitor to listen. At times like these I felt a deep disassociation between place and sound; nothing in my twenty years in Morocco had prepared me for listening to cosmic Afro-centric experimental jazz within the confines and acoustics of a Moroccan traditional home in the medina of Tangier.

The soundscape was nothing if not various at Dar Gnawa. Sometimes we would listen to Malian music. Abdellah El Gourd was particularly impressed with the blind duo Amadou and Miriam, who, he told me, overcame hardship and initial rejection by Malian audiences to become well-known international recording artists. We listened to world music compilations with pieces that mixed Celtic and African sounds. One day I arrived to a pulsing Latin beat.

"You listen to salsa music?" I asked, surprised and delighted. Abdellah El Gourd didn't understand the word "salsa." "Latin music! *al-musiqa al-la-tiniyya*," I clarified. "You like Latin music?"

"*Ma'lum!* Of course," he answered. "The origin of that music is Andalusian. *aṣl-u andalusi*. It's Andalusian music, *dyal-nah*, it is ours, it belongs to us." Here the *m'allem* was constructing his identity as a Moroccan more than an African. The Andalusian culture came down from Spain with the Moors (Berbers and Arabs) in the fourteenth and fifteenth centuries in the wake of the Reconquest and is most often associated with Fes and Tetouan, though Andalusians live in all major cities.

The music that Abdellah played in Dar Gnawa did not issue from a homogenous Gnawa aesthetic (the kind of style that is appropriated and recognized in world music, for example), but, echoing the diverse pantheon of spirits, represented a musical polytheism of sorts, or a polymusicalism. I realized that Dar Gnawa exists in part for the dissemination of global sounds to a *local* audience. It is a locale where transnational musics are played, displayed, and consumed. In this musical and very pedagogical space, Abdellah creates links between different musical traditions.[5]

Since I was there in the summer, there were a lot of visitors to Dar Gnawa: Moroccans living in other parts of the country who came back to visit family in Tangier and Moroccans living in Europe who make their annual pilgrimage across the Straits on massive ferries to the *bled*, the homeland. The young Gnawis always sat unimposingly against the wall, patiently waiting for the moment when they would rehearse the ceremonial songs. A long-time friend of Abdellah El Gourd's from Tetouan was often there, a tall man who, once he had smoked a bit, was extremely gregarious. I had the feeling that he came to Dar Gnawa to get out of the house and be with the boys. Illegal Nigerians waiting to cross the Straits and who only spoke English sometimes heard the music from the street and wandered in. They were welcomed by Abdellah El Gourd in English. Another m'allem frequented Dar Gnawa—a thin, light-skinned man with large eyes. Once the music got started this m'allem played a beautiful pair of rare wooden qraqab. There was also a saxophone player from the Royal Orchestra who was on vacation in the north. He came without his horn but often played the conga drums. Apart from one young European woman who wore a jellaba and smoked cigarettes with her Moroccan boyfriend one evening, I was the only woman present in Dar Gnawa that summer. I was always introduced as professora,[6] which alerted the other visitors to my status and explained my presence.

Other visitors to Dar Gnawa that summer included a Moroccan Jew, a flute player who had grown up with the m'allam in Tangier but now lived in Paris. The two men spoke fluent Spanish with each other. Maurice brought his flute and played jazz riffs over the Gnawa songs. He had lived in New York in his youth and had attended the Manhattan School of Music jazz program. Abdellah El Gourd was looking forward to the visit of Archie Shepp and Randy Weston in early September when they would all play at the Tangier Jazz Festival. (The festival was subsequently cancelled because of the events of September 11.)

This was the ambiance at Dar Gnawa, a salon for local residents of Tangiers, for immigrants returning from abroad, for artists in the community, for clandestine Africans, for foreign researchers, and, several times a year, for world-renown musicians. And at 9:00, as if everyone knew that the museum was closing, people packed up, said their good-byes, and left.

EXHIBIT TWO: CREATING MUSICAL HISTORY IN IMAGES

It is very important to try to understand the operation of a selective tradition. . . . In a society as a whole, and in all particular activities, the cultural tradition can be seen as a continual selection and re-selection of ancestors. Particular lines will be drawn, often for as long as a century, and then suddenly with some new stage in growth these will be cancelled or weakened, and new lines drawn. —Raymond Williams (1975 [1961])

The history of the Gnawa is largely oral. Apart from a corpus of books in French and some articles in English,[7] there is little scholarship on the Gnawa. Even the slave records from that time period are difficult to access.[8] Unlike other Sufi-influenced groups in Morocco—like the Aissawa (Dermenghem 1954), for example, or the Hamadsha (Crapanzano 1973)—there is no *shaykh* who has left writings and only a scant oral hagiography of a few saints is passed on from generation to generation (Hell 2002b). The transmission of Gnawa culture has been in the gestures, movements, and attitudes of the body possessed—and in the musical and aesthetic repertoire, of course. The history is in the songs—all 243 of them according to Abdellah's count. But even the songs themselves do not recount stories. There are few narrative lines in the lyrics, but mostly invocations to the different saints and spirits recognized by the Gnawa: Sidi Bilal, 'Abdalqadr Jilani, Sidi Musa, Lalla Aisha, Si Buhali, and others. The names of these *mluk* (or possessors) are repeated over and over, their qualities praised, their aid solicited. The spirits of the ancestors are still alive. Why then would they need to be conjured in books when their presence is conjured regularly in the bodies of the entranced, the *majdubin*? As philosopher Edward Casey notes, the body remembers the past as a form of presence (1987). Body memory experiences the past as co-immanent with the present. By dancing to the spirits, moving to their dictates and rhythms, history is embodied and made to live in the present (Browning 1995).

In part, the absence of any written history protects the Gnawa from criticism from other Moroccans, as the syncretic beliefs of the Gnawa, expressed in a system of African aesthetics, are not what most in Morocco consider to be mainstream Islam. Indeed, of all the mystic cults in Morocco that employ trance as a way of communing with the spiritual world, the Gnawa are the least understood. The Gnawa have reason to be circumspect about their manner of practicing devotion. They are often compared to magicians and are also the targets of racism. Although the masters of a generation or two ago are still remembered in conversation, they are not reified.

The pantheon of spirits is not represented in any of the images displayed in Dar Gnawa. Moroccans do not portray the spirits in images except as they incarnate in the bodies of the possessed. In the Gnawa worldview, the spirits are all around us, sometimes taking fleshly form, sometimes not. The images we do see on the wall in Dar Gnawa, however, are somewhat surprising. Abdellah El Gourd refers to them as the "ancestors."

"*Ha huma an-nass al-qdam*, those are the ancestors," the *m'allem* remarked when I approached the photographs to read the inscriptions in small print on the bottom. There were pictures of Rahsaan Roland Kirk, Eric Dolphy, Dexter Gordon, Thelonius Monk, Milt Hinton, Roy Eldridge, Johnny Copeland, Ben Webster, Archie Shepp, and, of course, Randy Weston, who is surrounded by

FIGURE 17: "The ancestors" in Dar Gnawa (pictures of Rahsaan Roland Kirk, Eric Dolphy, Dexter Gordon, Thelonius Monk, Milt Hinton, Roy Eldridge, Johnny Copeland, and Ben Webster). Photograph, Deborah Kapchan

pictures of Gnawa masters. How is it that African Americans jazz legends come to define the ancestors in Dar Gnawa?

Abdellah told me that one could not just decide to "become" a Gnawi (ṣbaḥ Gnawi). A Gnawi endures a long process of induction, initiation, and instruction. On the other hand, he said, there are people who are linked, marṭabit, to saints and spirits of the Gnawa pantheon. "Randy Weston," said the m'allem, "came all the way from Brooklyn marṭabat, or linked, to the spirit Sidi Musa and to the color blue." As discussed in chapter nine, Sidi Musa is another name for Moses, who delivered the Jews from slavery in ancient Egypt and into freedom. There are links between the pantheon of spirits in Morocco, who, like Sidi Musa, are ancestors, and the ancestors of jazz. One clear contiguity is between the slaves that went to the Americas and those who stopped earlier in the journey, at the tip of North Africa. Commenting on the lack of a written record of history, Abdellah El Gourd told me that the slaves in Morocco would go through the city singing certain songs, songs known only to them, in order to be reunited with their loved ones that had been separated from them in slavery. "There were no telephones, then," he said jokingly, "no portables (or cell phones). Slaves had their own language in song. When they would come into

FIGURE 18: "The ancestors" in Dar Gnawa. Photograph, Deborah Kapchan

a new city, they would sing the songs, trying to find their own." Songs served as auditory icons of identity, as sound "links." Weston found such a link to Africa in Morocco.

For Weston, Africa is the source (to invoke Abdellah El Gourd's term), the birthplace of all traditions. Linking his music to Africa is also making a claim to authenticity.[9] Yet, encountering Sidi Musa was also an encounter with the great jazz masters, since when Weston first heard the Gnawa he also heard "the black church, the blues, and jazz all at the same time" (see chapter nine). What's more, it was an opening into a different mode of being in the world. "When I heard this particular [version of] Sidi Musa, after the ceremony I was in trance for about a week. And when I say trance, I was functioning. . . . I was moving, but the music took me to a very high level, it took me to another dimension" said Weston, adding, "I really realized that we're just little leaves of the branch of mother Africa."

There is an inversion, as well as a complementarity to the way Abdellah El Gourd and Randy Weston define and pay homage to the ancestors. Both acknowledge the source in Africa itself: Abdellah El Gourd by invoking the m'allemin (pl.), the early Gnawa masters who left their legacy to the present in the *bodies and songs* of those who possess *tagnawit* today, and Randy Weston by making frequent reference in his performances and presentations to mother Africa—the place—also defined as the "source" of musical and spiritual tradition. When I asked Randy Weston, for example, what he found so powerful about Moroccan Gnawa music he responded, "It's like after being away from your parents for a long time, your mother and father, whom who love very deeply. And you know they are there, but you may never see them, or maybe you have seen them but you've been away a long time. When you do see them and you realize that what you have, they *gave* you, you become very humble." For Randy Weston, Africa becomes the primary place of return, whereas for Abdellah El Gourd, at least in Dar Gnawa, the ancestors that crossed the Atlantic become primary symbols of genealogical display. These ancestors—African American jazz men—are, we can postulate, just as tied to Africa (*marṭabtin*) as Mr. Weston himself—possessed or inhabited by the spirits of Africa who know no spatial limitations, who don't recognize borders, who are, in effect, outside of time. "You can't say that the mluk [the owners or spirits] were once alive and are now dead," the m'allem once chided me. "No! They were alive and are still alive today; *baqi ḥayyin ḥetta lyum, huma ma'-na*; they are with us." The spirits corporealize in different forms and bodies, but the spirit of Sidi Musa, for example, animates and literally inspires—breathes life into—the jazz music of Randy Weston just as it animates the ritual music of Abdellah El Gourd.

The visitor to Dar Gnawa also sees the history of Abdellah El Gourd's career as it took him and his musicians to Spain, to France, and to the United States. These last images are like postcards sent back home from abroad. They are not images for export; rather they document "there" in the "here" of Dar Gnawa, a self-reflexive display of cultural tourism as enacted by the Gnawa (Kirshenblatt-Gimblett 1998). The photos are emblems of internationalism at the level of the local.

It was only upon visiting Randy Weston in his home in Brooklyn, however, that I understood the full importance of Abdellah's photographic gallery. Weston had invited me to his home to watch a movie about the Stambali—the equivalent of the Gnawa in Tunisia.[10] Before leaving he took me to his "music room," a room commemorated to musical and other heroes whose portraits in photographs graced the walls. Some of them (Langston Hughes) were photographed with Weston; others (Malcolm X) stood alone. There were dignitaries from the jazz world—performers like Melba Liston, who arranged several of his recordings, Etta Jones, and major influences like Thelonius Monk, as well as Weston's parents. As in Dar Gnawa, the photographs were on all four walls, creating a sacred space with visual presence, a kind of folk altar (K. Turner 1999). Both Weston and Abdellah had the fathers of jazz displayed on their walls, as well as contemporaries like Archie Shepp, with whom Abdellah still performs.

As Susan Sontag notes in *On Photography*, "One can't possess reality, [but] one can possess (and be possessed by) images—as according to Proust, most ambitious of voluntary prisoners, one can't possess the present but one can possess the past" (1989: 163). The images displayed in both Weston's house and in Dar Gnawa narrate a story of association, of links between past and present. They are intersigns of a sort, keeping a past moment alive in present memory and allowing both Weston and El Gourd to "possess the past." But whereas the photographs in Weston's gallery document the influential people in his life—people that he has known—the photographs in Dar Gnawa are of the old jazz masters, many of them (at least physically) deceased. Weston's photo gallery indexes a personal genealogy, while El Gourd's photographs create a racial and musical history for the Gnawa in general. This is particularly notable, as it breaks with Moroccan conventions of display. In Morocco (as in many places in the world), the photographs that usually hang on the walls of homes are those of patriarchs and sometimes matriarchs. (In public places, pictures of the king are *de rigueur*.) In sepia tones and yellowed with age, these photographs represent a kind of ancestor veneration and a document of family origins, "a portable kit of images that bears witness to [the family's] connectedness" (Sontag 1989: 8). The photographs in Dar Gnawa do bear witness, but not to life narrative so much as to a *genealogy of style and identity*. Not only is the repetition of musical styles (in both directions) paralleled by a repetition of visual practice in the form of a gallery of images, but the genealogy portrayed is also one based not upon bloodline, but upon aesthetic and spiritual links. Indeed, the gallery at Dar Gnawa is a portrayal of what Erlmann calls the "global imagination"; it exhibits not just the content of the photographs themselves, but the actual "means by which people shift the contexts of their knowledge and endow phenomena with significance beyond their immediate realm of personal experience"; what's more, we see in this display an "epistemological symbiosis between African and Western modernities" (Erlmann 1999: 4), as pasts are created in images and narrative.

As Raymond Williams notes in the quote above, "cultural tradition can be seen as a continual selection and re-selection of ancestors" (R. Williams 1975 [1961]). As new genealogies are drawn, different practices and discourses emerge.

When words are written down, they become social facts; they have a material power, a power to affect things, a power of contagion even. In Moroccan practices of magic, for example, words from the Qur'an are written on small pieces of paper and either worn on the body as amulets or put in a glass of water where the ink dissolves and is ingested. Words conjure presence.

Calligraphy is also a very developed art in the Islamic world. Although representational art is rare—as it is hubris to depict what God alone can create (and of course the images on the walls provide an interesting counterpoint to this)—centuries of care have been given to the art of calligraphy (Messick 1993). There are Sufi prayer exercises, for example, which instruct the believer to envision the word "God" (الله) as if projected behind their forehead. The letters themselves are used as portals to mystical experience. It is in this context of the power of print that we can read Si Abdellah El Gourd's luḥa.

A luḥa is technically a board or slate. It is what children write upon when they are memorizing verses from the Qur'an in Qur'anic School. A luḥa in this context is a place for the consecration of sacred words.

When I first discovered Abdellah El Gourd's luḥa I had an epiphany of my own. I had been attending lilas for years, had recorded all-night ceremonies on my Marantz, and had listened to my tapes for hours trying to get the order of the invocation to the spirits, to transcribe the words of the songs. I had interviewed Gnawis trying to get them to dictate the lila to me. We had some good starts but never got far. Here, however, in Dar Gnawa was a poster-size chart of the lila from beginning to end, the names of the myriad saints and spirits written out plainly. What's more, the m'allem was extremely articulate about his tradition and vocation. Well, Randy Weston had been telling to go to Dar Gnawa since I met him.

Usually Abdellah El Gourd wakes from his afternoon siesta, gets out his draftsman's tools—rulers, calipers, stencils—orders a large glass of steaming mint tea from the café across the street, and gets to work on his luḥa. This is a chart where Abdellah El Gourd meticulously records the progression of the lila, from the playful songs sung before the ceremony (la'ba), through all the spirits. There are 243 qiṭ'a ("cuts" or segments) in the Tangier lila, which, unlike Gnawa ceremonies in other cities, is performed over two days and nights. The chart is coded by color—white, green, black, red, pink, yellow, violet, and orange. Each spirit is associated with a color. There are several spirits in each group, all sharing the incense burned with that color. Each spirit

FIGURE 19: Abdulleh's *luḥa*. Photograph, Deborah Kapchan

has their own song, and each color, or group of spirits, has a food or drink associated with it, something that is imbibed or incorporated into the body (Diouri 1990).

There were three *luḥas* in Dar Gnawa when I was there. The *mʿallem* was working on a new one. There was an old one from 1980—he was not pleased with the aesthetic presentation of that—and a half-done *luḥa* that was, he realized well into his work, short one slot for the songs of the black spirits (each group of spirits has a color that unites them into a class or family). So he started again. Around the edges of the diagram in the older *luḥa*, Abdellah El Gourd had written the names of the countries where, he said, the Gnawa came from: Mauritania, Senegal, Gambia, Guinea-Bissau, Uganda, Conga, Kenya, Côte d'Ivoire, Zaire, Niger, Sudan, Guinea, Sierra Leone, Malawi, Central African Republic, Chad, Nigeria, and Burkina Faso. Inscribed in a small box on the lower-right-hand corner, he had written the following words, in English:

The Way of the Gnawa
The Ancestor's Heritage composed and ordered by Dar Gnawa
for [its] preservation from dust. Dedicated to all koyatis and Gnawa lovers.

Here was cultural preservation, self-conscious, self-proclaimed—a way to possess heritage and, tellingly, to order it. Abdellah El Gourd was creating precedent by committing the oral tradition to paper and ink, so that it would not turn to "dust" when the bodies of its bearers were no longer present. Ironically and predictably, his efforts come at a time when the ṭreq lila (literally the path or progression of the ceremony) is transforming dramatically because of its commodification, both at home and abroad. By consecrating the lila to script, Abdellah El Gourd possesses what he calls the "heritage," but he is also possessed by the act of documentation. The index that he is creating, much like the "folk maps" that Palestinians make of destroyed villages (Slyomovics 1998: 7), provides a symbolic placement for the Gnawa and their traditions. It is not an index to the imaginary and symbolic geography of an individual (Pandolfo 1997), but to what Abdellah El Gourd is careful to delineate as a regional tradition. "This is the Tangier lila," he repeated often. Writing, Abdellah El Gourd is propitiating the spirit that desires to capture tradition before it disappears with the last of its practitioners. Present-day Gnawis, it will be remembered, market the music but have little knowledge of the ritual context from which it sprang. Abdellah El Gourd still remembers. The consecration of this memory to writing creates what Pierre Nora calls a "lieu de mémoire," a symbolic residence for the Gnawa identity (Nora 1989). But El Gourd is also propitiating the spirit of capitalism, of rationality and modernity, entering the tradition-qua-tradition into a transnational index. For what is an index if not a way to locate, to define, and to classify? "While memory is the raw material of history," Slyomovics reminds us, "a document is what remains" (1998: 18). Much like a map, the index is the objectification of this memory. It "represents the unrepresentable: place and the desire to own it" (Bohlman 2000: 654). In this case, the luḥa makes the intangible tangible.

Not surprisingly, with the help of Si Said and his European agent, Jaap Haarlaar, Abdellah has created a website for Dar Gnawa (www.dargnawa .myweb.nl). His preoccupations with the luḥa are intricately related to giving order and—more importantly—public and official recognition to the Gnawa cultural identity.

My reactions were perhaps predictably tinged with eleventh-hour anxiety. I wanted to own this luḥa, to possess the "facts" that I had been trying to "get down" for so long. I wanted to lay claim to that luḥa and to Gnawa culture as I knew it had not been presented or codified before. Nor was I alone in my desire to possess this object. "I wish I could get a copy of that luḥa," the saxophonist from the Royal Orchestra said to the m'allem one night, gesturing to the chart. "No one gets a copy. No copies," said the m'allem. "It's not ready."

Abdellah El Gourd would not part with a copy of a luḥa (though he had several from previous years), nor would he allow me to photograph the whole thing. "It's not ready," he kept repeating. "*ma zal*, not yet."[11]

The *luḥa*, in fact, is not very useful to the noninitiated. It is an index, a *farras* in Arabic. Listing the names of the songs, it acts as a mnemonic device for those who already know the tunes and the lyrics. Implicit in the idea of an index is that there is a reality (a text, a performance, a repertoire) outside the index to which it faithfully corresponds. The concept of the "indexical" is inseparable from that of referential association (M. Silverstein 1976). But it is also true that the index (as a representation) constitutes its object (Hall 1980). For El Gourd's apprentices, it is an authoritative text. One can imagine that, generations hence, young Gnawi will consult it much as Breton musicians consult historical records for clues to the past and inspirations for its reconstruction. In fact, Abdellah El Gourd is codifying a ritual that, in corporeal practice, may be far more malleable than the index infers. What's more, the majority of the song names are the names of the spirits they are invoking. An index of proper names, the *luḥa* does not lend itself to translation. Following Derrida (1985), we know that proper names resist translation utterly. They are icons of difference. For whom, then, did Abdellah El Gourd create the index, and why?

Mastering the progression of these names and consecrating them to print, Abdellah becomes the author of the Tangier tradition. The more I got to know Abdellah El Gourd, however, the more I realized that he himself was possessed by documentation, almost obsessive about his task of writing down the path of the ceremony and protective about the knowledge that he alone has transcribed. I saw three *luḥas*, but there had been others. None of them were officially on display, as they had been discarded to make room for the new. The current *luḥa* was exhibited, but only as a work-in-progress. Yet every day for years, Abdellah El Gourd worked on his *luḥa* in the presence of the visitors and apprentices who frequented Dar Gnawa. It was an *idée fixe*.

Abdellah El Gourd is possessed not just by documentation, but by the creation of heritage. His task is all the more pressing, as he is documenting the ephemeral—music, song, and gestures (remember his choreographic chart). He, himself, is creating the "ethnographic object" (Kirshenblatt-Gimblett 1998: 30). If Weston is represented as a musical anthropologist in his liner notes (chapter nine), El Gourd is an ethnographer, researching his own traditions and creating the texts, the museum labels if you will, for the artifacts of Gnawa culture. These "artifacts" are immaterial—like spirits, they cannot be put in a frame or a box. Performances cannot be taken home. They are singular events. Their documentation, then, is always an estimate and a failure of representation (Phelan 1993a). The index, however, does not fail, as it does not attempt to evoke, only to describe. Its limits are clear. It does not pretend to be the thing itself. It is a map, and nothing more.

Why, when all the music and images in Dar Gnawa were so accessible to my photography and questions, was this luḥa coveted? Did Abdellah El Gourd's years at Voice of America sensitize him to the power of information? Did the act of writing imbue the luḥa with a special status? Or was it his travel in Europe and the United States that exposed him to the possibilities of eventually commodifying his knowledge in a form a foreigner might appreciate, even pay for, or at least publish? I didn't know, but I hoped to find out. I asked Abdellah El Gourd if he would mind if I interviewed him on tape, and he agreed.

I arrived at 4:00 the next day, an hour before Dar Gnawa opens its doors to the public. When I got there, DAT-recorder in hand, I found that Abdellah El Gourd had already set up a video camera and intended to record my recording of him.

"You don't mind, do you, if Si Said videos our interview?" he asked. Si Said was the m'allem's producer-in-training.

"ma kayn muškil, No problem," I said, not completely sincerely. I was already nervous about this interview, for although the m'allem was always polite and helpful, he insisted on speaking a formal Arabic with me, always maintaining a professional distance. For my part, I was fluent in Moroccan Arabic, but less practiced in classical Arabic. I felt like I was being interviewed. Okay. Postmodern ethnography. The camera turns on the anthropologist. I wondered how those images would be disseminated after my departure.

In our spoken interview the m'allem read from many parts of the luḥa, reciting to me the names of the African spirits, the ḥawsawiyyin (from Haussa) for example—Baba Madani, Fulani, Busunana, Malgatu, Mamario—and all the qiṭ'a in the color blue, Sidi Musa, the color that Randy Weston pays homage to at every concert. But he stopped short of reading all 243 titles. "Bizaf," he said. "That's too much [to recite]."

That Abdellah El Gourd wanted to capture my interview with him on film speaks to his awareness of film as an important medium of documentation. Yet day after day, year after year, he carefully writes the names of the songs to the saints and spirits on his luḥa. He does not film the ceremonies (though these days many do). Writing is, for him, a kind of meditation that he returns to daily. It is also a way for him to excavate what until now has only lived in the recesses of bodily memory. Whereas setting up a video camera at a lila would capture the order, the words, and the process of the ceremony, visual representation does not have the same effect. Images are like mirrors, and we may wander among their halls in a kind of somnambulism of the senses. Writing, on the other hand—especially the act of writing about the body and about the spirits that inhabit the body—demands reflexivity, what I referred to earlier as a "coming to terms" with culture. What's more, Abdellah El Gourd might be less able to control the circulation of video images, which are easier to reproduce.

Ironically, spending time at Dar Gnawa is not an immersion into tagnawit in the strict sense of the term. Surrounded by images of great jazz musicians, as well as photos of secular Gnawa performances in Spain, France, and the United States, there is no pervasive feeling of anything resembling "pure" Gnawa-ness. The soundscape is equally diverse. The music of jazz musicians, West Africans, Latinos, and others, fills the space, entering the body through the vibrations created by the high decibels. We might say that Abdellah El Gourd is inhabited by the spirits of the jazz ancestors just as Randy Weston is inhabited by the spirits of the African ancestors. Indeed, when I asked Abdellah El Gourd if his own music—the music in his nonritual repertoire—was affected by his encounter with jazz, his response was an immediate affirmative. The same is true for Randy Weston, who makes regular pilgrimages back to Morocco, and whose career and life path have changed definitively because of his encounters and inhabitations.

There is little anxiety about cultural loss in Dar Gnawa at the level of image and sound. The history portrayed there is an international one—not just Pan-African, but also one that reaches across the Straits to Andalusia in Spain and across the Atlantic to Brooklyn. There is no protectionism here. Historical influences are fluid. Like the spirits in the ceremonies, they come from different parts of the globe, from different time periods, and different regions. Some, like Sidi Musa or Moses, from the Levant; others, like Sidi Bilal, from Africa, still others, like Abdalqadr Jilani, from Iraq. And then Thelonius Monk, born in North Carolina but raised in New York, Lester Young, Dexter Gordon, and others. Inhabiting the bodies of those they possess, these spirits dance and sing history into the present. For the Gnawa there is no danger that spirits will be lost. They simply are. Their incarnation has always varied—Sidi Musa may possess a young Moroccan girl or an American-born African composer. The images, then, the representations of the spirits, will also always change. The photos are *symbols* for the spirits/ancestors. Since spirits never can be actually represented, however, Abdellah is free to engage in infinite substitution. Following Roland Barthes, he is helped by the medium of photography itself, which because it is invisible—we see through the photograph to the image—always points to the referent, "repeating mechanically what could never be repeated existentially" (1980: 15).

This is true of the sound as well. It comes through each musician differently. There is no one right way to play. For Abdellah El Gourd, if an embodied musical culture does not exist, tradition dies. This is why he has virtually created a school for the instruction and practice of Gnawa traditional music. After working on his luḥa, he always takes out his hajhuj, and though they listen to recorded music from all over the world, they always play their own songs. Yet the luḥa—as representation of the rational, the literate, the modern—becomes the object that is kept from circulation on the cultural market. It has, for Abdellah, great worth as an item of symbolic capital. Dedicated to the koyatis, the Gnawa dancers or apprentices, and to all those who love the culture—the written record of the luḥa exists to save what he calls (in English, it should be noted) the "Ancestor's Heritage" from dust. It is not the memory of the ancestors that he is preserving with the luḥa, for they are remembered perennially in the dances and songs, in the bodies and breath of the Gnawa; it is rather the tradition that they have bequeathed that is being preserved, it is a particular Tangier practice that he intends to save by codifying it in print—tagnawit. That he is the only one to consign such knowledge to print puts Abdellah in a privileged relation to this genealogy of ancestors. He is both a critic of Gnawa tradition as practiced nationally and a custodian of his particular tradition. The ṭreq lila, the path of the ceremony as Abdellah El Gourd learned it, is changing rapidly. In other cities, whole colors are deleted from the lila and parts of the ritual once considered essential are dispensed with completely. Abdellah El Gourd's luḥa is a memorial to a specifically local way of honoring the spirits. Disembodied and consecrated to the luḥa, the spirits would seem to inhabit a new medium in ink, and Abdellah El Gourd comes to possess the tradition. But does this act of authorship signal the death of the spirit?

INHABITING CULTURE

What does it mean to possess culture? What is possessed? Who is the owner? How is ownership declared, recognized, and experienced?

The exhibits at Dar Gnawa remind us that we inhabit our senses differently. Sometimes we are in possession of them, and sometimes they possess us. Certainly the question of power and agency arises in relation to these different senses—audition, specularity, the tactility and deliberateness of writing—though it would be facile to assume that being possessed by a spirit, a color, a culture, a genre of music, an image, or an idea necessarily implies domination by the same. Rather, we must analyze the relations of *desire* inherent in these (subjectifying and objectifying) encounters and the way cultural forms inhabit bodies and imaginations in different degrees of depth and compatibility in a kind of Weberian elective affinity.

Dar Gnawa exhibits not only the process of being possessed by several cultures somatically, but it also makes claims to the possession of culture, objectifying a notion of *tagnawit*, Gnawa tradition, by representing the specific Gnawa practices in Tangier in a written and official form. Here, in the luḥa, Abdellah El Gourd is unabashedly proprietary. Creating the index, he authors the tradition and inserts it into a local as well as a global history. We might posit that a codification of regional tradition is taking place in response to the centrifugal forces of transnationalism. Interestingly, however, the production of difference at the site of the local in Dar Gnawa has created a construction of similarity at the level of the global, the intercultural collaboration of Abdellah El Gourd and Randy Weston emphasizing the links of common history and a system of shared aesthetics. Yet Abdellah El Gourd's genealogical claims to authenticity encompass much more than a single musical trajectory, going back to the eighteen African countries that surround the luḥa, to the Moroccan masters who taught him, but also to the masters of jazz in the United States. There is no essentialism here. Rather, identity is a matter of "links" that are not spurious but determined by the possessing spirits. Some people are linked to the spirits and color of blue, others to red, green, white, yellow, and black. Affiliations are determined by desire (the spirits'), by the attractions that some spirits have to some people. Identity is not in the blood so much as it is in propensity.

Does the local, the particular Gnawa aesthetic, become a fetish for export in the case of Dar Gnawa? Or is it, rather, the international and especially the African American heritage that has been imported, festishized, and put on display for a local audience? I would suggest that both of these interpretations are too simplistic to account for the performances and displays at Dar Gnawa. The Gnawa have always experienced otherness in the bones, so to speak. Theirs is a hybrid tradition, composed of a diverse pantheon of spirits with whom they have a corporeal and spiritual relation. Following Gilroy (1993: 73), this makes them modern before even the advent of modernism. They are used to this relation to multiplicity. For them, it is not unusual to give passage to a different modality of being or for a possessing spirit to reorient one's sense of taste, touch, and smell, one's way of hearing and speaking, singing and moving, even one's way of interpreting the world. This is what it means to inhabit a realm that includes not only human beings but also the mluk, the possessing spirits, whether they are saints who were once embodied or spirits who have always lived in a parallel realm. The Gnawa and their followers are adept at this kind of habitus exchange. Perhaps this is why their display of culture is so inclusive of other traditions: the soundscape at Dar Gnawa is as various as the pantheon of spirits, each song coming from a different culture, each embodying its own history. The Gnawa recognize and respect the state of being possessed by difference (with all the power relations that implies), while nonetheless never losing the ability to return to the cultural self as they themselves define and "come to terms" with it.

Spirits inhabit our bodies, whether they are the spirits of Thelonius Monk or Moses. They take root not just in our consciousnesses, but also in the muscles of our fingers as we imitate their key strokes and movements and in our breathing patterns as we sway to their rhythms, their particular beat (daqqa). We taste them in the infusion of odors that they demand be released into the air. We breathe them in. Sometimes they cause us to expire, but always to experience, in Randy Weston's words, "another dimension." The same is true of cultural imaginations. Cultural memories live in the body as presence. We are possessed by the repetitions that we perform each day, by the sounds that reside in our soundscape. But we are also always involved in the coming to terms with cultural identity, the codification and objectification not only of other cultures, but also of our own. Like Fatna, whose narrative repeats the gestures and rhythms of trance time in her poetics but whose words objectify trance, the tension between the space of the body and the space of representation creates the rhythms of the now, the rhythms of travel and diaspora, the pull between home and antihome (Kapchan 2006). Embracing this dual possession of culture and this multiple relation to music and history, the Gnawa participate in a global economy of aesthetic tastes and styles while creating their particular relation to history and the ancestors.

♦ 11 ♦

CONCLUSION
THE ALCHEMY
OF THE MUSICAL
IMAGINATION

♦ ♦ ♦

In this book I have tracked the transformation of cultural imaginaries, from their embodiment in the gestures of possession trance through their poetic expression in narratives of possession, in their physical travels through space and time, and in their touchdowns and reconfigurations in dream narratives and narratives of epiphany. In the process, I've analyzed how concepts of race, identity, and history change and how "the racial imagination remains forever on the loose, subject to reformulation within the memories and imaginations of the social as it blurs into other categories constituting difference" (Radano and Bohlman 2000a: 5). We've witnessed the spiraling encounters of styles and identities, as well as the power of recursivity in these engagements—that is, how narrative, gestural, and musical poetics intertwine and return in different aesthetic guises.

Style may be one form of identity (Keil and Feld 1994); however there is more at stake in the global travels of Gnawa music than just a supplanting of one style with another or even a layering of styles and identities. The circulations and transformations of this music affect ontologies of difference. The body possessed by music is not the same as the body possessed by spirits, however easy it may be to spin a bridge of metaphor between these realms. Certainly there are striking continuities, as Judith Becker astutely notes (2004); listening to a line of music and becoming possessed by the spirit that passes through the sound involves relations between body, emotion, and sound that may be very similar to those experience by someone with a deep passion for the music. A different metaphysics is in play, however, with different assumptions about the world and its inhabitants (humans, spirits), as well as the agencies attributed to each. So while there is much to be gained from looking at the neuro-psychological continuities between trance and deep listening, it is important to recognize the differences—namely ways that subjects interpret experience to themselves. This is not just a matter of interpretation only, however, as insofar as experiences of the body are intertwined with an individual and cultural imaginary, they give rise to forms of action that have very real material consequences. Ways of being human—and tolerance for them—are at stake (Asad 2003: 112).

In the case of the Gnawa, the iconic relations between sound, affect, and body are specific. With the commodification of Gnawa music, some ontologies are privileged, and others fade away. Moreover, the ways of being that inhere in the ritual ceremony are the ones that tend to disappear, which those characterizing the "global imagination" are ascendant (Erlmann 1999). We know this not from theories of commodification (Jameson 1991), but from those who are bi-ontological, so to speak. The masters who move adeptly in both ritual and market worlds are also those who see the ritual world fading into a misty past as new Gnawi arise who may understand and mimic the style but do not comprehend the devotional import of the music. Style is certainly an index of identity, but the symbolic relations between these vectors are changing. In the ritual world of the Gnawa, music and spirits are in a nonarbitrary relationship wherein melodies, invocations, and spirits are intertwined. In this world, there are specific configurations of the sensorium that emphasize smell, commensality, and aurality. These motivated and iconic relations begin to unweave, however, when noninitiates take the music into other stylistic, cultural, and mediated realms. This is not to wax nostalgic for a time when a more holistic model reigned. Not at all. Indeed, there are many aspects of the ritual dispositions, the body hexi, of the Gnawa and those possessed that are shattering rather than unifying. I am not suggesting that time and tradition be arrested, nor do I promote a policing of the "jadba beat." Traditional practices change, as do notions of aesthetics and style. It is important to realize, however, that some aspects of sounding, being, and listening cannot be translated. While the Gnawa enjoy an internationally recognized connection to the African diaspora, their local practices are not immune from the effects of the spirits of fame, so to speak. It is not just the appropriation and transformation of a musical style that is at stake, but a different way of listening to, interpreting, and physically responding to the music. Trance is not the same for Randy Weston as it is for Si Mohammed Chaouqi, and yet trance music is represented and marketed as if it were.

Discourses about music do not simply reflect reality, but actively create identity, as well as a broad range of "projects"—political, cultural, and economic. They also create race and racism. They are historically contingent and instable (Guilbault 2000: 436). This means that although, for example, their pasts in slavery may always have been part of the way Gnawa have defined themselves, the salience of race as a discourse tied to their music is historically contingent. Surely the alignment with the larger African diaspora of the "black Atlantic" is fairly new.

TRANCE AND "THE SACRED"

Interest in the Gnawa arises not only from the world music market, but from international festival organizers and other culture brokers who actively create a transnational notion of "the sacred" in order to promote tourism, to facilitate religious understanding and tolerance, as well as to create phenomenological states (of trance, of ecstasy) that consumers find exotic and pleasurabllle (Kapchan in progress). The Gnawa are featured at the Fes Festival of Sacred Music, on a CD entitled *Trance* (that highlights trance music from across the globe), and on numerous other compact disc recordings with African American composers for whom the Gnawa represent an authentic African and spiritual voice. They have also participated in festivals all over Europe. Despite the fact that these collaborations and recontextualizations highlight the trance induced by the music, the postures and other sensory data from the ritual are usually absent (but see chapter nine). There is a rehierarchization of the senses at work. The spirits are alluded to but not ritually acknowledged, their emotional effects downplayed, yet "trance" as a vehicle for heightened emotional experience becomes a salient and appropriable feature.

In its recontextualization from a local context to a global one, "trance" transforms and reinvents "the sacred" in secular and market contexts. Sensory and emotional shifts occur as a result, shifts that point to changes in sociopolitical spheres as well. In "processes of historical transformations and/or cross cultural encounter, divergent sensory structures and commensalities can come into conflict with each other," notes C. Nadia Serematakis, "and some are socially repressed, erased or exiled into privatized recollections and marginal experience" (1994: 37). The commodification of ritual, for example, signals a national dependence on tourism with all that this entails, including the folklorization of tradition, the creation of "heritage," and an orientation toward the "other" (the tourist) in cultural performances. Moreover, the appropriation of only some aspects of a ritual produce a flattening of meaning that may result in the propagation of stereotypes and/or a religious fervor divorced from its historical base.

While visiting with the Gnawa in their Houston hotel room, I asked Abdellah about the consequences of taking sacred music to audiences unfamiliar with its meaning and power. He immediately became very serious. After a minute or so of consideration he replied in classical Arabic (changing the level of formality to a higher register), "There are more than 240 qit'a. We only play the ones that are clean (nqi). If we play the others, then we might cause harm to ourselves and to others. You have to know how to measure [khus-ak t-'arraf ki-fesh t-miyyaz]," he said, bringing his hand to his heart.

It is not unusual for recontextualizations of ritual and art forms to radically alter the meanings and effects of the same. What is particularly interesting is how these changes spiral back to the local context and affect transformation there. Whereas the order of the pantheon was once strict and inviolable, now some spirits may be dropped completely. The "Jewish spirits," for example, have for the most part fallen out of the ceremony altogether, whether because there are very few Jews left in Morocco or because these spirits are particularly difficult to master, drinking wine and handling prohibited substances. Although the Gnawa still heal the possessed in all-night ceremonies, the codification of the ritual, along with the emotional repertoire that it facilitates, are getting fuzzier. It would seem that having mastered the spirits and their concurrent emotional repertoires, the Gnawa are turning to the mastery of other things—material economies and self-representation. The fetishization of trance and of the Gnawa themselves is an obvious part of what happens when these traditions travel.

Gnawa spirit possession has traveled to new vistas as the Gnawa travel to Europe and the United States with European and African American recording artists, playing in venues as diverse as night clubs in Paris to festivals in Brittany and university concert halls in the United States. Their presence in these contexts, particularly in France where the audiences are in part of North African origin, means that possession trance occurs in quite different ways, with very different co-occurrence rules. Second generation immigrants in France, not brought up attending ceremonies, nonetheless seem to effect trance in these contexts, while other audience members are moved to dance by the music.

More than a fetishizing of sacred trance is at work in the cases examined here, however. There is also a fetishization of victimhood (and here I use the concept of fetish as much as a symbol of empowerment as it is of alienation). For the Gnawa, the emphasis on their past lives in slavery keeps alive a memory of the ancestors and provides a way to honor them and their suffering. Being a symbolic slave inheres in the bones as somatic memory—found in the gestures, in the lyrics of the songs, and in the relations of power the Gnawa have with their owners, the mluk. Working the spirits, as we have seen, is one way to symbolically master the presence of trauma in the past, allowing the Gnawa and their adepts and practitioners to change their status as victims into one of masters. For Weston, an acknowledged master of music, the link with the Gnawa is also related to a shared past in Africa and to a shared experience of loss and suffering. Returning to the music of the Gnawa is also a return to an African heritage and to a common history.

For the Bretons, on the other hand, the fetishization of victimhood takes a different form, involving a displacement of French North African politics onto the musical exchange and invoking ideologies of the Négritude and Celtitude movements. Partaking in the authenticity of the Gnawa trance music is a way of inserting their own musical performance in an international discourse that fetishizes trance and trance music as vehicles for creating the sacred extralocally. The Breton musicians are opening a space for themselves, and for Celtitude, in an already extant international discourse on sacred music and identity. This discourse—evident in the plethora of sacred music festivals all over the world, from Fes to Geneva to Los Angeles—transforms a secular space into a sacred one through sonic performance. Music thus becomes a liminar, at once creating and sacrilizing communities of audition and affect. The nature of this Durkheimian sacrilization is particular to this moment in history insofar as the sacred music (and, one imagines the sacred beliefs) of one local community is made to sanctify very different audiences. Disentangling the relations of power and desire in these contexts is no easy task, though the directions of import and export are telling. The Breton preoccupation with trance results from a lack in what might be called a cultural economy (indexed also by their anxiety about cultural loss), while the Gnawa's participation arises from a lack of a different kind—a lack of capital, trance being neither an exotic phenomenon for the Gnawa nor a rare one. Although Celtitude is very different than Négritude, the signs produced in this schismogenetic encounter enter a global economy and proceed to travel on their own.

The Gnawa may be said to participate in their own fetishization as exotic others as well. This was particularly poignant in the performances at the Divan de Monde, where the Gnawa performed segments from the lila that, recontextualized, were those most liable to be categorized as pagan, savage, and exotic. Such self-exotification was evident in Brittany as well, as the Gnawa danced to illustrate the theater piece created from Breton folklore and the *Thousand and One Nights*. The overwhelming parallel with minstrelsy in turn-of-the-century America was striking (Nyong'o 2002, 2005). That the Gnawa participate in their own commodification does not mean that they do so unintentionally. They are not pawns in the hands of the global music market. To the contrary, the Gnawa possess the ability to move with agility in both ritual and commercial realms. They are not only traveling spirit masters, but they also master the spirit of travel.

Change happens incrementally, as narratives are woven, words revoiced, and perceptions shaped through the production and consumption of sound, images, words, and gestures. The sacred is also constituted slowly and usually imperceptibly through ritual assemblages of sounds, icons, movements, smells, and tastes. As Ibn al-'Arabi notes, to taste is not only to perceive but also to become and to *be* the thing tasted. Subject and object unite in the sense of taste, as they do in possession trance. Tasting, music, and spirit possession are all ways of knowing the world and ways of being *in* the world. And they change our perception *of* the world, which is why understanding how these media travel is so important. Is this so different from Jacques Attali's assertion that music "is a way of perceiving the world" (1985: 4)?

That the Gnawa use aesthetic means to heal and empower themselves and others is not surprising. That they become symbols of the sacred on the world music market, however, is a result the Gnawa's lack of capital and the Euro-Americans' lack of access to forms of primary reality (in this case, trance). And where there is a vacuum, the winds rush in. Tracking the transformations of Gnawa rituals is thus also a measure of the reinvention of the sacred internationally. This does not necessarily entail a loss of tradition at the level of the local, only an ability on the part of the Gnawa to play several roles, to create history while also preserving memory in the bones of practice—*tagnawit*.

The forms the sacred is taking in the narratives, the movements, and the songs examined here index not only a fast-appearing transnational notion of the sacred, but an equally strong rift dividing what Weston has called "the voice of God" (sacred music) from "the noise of man" (market capitalism). The Gnawa act as bridges here, though whether the ways of being created in their traditions will eventually suffer from their adaptability is still unsure. "One thing about the Gnawa that I admire," Weston told me, "is that they always come home. No matter where they travel in the world, they always return to Morocco." For Weston, the return to one's place of origin is an essential aspect of sacred identity. Weston has great faith in the durability of the Gnawa culture in this regard. "They will be here when you and I are gone," he repeats like a mantra.

If music presages social structure (as Attali asserts), the desire for the experience of trance is telling. Indeed, "trance" elicits millions of entries on the World Wide Web, while "trance music" brings up nearly as many. Granted, the techno-genre of trance music is a far cry from the Afro-Celtic music produced in Brittany (T. Taylor 2001). Nonetheless, sound that produces trance (whether through rhythm or suggestion) is a fetish that many communities want to own. Furthermore, its "possession," so to speak, cannot simply be dismissed as an illusion or misrecognition; rather, it is an event that actively creates communities of affect that are sometimes quite diverse. Ironically, the entry into the global identity is through the appropriation of an extralocal but nonetheless culturally specific other for whom trance is a naturalized concept and experience. One local is made to authenticate another and swirls both into the spiral of global music and identity via the fetish of trance.

In this work I have examined the creation of the sacred in the aesthetic domain related to trance, in which emotions of passion, anguish, rapture, abjection, and others co-occur with certain smells, gestures, sounds, and rhythms. They also co-occur with images, though the relation to the specular has a marked status—objectifying and mediating, creating history, as Nora says, out of memory—that is, out of practice. I examined how a strand of African American history is appropriated into a Moroccan historical narrative of identity and, further, how the commemoration of this history (in sound, images, and words) affects this. *Dream narratives as well as narratives of possession* are other ways that history is revoiced and selves and worlds are created. Indeed, these narratives, along with *narratives of epiphany* demonstrate how hybrid cultural imaginations, spawned largely through processes of mediation, are authored and how they, in turn, come to inhabit us as if possessing independent agency. This not only attests to the power of performance to create political shifts at the national and the transnational levels through the harnessing of affect-laden aesthetic forms, but it also elucidates how both local and transnational imaginations are formed through music and discourse and the impact of such forms on the global marketplace. It also furthers our understanding of trance, explaining the contemporary fascination of such heightened affective experience in terms of global economies of desire that actively create the transnational category of the "sacred."

Geertz has noted that all ethnography is ultimately about the ethnographer—or at least about how the experience of ethnography has changed the ethnographer (1988). This book is no exception. I hope to have shown as well, however, the subtle and complex alchemy of the imagination as it inhabits and transforms aesthetic culture and, perhaps more importantly, the power of aesthetic forms to change cultural imaginaries. The *mundus imaginalis* does not belong only to the Gnawa or to the Islamic world. Far from it. It is a symbolic realm, sometimes an oneiric realm, which actively creates material realities. It is inhabited by some Gnawa, desired by some, ignored by others, just as it is inhabited and inhabits musicians like Randy Weston, Neil Clark, and Talib Kibwe (T. K. Blue) while evading others. Spirits, it should be said, are also referred to as "winds"—*al riyaḥ*. They are literally the winds of change. What they change and how have been the subjects of this book. "The winds" are changing transnational concepts of the sacred and transforming notions and experiences of subjectivity. They do this through the media most able to permeate borders and bodies—incense, tears, and laughter, and most of all words and music.

EPILOGUE

Towards the end of writing this book, I got in touch with the photographer Ariane Smolderen to see if she had any pictures to contribute to the study. I had met Ariane through Randy Weston in 2001 when we all happened to be in Marrakech at the same time. Ariane was documenting both the Gnawa and Randy Weston's collaboration with the Gnawa in photographic images.

Ariane sent me her photographs in April 2006. When I opened the well-protected package, I was astonished. Ariane had done what I had never dared to do: she had photographed the spirits. Her photos were striking, almost eerie, as the bodies portrayed were (to me) clearly possessed by other entities. What's more, they illustrated the metaphoric and iconic gestures that I was describing in perfect detail.

Then the dreams began. Lucid dreams of course. One night two spirits were on the threshold of my bedroom. They were threatening presences, and I began to recite ritual verses in order that they leave. A few days later, a spirit that I recognized as Sidi Mimun appeared and bound my feet, dragging me off the bed. During that dream, my three-year-old son Nathaniel was lying next to me, as he often is in the wee hours of the morning, and I felt my mother's presence close by, just as I had felt her near me in the vision I had had of floating above Essaouira so many years ago. The *chora*.

"*Henaya n-sabaqu*," Sidi Mimun had told me in a vision that year. And in many ways, the spirits did "win out," just as Sidi Mimun had said they would. The man lying peacefully beside me at that time is no longer at my side. (Indeed, the materialization of a man who possessed many qualities of a *jinn* played a part in our divorce.) And I subsequently spent four years away from my daughter, just as the vision had portended. Not all in France, though that is where I write the concluding lines of this story.

Fortunately there are beneficent spirits, angels perhaps, and they have been generous. I now lie next to another peaceful man at night, and my daughter has come through our four years of separation with few scars due to the love she received from my mother (and from me and her father in absentia).

I have decided to include Ariane's photographs. I do so, however, in deference to Sidi Mimun. He clearly has not left the scene. I offer this book to him as a propitiation, as I continue to work. . . .

NOTES

◆ ◆ ◆

INTRODUCTION: INITIATION *(pages 1–8)*

1. See Chlyeh 1998; Fuson 2006; Hell 2002b; Pâques 1991a; Schuyler 1981.

2. It is one of the premises of this book that diverse notions of the sacred are in efflorescence at this juncture of history (de Vries and Weber 2001). The mediation of aesthetic forms deemed "sacred" in international music festivals, film, and cyberspace creates new markets for what might be called religious consumption and sacred tourism. Contrariwise, both local and transnational communities manipulate media to produce the sacred in novel ways. Discourses around trance and music are implicated in all these processes.

3. See also Boddy 1994 for a complete bibliography and an impressive overview of this literature. The following works are only examples. On possession as pathology see Bastide 1972 and Devereux 1980; on possession as written about by functionalists, see Lewis 1966; possession as therapy, Crapanzano 1973; possession as protest and resistance (Lewis 1966); possession as theater and performance (Leiris 1958; Rouget 1985); possession as cultural text (Boddy 1989; Lambek 1981, 1993; Kapferer 1983); possession as situated expression of local identity and gendered subjectivity (Boddy 1989); possession as embodied history (Stoller 1995). See also K. Brown 1991; Masquelier 2001; A. Ong 1987; Wafer 1991.

4. This is particularly the case when belief (*doxa*) is challenged by the introduction of difference (heterodoxy), and when the desire to create "heritage" is recognized and acted upon (Bourdieu 1977; Kirshenblatt-Gimblett 1998).

5. The title "master" is used in several contexts in Morocco. It refers to anyone who has mastered a trade, whether applied to a carpenter, an electrician or a blacksmith. The application of the honorific "master" for the Gnawa may emerge from the historical link between metallurgy and ritual musicians (Griaule and Dieterlen 1965; Pâques 1964, 1976, 1991). It certainly refers to one who has mastered the spirits and knows how to "work" them rather than being worked over by them. In this, a Gnawa master has overcome subjugation (to spirits, to former masters) and is able to subjugate others (Diouri 1984)—mostly with the performative force of his music, for a m'allem is above all an expert musician whose mastery extends to and has been proven in the spiritual world. A master is never self-designated; rather mastery (and the title "m'allem") is conferred by older and more experienced masters (Hell 2002b; Chlyeh 1998; Pâques 1991). It is an accomplishment acquired through discipline and designated by practice, a symbol of knowledge and a title of specialization and expertise.

6. Literally "one who goes before," a *mqaddema* (sing.) is a woman who has experience with the spirits and thus may take responsibility for overseeing the ceremony.

She is said to know how to "work" the spirits, like a *shuwwafa* or clairvoyant (see Chlyeh 1998).

7. Indeed, there are some that say that Gnawa identity itself is essentially feminine (*tagawit kul-u mra'*).

8. See Combs-Shilling 1989; Crapanzano 1973, 1980; Dwyer 1982; Eickelman 1976; Evers Rosander 1991; C. Geertz, H. Geertz, and Rosen 1978; Hammoudi 1993, 1997; Kapchan 1996; Ossman 1994; Pandolfo 1997; Rosen 1984. For other examples see J. Goodman 2005; Ossman 2002; P. Silverstein 2004; P. Silverstein and Tetreault 2005; Tetreault 2004.

9. See Boddy 1989; Bowen 1993, 2003; Eickelman 1976; Ewing 1997; Lambek 1993; Masquelier 2001.

10. Anthropologist and ethnomusicologist Steven Feld uses the trope "schizophonia to schismogenesis" to "describe some dynamics of the mutualistic process by which ever more commercial and noncommercial music is subsumed under the heading of 'global culture' (Featherstone 1990)" (Feld 1994: 258). Pairing Murray Schafer's term, shizophonia (the splitting of a sound from its source of origin) with Gregory Bateson's concept of shismogenesis (spiraling reactions and interactions that involve the "symbiotic interdependence of the parties" in complementary or destructive ways), Feld talks about the conundrums created by the commodification of music in the "global ecumene" (Feld 1995: 265; see also Bateson 1972; Schafer 1985).

CHAPTER 1: EMPLACEMENT *(pages 11–23)*

1. In Moroccan Arabic even Qur'anic citations are sometimes colloquialized. I have transcribed the words as they were spoken.

2. The *lila* (literally "night") lasts from 10:00 or 11:00 at night until after dawn the next morning. I have condensed the description here.

3. All of the spirits demand a blood sacrifice—in the form of chickens, goats, or sheep; however Sidi Hamu is particularly associated with the flowing of blood. He is the genie of the slaughterhouse.

4. The word may also be translated as "kings" or "angels" (Diouri 1990: 184n.27). The term *mluk* is used in the ritual ceremonies to refer to the spirits, *jnun* being the more colloquial nonritual term.

5. Hell notes: *"Qu'elles renvoient au berbère ('du pays des Noir'), à des qualicatifs géographiques ('de Djenné,' 'de Guinée') ou encore à des dialects africains (Songhay, etc.), toutes les etymologies possibles de leur nom reflètent une origine africaine"* (1999b: 385).

6. Cf. Pâques 1976: 171.

7. Hale notes that "slaves from Ghana, imported to Marrakech, Morocco, from the eleventh century onward passed through a still-standing city gate called the Bab Agenaou, or Gate of the People of Ghana. Some of them eventually reached Spain, where they were called *guineos*. When the French ships, following in the paths of the earlier Spanish and Portuguese fleets, arrived on the coast of Senegal in the early six-

teenth century, probably manned at least in part by Spanish sailors who knew the coast, the captains may have asked their most experienced crewmembers about the noisy musicians and praise-singers who announced visits by local rulers. The answer, I speculate, was that these highly audible Africans were 'just a group of guineos'—or Africans—a term that evolved into *guiriots* and later *griots*. If true, this theory makes griot a term that has both African and Western roots" (Hale 1998: 357–366).

8. Pâques asserts that the "field of cloudy skies" is a paraphrase to designate the star called amzil, or "Blacksmith," a fact that aligns the Gnawa with the African cosmology. Amzil is the star Aldebaran. Pâques says that the Gnawa considered themselves to have come from this star, and that they believe it to be the "place where the sky and the earth unite: this is how the Blacksmith Demiurge penetrates the sky and through a double tornado makes the two worlds communicate" (1976: 171).

9. Southern Morocco is a desert culture, based on trade routes, sub-Saharan exchange and cultivation. The presence of sub-Saharan peoples in southern Morocco dates from at least the third century when the Sanhadja (an indigenous Amazighi tribe) went south to expand their territory. Many black Africans speak Berber and live in southern Morocco. Despite the history of both conquests and peaceful coexistence, however, the twelfth century did see the results of a slave trade from sub-Saharan Africa in a conscripted military under the Almohades. This presence became more apparent in the sixteenth century when the Saadians went south in search of gold and salt, using slave labor for their exploits, conquering Timbuktu and the Songhay empire, and exporting both goods and populations back to Morocco and particularly to Marrakech.

10. "When Islam came to the Berbers, it transformed the land of the Blacks into the land of the 'infidels' or 'pagans.' The marginalized status of Blacks was reduced further to slave status. Only 'infidels' were legally allowed to be enslaved. Therefore, the best place to obtain slaves was across the closest borders of the infidels, in the Sudan. This borderline, with the contrast in physical type, contributed to the connection of skin colour with slavery. So, the ancient rivalry between nomadic Berbers and sedentary Blacks that led towards cultural and racial prejudice took an Islamic form after the conversion of the Berbers to Islam since the seventh century" (El Hamel 2002: 44).

11. See Pâques 1991; Laroui 1982).

12. "*Les Gnawa du Palais fourniront en effet un enseignement oral à tous les autres Gnawa, qu'ils fussent ou non d'origine saharienne*" (Pâques 1991: 27, translation mine: 27; cf. Claisse 2003).

13. C. Becker lucidly analyzes the Ismkhan populations in southern Morocco and their memories of slavery. The Ismkhan are Amazighi-speaking former slaves who distinguish themselves from the Gnawa on the basis of racial purity (saying those who call themselves Gnawa intermarry with Arabs and Berbers) and market forces (the Gnawa play for tourists, while the Ismkhan traditionally do not). Yet economic

hardship in the region has recently led to the Ismkhan registering as a national folk-loric group, renaming themselves the "Gnawa of Khamlia," and performing the *ḥaḍra*, or trance-dance for tourists. (2002)

14. In *The Ban of the Bori*, Tremearne examined the rituals of Hausa people in Tunisia, what he referred to as "demon-dancing" (1968 [1914]). For examples in Africa see Boddy 1989; Lewis 1989; Rasmussen 1995; Stoller 1995. For North Africa, see Jankowsky 2006; Pâques 1991; Tremearne 1968 [1914]; Dermenghem 1954. For the Caribbean and South America, see Bastide 1972, 1978; Browning 1995, 1998; Maghnia 1996; Métraux 1958; cf. K. Brown 1991. Lambek notes that although the Mayotte have experienced slavery, the thematization of slavery plays little part in their experiences of possession (1993).

15. However, see C. Becker 2002.

16. The middle class is a fast-expanding group in Morocco only within the last thirty years or so (Kapchan 1996). This class is defined by practices of consumption, and they are as likely to consume the services of the Gnawa as not; however there are many among the bourgeoisie and the educated who consider the Gnawa a backward and superstitious group from whom they want to distance themselves.

17. The historical relation between Islam, music, and slavery is significant. Despite the fact that the distinction between master and slave in Muslim history has not always rested on a racial distinction (See Pâques 1991: 24; cf. Mohammed Ennaji 1999; Lovejoy 2004), there is a clear and assumed association between music and the culture of slavery in early Islamic texts, where slaves represented the profane relation of music to the soul, even while being held up as an example of the possibility of a higher calling.

It may be hard for Western audiences to appreciate the power that such music contains. In the Middle Ages there were active debates among Muslim theologians about the place of music in religion. Noting its power to distract the believer from all religious devotion, some theologians advocated its prohibition. Al-Ghazzali, the eleventh century philosopher and preacher, worked against this view, however, persuading his contemporaries that knowledge of God was based on experience (not the intellect) and that music, among other phenomena, was instrumental in that quest. Interestingly much of the debate centered on the music of slaves and particularly women. When the early interpreters of the Hadith (the Prophetic sayings and customs) were deciding if music and dancing were lawful or not, whether they could be used to praise God or whether such activities took one's mind away from God, discussion often centered on the singing and dancing of slave girls. Quoting the theologian Ash-Shaf'i, al-Ghazzali says, "'If the possessor of a slave-girl gather men together to listen to her, he is of light understanding, you shall reject his testimony.' . . . And as for Malik (may God have mercy on him!), he has forbidden singing. He said, 'When a man buys a slave girl and finds that she is a singer, then it is his duty to send her back'" (al-Ghazzali 1909). Music was thought by many early Islamic thinkers to be akin to games, a distraction not worthy of the attention of the believer, whose time was better spent in prayer. There were those however—most notably the Sufis and their advocates, including al-Ghazzali—who not only found music to be permissible, but also desirable in that its power could bring the believer closer to the secrets of the heart. Indeed, rather than deny the latent power of music, al-Ghazzali acknowledged it fully, stating that music was, in effect, a mirror that made the secret desires of the heart manifest. Although the desires may be for God, or for other, less sacred unions, it was not music per se that was at fault. Speaking of music in terms that evoke alchemical metaphors, al-Ghazzali writes:

Lo! Hearts and inmost thoughts are treasuries of secrets and mines of jewels. Infolded in them are their jewels like as fire is infolded in iron and stone, and concealed like as water is concealed under dust and loam. There is no way to the extracting of their hidden things save by the flint and steel of listening to music and singing, and there is no entrance to the heart save by the ante-chamber of the ears. So musical tones, measured and pleasing, bring forth what is in it and make evident its beauties and defects. For when the heart is moved there is made evident that only which it contains like as a vessel drips only what is in it. And listening to music and singing is for the heart a true touchstone and a speaking standard; whenever the soul of the music and singing reaches the heart, then there stirs in the heart that which in it preponderates. (Ibid.: 199)

For al-Ghazzali, music made evident the hidden ponderings and workings of the heart. In his treatise on music and ecstasy, he describes them as active vehicles for communion with God. Nonetheless, the texts that he engages and refutes (in lengthy quotes within quotes) often describe music as akin to folly. Even when they do not, however, the association of music and slavery is pervasive: "'We have known Abu Marwan the Qadi, who had slave girls who chanted in public and whom he had prepared to sing to the Sufis,'" said al-Ghazzali, quoting Abu Talib al-Makki in his argument for the benefits of using music in the service of religion. And then, quoting Ibn Daoud, he racially marks another saint who, in the fourteenth century, wrote in favor of music and devotion: "Further he said, 'Abu-l-Hasan al-'Asqalani, the black, one of the Saints, was wont to listen to music and singing and to be distracted with longing thereat, and he wrote a book about it, and overthrew in that book those who blame music; and similarly, a number have written to overcome those blaming it" (Ibid.: 205). "Further, he [the Prophet] (whom God bless and save!) said, 'God listens more intently to a man with a beautiful voice reading the Qur'an than does the master of a singing slave-girl to his slave-girl.'" (Ibid.: 209).

There is no mention in these texts about the illegality of slavery under Islam. That 'Abu-l-Hasan al-'Asqalani, "the black," was a saint and not a slave, should warn us not to collapse the categories of race, gender, and slavery. Indeed, some of the slaves of this period were captives of other tribes and racially indistinguishable from their masters (often Circassian).

18. See Boddy 1989; Masquelier 2001; Rouch 1989 1960; Stoller 1989a).

19. "Face à cette prétendue «culture» des maîtres esclavagistes où «le triomphe de l'esprit économique sur l'imaginatif» provoqua «un schisme entre l'art et la vie», les esclaves noirs sauveg-ardèrent l'essence de la culture africaine où «il était, et il est toujours, inconcevable de séparer la musique, la danse, le chant ou tout autre produit de l'activité artistique de l'existence de l'homme ou de son culte des dieux. Toute expression étant un produit de la vie, était la beauté».

"Mais cette essence, ils la sauvegardèrent en créant des formes nouvelles, issues de leur vie, de leur environnement, de leur réalité concrète. Dans le très beau livre que nous citons sur «Le peuple du blues», Leroi Jones en apporte la démonstration. La musique ni la danse «ne produisent d'objets. C'est ce qui les sauva». Mais cette musique et cette danse devinrent, de l'esclave noir du Sud à l'ou-vrier noir des ghettos de Chicago jusqu'au combattant des «Black Panthers», le negro spiritual, le blues, puis le «free jazz». (Serfaty 1969, emphasis in the original).

For another discussion of the Pan-African Festival see J. Goodman 2005: 52–55.

20. See Monson 2003b [2000]: 331 for more examples.

21. Dialogism is not just a dialogue; it is a relativization—all the voices contribut-ing their (sometimes multiple and contradictory) messages, which are lived and in-terpreted differently by each participant (Bakhtin 1981). See Wafer 1991; cf. Boddy 1989; Browning 1995; Lambek 1993.

CHAPTER 2: INTOXICATION (pages 24–46)

1. For Frazer, in his work *The Golden Bough*, magic forces and constrains, while re-ligion conciliates.

2. Unlike these artisans, however, the realm of magic contained no causality like that of fire transforming clay into a pot; rather, in the realm of magic, techniques in one realm (incantations, for example) produced effects in another (healing the body).

3. Pels notes, "Anthropology, more than any other scholarly discourse on magic, was responsible for the interpretation of magic as an antithesis of modernity and for the production of the peculiar ambiguity and entanglement of magic and moder-nity . . . " (2003: 5).

4. See also Meyer and Pels 2003; Taussig 1997.

5. In his discussion of various forms of trance, Rouget (1985: 273) notes that sometimes even Sufi *dhikrs*, or remembrance ceremonies, exhibit the qualities of pos-session trance, particularly when the entranced person is identified (in trance) with his *shaykh* or with an ancestor.

6. The 'Aissawa follow the example of Ibn 'Aissa, also called Shaylh al-kamal, the complete *shaykh*. He is buried outside of Meknes. Their liturgy is codified and writ-ten, as are the writings of their saint. See Brunel 1926.

7. See Noyes 2003: 3 for an example of a festival that is defined as "addiction."

8. "Les Gnawa se dissent les gens du hla, cette partie cachee de la creation ou regnent les entites invisibles. Ils sont de ce fait, par essence, des marginaux jouant de cette image d'etrange etrangers (double sens que possede le terme arabe gherib). Porteurs d'un contre monde, les Gnawa se meuvent

la nuit et aux frontiers du licite. Marquee d'une ambiguitie fondamentale, ils sont des trans-gresseurs qui peuvent manipuler impunement le sang et controller les forces les plus dangereuses. Incarnant 'l'inquietante etrangete,' les descendants des esclaves noirs se voient investis des pouvoirs surnaturels les plus puissants" (Hell 2001: 160, translation mine).

9. "La science gnawi est une alchimie. Pour elle, le Démiurge est le grand forgeron dont le sacrifice fut à l'origine de l'univers, fragmenté et disperse. Tout le rituel d'une lila (nuit) a pour l'objet d'inviter l'adepte à rassembler les elements epars de l'univers, qui sont en meme temps ceux de sa personne—car l'homme est l'univers, qui est le Démiurge—afin de tenter, par la purification de ses composants, de reconstituer la grande unite primordiale de l'Eternel, du Mort-Vivant, du Forgeron." Pâques 1991: 80.

10. "Faire le derdeba c'est 'apprendre le métier,' c'est apprendre comment l'ame va de la vie a la mort pour revenir a la vie, en passant par les sept couleurs de lUnivers. Ces couleurs sont les etapes de l'annee et de la vie humaine, ainsi que celles de l'orge qui, comme l'homme, entre cru dans la mort et en resort cuit pour servir de nourriture au demiurge-cherif. La derdeba aidera l'adepte a franchir ces diverse etapes" (Pâques 1991: 255).

11. Gnawa science is alchemy. In it, the Demiurge is the great blacksmith who was sacrificed at the beginning of the universe, fragmented, and dispersed. The object of the entire ritual of the lila (night) is to invite the adept to reassemble the separate elements of the universe that are at the same time his own elements—as man is the universe, who is the Demiurge—in order to attempt, by the purification of these parts, to reconstitute the great primordial unity of the Eternal, of the Dead-Living, of the Blacksmith (Pâques 1991: 80, translation mine). ["La science gnawi est une alchimie. Pour elle, le Démiurge est le grand forgeron dont le sacrifice fut à l'origine de l'univers, fragmenté et disperse. Tout le rituel d'une lila (nuit) a pour l'objet d'inviter l'adepte à rassembler les elements epars de l'univers, qui sont en meme temps ceux de sa personne—car l'homme est l'univers, qui est le Démiurge—afin de tenter, par la purification de ses composants, de reconstituer la grande unite primordiale de l'Eternel, du Mort-Vivant, du Forgeron." (Ibid.)]. In this book I do not attempt to "reconstruct a unity" however, nor do I wish to generalize folk taxonomies of experience.

12. Michael Maier, quoted in Roob 2001: 11.

13. Chittick says, "Though more real and 'subtle' than the physical world, the World of the Imagination is less real and 'denser' than the spiritual world, which remains forever invisible as such. In Islam, the later intellectual tradition never tires of discussing the imaginal realm as the locus wherein spiritual realities are seen in visionary experience and all the eschatological events described in the Koran and the Hadith take place exactly as described. If on the Day of Resurrection, as reported by the Prophet, 'death is brought in the form of a salt-colored ram and slaughtered,' this is because imaginal existence allows abstract meanings to take on concrete form. And if all the works we performed during our lives are placed in the Scales, the good deeds in the right pan and the bad deeds in the left, this is because imagination brings about the subtlization of corporeal activities" (Chittick 1989: ix).

14. Alchemy was a potent metaphor for the early Sufi mystics. Muslim theologian Al-Ghazzali (1058–1111) in *The Alchemy of Happiness* (*Kimiya as-Sa'dat*) wrote of the purification of the soul whereby the human is purged of lower desires to ultimately become angelic in nature: "The spiritual alchemy which operates this change in him, like that which transmutes base metals into gold, is not easily discovered. . . . It is to explain that alchemy and its methods of operation that the author has undertaken this work" (1997: xv).

15. The belief in spiritual evolution and the ability to ascend in levels of gnosis is firmly rooted in the texts of Muslim philosophers like Ibn al-'Arabi and al-Ghazzali, which can be read as manuals for the aspiring Muslim saint. These texts have since entered a worldview that, while rarely articulated, provides conceptual and psychological maps for living a spiritual life in North Africa. In what follows I draw upon the epistemological and ontological visions of these two authors as I would on any contemporary social theorist to elucidate the tropes and experiences of the Gnawa who, themselves, do not espouse these ideologies in any explicit way.

16. In contemporary efforts to balance the mind/body bias in Western ideology, the body has entered analysis not just as an object but also as an agent of cultural production. Much emphasis has been put on the notion of performativity—the enactment of publicly recognized (and discursively constituted) meanings. Building upon Austin's notion of linguistic performativity (1962), wherein language does what it says (for example, "I promise"), the concept of performativity has been expanded to include embodied enactments of gender (Butler 1999) and religious identity (Mahmood 2005). Phelan (1993a) applies the term "performative writing" to writing that is evocative and transformative. In Performance Studies, in particular, the notion of performativity has enabled scholars to analyze cultural enactments that are ephemeral, part of a cultural "repertoire" rather than a cultural "archive" (D. Taylor 2003). The resurgence of interest in things performative has had many positive effects— the first among them, the restoration of the body to a place of importance in sociocultural analysis, illuminating how aesthetic practices create their object in performance. To insist that cultural meaning is constituted only at the intersection of the body and its history, however, is to elide some other equally important aspects of meaning making. Investigations of imagination, in particular, have suffered. As religious scholar William C. Chittick notes,

> In putting complete faith in reason, the West forgot that imagination opens up the soul to certain possibilities of perceiving and understanding not available to the rational mind. . . . By granting an independent ontological status to imagination . . . Islamic philosophy has gone against the mainstream of Western thought. (Chittick 1989: ix–x)

This viewpoint is not limited to scholars of religion. Phenomenologist Edward Casey begins his book *Imagining* (1976) by noting the neglect of the imagination in the history of Western philosophy. From Plato onwards, he says, it has been vilified as a lesser way of knowing. Although the imagination was celebrated by the Romantics and the surrealists, those movements did little to elucidate the epistemological aspects of imagination. It is necessary, Casey asserts, "to acknowledge the amplitude and intrinsic power of imagining" (1976: xi). For Casey, the imagination is "an autonomous mental act" that is nonetheless "specifically sensuous": "imaging occurs in the specific modalities of visualizing, audializing, smelling in the mind's nose, feeling in the mind's muscles, tasting with the mind's tongue, and so on" (1976: 41). He does not deny the integration of the mental faculties, but encourages us not to make them into a hierarchy:

> Any such hierarchy is *pre-evaluative* in the sense that it determines or expresses in advance which acts are more, and which less, important. . . . In order to avoid this kind of foreclosure, we must remain open to what can be called the *multiplicity of the mental*. Within this multiplicity there is no strict hierarchical structure—only a proliferation of unforeclosable possibilities. An acute and continuing sensitivity to the multiplicity of the mental will allow us to acknowledge what is unique in each mental act and thus to view imagination as nonderivative, as a phenomenon to be evaluated on its own terms. (1976: 19, emphasis in original)

If the imagination has suffered from a dearth of analysis, scholars are once again exploring its parameters. Anthropologist Vincent Crapanzano, for example, returns to Ibn al-'Arabi's notion of *barzakh*, or isthmus, to illustrate the "inter-space-time" of the ethnographic process, as well as the paradoxes that characterize the imagination and its analysis (2004: 6, 58; see also Pandolfo 1997). (There is nothing in existence but *barzakhs*," says Ibn al-'Arabi, "since a *barzakh* is the arrangement of one thing between two other things . . . and existence has no edges (*ṭaraf*)" [III 156.27, quoted in Chittick 1989: 14; cf. Crapanzano 2004; Pandolfo 1997]). He explores the ever-elusive "horizons" of cultural analysis, what Casey calls the "proliferation of unforeclosable possibilities," exemplified, in part, in Crapanzano's focus on "hope" (Crapanzano 2004; E. Casey 1976). Anthropologist Arjun Appadurai also makes the imagination a central aspect of cultural critique. The epoch of globalization, he asserts, is "marked by a new role for the imagination in social life" (2001: 140). Appadurai states that the

> imagination is no longer a matter of individual genius, escapism from ordinary life, or just a dimension of aesthetics. It is a faculty that informs the daily lives of ordinary people in myriad ways: It allows people to consider migration, resist state violence, seek social redress, and design new forms of civic association and collaboration, often across national boundaries. This view of the role of the imagination as a popular, social, collective fact in the era of globalization recognizes its split character. On the one hand, it is in and through the imagination that modern citizens are disciplined and controlled—by states, markets, and other powerful interests. But it is also the faculty through which collective patterns of dissent and new designs for collective life emerge. As the imagination as a social force itself works across national lines to produce locality as a spatial fact and as a sensi-

bility (Appadurai 1996), we see the beginnings of social forms without either the predatory mobility of unregulated capital or the predatory stability of many states. (2001: 6–7)

And literary critic and poet Susan Stewart invokes the eighteenth century philosopher Vico and his ideas of "corporeal imagination" to suggest that we not forget the interdependency of the senses with the imaginative process (2002: 15). For Vico, early humans were poets, and it was through language that the speaking subject emerged. Stewart notes: "Only when poetic metaphors make available to others the experience of the corporeal senses can the corporeal senses truly appear as integral experiences. The self (and here again the paradigm, is the self lost in the absolute darkness) is compelled to make forms—including the forms of persons striving to represent their corporeal imaginations to others" (2002: 15). In these authors and others, we see the emergence of what might be called the performativity of the imagination in cultural analysis.

17. Correspondences between Islamic and European worldviews are also present in the notion of *discordia concors*, "harmony created from dissimilarity." Such a cosmological understanding resonates with the philosophy of Sufi mystic Ibn al-'Arabi, for whom paradox was at the root of human existence. "No one will find true knowledge of the nature of things by seeking explanations in the 'either/or,'" Ibn al-'Arabi writes. "The real situation will have to be sought in 'both/and' or 'neither/not.' Ambiguity does not grow up simply from our ignorance: it is an ontological fact, inherent in the nature of the cosmos. Nothing is certain but Being Itself, yet It is the 'coincidence of opposites' (*jam' al-aḍḍād*), bringing all opposites together in a single reality" (Ibn al-'Arabi cited in Chittick 1989: 112).

For Ibn al-'Arabi, neither sense perception nor rationality can bring together opposites; only *imagination* possesses the strength to combine the two. Thus what Agrippa described as *discordia harmonia* was achieved via the imagination. Harnessing the power of the imagination is equivalent to working magic.

18. Cf. Lambek 1993: 315.

19. See J. Becker 2004; Crapanzano 2004; Eickelman 1976; Hell 2001, 2002b; Hirshkind 2001; Pandolfo 1997; Pâques 1991; Rouget 1985.

20. Tomlinson "explores those musico-magical practices and patterns of thought that have appeared to [him] to implicate music most profoundly in the theory and operation of magic, to involve music most centrally as itself a magical power (1993: xiii).

21. "Musical magic throughout the Renaissance tended to fall into classes. . . . There was, first, the magic of music's effects on sublunar objects: on inanimate things, on animals, on the human body, and even on the soul in its earthly exile. The natural magic of music embraced in part the rich story of music's effects on the psyche, though this had obvious celestial and supercelestial implications as well. Second came the role of music in governing the movement of heavenly bodies, the music of the spheres. Here music converged on astrology and astronomy, and its practice en-

tailed the mimesis of celestial musics in order to influence or enhance their effects on earth. Finally, music could bring about the most direct kinds of gnosis, inducing ecstatic trances and frenzied possessions" (Tomlinson 1993: 65). Tomlinson takes issue with Foucault, who defined the sixteenth-century episteme as one based on the similarities found in the *written* word (Tomlinson 1993; Foucault 1972).

22. Cf. Foucault 1972. Because there is apparent contradiction in the Names of God, Ibn al-'Arabi speaks of the Divine Conflict, which he asserts is also the source of all transformation. There are two kinds of servanthood described by Ibn al-'Arabi—the one toward the Divine Essence is compulsory (iḍṭirārī), while the one towards the divine names is voluntary (ikhtiyārī). He speaks of the names, the attributes of God, as having their own agency. Each name wants to possess the human being:

> Through compulsion and in reality they [the prophets] are the servants and the possession of the Essence. But the divine names seek them to make their effects manifest through them. So they have free choice (ikhtiyār) in entering under whichever name they desire. The divine names know this, so the divine names designate wages for them. Each divine name wants this slave of the Essence to choose to serve (khidma) it rather than the other divine names. It says to him, "Enter under my command, for I will give you such and such." Then he remains in the service of that name until he is called by the Lord in respect of his servanthood to the Essence. (Ibn al-'Arabi, quoted in Chittick 1989: 56)

23. Couliano notes that

> Renaissance culture was a culture of the phantasmic. It lent tremendous weight to the phantasms evoked by inner sense and had developed to the utmost the human faculty of *working actively upon and with phantasms*. It had created a whole dialectic of Eros in which phantasms, which at first foisted themselves upon inner sense, ended by being manipulated at will. It had a firm belief in the power of phantasms, which were transmitted by the phantasmic apparatus of the transmitter to that of the receiver. It also believed that inner sense was preeminently the locale for manifestations of transnatural forces—demons and the gods.
>
> By asserting the idolatrous and impious nature of phantasms, the Reformation abolished at one stroke the culture of the Renaissance. And since all Renaissance "sciences" were structures built on phantasms, they too had to be overpowered by the weight of the Reformation. (Couliano 1987: 193–194, emphasis in the original)

24. Indeed, "the cultural event that some call the 'twelfth-century Renaissance' signals the rediscovery of Greek Antiquity through Arab channels" (Couliano 1987: 10).

25. The concept of radiations has clear associations with the sympathetic magic of later centuries (Mauss 1972 [1902]).

26. "Eros" here is used in the Platonic sense to mean self-consciousness (Couliano 1987: 119, 127).

27. Tomlinson notes that for Ficino, "the spirit was the nexus of perception";

spirit, however perceived in *images*, including "music images." In effect, "Images were the link between sense perception and the soul's cognition—the passports, so to speak, across the spiritual borderline separating the sensible and intelligible realms" (Tomlinson 1993: 121). Music images were also *produced* by the musician, however, and following Ficino (influenced by al-Kindi), they went on to life a life of their own, sometimes as demons (Tomlinson 1993: 124–125).

28. Couliano notes that in the Renaissance, "Spirits are phantasms that acquire an autonomous existence through a practice of visualization resembling first and last the Art of Memory" (1987: 125).

29. Cf. Couliano 1987: 125. Tomlinson writes:

But for Ficino all magicians must have operated in the realm of images; they worked in a world dominated by image, putting into action al-Kindi's creative imagination, making phantasms that acquired true existence. In Ficino's view, in other words all magic came down to the magician's exercise of "demonic contrivances."

This must include the magic of sounds, of course, and with it the magic of music. Indeed in his eleventh summa for the Phaedrus, speaking of Socrates' inspiration, Ficino explained the demons' ability to move our imaginations through the sense of hearing. This must have happen, he surmised, in one of two ways:

Undoubtedly either [the demon] efficaciously propagates the imagined concept in the innermost hearing, or the demon itself forms the sound [*vocem*] by a certain marvelous motion in its own spiritual body and with this same motion strikes, almost as a kind of sound, on the spiritual body of Socrates. When this vibrates, the innermost hearing of Socrates is excited to the same vibration. (Allen, *Marsilio Ficino and the Phaedran Charioteer*, 1981: 139)

[. . .] Musical magic is therefore far from [an] utterly nondemonic force. . . . It is instead one of the many potent sonic images created by the demonic operation of our imagination. (Tomlinson 1993: 124–125, italics in original)

30. Here Rouget's distinction between communial trance and possession or fakirist trance is pertinent, the first being a trance entered into deliberately through the practice of chanting, the second an induced trance brought on by the possessing jinn. Yet, as Rouget notes, in practice, the final states are difficult to distinguish. A woman in a possession trance may lose herself in the *hal*, calling out for God, and be answered by someone nearby, an attendant: "He is." "*allah, allah, kayn!*" Such sacred performances exist in Gnawa possession ceremonies just as they do in more conservative Sufi *dhikrs*.

31. Viviana Pâques has aptly called this healing cult "the religion of slaves," evoking their history in slavery as well as their piety. In Islam, however, all the devout are referred to as worshippers, which is the same word as slave—'*abid*. The word Islam itself comes from the root, *sa la ma*, to submit. Faith is a higher station than submis-

sion and not one to which many can sincerely lay claim initially. On the other hand, all who worship God may be called ʻabid-llah, the slaves or servants of God. The verb ʻa ba da means "to worship," while the derivative noun, ʻabd, is often prefixed to the other ninety-nine nominatives of God and used as a first name: ʻabd allāh, the slave or servant of God, ʻabd al-majīd, the slave of the Glorious, ʻabd al-ghani, the slave of the Rich, ʻabd al-nāṣir, the slave of the Victorious, ʻabd al-ḥay, the slave of the Life Giving, ʻabd al-ḥāfiz, the slave of the Protector, ʻabd al-ḥamīd, the slave of the Blesser, ʻabd al-jabbār, the slave of the Powerful, ʻabd al-ṣamad, the slave of the Eternal, ʻabd al-ḥaqq, the slave of the Truth, and so forth.

The proximity that many slaves had to the royal family (themselves acknowledged as descendants of the Prophet Mohammed and thus possessors of baraka, or divine grace) somewhat reduced the stigma of slavery in one's past, especially since baraka is considered physically contagious—that is, closeness to those endowed with baraka makes one able to receive that baraka as well. What's more, many of the slaves brought to Morocco from Timbuktu in the fifteenth and sixteenth centuries became elite soldiers of Moulay Ismail. This is not to misrecognize the presence of racism in Morocco or to underestimate its effects. There is no doubt that among all the Sufi ṭuruq (recognized paths, or Sufi brotherhoods) and healing ṭawaʼif (groups) in Morocco, the Gnawa are at the very bottom of the hierarchy. (Though Sufi-influenced, the Gnawa do not consider themselves a Sufi brotherhood, nor are they recognized as such by any of the other Sufi lineages present in Morocco or elsewhere. The Gnawa are considered a ṭaʼifa, a group or community, devoted to healing the possessed.) They are considered magicians by some Moroccans—people who possess the power to manipulate the spirits to their own, and sometimes less-than-benevolent, advantage. Although I have heard the Gnawa refer to the spirits as helping them to achieve their desires, I have never heard them speak of harnessing the spirits' powers to hurt another. The popular conception of the Gnawa as dangerous among Moroccans is, in my estimate, based on fear, ignorance, and misrecognized racism. Although many Moroccans take pride in the diversity of their country and its lack of racism, racial intermarriage is not common. There is another result of their misperception by nonpractitioners, however—namely, the occulting of their traditions and their oral history. According to Pâques, the Gnawa themselves have cultivated the disdain in which they are held in order that their subtle religious and philosophical system of beliefs remain secret (1991: 22).

32. Caruth refers to post-traumatic stress disorder as "possession by the past" insofar as "overwhelming events of the past repeatedly possess, in intrusive images and thoughts, the one who has lived through them" (1995: 151).

33. Adapted from Welte and Aguadé 1996: 49.

34. Literally, the "owner of I."

35. Form III of the verb.

36. Form II of the verb.

37. See Briggs 1996; Desjarlais 1992; Laderman 1991; Laderman and Roseman 1996; Roseman 1991.

38. This discussion was recorded in Malika's home in the spring of 1995.

39. A *sherif* (masc.) or *sherifa* (fem.) is technically a descendant of the Prophet Mohammed, but the terms has been appropriated as a term of respect or politeness in Morocco. Waiters, for example, are often called to the table by the title sherif.

40. See also Bourguignon 1968.

41. See also Benjamin 1968.

42. This is as true of listening as it is of trance. As Judith Becker has shown in her comprehensive study of trance phenomena, music, emotion, and the brain, the trancelike states of those who become engrossed by listening to music is not that different from those of trancers:

> Both trancing and deep listening are physical, bodily processes, involving neural stimulation of specific brain areas that result in outward, visible physical reactions such as crying, or rhythmical swaying or horripilation. Deep listeners may stop there and remain physically still. Trancers seem to experience an even more intense neural stimulation that may be expressed in some form of gross physical behavior such as dancing. Both, I suspect, are initially aroused at a level of precognition that quickly expands in the brain to involve memory, feeling, and imagination. Deep listening and trancing, as processes, are simultaneously physical *and* psychological, somatic *and* cognitive. (2004: 29, emphasis in original)

The differences between trance and deep listening should not be elided; indeed, they have real material and ontological consequences (see conclusion). Nonetheless, both activities are active processes.

43. Perception requires both the perceived object and the perceiving subject. As Merleau-Ponty notes, perception is an ek-static act, actually reaching out into the world even as the world floods into the transcendent subject.

As an Islamic philosopher and theologian, al-Ghazzali helps explain a relation to the senses and to experience that is still applicable to understanding the aesthetics of spirit possession in Morocco. It is useful, however, to put these ideas into relation with ideas, namely phenomenology, that are in many ways complementary, particularly as delineated by Merleau-Ponty. As a philosophy that is not theistic, phenomenology nonetheless shares with Sufism the premise that all knowledge is based in experience. As a point of departure, phenomenology is a method, "a matter of describing, not of explaining or analyzing" ((Merleau-Ponty 1962: viii).

44. "[T]he sense of smell is the most important factor in the laying of spells on people; magic, in order to achieve its greatest potency, must enter through the nose" (Malinowski 1929: 449, quoted in Howes 1991b: 130). See also Lambek 1981 for a discussion of olfaction and transition.

45. Al-Ghazzali goes on to elaborate: "And, therefore, did al-Khadir, when he was

asked in the dream concerning Hearing, say, 'It is pure slipperiness, there stand not fast upon it save the feet of the learned.' This is because it moves the secret parts and the hidden places of the heart, and it disturbs it as that drunkenness which confounds the reason, disturbs it, and almost loosens the knot of fair behavior from the secret thoughts, except in those whom God Most High protects by light of His guidance and the benevolence of His protection" (1997: 711–712).

CHAPTER 3: "A GESTURE NARROWLY DIVIDES US FROM CHAOS"
(pages 47–80)

1. "*Tous ces jeux, ces sacrifices, ces danses, aux-quels tout le monde peut assister sont, bien sûr, en partie déstinés à cacher les connaissances secrètes des initiés, mais ils constituent en même temps des procédés mnémotechniques permettant de retrouver dans les moindres détails toute cette alchimie de l'âme humaine qui est celle du monde et de Dieu.*" (Pâques 1991: 24)

2. Feld notes the relation of tears and spirit possession among the Kaluli: "[A]udience members may burst into tears" upon recognizing the identity of a possessing spirit (1982: 182). In the Kaluli example, tears and the ability of song to move to tears is a manifestation of the mythic transformation of nature, symbolized by birds, to culture, symbolized by song (Feld 1990: 42).

3. Trancing bodies also rock, cry, and are soothed by the touch of others, though the body in trance is a more movement-filled body; trance resembles a frenetic dance, while lamentation and keening are usually engaged in while sitting.

4. Although men as well as women are possessed, the associations with the feminine genre of lamentation nonetheless exist, giving meaning to the statement by one m'allem, "tagnawit kul-ha mr'a, Gnawa identity is all [about] woman."

5. Moroccan psychoanalyst Mohammad Fouad, for example, told me that many of his patients have tried or try tradition forms of healing simultaneously with their psychoanalysis (Fouad 1995). He introduced me to one of his patients who had a long experience with the Gnawa, but who eventually left as she thought they were taking financial advantage of her distress and her possession by spirits.

6. This narrative does not recount a chronological sequence. Sidi Mimun comes before Sidi Musa.

7. In the following pages I describe these experiences but resist enclosing them in a definitive analysis. As Merleau-Ponty notes, description is the first and most important step in any phenomenological endeavor (1962). My perception and ways of perceiving changed when I entered the world of the Gnawa, and what may be called a different spatio-temporal orientation, and a different imaginary, has remained in my repertoire of emotions.

8. See J. Becker 2004: 30.

9. The link between experiences of time and the senses goes back to Plato, who argued "that time is not an aspect of eternity or a dimension of space and matter, but is rather a product of our *sensations* working in combination with our beliefs" (S.

Stewart 2002: 199, emphasis mine). Senses and beliefs are also shared and intersubjective. In part II, I explore how experiences of space and time change when these same sacred gestures are performed as spectacles in commercial performance venues.

10. See F. Goodman 1990 for a fascinating case study of gesture and emotion.

11. While examining the space of gesture and the gesture of space, I veer away from the majority of gesture studies in their preoccupation with what McNeill calls the "speech-gesture synchrony" (1992). These studies examine the interdependency of language and gesture and the meaning that emerges in their simultaneous performance and mutual constitution.

12. Since time "presupposes a view of time," of necessity it "arises from my relations to things" (Merleau-Ponty 1962: 411–412).

13. The past in slavery is mostly invoked in lyrics like "*jabu-ni man as-sudan;* they brought me from Sudan."

14. Among the bodily techniques for the spiritual transformation that al-Ghazzali advocates, music and ecstasy play a part. Indeed, the longing that music awakens in the soul for beauty is an essential factor in bringing the seeker to God. Not only must the lover know how to listen to the sound that inspires devotion, however, but the limbs must also move in sympathy.

> And the ecstasy of him who is consumed in love of God Most High is in proportion to his understanding, and his understanding is in proportion to his power of imagination, and what he imagines does not necessarily agree with what the poet meant or with his language. This ecstasy is truth and sincerity; and he who fears the peril of the destruction of the other world is fitted that his intellect should be disturbed in him and his limbs agitated. (al-Ghazzali, as translated by MacDonald 1901: 239)

Indeed, the seeker should not wait for an ecstatic state, or *hal*, to descend, but should, according to al-Ghazzali, adopt the physical gestures and emotional postures of what he calls the "Glorious States" of ecstasy even if they are not spontaneous. It is in such imitation, he says, that the spirit is trained and that states of grace and inspiration are ontologically produced.

> The division of ecstasy [*wājd*] is divided into that which itself attacks and that which is forced, and that is called affecting ecstasy [*tawajūd*]. Of this forced affecting ecstasy there is that which is blameworthy, and it is what aims at hypocrisy and at the manifestation of the Glorious States in spite of being destitute of them. And of it there is that which is praiseworthy, and it leads to the invoking of the Glorious States and the gaining of them for oneself and bringing them to oneself by device; for the Glorious States may be brought through such gaining for oneself. And therefore the Apostle of God commanded him who did not weep at the reading of the Qur'an that he should force weeping and mourning; for the beginning of these States is sometimes forced while their ends are thereafter true. And

how should forcing not be a cause that that which is forced should become in the sequel a matter of nature? Everyone who learns the Qur'an at first memorizes it by force, and recites it by force, in spite of completeness of meditation and presence of intelligence, and thereafter, that becomes a regular custom to the tongue, so that the tongue runs on through it in prayer, etc., while he who prays is inattentive. So he recites the whole of a Sura, and his soul returns to him after he has arrived at the end and he knows that he has recited it in a state of inattention. And so a writer writes at first with serious application, then his hand accustoms itself to penmanship and writing becomes to him nature. Then he writes many leaves while his heart is engrossed in thinking of something else.

So there is no path to gaining for oneself anything possible for the soul and the members except by effort and practice at first; and, thereafter, it becomes nature through custom. And that is what is meant by the saying of some, Custom is a fifth humour. [Footnote: al-'ada ṭabi'a khamisa. Ṭabi'a means "a humour" in the Hippocratic sense of the four humours, blood, phlegm, yellow bile, and black bile. It then comes to mean the mizaj, constitution or temperament of an animal body, literally, mixture.] Thus it is with the Glorious States. It is not fitting that despair of them should arise when they are lacking, but it is fitting that an effort should be made to acquire them for oneself through Hearing and its like. And, in truth, as to habit, the case has been seen of one desiring to love passionately an individual that at the time he does not love; then he does not cease repeating the mention of it to himself and keeping his gaze upon it and affirming to himself its amiable qualities and praiseworthy characteristics, until he does love it passionately, and that is fixed in his breast with a fixing that passes beyond the bound of his will. Then he may desire after that to be free of it and cannot get free of it. Like this is the love of God Most High and the longing to meet Him and the fear of His anger and other than that of the Glorious States; whenever a man misses them it is fitting that he should apply effort to bring them to himself by companioning with those who are characterized by them, and by witnessing their States and approving of their qualities in the soul and by sitting with them at the Hearing and by praying and beseeching God Most High that He would grant them the condition through making easy to him its causes. (al-Ghazzali, quoted in MacDonald 1901: 730–732.)

Adopting the postures of ecstasy actually creates the sensations and emotions associated with it. *Spirit follows form.* Or rather form and spirit are indivisible. This is true of other emotions as well.

Al-Ghazzali is describing the process of habituation, the way that an attitude—physical, emotional, or psychological—becomes incorporated so that it feels natural, even though it did not originate in spontaneity. Mimesis in this case is not only evocative but actively provocative (Tomlinson 1993: 112). For al-Ghazzali, the bodily comportments of mourning have co-occurrent emotional and spiritual states that may be produced by the posture itself. What's more, the gestures are methods, active techniques which take the initiate to another stage in his development, to a place of readiness, a place where longing for yet other states—states behind the states—is born. Witnessing an array of emotions, whether longing, fear, despair, or rapture, activates the emotions of the perceiver, acting "the part of a tinder-box which will light the fuel of his heart. Then its flames blaze up in him, and longing is strongly excited, and there assault him, because of it, states to which he is not accustomed" (al-Ghazzali 1997: 706–707). (This, at least is the jamāliyya path, the path of beauty. Other paths are less indulgent, bringing the propitiant to God through suffering, through the encounter with obstacles and the limits of one's humanity.) As a form of initiation, observation and imitation are active catalysts that ignite desire, yet fervent desire must be present to experience a transformation. Nīya (intention) is key. Like the elixir that the alchemists would add to copper to purportedly produce gold, intention (which in Morocco is not just conscious will but also sincere motivation) is an essential ingredient that transforms gesture into affect (Rosen 1984). Imitation is just the beginning of the path. Once the Glorious States are produced in the soul of an individual, the states themselves become guides, opening longings for states that before were not even imagined, ones that are indeed so new as to be experienced as assaults on the being. "For he that is debarred first from the Glorious States, thirsts for them; then, if he can obtain them, he thirsts for what is behind them" (al-Ghazzali 1997: 713). The postures and their co-occurent affective states are themselves materializations that lead to more subtle desires and realizations in the imaginal world.

The states that al-Ghazzali mentions may be compared to states achieved in trance ceremonies of the Moroccan Gnawa. The word "state" (ḥal) is often used in both contexts. But whereas the Glorious States that al-Ghazzali referred to were spiritual, the states in contemporary Gnawa ceremonies are spiritized—that is, they are thought to be produced not by postures but by the spirits that embody them. The difference is an ontological one: the "flint" that catalyzes the change of state is a spirit that is other than the self, but the material manifestation is nonetheless accompanied by postures and gestures that are codified and recognizable. Al-Ghazzali's treatise on gestures and emotions presages by several centuries Jerzy Growtowski's method of acting, in which the actor must assume the postures of different states in order to bring on the emotions and the understanding that comes from those states: "There is no contradiction between inner technique and artifice (articulation of a role by signs)," Growtowski asserts. "We believe that a spiritual process which is not supported and expressed by a formal articulation and disciplined structuring of the role will collapse in shapelessness. And we find that artificial composition not only does not limit the spiritual but actually leads to it" (Growtowski 1969: 190).

15. See chapter four. As Mauss notes in his discussion of alchemy, "we find over and over again that the transmutation of copper into gold is explained by a sacrificial allegory" (Mauss 1972 [1902]: 64).

16. See J. Becker 2004: 59 for a comparable example.

17. "It is usual to explain the motivation of those who enjoy dangerous activities as some sort of pathological need: they are trying to exorcize a deep-seated fear, they are compensating, they are compulsively reenacting an Oedipal fixation, they are 'sensation seekers.' While such motives may be occasionally involved, what is most striking when one speaks to specialists in risk, is how their enjoyment derives not from the danger itself, but from their ability to minimize it. So rather than a pathological thrill that comes from courting disaster, the positive emotion they enjoy is the perfectly healthy feeling of being able to control potentially dangerous forces" (Csikszentmihalyi 1990: 60).

18. *Hans Wehr Dictionary of Arabic.* Not to be confused with the verb "*fa ja 'a,*" to inflict suffering or distress.

19. My thanks to Yahya Tamezoujt for bringing the etymology of this word to my attention.

20. Csikszentmihalyi also defines flow as a lack of self-consciousness amidst awareness and, most importantly for this discussion, a change in one's relation to time (1990).

21. "The incipient trancer, through repeated participation in religious ritual, comes to know the script of the ritual and gradually comes to enact the script herself. As belief is intensified through action, the incipient trancer allows internal physical changes in the brain and body that may eventually also allow for trancing. The mind and body of the trancer becomes structurally coupled with the drama of the ritual. Her belief, imagination, sense of self and habitus of listening are coordinated with those of other human participants and the projected presences of holy beings, the cosmic drama that all enact" (J. Becker 2004: 121–122). Becker's explanations for trance phenomena have much in common with the work of anthropologist Victor Witter Turner (1974, 1982) and performance theorist Richard Schechner (1988) who employ a dramaturgical model to understand how ritual transforms social circumstances and creates community. Like Schechner and Turner, Becker bridges studies of neurology and cognition on the one hand and studies of trance (in both its subjective and social dimensions) on the other. All these studies demonstrate the extremely complex interplay between environment, aesthetic systems (learned ways of moving, listening, even breathing), memory, belief, subjectivity, and intersubjectivity and attest to the interdependency of all of these realms, an interdependency for which this study provides further proof.

22. In regard to falling and rising, Lefebvre notes that the "importance of places and space in gestural systems needs emphasizing. High and low have great significance: on the one hand the ground, the feet and the lower members, and on the other the head and whatever surmounts or covers it—hair, wigs, plumes, headdresses, parasols, and so forth. Right and left are similarly rich in meaning (in the West, the left hand has of course acquired negative—'sinister'—connotations). Variations in

the use of the voice, as in singing, serve to accentuate such meanings: shrill/deep, high/low, loud/soft" (1991: 215).

23. *La illāha illa allah wa muḥammadu rassullu-allah.* There is no God but God, and Muhammad is his messenger.

24. As Jaques Derrida makes clear in his oeuvre, there is often a play between an absence indexed in the present and a presence that alludes representation or any palpable existence in the "real" (Derrida 1978; Phelan 1993a). In Islamic ritual, on the other hand, presence (the presence of God, the presence of the self in relation to God and "his" creation) is brought about consciously by techniques of the body, while absence (to the self, to the community) is often less volitional (or at least less predictable), as visions and journeys out of the self occur seemingly spontaneously. The tension between absence and presence that exists in Derrida's worldview is applicable to the Islamic context, however; in both the deconstructionist and the mystical viewpoints—the two concepts define each other and give rise to discourses that continue to produce the dichotomy and the tension.

25. Anthropologist Judith Becker draws upon the work of neuroscientist Gerald Edelman to discuss the way trance activity is processed neurologically:

a single stimulus such as a sight or a sound may trigger multiple connectivities of bundles of neurons throughout the brain, resulting in what he calls "a global mapping." If a particular sound or sight results in the excitation of a global mapping, the individual may be associating the sound with a complex set of memories, emotions, inspirations to actions, beliefs, and even the experience of another realm of being. (2004: 115)

She goes on to elaborate:

Perception and action may become linked in a conjoining of sound with a cosmology that transforms the bodily/self experience of the individual. Edelman's diagram of a global mapping conjoins perception ("sensory sampling"/ "sensory sheets") in linked classification couples with many brain areas including those involved with emotion, memory, and the frontal lobes associated with complex intellectual processes (such as those necessary to construct cosmologies). Muscles, bodily movement are involved at both beginnings and endings of the circuit. Edelman is proposing a theory that connects perception, emotion, cognition, and action through multiple neuronal groups involved in multiple reentries, that is, two-way connections" (2004: 115).

26. Whereas trances provoked by spirit possession are often more violent in nature, they may have the same results. Keil calls this state of flow "primary reality." For him, primary reality is not acultural, but is rather a culturally-learned way of accessing states that dissolve the ego. "Healthy cultures, genuine cultures," he says alluding to Sapir, "give their infants access to primary reality because without cultural imprinting on our biological givens we can't enter into language, myth, music, dance,

poetry, wrights/rites, totemism, dreams, and other ego-dissolving primary-reality-engaging processes in the moment" (Sapir 1949; Keil 1995: 3–4).

27. Gestures do not isolate performances, but rather work to bring the entire community of participants into a new semantic domain, in this case that of ecstatic multiple subjectivity. Gesture has great power to create affective stances that inhabit not just the person but also the community. These gestures are, following Kendon, "emblematic" in that they are conventionalized signs. The body inhabits them with ease, and other bodies recognize and respond to them. What is particularly compelling about some of these gestures is that they enact root metaphors of space and body—"falling" and "rising," as well as "absence" and "presence"—metaphors that cognitive linguist Mark Johnson would call bodily "schemata" (1987). In other words, these gestures may be said to mimic, re-enact and reactivate cognitive and embodied categories that are learned at an early age.

28. Condillac noted in *Traité des Sensations* (1754) that judgment, reflection, and desire were transformations of sensations. Certainly emotions as well as spirit possessions are highly complex phenomena and cannot be reduced to "only sensations"; the language used to interpret sensations, however, is highly significant, as are the other semiotic symbols that co-occur with them.

29. As Langer notes, "musical duration is an image of what might be termed 'lived' or 'experienced' time—the passage of life that we feel as expectations become 'now,' and 'now' turns into an unalterable fact" (Langer 1953: 109; cf. Schade-Poulsen 1999: 119).

30. Music may be the catalyst for returning the subject to what Kristeva calls the "*chora*," that amorphous and maternal space of movement wherein and against which the subject is constituted. For Kristeva, the *chora* is prelinguistic, "analogous only to vocal or kinetic rhythm" (1982: 94). Kristeva describes the semiotic *chora* as follows:

> Discrete quantities of energy move through the body of the subject who is not yet constituted as such and, in the course of development, they are arranged according to various constraints imposed on this body—always already involved in the semiotic process—by family and social structures. In this way the drives, which are "energy" charges as well as "psychical" marks, articulate what we call a *chora*: a non-expressive totality formed by the drives and their stases in a motility that is as full of movement as it is regulated. . . .

> Although our theoretical description of the *chora* is itself part of the discourse of representation that offers it as evidence, the *chora*, as rupture and articulations (rhythm), precedes evidence, verisimilitude, spatiality and temporality. Our discourse—all discourse—moves with and against the *chora* in the sense that it simultaneously depends upon it and refuses it. Although the *chora* can be designated and regulated, it can never be definitely posited: as a result, one can situate the *chora* and, if necessary, lend it a typology, but one can never give it axiomatic form.

The *chora* is not yet a position that represents something for someone (i.e., it is not a sign); nor is it a *position* that represents someone for another position (i.e., it is not yet a signifier either); it is, however, generated in order to attain this signifying position. Neither model nor copy, the *chora* precedes and underlies figuration and thus specularization, and is analogous only to vocal and kinetic rhythm. We must restore this motility's gestural and vocal play (to mention only the aspect relevant to language) on the level of the socialized body in order to remove motility from ontology and amorphousness where Plato confines it in an apparent attempt to conceal it from the Democritean rhythm. The theory of the subject proposed by the theory on the unconscious will allow us to read in this rhythmic space, which has no thesis and no position, the process by which significance is constituted. Plato himself leads us to such a process when he calls this receptacle or *chora* nourishing and maternal, not yet unified in an ordered whole because deity is absent from it. Though deprived of unity, identity or deity, the *chora* is nevertheless subject to a regulating process [*réglementation*], which is different from that of symbolic law but nevertheless effectuates discontinuities by temporarily articulating them and then starting over, again and again.

The *chora* is a modality of significance in which the linguistic sign is not yet articulated as the absence of an object and as the distinction between the real and the symbolic. We emphasize the regulated aspect of the *chora*: its vocal and gestural organization is subject to what we shall call an objective ordering [*ordonnancement*], which is dictated by natural or socio-historical constraints such as the biological difference between the sexes or family structure. We may therefore posit that social organization, always already symbolic, imprints its constraint in a mediated form which organizes the *chora* not according to a law (a term we reserve for the symbolic) but through an *ordering*. What is this mediation? (1984: 93–94, emphases in original)

31. Gesture, asserts Kendon, "refers to that range of visible bodily actions that are, more or less, generally regarded as part of a person's willing expression. This differentiates it," he says, "from the expression of affect . . . which is typically seen as something we cannot help." Kendon finds that within the speech-gesture nexus, gesture determines intentionality in cases where speech may be ambiguous. Gesture concretizes and contextualizes meaning. "In all of the cases where gesture persists after speech," he says, "it would seem that the speaker is maintaining a display of the same frame of mind or intention that informed his last utterance" (1994: 49).

In the case of trance, gesture not only concretizes meaning, but may be said to cue or "key" a different state of being by invoking the embodied metaphor of falling. The gestures that co-occur with possession-trance are neither affect-free nor intentional; rather they "happen to" their subjects and then inhabit them with a different affective repertoire. In other words, the root metaphor of falling is experienced bodily and occurs with a repertoire of emotions and sensory dispositions that correspond to different spirits, colors, and smells. Falling is triggered by music as well—whether a particular Gnawa beat (or *dukka*), a melodic line, or the sung invocation of a spirit's name. These correspondences across sensory modalities are conventionalized. Steven Feld refers to such aesthetic configurations as "cross-modal homologies"— that is, correspondences across semiotic fields (the aural, the visual, the tactile, etc.)—based on iconicity—that is, similarity in form (1995b: 131). Thus a fall to the floor in a possession ceremony corresponds with the fall to the spirits, as well as with a particular color and a particular odor thought (or felt) to be structurally homologous. These homologies are also productive of emotional states. Speech also carries affect, of course; though it may be argued that the affective qualities of speech reside in its musical aspects—intonation, rhythm, and volume.

32. "The abject has only one quality of the object," says Kristeva, "that of being opposed to I" (1982: 1). It "is radically excluded and draws me toward the place where meaning collapses . . . and yet, from its place of banishment, the abject does not cease challenging its master. . . . A weight of meaninglessness, about which there is nothing insignificant, and which crushes me. On the edge of non-existence and hallucination, of a reality that, if I acknowledge it, annihilates me. There, abject and abjection are my safeguards. The primers of my culture" (Kristeva 1982: 2).

33. There are other ways to read this material. Crapanzano's work on trance cults in Morocco takes a psychoanalytic approach; trance is therapy treating common social ills that Crapanzano defines in part as unfulfilled Oedipus complexes on the part of Moroccan men who, because of the paternalistic structure of male socialization, never symbolically accede to the place of the father (1973). Abdellah Hammoudi concurs with this interpretation in his work on Moroccan authoritarianism; speaking of the master-disciple relationship of Sufi brotherhoods he says, "the service demanded by an initiating shaykh . . . can lead to the sheer negation of manhood and bring the male disciple to a radically altered state, namely femininity," the "renunciation of virility" (1997: 97, 91), as he calls it.

Clearly there are therapeutic aspects of trance phenomena and reasons, embedded in the unconscious habitus of both genders, for the expression of multiple subjectivities. As Weber looked for the way culture constrains meaning and interpretation, Crapanzano examines how genres constrain and determine subjectivity (1992). This is not very different from what Obeyesekere refers to as "the myth model," or "the idiom, or set of meanings, in which symbols are embodied" (1981: 102). Indeed, Obeyesekere is explicit about the relation to genre.

34. Cf. Combs-Schillings 1989; Rachik 1990.

35. From the *Oxford English Dictionary*:

"benzoin: belzoin, benjoin, bengwin, bengewyne, . . . -wine, . . . bengwine, benzwine, benswine, benioyn, benjoine, benjouin, benzoine, benzion, bezoin, . . . benione, . . . benzoin. (In 16th c. benjoin, a. F. benjoin [also benjaoy, quoted by Devic from Déterville Dict. Hist. Nat. 1816], repr. Sp. benjui, benjuy

(Barbosa 1516), Pg. beijoim [Vasco da Gama 1498], It. benzoi [Venetian records, 1461], for *lo-benzoi, *lo-benjuy, a. Arab. lubn jw 'frankincense of Jw' [Sumatra], by which name benzoin is called by Ibn Batuta c1350 [ed. Paris IV. 228]. The lo- appears to have been dropped in Romanic, as if it were the article. The word was naturally much corrupted in European langs.; later It. forms are belgivino, belzuino, mod.L. 1584 belzuinum, whence occas. Eng. belzoin. In Eng., benjoin was soon corrupted to benjamin, which still survives as a synonym. Benzoin, which is farther from the original, and appears to owe its z to the It., began to prevail c1650. From benzoin, was formed a1800 the chemical term benzoic [acid], whence at a later period benzin[e], benzol, and the numerous names of the benzene series.)

1. A dry and brittle resinous substance, with a fragrant odour and slightly aromatic taste, obtained from the Styrax benzoin, a tree of Sumatra, Java, etc. It is used in the preparation of benzoic acid, in medicine, and extensively in perfumery. For scientific distinction it is now termed gum benzoin. Also called by popular corruption benjamin."

36. Cf. Howes 1991a: 10

CHAPTER 4: WORKING THE SPIRITS (pages 81–105)

1. See Scanlon 2003: 510–553 on the influence of the blues on the poetry of Langston Hughes.

2. See Nuckolls 1996 and Erlmann 2004.

3. Erlmann notes that communities of style are formed around music that is phatic—that is, music that is not about meaning, but that is about marking the musical community as different (1999: 248). See also Erlmann 2003.

4. Arguments have been made for the referential function of music as well. See Feld and Fox 1994 for an overview of all of these arguments. See also Myers 2002: 118.

5. See Monson 1996; Voloshinov 1972.

6. "On n'a jamais vu personne 'tomber' possedé à la simple audition d'une cassette enregistrée" (Pâques 1991: 286).

7. Volosinov defines "inner speech" as consciousness: the word, he says, is "the semiotic material of inner life—of consciousness (inner speech) . . . the problem of individual consciousness as the inner word (as an inner sign in general) becomes one of the most vital problems in the philosophy of language" (Voloshinov 1972: 14, emphasis in original).

8. Voloshinov notes that different historical periods have different ways of treating reported speech. These ways are related to views of the subject or authorship and authority (Voloshinov 1972: 123).

9. But so does the entire oeuvre of performance theorist Richard Schechner. He notes that the "difference between performing myself—acting out a dream, reexperiencing a childhood trauma, showing you what I did yesterday—and more formal "presentations of self" (see Goffman 1959)—is a difference of degree, not kind"

(Schechner 1985: 37) It is clear that the anaphoric "I" has its counterpart in the repetitions of embodied performance.

10. See also Abbassi 1977.

11. See also Boddy 1989.

12. Nonetheless, she is not representative of the majority of women I met in the world of the Gnawa. Most others lived in more popular quarters, in humbler accommodations, and only just got by.

13. See Leiris 1958.

14. See Russell 1999 for more information on film and possession.

CHAPTER 5: ON THE THRESHOLD OF A DREAM (pages 106–120)

1. "This possible condition is, perhaps, that which the Sufis call "ecstasy" (ḥal)—that is to say, according to them, a state in which, absorbed in themselves and in the suspension of sense-perceptions, they have visions beyond the reach of intellect" (al-Ghazzali 1909: 17–18).

2. As ethnomusicologist Jean During notes, "Taken in the strictly religious sense, [ḥal] can be understood as the equivalent of 'communication with the divine.' Sufis and mystics define it as a state of transcendental grace that penetrates the heart of an individual without their volition" (2001: 92, translation mine). During goes on to say that the term "ḥal" is used in many different ways—by Sufis, by musicians, and by listeners. In the context of musical aesthetics, the ḥal produces a kind of contemplation in which a distance between two levels of being is perceived and transcendence attained (During 2001: 92–93).

3. In this context it is not hard to understand the logocentrism of Islam, which, like Christianity and Judaism, designates the word—discourse—as the carrier of revelation. For, like language, God is infinitely creative, embodying a myriad of meanings (parole), yet emerging from one source, one system (langue).

4. Si Mohammed was one of seven children born in Twarga, including his sisters Khadija and Mahjouba (who died in 1972 when she was seventeen years old) and his brothers al-Khadir, Hassan (who died in 2003), Abdelkader, and Abdelkabir.

5. Literally "Mbaraka the daughter of Bilal Samba, the daughter of Malika the Guinean." While Bilal is a male name (and the patron saint of the Gnawa), Malika is a female name. It is very unusual for names to recount a female genealogy. Nonetheless, this is what Si Mohammed told me. It is possible that because she was a slave and separated from her father, she was named after her mother, but this is conjecture.

6. Lalla Mimuna is a saint revered by both Jews and Muslims in Morocco. She exists in the hagiography of the Sufis as well. Her tomb is on the ramparts of the Marrakech medina near the Gate of the Tanners. She was from the Sahara and is often portrayed as a humble and illiterate woman of great faith whose only prayer was "Mimuna loves God, and God loves Mimuna" (Sometimes said: "Mimuna knows God and God knows Mimuna" (Pâques 1991: 64). The story goes that one day an angel,

knowing her level of devotion, descended to correct her prayers. When the angel left, Mimuna still had not memorized the entire prayer. She ran after the angel, up into the clouds, asking the angel to please repeat the verses. Seeing the great faith of Mimuna as she levitated into the air, the angel told her to continue as she had been doing, as her faith far surpassed most (Skali 1985). In some versions of this story, Mimuna walks on water to get to the angel. She is always portrayed as enacting miracles. Some of the Gnawa revere Lalla Mimuna and hold ceremonies expressly for her, though during the day.

7. In the substance of blood, the esoteric—what in Islamic mysticism is called *al-batin*, the interior realities (coming from "the belly")—and the exoteric—*zahir*, or exterior things—meet (Corbin 1966 : 382).

8. Howes notes that an anthropology of the senses is one that seeks to "liberate us from the hegemony which sight has for so long exercised over our own culture's social, intellectual, and aesthetic life" (1991a: 4). Furthermore, it sensitizes us to the different sensory modalities of other cultures.

9. See Schroeter 1988, 2002.

CHAPTER 7: MONEY AND THE SPIRIT (*pages 129–150*)

1. See also Gates 1988; Floyd 1995; Keil and Feld 1994; Szwed 2005. As Keil notes, music is one force among others that connects humans to a "primary reality." He says: "Healthy cultures, genuine cultures (Sapir 1949), give their infants access to primary reality because without cultural imprinting on our biological givens we can't enter into language, myth, music, dance, poetry, wrights/rites, totemism, dreams, and other ego-dissolving primary-reality-engaging processes in the moment" (1995: 3–4).

2. Chernoff 1979; Erlmann 1995; Guilbault 1993; Meintjes 2003; Turino 2000; Waterman 1990 to name but a few.

3. Radano and Bohlman remark that "It is in this ever-increasing proliferation of sonic fragmentation—and the new densities of space and place it constructs—that one finds attached corresponding formations of the authentic and real; with each displacement the 'truth' of place and origin seems to rise in value" (Radano and Bohlman 2000a: 32).

4. "*Trop souvent, cependant, on avait emprunté les procédés techniques plus que les valeurs: plus que l'âme. C'est Marcel Griaule et son École qui ont appris, par-delà les paroles, par-delà le style des images symboliques, des melodies et des rhythmes, à pénétret jusqu'au Coeur, jusqu'à l'âme meme de la Négritude*" (Senghor 1987: vii).

5. See Pâques 1964a. "L'arbre cosmique" is the name Pâques gives to the cosmology she finds across this expanse of Africa. Her work is a monumental piece of comparative ethnography, rooted deeply in the Griaulian methodology of comprehensive and long-term study. See also her predecessors in these studies: Dermenghem 1954; Doutté 1909; Griaule 1947; Tremearne 1968 [1914]; Monteil 1924. See also her con-

temporaries: Dieterlen 1988 [1951]; Leiris 1958; Rouch 1960. See also Pâques's student Bertrand Hell 1994, 1999b, 2002b.

6. Says Gnawi Abdenbi Binizi, cited in the liner notes of *Trance*, "there must be a woman there. The Ganawa [*sic*] are called in by women." (Hakmoun 1993: 21).

7. Timothy Taylor goes on to say that following

Baudrillard . . . [the] process of transformation is reversed in the consumption of world music: the music is not familiar-made-monstrous, but the monstrous-made-familiar: noise transformed into music. This transformation occurs by aestheticization, the unfamiliar music harnessed for western consumption by its incorporation into the interlinked realms of the commodity and the aesthetic. There is some irony in the fact that to "understand" or "appreciate" world music, it has not only to be presented by an intermediary but commodified as well, as if commodification somehow refines world music into a familiar and intelligible consumable item" (1997: 30–31).

8. It may be argued that trance is in the body and that the stories woven around it have little impact on the experience of *communitas* that it affords. Yet for Moroccans, the difference between Sufi communion with God and being possessed by Aisha Qandisha is palpable.

CHAPTER 9: NARRATIVES OF EPIPHANY (*pages 176–209*)

1. See Crain 1991; A. Ong 1987; Taussig 1993, 1997.

2. Cf. Abu-Lughod 1986.

3. From Bowles and Wanklyn 1966: 22–26. Another version of this song was performed by the late m'allem Sam (Mohammed Zourbat) on the nights of December 5 and 6, 1993, recorded and transcribed by Antonio Baldassare (there is no Arabic given):

They took us away, Oh Lord, they took us away
They took us away from the land of the Blacks
Oh my Lord forgive them
The Arabs took us away, Oh Lord
They took us away trapped in sacks
In the knapsacks on the camel's back
And they sold us at the wool market
My Lord forgive them
The children of the prophet bought us
They covered us in trinkets
They covered us with the scent of orange blossom and jasmine
Alas Sidi Rahal, they took us away from our land
They separated us from our parents
They took us to the wool market
They sold us like little lost children
Oh God of Princes, forgive them.

4. These words come from a transcription in both transliterated Arabic and German in Welte and Aguadé 1996: 72. Welte recorded and transcribed an entire ceremony. My translation is from the Arabic transliteration that he provides. I also recorded an entire ceremony twice—but both times the volume of the qraqab, the metal cymbals, drowned out the words on my tapes.

5. Maghnia draws the link between the spirit Bala Bala Dima in the Gnawa pantheon, the spirit Damballah in Haitian Voudun and the spirit Da in Dahomey (1996).

6. Fouzia El-Belkani, a daughter of a well-known m'allem in Marrakech notes in her Master's thesis that "many of the great masters of the Gnawa music do not fully understand words and expressions in certain songs. In fact, they have kept the same music, the same tune but tried to adopt different lyrics that, for them, most suit or correspond to the original meanings. However, there remain so many terms to which they were unable to find close equivalents and they were obliged to keep them as they are like African proper names, names of their saints and a number of refrains" (2000: 22).

7. In the song "bala kinba," the words "kinba" and "bala" are of African origin, while the word "salawi" means "the one from Salé": "kinba Sidi Musa bala / oh one from Salé, Sidi Musa Bala / kinba Sidi Musa Bala / spirit of the sky Sidi Musa Bala / spirit of the sea Sidi Musa Bala" (Welte and Aguadé 1996: 74–75; my translation from the Arabic transliteration).

8. This, says Pâques, represents a spring frothing up at the summit of the mountain: "During the dance the water falls on the possessed like rain and returns to the sea," she says, "where it rises up again in evaporation. . . . The dancer that carries the bowl eventually lowers himself a bit, finally lying on the ground pretending to swim. In that way he invites . . . the genies—to come and drink from this spring. Swimming brings them to enter into the ocean. . . . The rainwater will replenish the earth, which is dead and dry, and make it green again" (Pâques 1991: 293–924, translation mine).

9. "Barakati lalla Fatima / mulay Muḥammad / sidi ya rasul llah / mulay Muḥammad / nẕuru mekka wa l-madīna / mulay Muḥammad / syadi daba y-nub allah / mulay Muḥammad" (Welte and Aguadé 1996: 57).

10. Howes also calls attention to the role of olfaction in change of states (1991a). Crapanzano emphasizes that trance is a kind of semiotic system, "an idiom for articulating a certain range of experience (1973: 10); it is also a system of meaning and interpretation (Boddy 1994: 412).

11. Cf. Browning 1995.

12. Of epiphany in the work of James Joyce, Trilling notes:
To emphasize the intractable material necessity of common life and what this implies of life's wonderlessness is to make all the more wonderful such moments of transcendence as may now and then occur. This, it will be recognized, is the basis of Joyce's conception of the "epiphany," literally a "showing forth." The assumption of the epiphany is that human existence is in largest part compounded of the

dullness and triviality of its routine, devitalized or paralyzed by habit and the weight of necessity, and that what is occasionally shown forth, although it is not divinity as the traditional Christian meaning of the word would propose, is nevertheless appropriate to the idea of divinity: it is what we call spirit. Often what is disclosed is spirit in its very negation, as it has been diminished and immobilized by daily life. But there are times when the sudden disclosure transfigures the dull and ordinary, suffusing it with significance. So far as Joyce thinks of the epiphany as a genre in itself, he stays close to one of the established implications of the word, that the revelation takes place suddenly, in a flash. Yet we can perhaps consider the whole of *Ulysses* as an epiphany, the continuous showing forth of the spirit of Leopold Bloom out of the intractable commonplaceness of his existence. (Trilling 1972: 89–90)

Trilling notes in a footnote that critic Richard Ellman distinguishes between "lyrical epiphanies" and "bald, under-played epiphanies" in his book *James Joyce.* (1959. New York: Oxford University Press, 1959): 169. He quotes Ellman as saying, "Sometimes the epiphanies are 'eucharistic,' another term arrogantly borrowed by Joyce from Christianity and invested with secular meaning. These are moments full of passion. Sometimes the epiphanies are rewarding for another reason, that they convey precisely the flavor of unpalatable experiences. The spirit, as Joyce characteristically held, manifested itself at both levels" (87).

13. This agency is often referred to a "performativity" in anthropological discourse (Austin 1962).

14. See Ossman 2002 on "linked comparisons."

15. Says Braidoti,
The nomadic subject is a myth, that is to say a political fiction, that allows me to think through and move across established categories and levels of experience: blurring boundaries without burning bridges. Implicit in my choice is the belief in the potency and relevance of the imagination, of myth-making, as a way to step out of the political and intellectual stasis of these postmodern times. Political fictions may be more effective, here and now, than theoretical systems. The choice of an iconoclastic, mythic figure such as the nomadic subject is consequently a move against the settled and conventional nature of theoretical and especially philosophical thinking. This figuration translates therefore my desire to explore and legitimate political agency, while taking as historical evidence the decline of metaphysically fixed, steady identities. One of the issues at stake here is how to reconcile partiality and discontinuity with the construction of new forms of interrelatedness. (1994: 4–5)

16. Drawing on Deleuze's notion of the "nomadic subject," feminist scholar Rosi Braidoti notes, "Drawing a flow of connections need not be an act of appropriation. On the contrary, it marks transitions between communicating states or experiences . . . nomadic becoming is neither reproduction nor just imitation, but rather

emphatic proximity, intensive interconnectedness. . . . Nomadic shifts designate therefore a creative sort of becoming; a performative metaphor that allows for otherwise unlikely encounters and unsuspected sources of interaction of experience and of knowledge" (1994: 5–6).

17. Jackson defines the "blues aesthetic" as "the sum of the reflective and normative assertions that musicians have made regarding processes of performance, interaction, and evaluation. In the simplest terms, it is constituted by (learned) practices derived from and continually fed by African American musics and culture. It is not, however, racially based, nor is it 'coded' in the genes of any group of individuals. Rather it is learned through the engagement of individuals with those musics and culture" (Jackson 2003: 52).

18. As Randy Weston told Rhashidah E. McNeill for the liner notes to *Well You Needn't—Portraits of Thelonious Monk:*

"'Always know' was one of Thelonious Monk's themes. And he knew. When people told Monk that his music was weird he always replied that it was logical.

"His predilection toward logic may have precipitated from the fact that he excelled in physics and math as a high school student. It may also account for the many enigmatic or paradoxical answers or responses that Monk gave when questioned. 'All jazz musicians are mathematicians unconsciously' was a favorite theory of Monk's. Those who have studied his compositions have found them to be perfectly structured.

"Monk also knew that his music and its secret messages would remain an enigma long after its exposure to the world for years to come. The 'High Priest of Bop,' as he was later dubbed, remarked in 1959 that he had always been content to play his music his way and let the public catch up to him . . . 'even if it does take them 15, 20 years' which, of course, it did!"

Randy Weston, a Monk exponent, did a little catching up, too! Randy thought that the pianist just couldn't play the first time he heard Monk. But Weston s admiration for Coleman Hawkins, his idol, made Weston lend a more discerning ear to Monk's offbeat playing.

"Thelonious Monk was probably the most original pianist I ever heard. I first heard him play with Coleman Hawkins in the late '40s. They were playing on 52nd Street. Hawkins was my idol. He was the first man to play jazz on a tenor saxophone and he was so brilliant. Not only that but Hawkins always played with the young, advanced musicians. And, they were all great talents. So, that's how I discovered Monk and ironically, the first song I heard him play was, 'Ruby, My Dear.'"

"Ruby, My Dear," a Monk composition, and a hauntingly beautiful ballad was inspired by Thelonious' first love, Ruby Richardson, a dietician and his sister Marion's best friend.

Monk himself had been influenced by the grand Duke Ellington, and the great stride pianist, James P. Johnson. Though he rarely talked about his influences

Monk was quoted as saying of his blues improvisation, "Functional," "I sound just like James P." James P Johnson had lived near the Monk family in the San Juan section of Manhattan, New York, a primarily Black area, and befriended Thelonious in the early '30s. San Juan was a thriving center of rich Black culture and was home for many musicians, writers, and other artists, including Eubie Blake.

Randy Weston proved to be a most loyal, engaging disciple of Monk's. "I went to Monk's house, asked him if I could visit him. He said, 'Yes.' I went by to see him, spent nine hours in his home. He didn't speak at all, just sent vibrations like the great Sufi masters. And, he refused to answer any of my questions."

Though perplexed by Monk, Randy would later learn in his travels to Africa that Monk's way of communicating was the traditional African way of the elders and the ancient African ancestors.

Although he notated all his compositions, Monk often refused to let even his sidemen see his sheet music, preferring to let them learn his tunes by playing them rather than reading them, which was also the African way, Randy would later discover.

"When I got ready to leave, Monk invited me to come back again. About a month later, he played about three hours for me on the piano.

"When I heard him play I realized that this was the direction for me to go. That really opened my eyes."

This encounter allowed Randy to free up his own style and creativity. He suddenly realized that, with Monk, as he would recognize again later with Duke's piano playing, there were no time or style barriers.

In the early to mid 1950's Monk couldn't work in the New York clubs because his cabaret card had been revoked for six years. "For three years," Randy recalls, "I used to pick Monk up in my car and bring him to Brooklyn because in Brooklyn we always had that community spirit. He couldn't work but he never complained. Monk just continued to write and play his music. In 1957, Monk was rediscovered as a major composer and musician and in 1964 he became the first Black jazz musician to make the front cover of *Time Magazine*. 1976 was Monk's last public appearance, at the Newport Jazz Festival of 1976, due to illness.

"He made a heavy impact on me because he taught me perseverance. He taught me, also, no compromise—never compromise your Music.

"You see," Randy observes, "these men are like great prophets. What the Creator has done is bring them to us bringing all these gifts of music and these gifts are like almost a place that has no boundaries. If you can, imagine a building that has no walls and no ceiling but yet, it's a building. But it's so vast and so expanding.

"So, they came and brought us all this music. And with all they gave we can take what they gave and go in our own direction." Which is exactly what Randy Weston did becoming one of the music's most valuable assets and most important composer/musicians, as a modern pianist.

Although Monk's influence is easily recognizable, there is no question that Weston has developed his own style and his own audience. Following the tradition of all the great masters, he has taken the best of what he has learned from all his influences and melded them, to create fresh new music for our future generations.

Though, *Portraits of Monk*, is a tribute to one of the world's most revered composer/pianists Weston does not attempt to imitate Monk. With musicians Idris Muhammad, drummer, Jamil Nasser, bassist, and Eric Asante, percussionist, Randy plays some of Monk's compositions, Weston style. He combines the sounds and rhythms that he has gathered in his thirty years as a musician with the New-Orleans sound of Muhammad, a touch of Africa from Asante, and the deep, bluesy Memphis sound of Jamil Nasser.

Together, in the Ferber Studio, Paris, they produced a bit of magic, all in a single day and with no prior rehearsal, no music sheets, just sheer joy! All of the funk, the beauty, the unexpected, and of course, the mystery that one would associate with Monk's music is here. At the bottom of it all is the ever present blues. Deep!

"The way I played these songs was spontaneous. We just decided we'd get together and play. We didn't particularly do any arrangements. We just played the way we felt.

"I'm not copying Monk. What I'm trying to do is create a musical portrait of him, taking some of his compositions, using some of his riffs, some of his phrases. But, it's a way of, through music, describing him.

"The songs I chose were chosen either because they had a particular history or because they were just songs that I heard growing up and loved. These are all songs that Monk wrote before I met him or during the time that I spent with him." These songs also represent part of a time of great, great creativity in the history of the music—the 20's to the 60's when much of the most influential, greatest music in history was written and performed by the best! (Weston 1990b, liner notes as told to Rhashidah E. McNeill)

19. These axioms are: (1) The Principle of Mentalism, "The All is Mind; The Universe is Mental; (2) The Principle of Correspondence "As above, so below; as below, so above; (3) The Principle of Vibration, "Noting rests; everything moves; everything vibrates"; (4) The Principle of Polarity, "Everything is dual; everything has poles; everything has its pair of opposites; like and unlike are the same; opposites are identical in nature, but different in degree; extremes meet; all truths are but half-truths; all paradoxes may be reconciled"; (5) The Principle of Gender, "Gender is everything; everything has its Masculine and Feminine Principles; Gender manifests on all planes"; (6) The Principle of Rhythm, "Everything Flows out and in; everything has its tides; all things rise and fall; the pendulum swing manifests in everything; the measure of the swing to the right is the measure of the swing to the left; rhythm compensates"; (7) The Principle of Cause and Effect, "Everything has its Effect; every

Effect has its cause; everything happens according to Law; Chance is but a name for Law not recognized; there are many planes of causation but nothing escapes the Law" (Three Initiates 1940 [1912]: 25–41).

20. Cf. Szwed 1997: 132, 138; Three Initiates 1940 [1912].

21. Malcolm Chapman says that in a small Breton village, it is entirely typical that "traditional Breton music," as played on "traditional Breton instruments," should be totally absent; if it is indeed present, then it is in all probability the province of either the intellectual incomers with folkloric tastes, or of some small part of the university-educated local youth who might listen to such music. . . . Locally born, full-time residents, and (crucially perhaps) speakers of the local Celtic language, that is, the great majority of local people, often know little or nothing about this music, and have no interest in it. (1994: 30)

22. While no mention is made of North Africa in the discussion of genetics, it is clear that Quinn believes the Berbers may have originated in what today is Europe and migrated to North Africa by sea. Of course, the Berbers were in Spain in the Middle Ages.

23. Silverstein does note that the organic intellectuals in Brittany did recognize the difference between their plight and that of the Algerians, "namely that the latter enjoyed full political and civil rights" (2004: 73).

24. Sidi Musa is described as the "wellspring or source of life" (Pâques 1991); Stivell, a self-chosen name, also means "wellspring" (Wilkinson 2003).

25. Alan Stivell, "Délivrance," the second track on his *Live in Dublin* CD (first released 1975 by Keltia III, rereleased by Dreyfus in 1988). My thanks to Ellen Badone for calling my attention to this song. The full lyrics are as follows:

Voici venu le temps de délivrance
Loin de nous toute idée de vengeance
Nous garderons notre amitié avec le peuple de France
Puis nous abattrons les murailles honteuses qui nous empêchent de
regarder la mer
Les miradors qui nous interdisent nos plus proches frères de Galles,
d'Ecosse, d'Irlande
Et nous, dont le nom connu des goëlands et des cormorans, fut banni de
toutes les cartes terrestres,
Nous ouvrirons nos coeurs de paysans et de marin-pêcheurs à tous les
peuples de la planète Terre
Et nous offrirons nos yeux au Monde
Est-ce prétentieux de nous croire égaux?
Est-ce trop demander que de vouloir vivre?
Nous ferons tomber la pluie sur le monde meurtri
Et nettoyer le sang graisseux dont se nourrissent les soi-disant
puissants

Et donner à boire aux assoiffés de justice

Et les feuilles repousseront de Bretagne en Espagne, du Mali au Chili,
d'Indochine en Palestine

Bretagne, centre du monde habité, tu seras un refuge pour les oiseaux
chassés pétrolés

Pour les femmes torturées en prison

Pour les vieillards bombardés

Celtie, au croisement des peuples du Nord et du Sud, aux confins dus
vieux monde et du nouveau monde, aux frontières de la terre et de la
mer, à la limite du monde visible et du monde invisible?

26. For analysis of the Celtic movement, see Ellen Badone's review of Maryon McDonald's *"We Are Not French!"* (New York: Routledge, 1989): Badone 1989b.

For other viewpoints on the "Celtic question," see Grall 1977; Lebesque 1970; Le Coadic, Denis, and Wieviorka 1998. My thanks to Ellen Badone for her helpful insights.

27. See also Spyer 1998.

28. In that world," continues Marx: "the productions of the human brain appear as independent beings endowed with life, and entering into relation both with one another and the human race. So it is in the world of commodities with the products of men's hands. This I call the Fetishism which attaches itself to the products of labour so soon as they are produced as commodities, and which is therefore inseparable from the production of commodities" (Marx 1977).

29. This recalls the ritual of *sama'* (literally "audition") in Sufi tradition, wherein the believer listens to the chanting of the names of God until she falls into an ecstatic state where visions and revelations may be received.

30. I am grateful to Barbara Kirshenblatt-Gimblett for her insights on this subject.

CHAPTER 10: POSSESSING GNAWA CULTURE *(pages 210–231)*

1. "The invocation of utopia references what, following Seyla Benhabib's suggestive lead, I propose to call the politics of transfiguration. This emphasizes the emergence of qualitatively new desires, social relations, and modes of association within the racial community of interpretation and resistance and between that group and its erstwhile oppressors. It points specifically to the formation of a community of needs and solidarity which is magically made audible in the music itself and palpable in the social relations of its cultural utility and reproduction. Created under the very nose of its overseers, the utopian desires which fuel the complementary politics of transfiguration must be invoked by other, more deliberately opaque means. This politics exists on a lower frequency when it is played, danced, and acted, as well as sung and sung about, because words, even words stretched by melisma and supplemented or mutated by the screams which still index the conspicuous power of the slave sublime, will never be enough to communicate its unsayable claims to truth. The willfully

damaged signs which betray the resolutely utopian politics of transfiguration therefore partially transcend modernity, constructing both an imaginary anti-modern past
and a postmodern yet-to-come. This is not a counter-discourse but a counterculture
that defiantly reconstructs its own critical, intellectual and moral genealogy in a partially hidden public sphere of its own. The politics of transfiguration therefore reveals the hidden fissures in the concept of modernity. The bounds of politics are extended precisely because this tradition of expression refuses to accept that the
political is a readily separable domain. Its basic desire is to conjure up and enact new
modes of friendship, happiness and solidarity that are consequent on the overcom-
ing of the racial oppression on which modernity and its antimony of rational, western progress as excessive barbarity relied." (Gilroy 1993: 37–38)

2. An international port before WWII, Tangier attracted artists from Europe and
America, as well as the ultra-rich. One thinks of the luxuriously colored paintings of
Eugene De la Croix, the seedy novels of Paul Bowles, and the decadent parties of Malcolm Forbes, for example. Literary depictions of Tangier usually portray the city
through the lens of expatriate fantasy, citing intrigue, danger, and seduction. And
certainly there is a bit of all three in Tangier, mostly due to the drug trade. On the
other hand, Tangier today is a city with a huge illegal immigrant population, poor
sanitation, and few cultural resources. Fortunately the winds from the surrounding
waters blow most of the pollution away. But the winds in some seasons do not let the
people rest. The *chergi*, the east wind, blows (if not eternal, at least) often.

3. "One effective way to analyze the logics of inclusions and exclusion that have informed the production of racialized music histories is to examine music that springs
from, circulates around, and seeps through the interstices of racial categories" (Waterman 2000: 167–168).

4. Pâques notes that "with the Gnawa as in all of North Africa we don't find ourselves in the presence of a fixed and clearly exposed dogma, but before a corpus of beliefs and interpretations that vary according to the adept and the ceremonial leader
but which follow a known schema recognized by the Gnawa and members of other
sects" (1976: 177, translation mine).

5. Cf. cooke and Lawrence 2005.

6. Abdellah is a fluent speaker of Moroccan Arabic, French, and Spanish. He also
speaks English with quite a bit of proficiency (I discovered this when I heard him
speaking on the United States tour). He reads and writes classical Arabic and can el-
evate his dialect to a more formal Arabic with ease.

7. See Hell 1999b, 2002b, Lapassade 1990, 1998; Pâques 1991 for books in French.
See C. Becker 2002; Fuson 2001, Schuyler 1981 for articles in English.

8. But see El Hamel 2002; Mohammed Ennaji 1999; Lovejoy 2000, 2004; Wright
2002.

9. "The assertion that certain traits of African-American music are fundamentally
African is fundamental to claims of authenticity in the African diaspora, whether in

North America and South America, or along the Atlantic littoral" (Radano and Bohl-man 2000a: 29).

10. "Stambali" comes from the word "Istanbul" (Hell 2002b).

11. Abdellah was not opposed to me publishing the photographs here, since the names are indistinguishable. His concern is with disseminating information that is not exact concerning the Tangier lila.

ACKNOWLEDGMENTS

◆ ◆ ◆

This research was conducted under the auspices of several granting agencies, to which I am indebted: the Fulbright-Hays Foundation, the Social Science Research Council, the American Institute for Maghreb Studies, the John Simon Guggenheim Foundation, and the University of Texas at Austin. New York University supported a research leave in 2003.

The book has benefited from dialogues with several of my colleagues and friends, particularly Ellen Badone, Jamila Bargach, Pierre Alain Claisse, Abdelhai Diouri, Veit Erlmann, Bob and B. J. Fernea, Tim Fuson, Bertrand Hell, Barbara Kirshenblatt-Gimblett, Michael Lambek, Ahmed Lemsyeh, Stefania Pandolfo, John Schaefer, Philip Schuyler, Jonathan Shannon, Ted Swedenburg, Yahya Tamezoujt, and Katharine Young. Katherine Young invested her time and brilliance in reading the manuscript closely and drawing attention to new lines of connection. Veit Erlmann showed me my blind spots (there are, I'm sure, still ones I do not see). My thanks as well to the reader who chose to remain anonymous. My intellectual debts are evident in the text that follows, but clearly the scholars who were colleagues at the University of Texas at Austin have left a deep imprint: Veit Erlmann, Steven Feld, Ward Keeler, Joel Sherzer, Katie Stewart, and Greg Urban. My writing "sisters" in Austin—Françoise DeBacker, Martha Norkunas, Sheree Scarborough, and Suzy Seriff—have shown the way more than once. Also dyed in the narrative wool is the scholarship of Roger Abrahams, Richard Bauman, Margaret Mills, and Susan Slyomovics. My new colleagues at the Department of Performance Studies at New York University have also been a source of great inspiration—Barbara Browning, Barbara Kirshenblatt-Gimblett, André Lepecki, José Muñoz, Tavia Nyong'o, Ann Pellegrini, Richard Schechner, Karen Shimakawa, Diana Taylor, Allen Weiss. These colleagues give new meaning to the words "faculty meeting." Michael Gilsenan, Faye Ginsberg, Zachary Lockman, Fred Myers, Shiva Belaghi, Bambi Schieffelin, and Angela Zito have made sure I feel welcome in a larger NYU community. My thanks.

I couldn't have done this work without the generosity of the Gnawa themselves—Si Mohammed Chaouqi (al-'Abdi) and the Chaouqi brothers, Khadir, and the late Hassan, and the sons—Younis and Muṣbaḥ. The mqaddemat—who preferred to be known as Mbaraka, Malika, and Fatima—gave of their time and counsel. In Tangier, Abdellah El Gourd (Bu-al-khir) and his group—Abdelkadr El Khlyfy and Nour Eddine Touati—were particularly obliging.

Randy Weston, Neil Clark, Talib Kibwe (T. K. Blue) and James Clark were generous interlocutors and have taught me much about music and the spirit. Jaap Harlaar opened stage doors to me in numerous cities. The Breton musicians that gave so generously of their time, ideas, and music carry pseudonyms in this manuscript. I regret that in the intervening years between fieldwork and write-up, their street addresses and telephone and fax numbers changed, and neither telephone directories nor Google searches have produced any sign of them. They gave me much to contemplate, and they have my deep appreciation. Antonio Baldassare expeditiously sent me transcriptions of the song lyrics for *Sidi Musa* and *Ulad Bambara*, and Tim Fuson shared his recordings.

It has been a unique and very rewarding experience for me to be with my students "in the field" in Morocco. Dr. Mieke Curtis, Miriam Robinson Gould, David Lynch, Alisa Perkins, John Schaefer, Dr. Chantal Tetreault, and Lauren Wagner have enriched my life and scholarship in untold ways, as have my students working in other parts of the Middle East and Asia, Dr. Adam Frank, Dr. Faedah Totah, and Mark Westmoreland. Tina Majkowski and Sarah Kozinn helped with the bibliography, and Brigitte Sion pulled it all together, compiling, and formatting it.

Water spirit Nancy Venute is a constant support. My daughter Hannah Joy Tamezoujt, and my son Nathaniel (Nadim) Jackson Shannon are the biggest joys of my life. Finally, my thanks to Jonathan Shannon, whose companionship provides the *baraka* and *ilham* that make living a creative life possible.

BIBLIOGRAPHY

◆ ◆ ◆

BOOKS

Abbassi, Abdelaziz. 1977. *A Sociolinguistic Analysis of Multilingualism in Morocco.* Unpublished dissertation, University of Texas at Austin.

Abrahams, Roger D. 2005. *Everyday Life: A Poetics of Vernacular Practices.* Philadelphia: University of Pennsylvania Press.

———. 1986. "Ordinary and Extraordinary Experience." In *The Anthropology of Experience,* edited by Victor Turner and Edward M. Bruner, 45–72. Urbana: University of Illinois Press.

———. 1983. *The Man-of-Words in the West Indies: Performance and the Emergence of Creole Culture.* Johns Hopkins Studies in Atlantic History and Culture. Baltimore, Md.: Johns Hopkins University Press.

Abrahams, Roger D., and Richard Bauman. 1981. *"And Other Neighborly Names": Social Process and Cultural Image in Texas Folklore.* Austin: University of Texas Press.

Abu-Lughod, Janet L. 1980. *Rabat, Urban Apartheid in Morocco.* Princeton Studies on the Near East. Princeton, N.J.: Princeton University Press.

Abu-Lughod, Lila. 2005. *Dramas of Nationhood: The Politics of Television in Egypt.* The Lewis Henry Morgan Lectures. Vol. 2001. Chicago, Ill.: University of Chicago Press.

———. 1989. "Zones of Theory in the Anthropology of the Arab World." *Annual Review of Anthropology* 18: 267–306.

———. 1986. *Veiled Sentiments: Honor and Poetry in Bedouin Society.* Berkeley: University of California Press.

Abu-Lughod, Lila, and Catherine Lutz. 1990. *Language and the Politics of Emotion.* Studies in Emotion and Social Interaction. Cambridge, England: Cambridge University Press; Editions de la maison des sciences de l'homme.

Adorno, Theodor W. 1991. "On the Fetish Character in Music and the Regression of Listening." In *The Culture Industry: Selected Essays on Mass Culture,* edited by J. M. Bernstein, 35–36. London: Routledge.

Agawu, V. Kofi. 2003. *Representing African Music: Postcolonial Notes, Queries, Positions.* New York: Routledge.

Akhmisse, Mustapha. 2000. *Médecine, Magie Et Sorcellerie Au Maroc, Ou, L'Art Traditionnel De Guérir.* 4, § rev. et augm ed. Casablanca: Dar Kortoba.

Allali, Réda, and Yassine Zizi. 2002. "Essaouira Spirit." *Telquel* 33: 17.

Althusser, Louis. 1994. *Écrits Philosophiques et Politiques* [Selections]. Paris: Stock/IMEC.

Appadurai, Arjun, ed. 2001. *Globalization.* Millennial Quartet Book. Durham, N.C.: Duke University Press.

————. 1990. "Disjuncture and Difference in the Global Economy." *Public Culture* 2, no. 2: 1–24.

————. 1996. *Modernity at Large: Cultural Dimensions of Globalization*. Public Worlds. Vol. 1. Minneapolis: University of Minnesota Press.

————. 1986. *The Social Life of Things: Commodities in Cultural Perspective*. Cambridge, England: Cambridge University Press.

————. 1981. *Worship and Conflict Under Colonial Rule: A South Indian Case*. Cambridge South Asian Studies. Vol. 27. Cambridge, England: Cambridge University Press.

Artaud, Antonin. 1958. *The Theater and Its Double* [Théâtre et son double]. New York: Grove Press.

Asad, Talal. 2003. *Formations of the Secular: Christianity, Islam, Modernity*. Cultural Memory in the Present. Stanford, Calif.: Stanford University Press.

Attali, Jacques. 1985. *Noise: The Political Economy of Music*. Theory and History of Literature [Bruits]. Vol. 16. Minneapolis: University of Minnesota Press.

Austin, J. L. 1962. *How to Do Things with Words*. William James Lectures. Vol. 1955. Cambridge: Harvard University Press.

Badone, Ellen, ed. 1990. *Religious Orthodoxy and Popular Faith in European Society*. Princeton, N.J.: Princeton University Press.

————. 1989a. *The Appointed Hour: Death, Worldview, and Social Change in Brittany*. Berkeley: University of California Press.

————. 1989b. "'We Are Not French!'" *American Ethnologist* 19: 806–817.

Badone, Ellen, and Sharon R. Roseman, eds. 2004. *Intersecting Journeys: The Anthropology of Pilgrimage and Tourism*. Urbana: University of Illinois Press.

Bakhtin, M. M. 1986. *Speech Genres and Other Late Essays*. Edited by Caryl Emerson and Michael Holquist. Translated by Vern W. McGee. University of Texas Press Slavic Series. Vol. 8. Austin: University of Texas Press.

————(P. N. Medvedev). 1985. *The Formal Method in Literary Scholarship: A Critical Introduction to Sociological Poetics* [Formalny_ metod v literaturovedenii]. Translated by Albert J. Wehrle. Cambridge, Mass.: Harvard University Press.

————. 1984. *Rabelais and His World*. Translated by Hélène Iswolsky. 1st Midland ed. Bloomington: Indiana University Press.

————. 1981. *The Dialogic Imagination: Four Essays*. Edited by Michael Holquist. Translated by Caryl Emerson and Michael Holquist. University of Texas Press Slavic Series. Vol. 1. Austin: University of Texas Press.

Baldwin, James. 1956. *Giovanni's Room; a Novel*. New York: Dial Press.

Baraka, Imamu Amiri. 1991. "'The Blues Aesthetic' And the 'Black Aesthetic': Aesthetics as the Continuing Political History of a Culture." *Black Music Research Journal* 11, no. 2: 101–109.

————. 1963. *Blues People: Negro Music in White America*. New York: W. Morrow.

Barnwell, Randell, and William Lawrence. 1995. Liner Notes, Trance (Ellipsis Records).

Barthes, Roland. 1985. *The Grain of the Voice: Interviews 1962–1980* [Grain de la voix]. New York: Hill and Wang.

———. 1980. *La Chambre Claire: Note sur la Photographie*. Paris: Cahiers du cinéma.

Bastide, Roger. 1978. *The African Religions of Brazil: Toward a Sociology of the Interpenetration of Civilizations*. Johns Hopkins Studies in Atlantic History and Culture [Religions afro-brésiliennes]. Baltimore, Md.: Johns Hopkins University Press.

———. 1972. *Le Rêve, La Transe et la Folie*. Nouvelle Bibliothèque Scientifique. Paris: Flammarion.

Bataille, Georges. 1986. *Erotism: Death and Sensuality* [Erotisme]. San Francisco: City Lights Books.

Bateson, Gregory. 1972. *Steps to an Ecology of Mind*. New York: Ballantine Books.

Bauman, Richard. 1986. *Story, Performance, and Event: Contextual Studies of Oral Narrative*. Cambridge Studies in Oral and Literate Culture. Vol. 10. Cambridge, England: Cambridge University Press.

———. 1977. *Verbal Art as Performance*. Boston: Newbury House.

Bauman, Richard, Inta Gale Carpenter, and Patricia Sawin. 1992. *Reflections on the Folklife Festival: An Ethnography of Participant Experience*. Special Publications of the Folklore Institute. Vol. 2. Bloomington: Folklore Institute, Indiana University.

Becker, Cynthia. 2002. "'We are Real Slaves, Real Ismkhan': Memories of the Trans-Saharan Slave Trade in the Tafilalet of South-Eastern Morocco." *The Journal of North African Studies* 7, no. 4: 97–121.

Becker, Judith. 2004. *Deep Listeners: Music, Emotion, and Trancing*. Bloomington: Indiana University Press.

Ben Driss, Karim. 2002. *Sidi Hamza Al-Qadiri Boudchich: Le Renouveau Du Soufisme Au Maroc*. Beirut and Milan: Albouraq-Archè.

Benjamin, Walter. 1968. *Illuminations* [Illuminationen]. Edited and with an introduction by Harry Zohn. Translated by Hannah Arendt. New York: Schocken Books.

Benveniste, Emile. 1971 [1958]. "Subjectivity in Language." In *Problems in General Linguistics*, translated by M. E. Meek, 223–230. Miami: University of Miami Press.

———. 1971 [1956]. "The Nature of Pronouns." In *Problems in General Linguistics*, translated by M. E. Meek, 217–222. Miami: University of Miami Press.

Bergson, Henri. 1910. *Time and Free Will; an Essay on the Immediate Data of Consciousness*. Translated by Frank Lubecki Pogson. Library of Philosophy. Edited by J. H. Muirhead. London: S. Sonnenschein and Co.

———. 1911. *Matter and Memory*. Translated by Nancy Margaret Paul and William Scott Palmer. Library of Philosophy. London: S. Sonnenschein and Co.

Berlant, Lauren Gail, ed. 2000. *Intimacy*. Chicago: University of Chicago Press.

Besmer, Fremont E. 1982. *Horses, Musicians, and Gods: The Hausa Cult of Possession-Trance*. South Hadley, Mass.: Bergin and Garvey Publications.

Besnier, Niko. 1990. "Language and Affect." *Annual Review of Anthropology* 19: 419–451.

Birdwhistell, Ray L. 1970. *Kinesics and Context; Essays on Body Motion Communication.* University of Pennsylvania Publications in Conduct and Communication [no. 2]. Philadelphia: University of Pennsylvania Press.

Bithell, Caroline. 2003. "Shared Imaginations: Celtic and Corsican Encounters in the Soundscape of the Soul." In *Celtic Modern: Music at the Global Fringe,* edited by Martin Stokes and Philip Vilas Bohlman, 27–72. Lanham, Md.: Scarecrow Press.

Boddy, Janice. 1994. "Spirit Possession Revisited: Beyond Instrumentality." *Annual Review of Anthropology* 23: 407–434.

———. 1989. *Wombs and Alien Spirits: Women, Men, and the Zar Cult in Northern Sudan.* New Directions in Anthropological Writing. Madison, Wis.: University of Wisconsin Press.

Bohlman, Philip Vilas. 2000. "The Remembrance of Things Past: Music, Race and the End of History in Modern Europe." In *Music and the Racial Imagination,* edited by Ronald Michael Radano and Philip Vilas Bohlman, 644–676. Chicago: University of Chicago Press.

Bourdieu, Pierre. 1984. *Distinction: A Social Critique of the Judgment of Taste* [Distinction]. Cambridge, Mass.: Harvard University Press.

———. 1977. *Outline of a Theory of Practice.* Cambridge Studies in Social Anthropology. Cambridge, England: Cambridge University Press.

Bourguignon, Erika. 1976. *Possession.* Chandler & Sharp Series in Cross-Cultural Themes. San Francisco: Chandler and Sharp Publishers.

———. 1968. "World Distribution and Patterns of Possession States." In *Trance and Possession States,* edited by Raymond Prince, 3–34. Montreal: R. M. Bucke Memorial Society.

Bowen, John Richard. 2003. *Islam, Law, and Equality in Indonesia: An Anthropology of Public Reasoning.* Cambridge, England: Cambridge University Press.

———. 1998. *Religions in Practice: An Approach to the Anthropology of Religion.* Boston: Allyn and Bacon.

———. 1993. *Muslims through Discourse: Religion and Ritual in Gayo Society.* Princeton, N.J.: Princeton University Press.

Bowles, Paul, and Christopher Wanklyn. 1966. Liner Notes, *Morocco: Music of Morocco.* Recording and Notes by Christopher Wanklyn (Folkways FE 4339).

Boyer, Gaston. 1953. *Un Peuple de l'Ouest Soudanais, Les Diawara.* Dakar: Ifan.

Braidoti, Rosi. 1994. *Nomadic Subjects: Embodiment and Sexual Difference in Contemporary Feminist Theory.* New York: Columbia University Press.

Brandes, Stanley H. 1988. *Power and Persuasion: Fiestas and Social Control in Rural Mexico.* Philadelphia: University of Pennsylvania Press.

Breckenridge, Carol, Sheldon Pollock, Homi K. Bhabha, and Dipresh Chakrabarty. 2002. *Cosmopolitanism.* Durham, N.C.: Duke University Press.

Brenner, Louis. 1993. "Constructing Muslim Identities in Mali." In *Muslim Identity*

and *Social Change in Sub-Saharan Africa*, edited by Louis Brenner, 59–78. Bloomington: Indiana University Press.

Briggs, Charles L. 1996. "The Meaning of Nonsense, the Poetics of Embodiment,
and the Production of Power in Warao Healing." In *The Performance of Healing*,
edited by Carol Laderman and Marina Roseman, 185–232. New York:
Routledge.

Brown, Karen McCarthy. 1991. *Mama Lola: A Vodou Priestess in Brooklyn*. Comparative
Studies in Religion and Society. Vol. 4. Berkeley: University of California Press.

Brown, Laura S. 1995. "Not Outside the Range: One Feminist Perspective on Psychic
Trauma." In *Trauma: Explorations in Memory*, edited by Cathy Caruth, 100–112.
Baltimore, Md.: Johns Hopkins University Press.

Browning, Barbara. 1998. *Infectious Rhythm: Metaphors of Contagion and the Spread of
African Culture*. New York: Routledge.

———. 1995. *Samba: Resistance in Motion*. Arts and Politics of the Everyday. Bloomington: Indiana University Press.

Brunel, René. 1926. *Essai sur la Confrérie Religieuse des 'Aissaoua au Maroc*. Paris:
P. Geuthner.

Butler, Judith. 1990. *Gender Trouble: Feminism and the Subversion of Identity*. New York:
Routledge.

———. 1993. *Bodies that Matter: On the Discursive Limits of "Sex."* New York: Routledge.

———. 1996. *Excitable Speech: A Politics of the Performative*. New York: Routledge.

Caillois, Roger. 1960. *Man and the Sacred* [Homme et le sacré]. Glencoe, Ill.: Free
Press of Glencoe.

Callaway, Barbara. 1987. *Muslim Hausa Women in Nigeria: Tradition and Change*. Syracuse, N.Y.: Syracuse University Press.

Canetti, Elias. 1978. *The Voices of Marrakesh: A Record of a Visit*. A Continuum Book.
New York: Seabury Press.

Cantwell, Robert. 1993. *Ethnomimesis: Folklife and the Representation of Culture*. Chapel
Hill: University of North Carolina Press.

Caruth, Cathy. 1996. *Unclaimed Experience: Trauma, Narrative, and History*. Baltimore,
Md.: Johns Hopkins University.

———, ed. 1995. *Trauma: Explorations in Memory*. Baltimore, Md.: Johns Hopkins
University Press.

Casanova, José. 1994. *Public Religions in the Modern World*. Chicago: University of Chicago Press.

Casey, Conerly. 1997. "Medicines for Madness: Suffering, Disability and the
Identification of Enemies in Northern Nigeria." Ph.D. dissertation, University of
California, Los Angeles.

Casey, Edward S. 1997. *The Fate of Place: A Philosophical History*. Berkeley: University of
California Press.

———. 1987. *Remembering: A Phenomenological Study.* Studies in Phenomenology and Existential Philosophy. Bloomington: Indiana University Press.

———. 1976. *Imagining: A Phenomenological Study.* Studies in Phenomenology and Existential Philosophy. Bloomington: Indiana University Press.

Caton, Steven C. 1990. *"Peaks of Yemen I Summon": Poetry as Cultural Practice in a North Yemeni Tribe.* Berkeley: University of California Press.

———. 1987. "Contributions of Roman Jakobson." *Annual Review of Anthropology* 16: 223–260.

Chandler, Wayne. 1999. *Ancient Future: The Teachings and Prophetic Wisdom of the Seven Hermetic Laws of Ancient Egypt.* Atlanta, Ga.: Black Classic Press.

Chapman, Malcolm. 1994. "Some Thoughts on Celtic Music." In *Ethnicity, Identity, and Music: The Musical Construction of Place,* edited by Martin Stokes, 29–44. Oxford: Berg.

Chebel, Malek. 2002. *Le Sujet en Islam.* Paris: Seuil.

Chernoff, John Miller. 1979. *African Rhythm and African Sensibility: Aesthetics and Social Action in African Musical Idioms.* Chicago: University of Chicago Press.

Chittick, William C. 1989. *The Sufi Path of Knowledge: Ibn Al Arabi's Metaphysics of Imagination.* Albany, N.Y.: State University of New York Press.

Chlyeh, Abdelhafid, ed. 2000. *La Transe.* Casablanca: Marsam.

———. 1999. *L'Univers des Gnaouas.* Paris: Editions Le Fennec/La Pensée sauvage.

———. 1998. *Les Gnawa du Maroc: Itinéraires Initiatiques, Trance et Possession.* Paris: Editions le Fennec, La Pensée sauvage.

Claisse, Pierre-Alain. 2003. *Les Gnawa Marocains De Tradition Loyaliste.* Paris: L'Harmattan.

Classen, Constance. 1993. *Worlds of Sense: Exploring the Senses in History and Across Cultures.* New York: Routledge.

Comaroff, Jean, and John Comaroff. 1993. "Introduction." In *Modernity and Its Malcontents: Ritual and Power in Postcolonial Africa,* edited by Jean Comaroff, and John Comaroff, xi–xxxvii. Chicago: University of Chicago Press.

Combs-Schilling, M. E. 1989. *Sacred Performances: Islam, Sexuality, and Sacrifice.* New York: Columbia University Press.

Condillac, Abbé de. 1754. *Traité des Sensations.* Vol. 2. London: De Bure L'Aîné.

Connerton, Paul. 1989. *How Societies Remember.* Themes in the Social Sciences. Cambridge, England: Cambridge University Press.

cooke, miriam, and Bruce B. Lawrence. 2005. *Muslim Networks from Hajj to Hip Hop.* Islamic Civilization and Muslim Networks. Chapel Hill: University of North Carolina Press.

Corbin, Henry. 1998. *Alone with the Alone: Creative Imagination in the Sufism of Ibn 'Arabi.* Princeton/Bollingen Paperbacks. [*Imagination créatrice dans le soufisme d'Ibn 'Arabi*]. Vol. 91. Princeton, N.J.: Princeton University Press.

————. 1996. "The Visionary Dream in Islamic Spirituality." In *The Dream in Human Societies*, edited by G. E. von Grunebaum and Roger Caillois, 381–407. Berkeley: University of California Press.

Cornell, Vincent J. 1998. *Realm of the Saint: Power and Authority in Moroccan Sufism.* Austin, Tex.: University of Texas Press.

Couliano, Ioan P. 1987. *Eros and Magic in the Renaissance.* Translated by Margaret Cook. Chicago: University of Chicago Press.

Crain, Mary. 1991. "Poetics and Politics in the Ecuadorian Andes: Women's Narratives of Death and Devil Possession." *American Ethnologist* 18, no. 1: 67–89.

Crapanzano, Vincent. 2004. *Imaginative Horizons: An Essay in Literary-Philosophical Anthropology.* Chicago: University of Chicago Press.

————. 1992. *Hermes' Dilemma and Hamlet's Desire: On the Epistemology of Interpretation.* Cambridge, Mass.: Harvard University Press.

————. 1980. *Tuhami, Portrait of a Moroccan.* Chicago: University of Chicago Press.

————. 1973. *The Hamadsha; a Study in Moroccan Ethnopsychiatry.* Berkeley: University of California Press.

Csikszentmihalyi, Mihaly. 1990. *Flow: The Psychology of Optimal Experience.* New York: Harper and Row.

Csordas, Thomas J. 1996. "Imaginal Performance and Memory in Ritual Healing." In *The Performance of Healing*, edited by Carol Laderman and Marina Roseman. New York: Routledge.

————. 1994a. *Embodiment and Experience: The Existential Ground of Culture and Self.* Cambridge Studies in Medical Anthropology. Vol. 2. New York: Cambridge University Press.

————. 1994b. *The Sacred Self: A Cultural Phenomenology of Charismatic Healing.* Berkeley: University of California Press.

————.1993. "Somatic Modes of Attention." *Cultural Anthropology* 8, no. 2: 135–156.

Curtis, Maria. Forthcoming. "The Fes Festival of World Sacred Music: Spirituality, Music, and Diplomacy on an Emerging Global Stage." Doctoral Dissertation, University of Texas at Austin.

————. 2002. "Sound Faith: The Fes Festival of World Sacred Music: Music and Diplomacy on a Global Stage." Paper presented at the American Association of Anthropology, New Orleans, La.

De Certeau, Michel. 1992. *The Mystic Fable: The Sixteenth and Seventeenth Centuries.* Translated by Michael B. Smith. Chicago: University of Chicago Press.

de Heusch, Luc. 1986. *Le Sacrifice Dans Les Religions Africaines.* Bibliothèque Des Sciences Humaines. Paris: Gallimard.

De Vries, Hent. 2001. "In Media Res: Global Religion, Public Spheres, and the Task of Contemporary Comparative Religious Studies." In *Religion and Media*, edited by Hent De Vries and Samuel Weber, chap. 3–41. Ithaca, N.Y.: Cornell University Press.

De Vries, Hent, and Samuel Weber. 2001. *Religion and Media*. Cultural Memory in the Present. Stanford, Calif.: Stanford University Press.

Delafosse, M. 1924. "Les Relations Du Maroc Avec Le Soudan à Travers Les Ages." *Hesperis* 41: 153–174.

———. 1923. "Les Débuts Des Troupes Noires Au Maroc." *Hesperis* 2: 1–11.

Deleuze, Gilles, and Félix Guattari. 1980. *Mille Plateaux: Capitalisme Et Schizophrénie*. Paris: Minuit.

———. 1977. *Anti-Oedipus: Capitalism and Schizophrenia*. New York: Viking Press.

Dent, Michelle, and M. J. Thompson. 2004. "Introduction: Falling." *Women and Performance: A Journal of Feminist Theory* 27, no. 14: 7–11.

Deren, Maya. 1983. *Divine Horsemen: The Living Gods of Haiti*. New Paltz, N.Y.: McPherson.

Dermenghem, Émile. 1954. *Le Culte Des Saints Dans l'Islam Maghrebin*. Paris: Gallimard.

Derrida, Jacques. 2001. "'Above all, no Journalists!'" In *Religion and Media*, edited by Hent De Vries and Samuel Weber, 56–93. Stanford, Calif.: Stanford University Press.

———. 1994. *Specters of Marx: The State of the Debt, the Work of Mourning, and the New International*. Translated by Peggy Kamuf. New York: Routledge.

———. 1985. "Des Tours De Babel." In *Difference in Translation*, edited by Joseph Graham, 165–248. Ithaca, N.Y.: Cornell University Press.

———. 1978. *Writing and Difference* [Ecriture et la différence]. Chicago: University of Chicago Press.

Desjarlais, Robert R. 1992. *Body and Emotion: The Aesthetics of Illness and Healing in the Nepal Himalayas*. Series in Contemporary Ethnography. Philadelphia: University of Pennsylvania Press.

Devereux, George. 1980. *Basic Problems of Ethnopsychiatry*. Chicago: University of Chicago Press.

Diawara, Mamadou. 2002. *L'Empire Du Verbe et l'Eloquence du Silence: Vers une Anthropologie du Discours dans les Groupes dits dominés au Sahel*. Studien Zur Kulturkunde. Vol. 120. Wiesbaden: F. Steiner.

Diehl, Keila. 2002. *Echoes from Dharamsala: Music in the Life of a Tibetan Refugee Community*. Berkeley: University of California Press.

Dieterlen, Germaine. 1999. *Les Dogon: Notion De Personne et Mythe de la Création*. Passerelles De La Mémoire. Paris: L'Harmattan.

———. 1988 [1951]. *Essai sur la Religion Bambara*. Anthropologie Sociale. 2nd ed. Bruxelles: Editions de l'Université de Bruxelles.

———. 1960. *An Essay on the Religion of the Bambara = Essai Sur La Religion Bambara* [Essai sur la religion bambara]. New Haven, Conn.: Human Relations Area File.

Diouri, Abdelhai. 1990. *Lahlou: Nourriture Sacrificielle des Gnaouas du Maroc*. Agencia Española de Cooperación Internacional.

————. 1984. "La Résistance du Nom." *Bulletin Economique et Social du Maroc*: 153–154.

————. 1979. "Transe, Écriture: Contributions à une Lecture Socio-sémiotique de Quelques Faits de Culture Orale et Écrite au Maroc." Doctoral thesis, Ecole des hautes etudes en sciences sociales.

Djebar, Assia. 1999. *Ces Voix Qui M'Assiègent: En Marge De Ma Francophonie*. Collection "L'Identité Plurielle." Paris: Albin Michel.

Doutté, Edmund. 1909. *Magie et Religion dans l'Afrique du Nord*. Alger: A. Jourdan.

Duncan B. MacDonald. 1901. "Al-Ghazzali on Music and Ecstasy: Emotional Religion in Islam as Affected by Music and Singing; being a Translation of a Book by the Ihya Ulum Ad-Din of Al-Ghazzali with Analysis, Annotation and Appendices." *Journal of the Royal Asiatic Society*.

Duranti, Alessandro. 1986. "The Audience as Co-Author: An Introduction." *Text* 6: 239–247.

During, Jean. 2001. *L'Âme Des Sons: L'Art Unique d'Ostad Elahi*. Paris: Editions du Relié.

————. 1988. *Musique et Extase: L'Audition Mystique dans la Tradition Soufie*. Paris: Albin Michel.

Durkheim, Emile. 1915. *The Elementary Forms of the Religious Life, a Study in Religious Sociology*. London: G. Allen & Unwin.

Dwyer, Kevin, and Faqir Muhammad. 1982. *Moroccan Dialogues: Anthropology in Question*. Baltimore, Md.: Johns Hopkins University Press.

Efron, David. 1972. *Gesture, Race and Culture; a Tentative Study of the Spatio-Temporal and "Linguistic" Aspects of the Gestural Behavior of Eastern Jews and Southern Italians in New York City, Living Under Similar as Well as Different Environmental Conditions*. Approaches to Semiotics. [Gesture and environment]. Vol. 9. The Hague: Mouton.

Eickelman, Dale F. 1977. "Time in a Complex Society: A Moroccan Example." *Ethnology* 16, no. 1: 39–55.

————. 1976. *Moroccan Islam: Tradition and Society in a Pilgrimage Center*. Modern Middle East Series. No. 1. Austin: University of Texas Press.

Eickelman, Dale F., and Jon W. Anderson. 1999. *New Media in the Muslim World: The Emerging Public Sphere*. Indiana Series in Middle East Studies. Bloomington: Indiana University Press.

Ekman, Paul, and Wallace Friesen. 1969. "The Repertoire of Non-Verbal Behavior: Categories, Origins, Usage and Coding." *Semiotica* 1, no. 1: 49–98.

El-Belkani, Fouzia. 2000. "Trance and Music among the Gnawa of Marrakech: A Sociolinguistic Approach." Master's Thesis, Department of English, University of Cadi Ayad, Faculty of Letters, Abdullah Koucha, Director.

El Hamel, Chouki. 2002. "'Race,' Slavery and Islam in the Maghribi Mediterranean Thought: The Question of the Haratin in Morocco." *Journal of North African Studies* 29, no. 38: 29–52.

Ellison, Ralph. 1964. *Shadow and Act*. New York: Random House.

El Shaheed, Patrick Jabbar. 1993. Liner Notes, *Shabeesation*. Rykodisc. http://worldmusiccentral.org/artists/artist_page.php?id=1928.

Ennaji, Moha. 2005. *Multilingualism, Cultural Identity, and Education in Morocco*. New York: Springer.

———. 1985. *Contrastive Syntax: English, Moroccan Arabic, and Berber Complex Sentences*. Würzburg: Königshausen and Neumann.

Ennaji, Mohammed. 1999. *Serving the Master: Slavery and Society in Nineteenth-Century Morocco* [Soldats, domestiques et concubines]. New York: St. Martin's Press.

———. 1994. *Soldats, Domestiques et Concubines: L'Esclavage Au Maroc Au XIXe Siècle*. Collection Le Nadir. Paris: Balland.

Erlmann, Veit, ed. 2004. *Hearing Cultures: Essays on Sound, Listening, and Modernity*. Wenner-Gren International Symposium Series. Oxford: Berg.

———. 2003. "Communities of Style: Musical Figures of Black Diasporic Identity." In *The Black Diaspora: A Musical Perspective*, edited by Ingrid Monson, 83–102. New York: Routledge.

———. 1999. *Music, Modernity, and the Global Imagination: South Africa and the West*. New York: Oxford University Press.

———. 1996. "The Aesthetics of the Global Imagination: Reflections on World Music in the 1990s." *Public Culture* 8 (Spring): 467–487.

———. 1995. *Nightsong: Performance, Power, and Practice in South Africa*. Chicago Studies in Ethnomusicology. Chicago: University of Chicago.

———. 1993. "The Politics and Aesthetics of Transnational Music." *The World of Music* 35, no. 2: 3–15.

———. 1986. *Music and the Islamic Reform in the Early Sokoto Empire: Sources, Ideology, Effects*. Abhandlungen Für Die Kunde Des Morgenlandes. Vol. 48, 1. Stuttgart: Deutsche Morgenländische Gesellschaft: Kommissionsverlag Franz Steiner Wiesbaden GmbH.

Erlmann, Veit, and Magagi Habou. 1989. *Girkaa: Une Cérémonie d'Initiation Au Culte De Possession Boorii Des Hausa De La Région De Maradi (Niger)*. Berlin: Dietrich Reimer Verlag.

Errington, Shelly. 1998. *The Death of Authentic Primitive Art and Other Tales of Progress*. Berkeley: University of California Press.

Evans-Pritchard, E. E. 1966. *Theories of Primitive Religion*. Oxford: Clarendon Press.

———. 1937. *Witchcraft, Oracles, and Magic among the Azande*. Oxford: Clarendon Press.

Evers Rosander, Eva. 1991. *Women in a Borderland: Managing Muslim Identity Where Morocco Meets Spain*. Stockholm Studies in Social Anthropology. Vol. 26. Stockholm: Department of Social Anthropology, Stockholm University.

Ewing, Katherine P. 1998 [1990]. "The Illusion of Wholeness: 'Culture,' 'Self,' and the Experience of Inconsistency." In *The Art of Medical Anthropology: Readings*, edited by Sjaak van der Geest and Adri Rienks, 296–310. Amsterdam: Het Spinhaus.

———. 1997. *Arguing Sainthood: Modernity, Psychoanalysis and Islam.* Durham, N.C.: Duke University Press.

———. 1990. "The Dream of Spiritual Initiation and the Organization of Self Representations among Pakistani Sufis." *American Ethnologist* 17, no. 1: 56–57.

———. 1988. *Shari'at and Ambiguity in South Asian Islam.* Berkeley: University of California Press.

Fabian, Johannes. 2002. *Time and the Other: How Anthropology Makes Its Object.* New York: Columbia University Press.

———. 1991. *Time and the Work of Anthropology: Critical Essays, 1971–1991.* Studies in Anthropology and History. Vol. 3. Chur, Switzerland: Harwood Academic Publishers.

Fahd, Toufy. 1966. "The Dream in Medieval Islamic Society." In *The Dream in Human Societies,* edited by G. E. von Grunebaum and R. Caillois. Berkeley: University of California Press.

Falassi, Alessandro. 1987. *Time Out of Time: Essays on the Festival.* Albuquerque: University of New Mexico Press.

Fanon, Frantz. 1967. *Black Skin, White Masks* [Peau noire, masques blancs]. An Evergreen Book. New York: Grove Press.

Featherstone, Mike. 1990. *Global Culture: Nationalism, Globalization and Modernity.* London: Sage in Association with Theory, Culture and Society.

Feld, Steven. 1996. "Waterfalls of Song: An Acoustemology of Place Resounding in Bosavi, Papua New Guinea." In *Senses of Place,* edited by Steven Feld and Keith H. Basson, 91–136. Santa Fe: School of American Research Press.

———. 1995a. "From Schizophonia to Schismogenesis." In *Music Grooves,* edited by Steven Feld and Charles Keil, 257–289. Chicago: University of Chicago Press.

———.1995b. "Aesthetics as Iconicity of Style (Uptown Title); or (Downtown Title) 'Left-Up-Over-Sounding': Getting Into the Kaluli Groove." In *Music Grooves,* edited by Steven Feld and Charles Keil, 109–150. Chicago: University of Chicago Press.

———. 1990. "Wept Thoughts: The Voicing of Kaluli Memories." *Oral Tradition* 5, no. 2/3: 241–266.

———. 1982. *Sound and Sentiment: Birds, Weeping, Poetics, and Song in Kaluli Expression.* Publications of the American Folklore Society. Vol. 5. Philadelphia: University of Pennsylvania Press.

Feld, Steven, and Aaron Fox. 1994. "Music and Language." *Annual Review of Anthropology* 23: 25–53.

Ferchiou, Sophie. 1991. "The Possession Cults of Tunisia: A Religious System Functioning as a System of Reference and a Social Field for Performing Actions."

In *Women's Medicine: The Zar-Bori Cult in Africa and Beyond*, edited by I. M. Lewis, Ahmed Al-Sa, and Sayyid Hurreiz, 209–218. Edinburgh: Edinburgh University Press.

Fernandez, James W. 1991. *Beyond Metaphor: The Theory of Tropes in Anthropology*. Stanford, Calif.: Stanford University Press.

———. 1986. *Persuasions and Performances: The Play of Tropes in Culture*. Bloomington: Indiana University Press.

Ficino, Marsilio, and Michael J. B. Allen. 1981. *Marsilio Ficino and the Phaedran Charioteer: Introduction, Texts, Translations*. Berkeley: University of California Press.

Fine, Elizabeth C. 1984. *The Folklore Text: From Performance to Print*. Bloomington: Indiana University Press.

Floyd, Samuel A. 1995. *The Power of Black Music: Interpreting Its History from Africa to the United States*. New York: Oxford University Press.

Forman, Murray. 2002. "Soundtrack to a Crisis: Music, Context, Discourse." *Television and New Media* 3, no. 2 (May): 191–204. Available at http://www.csa.com/ids70/gateway.php?mode=pdf&doi=10.1177%2F152747640200300201l&db=sagecom-set-c&s1=0481a105f171b290704da15e7194365a&s2=7f5ce68f43f7dcfa89d70fe8b3cf1114.

Fouad, Mohammed. 1995. Personal Communication.

Foucault, Michel. 1972. *The Archaeology of Knowledge and the Discourse on Language*. Translated by A. M. Sheridan Smith. New York: Pantheon Books.

Fox, Aaron A. 2004. *Real Country: Music and Language in Working-Class Culture*. Durham, N.C.: Duke University Press.

Frazer, James George. 1922. *The Golden Bough: A Study in Magic and Religion*. New York: MacMillan.

Freud, Sigmund. 1899. "Screen Memories." In *Standard Edition*. Vol. 34: 301–322. London: The Hogarth Press.

Fuson, Tim Abdellah. 2001. "'Where are You, Children of the Sudan?': The Recollection of Slavery in the Lila Ritual of the Gnawa of Morocco." Paper Presented at the conference "Slavery and Religion in the Modern Era," Essaouira.

Ganay, Soange de, et al. 1987. *Ethnologiques: Hommages à Marcel Griaule*. Paris: Hermann.

Gates, Henry Louis. 1988. *The Signifying Monkey: A Theory of Afro-American Literary Criticism*. New York: Oxford University Press.

Geertz, Clifford. 1988. *Works and Lives: The Anthropologist as Author*. Cambridge, England: Polity Press.

Geertz, Clifford, Hildred Geertz, and Lawrence Rosen. 1978. *Meaning and Order in Moroccan Society: Three Essays in Cultural Analysis*. Cambridge, England: Cambridge University Press.

Gell, Alfred. 1992. *The Anthropology of Time: Cultural Constructions of Temporal Maps and Images*. Explorations in Anthropology. Oxford: Berg.

al-Ghazzali. 1997. *The Alchemy of Happiness*. Wisdom of the East Series. Translated from the Hindustani by Claude Field. Lahore: Sh. Muhammad Ashraf.

———. 1909. *The Confessions of Al-Ghazzali*. Translated by Claude Field. London: John Murray.

Gilroy, Paul. 1994. "Sounds Authentic: Black Music, Ethnicity, and the Challenge of a Changing Same." In *Imagining Home: Class, Culture, and Nationalism in the African Diaspora*, edited by Sidney J. Lemelle and Robin D. G. Kelley. New York: Verso.

———. 1993. *The Black Atlantic: Modernity and Double Consciousness*. Cambridge, Mass.: Harvard University Press.

Ginsburg, Faye D., Lila Abu-Lughod, and Brian Larkin, eds. 2002. *Media Worlds: Anthropology on New Terrain*. Berkeley: University of California Press.

Girard, René. 1972. *La Violence Et Le Sacré*. Paris: Grasset.

Goffman, Erving. 1963. *Behavior in Public Places; Notes on the Social Organization of Gatherings*. New York: Free Press of Glencoe.

———. 1959. *The Presentation of Self in Everyday Life*. Doubleday Anchor Books, A174. Revised and enlarged ed. Garden City, N.Y.: Doubleday.

———. 1954. "Communication Conduct in an Island Community." Doctoral Dissertation, University of Chicago.

Goodman, Felicitas D. 1990a. "A Trance Dance with Masks: Research and Performance at the Cuyamungue Institute." *The Drama Review* 34, no. 1: 102–114.

Goodman, Jane E. 2005. *Berber Culture on the World Stage: From Village to Video*. Bloomington: Indiana University Press.

Gordon, Avery. 1997. *Ghostly Matters: Haunting and the Sociological Imagination*. Minneapolis: University of Minnesota Press.

Gouk, Penelope. 2004. "Raising Spirits and Restoring Souls: Early Modern Medical Explanations for Music's Effects." In *Hearing Cultures: Essays on Sound, Listening and Modernity*, edited by Veit Erlmann, 87–106. New York: Berg.

———. 2000. *Musical Healing in Cultural Contexts*. Aldershot: Ashgate.

———. 1999. *Music, Science, and Natural Magic in Seventeenth-Century England*. New Haven, Conn.: Yale University Press.

Gouk, Penelope, and Helen Hills. 2005. *Representing Emotions: New Connections in the Histories of Art, Music, and Medicine*. Aldershot: Ashgate.

Goux, Jean-Joseph. 1990. *Symbolic Economies: After Marx and Freud*. Ithaca, N.Y.: Cornell University Press.

Graham, Laura R. 1995. *Performing Dreams: Discourses of Immortality among the Xavante of Central Brazil*. Austin: University of Texas Press.

Grall, Xavier. 1977. *Le Cheval Couché*. Paris: Hachette.

Greene, Paul D., and Thomas Porcello. 2005. *Wired for Sound: Engineering and Technologies in Sonic Cultures*. Music/Culture. Middletown, Conn.: Wesleyan University Press.

Greenhouse, Carol J. 1996. *A Moment's Notice: Time Politics Across Cultures*. Ithaca, N.Y.: Cornell University Press.

Griaule, Marcel. 1957. *Methode de l'Ethnographie*. Oarus: Presses Universitaires de France.

———. 1947. *Arts De l'Afrique Noire*. Paris: Éditions du Chêne.

———. 1938. *Masques Dogons*. Paris: Institut d'Ethnologie.

Griaule, Marcel, and Germaine Dieterlen. 1965. *Le Renard Pâle*. Paris: Institut d'Ethnologie.

Grice, H. P. 1989. *Studies in the Way of Words*. Cambridge, Mass.: Harvard University Press.

Grotowski, Jerzy. 1969. "Towards the Poor Theatre." In *Public Domain: Essays on the Theatre*, edited by Richard Schechner, 190. Indianapolis and New York: The Bobbs Merrill Co.

Guilbault, Jocelyne. 2000. "Racial Projects and Musical Discourses in Trinidad, West Indies." In *Music and the Racial Imagination*, edited by Ronald Michael Radano and Philip Vilas Bohlman, 435–458. Chicago: University of Chicago Press.

———. 1993. *Zouk: World Music in the West Indies*. Chicago Studies in Ethnomusicology. Chicago: University of Chicago Press.

Hakmoun, Hassan. 2004. Personal Communication.

Hale, Thomas A. 1998. *Griots and Griottes: Masters of Words and Music*. Bloomington: Indiana University Press.

Hall, Stuart. 1980. *Culture, Media, Language: Working Papers in Cultural Studies, 1972–79*. London: Hutchinson.

Hammoudi, Abdellah. 1997. *Master and Disciple: The Cultural Foundations of Moroccan Authoritarianism* [Maître et disciple]. Chicago: University of Chicago Press.

———. 1993. *The Victim and Its Masks: An Essay on Sacrifice and Masquerade in the Maghreb*. Chicago: University of Chicago Press.

Hanks, William F. 1990. *Referential Practice: Language and Lived Space among the Maya*. Chicago: University of Chicago Press.

Hannerz, Ulf. 1989. "Notes on the Global Ecumene." *Public Culture* 1, no. 2: 66–75.

Hartman, Saidiya V. 1997. *Scenes of Subjection: Terror, Slavery, and Self-Making in Nineteenth-Century America*. Race and American Culture. New York: Oxford University Press.

Haviland, John Beard. 1977. *Gossip, Reputation, and Knowledge in Zinacantan*. Chicago: University of Chicago Press.

Heath, Jeffrey. 1989. *From Code-Switching to Borrowing: Foreign and Diglossic Mixing in Moroccan Arabic*. Library of Arabic Linguistics. Vol. monograph, no. 9. London: Kegan Paul International.

———. 1987. *Ablaut and Ambiguity: Phonology of a Moroccan Arabic Dialect*. SUNY Series in Linguistics. Albany, N.Y.: State University of New York Press.

Hebdige, Dick. 1979. *Subculture, the Meaning of Style*. New Accents. London: Methuen.

Hélias, Pierre Jakez, and June Guicharnaud. 1978. *The Horse of Pride: Life in a Rural Breton Village*. New Haven, Conn.: Yale University Press.

Hell, Bertrand. 2002a. "Honnis Mais Efficaces! Inversion Sociale et Pouvoir Thérapeutique dans le Système de la Possession au Maroc." In *Convocations Thérapeutique du Sacré*, edited by Raymond Massé and Jean Benoist. Paris: Karthala.

———. 2002b. *Le Tourbillon des Génies: au Maroc avec les Gnawa*. Paris: Flammarion.

———. 2001. "L'Esclave Et Le Saint. Les Gnawa Et La Baraka De Moulay Abdallah Ben Hsein (Maroc)." In *Saints, Sainteté Et Martyre: La Fabrication De l'exemplarité*, edited by P. Centlivres, 149–174. Paris: Editions de la Maison des Sciences de l'Homme.

———. 2000. "'Travailler' Avec Ses Genies: De La Possession Sauvage à La Possession Maîtrisée Chez Les Gnawa Du Maroc." In *La Politique Des Esprits: Chamanismes Et Religions Universalistes*, edited by Denise Aigle, Benédicte Brac de la Perrière, and Jean-Pierre Chaumeil. Nanterre: Societé d'Ethnologie.

———. 1999a. "'Ouvrir Toutes Les Portes': Le Sang Sacrificiel chez les Gnawa du Maroc." In *Sacrifices en Islam: Espaces et Temps d'un Rituel*, edited by, Pierre Bonte, Anne-Marie Brisebarre, and Altan Gokalp. Paris: Centre National de la Recherche Scientifique.

———. 1999b. *Possession et Chamanisme: Les Maîtres des Désordres*. Paris: Flammarion.

Herskovits, Melville J. 1966. *The New World Negro; Selected Papers in Afroamerican Studies*. Edited by Frances S. Herskovits. Bloomington: Indiana University Press.

Herzfeld, Michael. 1997. *Cultural Intimacy: Social Poetics in the Nation-State*. New York: Routledge.

———. 1985. *The Poetics of Manhood: Contest and Identity in a Cretan Mountain Village*. Princeton, N.J.: Princeton University Press.

Hirshkind, Charles. 2001. "The Ethics of Listening: Cassette-Sermon Audition in Contemporary Egypt." *American Ethnologist* 28, no. 3: 623–649.

Hobsbawm, E. J., and T. O. Ranger. 1983. *The Invention of Tradition*. Past and Present Publications. Cambridge, England: Cambridge University Press.

Hodgson, Dorothy. 1997. "Embodying the Contradictions of Modernity: Gender and Spirit Possession among Maasai Women in Tanzania." In *Gendered Encounters: Challenging Cultural Boundaries and Social Hierarchies in Africa*, edited by Maria Grosz-Ngate and Omari H. Kokole, 111–129. New York: Routledge.

Hourani, Albert Habib. 1992. *A History of the Arab Peoples*. New York: Warner Books.

———. 1991. *Islam in European Thought*. Cambridge, England: Cambridge University Press.

Howes, David. 1991a. "Olfaction and Transition." In *The Varieties of Sensory Experience: A Sourcebook in the Anthropology of the Senses*, edited by David Howes, 128–147. Toronto: University of Toronto Press.

————, ed. 1991b. *The Varieties of Sensory Experience: A Sourcebook in the Anthropology of the Senses.* Anthropological Horizons. Toronto: University of Toronto Press.

Hubert, Henri, and Marcel Mauss. 1964. *Sacrifice: Its Nature and Function.* Chicago: University of Chicago Press.

Hymes, Dell H. 1974. *Foundations in Sociolinguistics; an Ethnographic Approach.* Philadelphia: University of Pennsylvania Press.

Irvine, Judith. 1990. "Registering Affect: Heteroglossia in the Linguistic Expression of Emotion." In *Language and the Politics of Emotion*, edited by Catherine Lutz and Lila Abu-Lughod, 126–161. Cambridge, England: Cambridge University Press.

Jackson, Travis A. 2003. "Jazz Performance as Ritual: The Blues Aesthetic and the African Diaspora." In *The African Diaspora: A Musical Perspective*, edited by Ingrid T. Monson, 23–82. New York: Routledge.

Jakobson, Roman. 1987. *Language in Literature.* Edited by Krystyna Pomorska, and Stephen Rudy. Cambridge, Mass.: Belknap Press.

————. 1981. "Poetry of Grammar and Grammar of Poetry." In *Selected Writings*, vol. 3, edited by S. Rudy, 751–756. The Hague: Mouton.

————. 1960. "Closing Statement: Linguistics and Poetics." In *Style in Language*, edited by T. A. Sebeok, 350–377. Cambridge: MIT Press.

————. 1957. *Shifters, Verbal Categories, and the Russian Verb.* Cambridge: Harvard University Russian Language Project.

Jakobson, Roman, and Morris Halle. 1971. *Fundamentals of Language.* Janua Linguarum. 2nd revised ed. Vol. 1. The Hague: Mouton.

Jameson, Frederic. 1991. *Postmodernism, or, The Cultural Logic of Late Capitalism.* Durham, N.C.: Duke University Press.

Jankowsky, Richard. 2006. "Black Spirits, White Saints: Music, Spirit Possession, and Sub-Saharans in Tunisia." *Ethnomusicology* 50 vol. 3: 373–410.

Johnson, Mark. 1987. *The Body in the Mind: The Bodily Basis of Meaning, Imagination, and Reason.* Chicago: University of Chicago Press.

Jung, C. G. 1963. *Memories, Dreams, Reflections* [Erinnerungen, Träume, Gedanken]. Edited by and Aniela Jaffé. Translated by Clara Winston and Richard Winston. New York: Vintage Books.

Kapchan, Deborah. In Progress. "Creating the Transnational Sacred: Festival, Hope and the Promise of Sonic Translation."

————. 2006. "Talking Trash: Creating Home and Anti-Home in Austin's Salsa Culture." *American Ethnologist* 33, no. 3: 361–377.

————. 2002. "Possessing Gnawa Culture: Displaying Sound, Creating History in an Unofficial Museum." *Music and Anthropology* 7.

————. 2000a. "Following the Entranced Ones: Gnawa Performances and Trance in Rabat." *Garland Encyclopedia of Middle Eastern Folklore.* Vol. 6. New York: Routledge.

————. 2000b. "Le Marché De Transe: Le Cas Des Gnaoua Marocains." In *La Transe*, edited by Abdelhafid Chlyeh, 157–168. Casablanca: Marsam.

———. 1996. *Gender on the Market: Moroccan Women and the Revoicing of Tradition.* University of Pennsylvania Press New Cultural Studies. Philadelphia: University of Pennsylvania Press.

Kapferer, Bruce. 1983. *A Celebration of Demons: Exorcism and the Aesthetics of Healing in Sri Lanka.* Bloomington: Indiana University Press.

Kaplan, Caren. 1992. "Resisting Autobiography." In *De-Colonizing the Subject: The Politics of Gender in Women's Autobiography,* edited by Sidonie Smith and Julia Watson. Minneapolis: University of Minnesota Press.

Keil, Charles. 1995. "The Theory of Participatory Discrepancies: A Progress Report." *Ethnomusicology* 39, no. 1: 1–19.

———. 1991 [1966]. *Urban Blues.* Chicago: University of Chicago Press.

Keil, Charles, and Steven Feld. 1994. *Music Grooves: Essays and Dialogues.* Chicago: University of Chicago Press.

Kelley, Robin D. G. 2002. *Freedom Dreams: The Black Radical Imagination.* Boston: Beacon Press.

———. 2001."Finding Jazz's Soul in Africa's Music: Randy Weston Archives a Synthesis of African and African-American, of Benin and Brooklyn." *New York Times,* July 8. http://select.nytimes.com/search/restricted/article?res= F40915FB355D0C7B8CDDAE0894D9404482.

———. 1998. "Check in the Technique: Black Urban Culture and the Predicament of Social Science." In *In Near Ruins,* edited by Nicholas B. Dirks, 39–66. Minneapolis: University of Minnesota Press, 1998.

———. 1997. *Yo' Mama's Disfunktional!: Fighting the Culture Wars in Urban America.* Boston: Beacon Press.

———. 1995. *Into the Fire—African Americans since 1970/by Robin D.G. Kelley.* The Young Oxford History of African Americans. Vol. 10. New York: Oxford University Press.

———. 1994. *Race Rebels: Culture, Politics, and the Black Working Class.* New York: Free Press.

Kelley, Robin D. G., and Earl Lewis. 2000. *To Make Our World Anew: A History of African Americans.* New York: Oxford University Press.

Kendon, Adam. 1995. "Gestures as Illocutionary and Discourse Structure Markers in Southern Italian Conversation." *Journal of Pragmatics* 23, no. 3: 247–279.

———. 1994. "Do Gestures Communicate? A Review." *Research on Language and Social Interaction* 27, no. 3: 175–200.

———. 1993a. "An Agenda for Gesture Studies." *Semiotic Review of Books* 7, no. 3: 7–12.

———. 1993b. "Human Gesture." In *Tools, Language and Cognition in Human Evolution,* edited by K. R. Gibson and T. Ingold. Cambridge: Cambridge University Press.

———. 1993c. "Space, Time and Gesture." *Degrés* 74: 3a–16a.

———. 1982. "The Study of Gesture: Some Observations on Its History." *Recherches Sémiotiques/Semiotic Inquiry* 2, no. 1: 45–62.

———. 1981a. "Behavioural Foundations for the Process of Frame Attunement in Face-to-Face Interaction." In *Discovery Strategies in the Psychology of Action*, edited by G. P. Ginsburg, M. Brenner, and M. von Cranach. London: Academic Press.

———. 1981b. "Geography of Gesture." *Semiotica* 37, no. 1/2: 129–163.

Kenyon, Susan. 1995. "Zar as Modernization in Contemporary Sudan." *Anthropological Quarterly* 68, no. 2: 107–120.

———. 1991. *Five Women of Sennar: Culture and Change in Central Sudan.* Oxford Studies in African Affairs. Oxford: Oxford University Press.

Kirshenblatt-Gimblett, Barbara. 1998. *Destination Culture: Tourism, Museums, and Heritage.* Berkeley: University of California Press.

Kirshenblatt-Gimblett, Barbara, and Anthony E. Backhouse. 1976. *Speech Play: Research and Resources for Studying Linguistic Creativity.* University of Pennsylvania Publications in Conduct and Communication. Philadelphia: University of Pennsylvania Press.

Kisliuk, Michelle Robin. 1998. *Seize the Dance! BaAka Musical Life and the Ethnography of Performance.* New York: Oxford University Press.

Koestenbaum, Wayne. 1993. *The Queen's Throat: Opera, Homosexuality, and the Mystery of Desire.* New York: Poseidon Press.

Kristeva, Julia. 1984. *Revolution in Poetic Language.* New York: Columbia University Press.

———. 1982. *Powers of Horror: An Essay on Abjection.* European Perspectives. New York: Columbia University Press.

———. 1980. *Desire in Language: A Semiotic Approach to Literature and Art.* European Perspectives. New York: Columbia University Press.

Kristeva, Julia. 1986. *The Kristeva Reader.* Edited by Toril Moi. New York: Columbia University Press.

Laderman, Carol. 1991. *Taming the Wind of Desire: Psychology, Medicine, and Aesthetics in Malay Shamanistic Performance.* Comparative Studies of Health Systems and Medical Care. Berkeley: University of California Press.

Laderman, Carol, and Marina Roseman, eds. 1996. *The Performance of Healing.* New York: Routledge.

Laidler, Keith. 1998. *The Head of God.* London: Weidenfeld.

Lambek, Michael. 2001. "The Value of Coins in a Sakalava Polity: Money, Death, and Historicity in Mahajanga, Madagascar." *Comparative Studies in Society and History* 43, no. 4: 735–762.

———. 1993. *Knowledge and Practice in Mayotte: Local Discourses of Islam, Sorcery, and Spirit Possession.* Anthropological Horizons. Toronto: University of Toronto Press.

———. 1981. *Human Spirits: A Cultural Account of Trance in Mayotte.* Cambridge Studies in Cultural Systems. Vol. 6. Cambridge, England: Cambridge University Press.

Langer, Susanne Katherina Knauth. 1957. *Philosophy in a New Key; a Study in the Symbolism of Reason, Rite, and Art.* 3d ed. Cambridge, Mass.: Harvard University Press.

———. 1953. *Feeling and Form; a Theory of Art.* New York: Scribner.

Lapassade, Georges. 1998. *Derdeba: La Nuit Des Gnaoua.* Marrakech: Traces du Présent.

———. 1997. *Les Rites De Possession.* Paris: Anthropos.

———. 1990. *La Transe.* Paris: Presses Universitaires de France.

Larkin, Brian. 2002. "The Materiality of Cinema Theaters in Northern Nigeria." In *Media Worlds: Anthropology on New Terrain,* edited by Faye D. Ginsburg, Lila Abu-Lughod, and Brian Larkin. Berkeley: University of California Press.

———. 1997. "Indian Films and Nigerian Lovers: Media and the Creation of Parallel Modernities." *Africa* 67, no. 3: 406–440.

Laroui, Abdullah. 1982. *L'Histoire Du Maroc.* Paris: Maspero.

Lawrence, William. 1999. Personal Communication. Boston, Mass.

Le Coadic, Ronan, Michel Denis, and Michel Wieviorka. 1998. *L'Identité Bretonne. Essais.* Rennes France: Terre de Brume Editions, Presses universitaires de Rennes.

Lebesque, Morvan. 1970. *Comment Peut-on Être Breton: Essai Sur La Démocratie Française.* Paris: Seuil.

Leder, Drew. 1990. *The Absent Body.* Chicago: University of Chicago Press.

Lee, Benjamin. 1997. *Talking Heads: Language, Metalanguage, and the Semiotics of Subjectivity.* Durham, N.C.: Duke University Press.

Lefebvre, Henri. 1991. *The Production of Space.* Oxford: Blackwell.

Leiris, Michel. 1958. *La Possession et ses Aspects théâtraux Chez Les Éthiopiens De Gondar.* Paris: Plon.

———. 1934. *L'Afrique fantôme [de Dakar à Djibouti, 1931–1933].* Paris: Gallimard.

Lemelle, Sidney J., and Robin D. G. Kelley, eds. 1994. *Imagining Home: Class, Culture, and Nationalism in the African Diaspora.* The Haymarket Series. New York: Verso.

Lenneberg, Eric H. 1967. *Biological Foundations of Language.* New York: Wiley.

Lepecki, André. 2006. *Exhausting Dance: Performance and the Politics of Movement.* New York: Routledge,.

———. 2004. *Of the Presence of the Body: Essays on Dance and Performance Theory.* Middletown, Conn.: Wesleyan University Press.

Lévi-Strauss, Claude. 1969a. *The Naked Man [Homme nu].* New York: Harper and Row.

———. 1969b. *The Raw and the Cooked.* His Introduction to a Science of Mythology, I. [Le cru et le cuit]. New York: Harper & Row.

Lewis, I. M. 1996. "Spirit Possession and Deprivation Cults." *Man* 19: 307–329.

———. 1989 [1987]. *Ecstatic Religion: A Study of Shamanism and Spirit Possession.* 2nd ed. New York: Routledge.

———. 1986. *Religion in Context: Cults and Charisma.* Cambridge, England: Cambridge University Press.

———. 1983. "The Past and the Present in Islam: The Case of African 'Survivals.'" *Temenos* 19: 55–67.

―――. 1971. *Ecstatic Religion: An Anthropological Study of Spirit Possession and Shamanism*. Baltimore, Md.: Penguin Books.

Lidov, D. 1980. "Musical and Verbal Semantics." *Semiotica* 31, no. 3/4: 369–391.

Lipsitz, George. 1998. *The Possessive Investment in Whiteness: How White People Profit from Identity Politics*. Philadelphia: Temple University Press.

―――. 1994. *Dangerous Crossroads: Popular Music, Postmodernism, and the Poetics of Place*. New York: Verso.

Lovejoy, Paul E. 2004. *Slavery on the Frontiers of Islam*. Princeton, N.J.: Markus Wiener Publishers.

―――. 2000. *Identity in the Shadow of Slavery*. The Black Atlantic. New York: Continuum.

―――. 1997. "The African Diaspora: Revisionist Interpretations of Ethnicity, Culture, and Religion Under Slavery." *Studies in the World History of Slavery, Abolition, and Emancipation* 2. http://www.yorku.ca/nhp/publications/Lovejoy_Studies%20in%20the%20world%20History%20of%20Slavery.pdf.

―――. 1983. *Transformations in Slavery: A History of Slavery in Africa*. African Studies Series. Vol. 36. Cambridge, England: Cambridge University Press.

Lovejoy, Paul E., and Pat Ama Tokunbo Williams, eds. 1997. *Displacement and the Politics of Violence in Nigeria*. New York: Brill.

Low, Setha M. 1994. "Embodied Metaphors: Nerves as Lived Experience." In *Embodiment and Experience: The Existential Ground of Culture and Self*, edited by Thomas J. Csordas, 139–162. Cambridge, England: Cambridge University Press.

Lutz, Catherine. 1988. *Unnatural Emotions: Everyday Sentiments on a Micronesian Atoll and Their Challenge to Western Theory*. Chicago: University of Chicago Press.

Lutz, Catherine, and Geoffrey White. 1986. "The Anthropology of Emotions." *Annual Review of Anthropology* 15: 405–436.

Lyotard, Jean François. 1992. *The Postmodern Explained: Correspondence, 1982–1985*. Translated by Julian Pefanis and Morgan Thomas. Sydney: Power Publications.

MacCannell, Dean. 1999. *The Tourist: A New Theory of the Leisure Class*. Berkeley: University of California Press.

MacDonald, Duncan B. 1901. "Al-Ghazzali on Music and Ecstasy: Emotional Religion in Islam as Affected by Music and Singing; being a Translation of a Book of the Ihya Ulum Ad-Din of Al-Ghazzali with Analysis, Annotation, and Appendices." *Journal of the Royal Asiatic Society*.

Maghnia, Abdelghani. 1996. "Un Génie Ophidien de la Forêt." Rabat, Université Mohammed V, Publications de l'Institut des Études Africaines.

Mahmood, Saba. 2005. *Politics of Piety: The Islamic Revival and the Feminist Subject*. Princeton, N.J.: Princeton University Press.

Malinowski, Bronislaw. 1963. *The Family among the Australian Aborigines, a Sociological Study*. New York: Schocken Books.

―――. 1929. *The Sexual Life of Savages in North-Western Melanesia; an Ethnographic Account of Courtship, Marriage and Family Life among the Natives of the Trobri and Islands, British New Guinea*. New York: Eugenics Pub. Co.

Marcus, George E. 1998. *Ethnography through Thick and Thin*. Princeton, N.J.: Princeton University Press.

Marcus, George E., and Fred R. Myers. 1995. *The Traffic in Culture: Refiguring Art and Anthropology*. Berkeley: University of California Press.

Martin, Randy. 1998. *Critical Moves: Dance Studies in Theory and Politics*. Durham, N.C.: Duke University Press.

―――. 1990. *Performance as Political Act: The Embodied Self*. Critical Perspectives in Social Theory. New York: Bergin and Garvey.

―――. 1985. "Dance as a Social Movement." *Social Text* 12: 54–70.

Marx, Karl. 1977. *Capital*. New York: Vintage.

Masquelier, Adeline. 2001. *Prayer Has Spoiled Everything: Possession, Power, and Identity in an Islamic Town of Niger*. Body, Commodity, Text. Durham, N.C.: Duke University Press.

―――. 1994. "Lightning, Death, and the Avenging Spirits: Bori Values in a Muslim World." *Journal of Religion in Africa* 24, no. 1, 2–51.

―――. 1993. "Narratives of Power, Images of Wealth: The Ritual Economy of Bori in the Market." In *Modernity and its Malcontents: Ritual and Power in Post-Colonial Africa*, edited by Jean and John Comaroff, 3–33. Chicago: University of Chicago Press.

Mauss, Marcel. 1979 [1935]. "Techniques of the Body." In *Sociology and Psychology*, edited by Marcel Mauss, 97–123. London: Routledge and Kegan.

―――. 1972 [1902]. *A General Theory of Magic*. Translated by Robert Brain. New York: Routledge.

Mbiti, John S. 1969. *African Religions and Philosophy*. New York: Praeger.

McNeill, David. 1992. *Hand and Mind: What Gestures Reveal about Thought*. Chicago: University of Chicago Press.

Mead, George Herbert, and Charles William Morris. 1963. *Mind, Self, and Society From the Standpoint of a Social Behaviorist*. Chicago, Ill.: University of Chicago Press.

Meintjes, Louise. 2003. *Sound of Africa! Making Music Zulu in a South African Studio*. Durham, N.C.: Duke University Press.

Merleau-Ponty, Maurice. 1962. *Phenomenology of Perception* [Phénoménologie de la perception]. International Library of Philosophy and Scientific Method. New York: Humanities Press.

Messick, Brinkley Morris. 1993. *The Calligraphic State: Textual Domination and History in a Muslim Society*. Comparative Studies on Muslim Societies. Vol. 16. Berkeley: University of California Press.

Métraux, Alfred. 1958. *Le Vaudou Haïtien*. Paris: Gallimard.

Meyer, Birgit. 1999. *Translating the Devil: Religion and Modernity among the Ewe in Ghana*. Trenton, N.J.: Africa World Press.

Meyer, Birgit, and Annelies Moors. 2006. *Religion, Media, and the Public Sphere*. Bloomington: Indiana University Press.

Meyer, Birgit, and Peter Pels, eds. 2003. *Magic and Modernity: Interfaces of Revelation and Concealment*. Stanford, Calif.: Stanford University Press.

Michotte, A. E. 1950. "The Emotions Regarded as Functional Connections." In *Feelings and Emotions*, edited by M. L. Reymert, 114–126. New York: McGraw Hill.

Monson, Ingrid T. 2003a [2000]. "Introduction." In *The African Diaspora: A Musical Perspective*, edited by Ingrid T. Monson, 329–352. New York: Routledge.

———. 2003b [2000]. "Art Blakely's African Diaspora." In *The African Diaspora: A Musical Perspective*, edited by Ingrid T. Monson, 1–22. New York: Routledge.

———, ed. 1996. *Saying Something: Jazz Improvisation and Interaction*. Chicago Studies in Ethnomusicology. Chicago: University of Chicago Press.

Monteil, Charles. 1924. *Les Bambara du Ségon et du Kaarta: Etude Historique, Ethnographique et Littéraire d'une Peuplade du Soudan Français*. Paris: Larose.

Morris, Charles William. 1964. *Signification and Significance; a Study of the Relations of Signs and Values*. Studies in Communication. Cambridge, Mass.: Massachusetts Institute of Technology Press.

Mudimbe, V. Y. 1988. *The Invention of Africa: Gnosis, Philosophy, and the Order of Knowledge*. African Systems of Thought. Bloomington: Indiana University Press.

Munn, Nancy D. 1992. "The Cultural Anthropology of Time: A Critical Essay." *Annual Review of Anthropology* 21: 93–123.

Muñoz, José Esteban. 2000. "Feeling Brown: Ethnicity and Affect in Ricardo Bracho's the Sweetest Hangover (and Other STDs)." *Theatre Journal* 52: 67–79.

Myers, Fred R. 2002. *Painting Culture: The Making of an Aboriginal High Art*. Durham, N.C.: Duke University Press.

Naficy, Hamid. 1993. *The Making of Exile Cultures: Iranian Television in Los Angeles*. Minneapolis: University of Minnesota Press.

Needham, Rodney. 1967. "Percussion and Transition." *Man* 2: 606–614.

Nelson, Kristina. 1985. *The Art of Reciting the Qur'an*. Modern Middle East Series. Vol. 11. Austin: University of Texas Press.

Nora, Pierre. 1989. "Between Memory and History: Lieux de Mémoire." *Representations* 26, no. 12: 7–25.

Noyes, Dorothy. 2003. *Fire in the Plaça: Catalan Festival Politics After Franco*. Philadelphia: University of Pennsylvania Press.

Nuckolls, Janis B. 2004. "Language and Nature in Sound Alignment." In *Hearing Cultures: Essays on Sound, Listening and Modernity*, edited by Veit Erlmann, 65–86. Oxford: Berg.

———. 1996. *Sounds Like Life: Sound-Symbolic Grammar, Performance, and Cognition in*

Pastaza Quechua. Oxford Studies in Anthropological Linguistics. Vol. 2. New York: Oxford University Press.

Nyong'o, Tavia. 2005. "Black Theatre's Closet Drama." *Theatre Journal* 57, no. 4: 590–592.

———. 2002. "Racial Kitsch and Black Performance." *Yale Journal of Criticism* 15, no. 2: 371–91.

Obeyesekere, Gananath. 1981. *Medusa's Hair: An Essay on Personal Symbols and Religious Experience*. Chicago: University of Chicago Press.

O'Brien, Susan. 2000. "Gender, Islam, and Healing: The Spirit Possession Cult of Bori and Muslim Hausa History in Northern Nigeria." Ph.D. dissertation, University of Wisconsin, Madison.

Ochs, E., and Capps, L. 1996. "'Narrating the Self.'" *Annual Review of Anthropology* 25: 19–43.

Ondaatje, Michael. 2000. *Anil's Ghost*. New York: Vintage Press.

Ong, Aihwa. 1987. *Spirits of Resistance and Capitalist Discipline: Factory Women in Malaysia*. State University of New York Series in the Anthropology of Work. Albany: State University of New York Press.

Ong, Walter J. 1982. *Orality and Literacy: The Technologizing of the Word*. New Accents. London: Methuen.

Ortner, Sherry B. 1999. *The Fate of "Culture": Geertz and Beyond*. Representations Books. Vol. 8. Berkeley: University of California Press.

Ossman, Susan. 2002. *Three Faces of Beauty: Casablanca, Paris, Cairo*. Durham, N.C.: Duke University Press.

———. 1994. *Picturing Casablanca: Portraits of Power in a Modern City*. Berkeley: University of California Press.

Palmer, Robert. 1973. "Tangier." *Rolling Stones Magazine* (May 1973).

Pamuk, Orhan. 1994. *The Black Book*. New York: Farrar, Straus and Giroux.

Pandolfo, Stefania. 1997. *Impasse of the Angels: Scenes from a Moroccan Space of Memory*. Chicago: University of Chicago Press.

Pâques, Viviana. 1991. *La Religion des Esclaves: Recherches Sur La Confrérie Marocaine Des Gnawa*. Rome: Vitalli Press.

———. 1976. "Le Monde Des Gnawa." In *L'Autre Et Ailleurs. Hommage à Roger Bastide*, edited by J. Poirier et F. Raveau, 169–182. Paris: Berger-Levrault.

———. 1964. *L'Arbre Cosmique Dans La Pensée Populaire Et Dans La Vie Quotidienne Du Nord-Ouest Africain*. Paris: Institut d'Ethnologie.

Peirce, Charles S., and Max Harold Fisch. 1982. *Writings of Charles S. Peirce: A Chronological Edition*. Bloomington: Indiana University Press.

Pels, Peter. 2003. "Introduction: Magic and Modernity." In *Magic and Modernity: Interfaces of Revelation and Concealment*, edited by Brigit Meyer and Peter Pels, 1–38. Stanford, Calif.: Stanford University Press.

Phelan, Peggy. 1993a. *Unmarked: The Politics of Performance*. New York: Routledge.

———. 1993b. "Writing and Difference." In *Acting Out: Feminist Performances*, edited by Peggy Phelan and Lynda Hart, 000–000. Ann Arbor: University of Michigan Press. [Comp: Please carry: Au: page nos.?]

Piscatori, James P., and Dale F. Eickelman. 1990. *Muslim Travellers: Pilgrimage, Migration, and the Religious Imagination*. Berkeley: University of California Press.

Plato. 1936. *The Works of Plato*. Edited by B. Jowett. 4 volumes. New York: Tudor.

Poirot, Luis. 1990. *Pablo Neruda: Absence and Presence*. Translated by Alasteir Reid. New York: W. W. Norton and Co.

Proust, Marcel. 1993. *Search of Lost Time: Volume III. The Guermantes Way*. Translated by C.K. Scott Moncrieff and Terence Kilmartin. New York: Modern Library.

Quinn, Bob. 2005. *The Atlantean Irish: Ireland's Oriental and Maritime Heritage*. Dublin: Lilliput Press.

Rachik, Hassan. 1990. *Sacrâe Et Sacrifice Dans Le Haut Atlas Marocain*. Sociologie Collection. Casablanca: Afrique Orient.

Radano, Ronald Michael. 2000. "Hot Fantasies: American Modernism and the Idea of Black Rhythm." In *Music and the Racial Imagination*, edited by Ronald Michael Radano and Philip Vilas Bohlman, 459–482. Chicago: University of Chicago Press.

Radano, Ronald Michael, and Philip Vilas Bohlman. 2000a. "Music and Race, Their Past, Their Presence." In *Music and the Racial Imagination*, edited by Ronald Michael Radano and Philip Vilas Bohlman, 1–53. Chicago: University of Chicago Press.

———, eds. 2000b. *Music and the Racial Imagination*. Chicago: University of Chicago Press.

Rasmussen, Susan J. 1995. *Spirit Possession and Personhood among the Kel Ewey Tuareg*. Cambridge Studies in Social and Cultural Anthropology. Vol. 94. Cambridge, England: Cambridge University Press.

Reddy, William M. 2001. *The Navigation of Feeling: A Framework for the History of Emotions*. New York: Cambridge University Press.

Roob, Alexander. 2001. *The Hermetic Museum: Alchemy & Mysticism* [Alchemie & Mystik]. New York: Taschen.

Rosaldo, Renato. 1989. *Culture and Truth: The Remaking of Social Analysis*. Boston: Beacon Press.

Rose, Tricia. 1994. *Black Noise: Rap Music and Black Culture in Contemporary America*. Music/Culture. Hanover, N.H.: Wesleyan University Press/University Press of New England.

Rosello, Mireille. 2005. *France and the Maghreb: Performative Encounters*. Gainesville: University Press of Florida.

Roseman, Marina. 1991. *Healing Sounds from the Malaysian Rainforest: Temiar Music and Medicine*. Comparative Studies of Health Systems and Medical Care. Berkeley: University of California Press.

Rosen, Lawrence. 1984. *Bargaining for Reality: The Construction of Social Relations in a Muslim Community*. Chicago: University of Chicago Press.

Rouch, Jean. 2003. *Ciné-Ethnography*. Translated by Steven Feld. Visible Evidence. Vol. 13. Minneapolis: University of Minnesota Press.

———. 1997. *Les Hommes et les Dieux du Fleuve: Ethnographique sur les Populations Songhay du Moven Niger, 1941–1983*. Paris: Artcom.

———. 1960. *La Religion et la Magie Songhay*. Paris: Presses Universitaires de France.

Rouget, Gilbert. 1985. *Music and Trance: A Theory of the Relations between Music and Possession* [Musique et la transe]. Chicago: University of Chicago Press.

Rudolph, Adam. 2001. Personal Communication. Marrakech.

Russell, Catherine. 1999. *Experimental Ethnography: The Work of Film in the Age of Video*. Durham, N.C.: Duke University Press.

Sadiqi, Fatima. 2003. *Women, Gender, and Language in Morocco*. Woman and Gender, the Middle East and the Islamic World. Vol. 1. Boston: Brill.

Samuels, David William. 2004. *Putting a Song on Top of It: Expression and Identity on the San Carlos Apache Reservation*. Tucson: University of Arizona Press.

Sapir, Edward. 1949. *Language, an Introduction to the Study of Speech*. Harvest Books. Vol. HB7. New York: Harcourt, Brace and World.

Sawyers, June Skinner. 2000. *The Complete Guide to Celtic Music: From the Highland Bagpipe and Riverdance to U2 and Enya*. London: Aurum.

Scanlon, Larry. 2003. "'Death Is a Drum': Rhythm, Modernity, and the Negro Poet Laureate." In *Music and the Racial Imagination*, edited by Ronald Michael Radano and Philip Vilas Bohlman, 510–553. Chicago: University of Chicago Press.

Schade-Poulsen, Marc. 1999. *Men and Popular Music in Algeria: The Social Significance of Raï*. Modern Middle East Series. Vol. 20. Austin: University of Texas Press.

Schafer, Murray. 1985. "Acoustic Space." In *Dwelling , Place, and Environment*, edited by D. Seamon and R. Mugerauer, 87–98. Dordrecht, Netherlands: M. Nijhoff.

Schechner, Richard. 2002. *Performance Studies: An Introduction*. New York: Routledge.

———. 1988. *Performance Theory*. Revised and expand ed. New York: Routledge.

———. 1985. *Between Theater and Anthropology*. Philadelphia: University of Pennsylvania Press.

———. 1969. *Public Domain: Essays on the Theater*. Indianapolis: Bobbs-Merrill.

Scheper-Hughes, Nancy. 1992. *Death without Weeping: The Violence of Everyday Life in Brazil*. Berkeley: University of California Press.

Schieffelin, Edward. 1996. "On Failure and Performance: Throwing the Medium Out of the Seance." In *The Performance of Healing*, edited by Carol Laderman and Marina Roseman, 59–90. New York: Routledge.

———. 1976. *The Sorrow of the Lonely and the Burning of the Dancers*. New York: St. Martin's Press.

Schimmel, Annemarie. 1975. *Mystical Dimensions of Islam*. Chapel Hill, N.C.: University of North Carolina Press.

Schneider, Rebecca. 1997. *The Explicit Body in Performance*. New York: Routledge.

Schneider, Rebecca, and Gabrielle H. Cody. 2002. *Re:Direction: A Theoretical and Practical Guide*. Worlds of Performance. New York: Routledge.

Schroeter, Daniel J. 2002. *The Sultan's Jew: Morocco and the Sephardi World*. Stanford Studies in Jewish History and Culture. Stanford, Calif.: Stanford University Press.

———. 1988. *Merchants of Essaouira: Urban Society and Imperialism in Southwestern Morocco, 1844–1886*. Cambridge Middle East Library. Cambridge, England: Cambridge University Press.

Schuyler, Philip. 2000. "Jajouka/Jahjouka/Zahjouka." In *Mass Mediations: New Approaches to Popular Culture in the Middle East and Beyond*, edited by Walter Armbrust, 146–160. Berkeley: University of California Press.

———. 1981. "Music and Meaning among the Gnawa Religious Brotherhood of Morocco." *The World of Music* 23, no. 1: 3–10.

———. 1975. *Morocco I: Music of Islam and Sufism in Morocco*. Kassel: Bärenreiter Musicaphon.

Searle, John. 1976. "The Classification of Illocutionary Acts." *Language in Society* 5: 1–23.

Senghor, Léopold Sédar. "Preface." *Ethnologiques: Hommages à Marcel Griaule*. Edited by Solange de Ganay, Annie Lebeuf, and Jean-Paul Lebeuf. Paris: Hermann.

Seremetakis, C. Nadia. 1994. *The Senses Still: Perception and Memory as Material Culture in Modernity*. Boulder, Colo.: Westview Press.

Serfaty, Abraham. 1969. "Salut Aux Afro-Américains." *Souffles* 15: 32–33.

Sharp, Lesley Alexandra. 1993. *The Possessed and the Dispossessed: Spirits, Identity, and Power in a Madagascar Migrant Town*. Comparative Studies of Health Systems and Medical Care. Vol. 37. Berkeley: University of California Press.

Sherzer, Joel. 2002. *Speech Play and Verbal Art*. Austin: University of Texas Press.

———. 1987. "A Discourse-Centered Approach to Language and Culture." *American Anthropologist* 89: 295–309.

———. 1983. *Kuna Ways of Speaking: An Ethnographic Perspective*. Texas Linguistics Series. Austin: University of Texas Press.

———. 1972. "Verbal and Nonverbal Deixis: The Pointed Lip Gesture among the San Blas Cuna." *Language in Society* 2, no. 1: 117–131.

Shimakawa, Karen. 2002. *National Abjection: The Asian American Body on Stage*. Durham, N.C.: Duke University Press.

Shohat, Ella. 1988. "Sephardim in Israel: Zionism from the Standpoint of Its Jewish Victims." *Social Text* 19/20: 1–35.

Shuman, Amy. 2005. *Other People's Stories: Entitlement Claims and the Critique of Empathy*. Urbana: University of Illinois Press.

———. 2004. Personal Communication.

Silverstein, Michael. 1996. "The Secret Life of Texts." In *Natural Histories of Discourse*, edited by Michael Silverstein and Greg Urban, 81–105. Chicago: University of Chicago Press.

———. 1976. "Shifters, Linguistic Categories, and Cultural Description." In *Meaning in Anthropology*, edited by Keith Basso and Henry Selby, 11–55. Albuquerque: University of New Mexico Press.

Silverstein, Paul, and Chantal Tetreault. 2006. "Postcolonial Urban Apartheid." *Items and Issues. Quarterly for the Social Science Research Council.*

———. 2005. *Postcolonial Urban Apartheid.* Social Science Research Council Forum http://riotsfrance.ssrc.org (accessed October 12, 2006).

———. "Urban Violence in France." Middle East Report. http://www.merip.org/ mero/interventions/silverstein_tetreault_interv.htm (accessed October 12, 2006).

Silverstein, Michael, and Greg Urban, eds. *Natural Histories of Discourse.* Chicago: University of Chicago Press.

Silverstein, Paul A. 2004. *Algeria in France: Transpolitics, Race, and Nation.* New Anthropologies of Europe. Bloomington: Indiana University Press.

Singer, Milton. 1989. "Pronouns, Persons, and the Semiotic Self." In *Semiotics, Self, and Society*, edited by Benjamin Lee and Greg Urban, 229–296. New York: Mouton de Gruyter.

———. 1984. *Man's Glassy Essence: Explorations in Semiotic Anthropology.* Advances in Semiotics. Bloomington: Indiana University Press.

———. 1980. "Signs of the Self: An Exploration in Semiotic Anthropology." *American Anthropologist* 82, no. 3: 485–507.

Sisario, Ben. 2002. "Marrying a Moroccan Sound to the World's Music." *New York Times*, August 11. http://select.nytimes.com/search/restricted/article?res =F30B14F93A5f0C728DDDA10894DA404482.

Skali, Faouzi. 2004a. "La Cité de Moulay Idris." In *L'Esprit De Fes*, edited by Nathalie Callamné, 000–000. Paris: Editions du Rocher. [Comp: Please carry: Au: page numbers for article?]

———. 2004b. Personal Communication. Fes, Morocco.

———. 2002. *Le Face-à-Face Des Coeurs: Le Soufisme aujourd'hui.* Paris: Pocket.

———. 1998. *Traces De Lumières.* Paris: Albin Michel.

———. 1989. *Futuwah: Traité De La Chevalerie Soufie De Muhammad Ibn Al-Husayn Sulami.* Paris: Albin Michel.

———. 1985. *La Voie Soufie.* Paris: Albin Michel.

Sklar, Deidre. 2001. *Dancing with the Virgin: Body and Faith in the Fiesta of Tortugas, New Mexico.* Berkeley: University of California Press.

Slyomovics, Susan. 1998. *The Object of Memory: Arab and Jew Narrate the Palestinian Village.* Philadelphia: University of Pennsylvania Press.

Smith, Bruce R. 1999. *The Acoustic World of Early Modern England: Attending to the O-Factor.* Chicago: University of Chicago Press.

Sontag, Susan. 1989. *On Photography*. New York: Farrar, Straus and Giroux.

Spillers, Hortense J. 2003. *Black, White, and in Color: Essays on American Literature and Culture*. Chicago: University of Chicago Press.

Spyer, Patricia. 1998. *Border Fetishisms: Material Objects in Unstable Spaces*. Zones of Religion. New York: Routledge.

Stallybrass, Peter, and Allon White. 1986. *The Politics and Poetics of Transgression*. Ithaca, N.Y.: Cornell University Press.

Steiner, George. 1998. *After Babel: Aspects of Language and Translation*. 3rd ed. Oxford: Oxford University Press.

Stewart, Kathleen. 2000. "Still Life." In *Intimacy*, edited by Lauren Gail Berlant, 405–420. Chicago: University of Chicago Press.

———. 1996. *A Space on the Side of the Road: Cultural Poetics in an "Other" America*. Princeton, N.J.: Princeton University Press.

Stewart, Susan. 2002. *Poetry and the Fate of the Senses*. Chicago: University of Chicago Press.

Stokes, Martin, ed. 1994. *Ethnicity, Identity, and Music: The Musical Construction of Place*. Berg Ethnic Identities Series. Oxford: Berg.

Stoller, Paul. 1997. *Sensuous Scholarship*. Contemporary Ethnography. Philadelphia: University of Pennsylvania Press.

———. 1995. *Embodying Colonial Memories: Spirit Possession, Power, and the Hauka in West Africa*. New York: Routledge.

———. 1992. *The Cinematic Griot: The Ethnography of Jean Rouch*. Chicago: University of Chicago Press.

———. 1989a. *Fusion of the Worlds: An Ethnography of Possession among the Songhay of Niger*. Chicago: University of Chicago Press.

———. 1989b. *The Taste of Ethnographic Things: The Senses in Anthropology*. Contemporary Ethnography Series. Philadelphia: University of Pennsylvania Press.

Stoller, Paul, and Cheryl Olkes. 1987. *In Sorcery's Shadow: A Memoir of Apprenticeship among the Songhay of Niger*. Chicago: University of Chicago Press.

Straus, Erwin W. 1966. *Phenomenological Psychology*. New York: Basic Books.

Szwed, John F. 2005. *Crossovers: Essays on Race, Music, and American Culture*. Philadelphia: University of Pennsylvania Press.

———. 2002. *So What: The Life of Miles Davis*. New York: Simon and Schuster.

———. 1997. *Space is the Place: The Lives and Times of Sun Ra*. New York: Pantheon Books.

Tambiah, Stanley Jeyaraja. 1990. *Magic, Science, Religion, and the Scope of Rationality*. The Lewis Henry Morgan Lectures. Vol. 1984. Cambridge, England: Cambridge University Press.

Tapper, Nancy. 1990. "Ziyaret: Gender, Movement and Exchange in a Turkish Community." In *Muslim Travellers: Pilgrimage, Migration, and the Religious Imagination*, edited by Dale F. Eickelman and James Piscatori, 236–255. New York: Routledge.

Taussig, Michael T. 1997. *The Magic of the State*. New York: Routledge.

———. 1993. *Mimesis and Alterity: A Particular History of the Senses*. New York: Routledge.

———. 1980. *The Devil and Commodity Fetishism in South America*. Chapel Hill: University of North Carolina Press.

Taylor, Diana. 2003. *The Archive and the Repertoire: Performing Cultural Memory in the Americas*. Durham, N.C.: Duke University Press.

Taylor, Timothy Dean. 2001. *Strange Sounds: Music, Technology and Culture*. New York: Routledge.

———. 1997. *Global Pop: World Music, World Markets*. New York: Routledge.

Tazi, Neila. 2004. Personal Communication. Essaouira, Morocco.

Tetreault, Chantal. 2004. "Communicative Performances of Social Identity in an Algerian-French Neighborhood in Paris." Ph.D. dissertation, University of Texas at Austin.

———. 2002. "'You Call that a Girl?': Borderwork in a French Cité." In *Gendered Practices in Language*, edited by Mary Rose, et al., 237–254. Stanford, Calif.: Center for the Study of Language and Information, Stanford University.

———. 2001. "Ambiguous Authority: Adolescent Girls of Algerian Descent Performing French Cité Styles." In *Europaea: Journal of the Europeanists, Special Issue on Youth in Europe* (edited by Levent Soysal) 1, no. 2:117–130.

Tharaud, Jérôme. 1921. *Rabat, Ou, Les Heures Marocaines*. Paris: Librairie Plon.

Thiong'o, Ngugi wa. 1998. *Penpoints, Gunpoints, and Dreams: Towards a Critical Theory of the Arts and the State in Africa*. Clarendon Lectures in English Literature. Oxford: Oxford University Press.

Three Initiates. 1940 [1912]. *The Kybalion*. Chicago: The Yoga Publication Society.

Tomlinson, Gary. 1993. *Music in Renaissance Magic: Toward a Historiography of Others*. Chicago: University of Chicago Press.

Trawick, Margaret. 1991. "Wandering Lost: A Landless Laborer's Sense of Place and Self." In *Wandering Lost: A Landless Laborer's Sense of Place and Self*, edited by Arjun Appadurai, Frank Korom, and Margaret Mills, 224–266. Philadelphia: University of Pennsylvania Press.

———. 1990. *Notes on Love in a Tamil Family*. Berkeley: University of California Press.

Tremearne, A. J. N. 1968 [1914]. *The Ban of the Bori: Demons and Demon-Dancing in West and North Africa*. Cass Library of African Studies. Vol. 74. London: Cass.

Trilling, Lionel. 1972. *Sincerity and Authenticity: The Charles Eliot Norton Lectures, 1969–1970*. Cambridge, Mass.: Harvard University Press.

———. 1959. *James Joyce*. New York: Oxford University Pres.

Trimingham, J. Spencer. 1961. *Islam in West Africa*. Oxford: Clarendon Press.

———. 1949. *Islam in the Sudan*. London: Oxford University Press.

Tristam, H. B. 1985. *The Great Sahara: Wanderings South of the Atlas Mountains*. London: Darf Publishers.

Turino, Thomas. 2000. *Nationalists, Cosmopolitans, and Popular Music in Zimbabwe*. Chicago Studies in Ethnomusicology. Chicago: University of Chicago.

Turner, Kay. 1999. *Beautiful Necessity: The Art and Meaning of Women's Altars*. New York: Thames and Hudson.

Turner, Victor Witter. 1982. *From Ritual to Theatre: The Human Seriousness of Play*. Performance Studies Series. New York City: Performing Arts Journal Publications.

———. 1975. *Revelation and Divination in Ndembu Ritual*. Symbol, Myth, and Ritual Series. Ithaca, N.Y.: Cornell University Press.

———. 1974. *Dramas, Fields, and Metaphors; Symbolic Action in Human Society*. Symbol, Myth, and Ritual. Ithaca, N.Y.: Cornell University Press.

Turner, Victor Witter, and Edward M. Bruner. 1986. *The Anthropology of Experience*. Urbana: University of Illinois Press.

Urban, Greg. 1996. *Metaphysical Community: The Interplay of the Senses and the Intellect*. Austin: University of Texas Press.

———. 1993. "Culture's Public Face." *Public Culture* 5: 213–238.

———. 1991. *A Discourse-Centered Approach to Culture: Native South American Myths and Rituals*. Texas Linguistics Series. Austin: University of Texas Press.

———. 1989. "The 'I' of Discourse." In *Semiotics, Self, and Society*, edited by Benjamin Lee and Greg Urban, 27–52. New York: Mouton de Gruyter.

———. 1988. "Ritual Wailing in Amerindian Brazil." *American Anthropologist* 90: 385–400.

———. 1984a. "The Semiotics of Two Speech Styles in Shokleng." In *Semiotic Mediation: Sociocultural and Psychological Perspectives*, edited by Elizabeth Mertz and Richard J. Parmentier, 311–329. Orlando, Fla.: Academic Press.

———. 1984b. "Speech about Speech in Speech about Action." *Journal of American Folklore* 97, no. 385: 310–328.

Valéry, Paul. 1961. *The Art of Poetry*. Translated by Denise Folliot. New York: Vintage Books.

Voloshinov, V. N. 1972. *Marxism and the Philosophy of Language* [Marksizm i filosofiëiìa ëiìazyka]. Janua Linguarum. Series Anastatica. Vol. 5. The Hague: Mouton.

von Grunebaum, G. E. 1966. "The Cultural Function of the Dream as Illustrated by Classical Islam." In *The Dream in Human Societies*, edited by G. E. von Grunebaum and R. Caillois, 3–21. Berkeley: University of California Press.

Wafer, James William. 1991. *The Taste of Blood: Spirit Possession in Brazilian Candomblé*. Contemporary Ethnography Series. Philadelphia: University of Pennsylvania Press.

Wagner, Daniel A. 1993. *Literacy, Culture, and Development: Becoming Literate in Morocco*. Cambridge, England: Cambridge University Press.

Waterman, Christopher Alan. 2000. "Corrine Corrina, Bo Chatman, and the Excluded Middle." In *Music and the Racial Imagination*, edited by Ronald Michael Radano and Philip Vilas Bohlman, 167–205. Chicago: University of Chicago Press.

———. 1990. *Jùjú: A Social History and Ethnography of an African Popular Music*. Chicago Studies in Ethnomusicology. Chicago: University of Chicago Press.

Waugh, Earle H. 2005. *Memory, Music, and Religion: Morocco's Mystical Chanters*. Studies in Comparative Religion. Columbia, S.C.: University of South Carolina Press.

Weber, Max. 1963. *The Sociology of Religion*. Boston: Beacon Press.

Webster, Charles. 1982. *From Paracelsus to Newton: Magic and the Making of Modern Science*. The Eddington Memorial Lectures. Vol. 1980. Cambridge: Cambridge University Press.

Weiner, Annette B. 1992. *Inalienable Possessions: The Paradox of Keeping-while-Giving*. Berkeley: University of California Press.

Welte, Frank Maurice. 1990. *Der Gnâawa-Kult: Trancespiele, Geisterbeschwèorung Und Besessenheit in Marokko*. European University Studies. Series 19, Anthropology-Ethnology. Section B, Ethnology. Vol. 18. Frankfurt am Main: P. Lang.

Welte, Frank, and Jordi Aguadé. 1996. *Die Lieder Der Gnawa Aus Meknes*. Marburg: Diagonal-Verlag.

West, Cornel. 1993. *Race Matters*. Boston: Beacon Press.

Weston, Randy. 1994. Liner Notes, *The Splendid Master Gnawa Musicians of Morocco* (Verve).

Wilkinson, Desi. 2003. "'Celtitude,' Professionalism, and the Fest Noz in the Traditional Music in Brittany." In *Celtic Modern: Music at the Global Fringe*, edited by Martin Stokes and Philip Vilas Bohlman, 219–256. Lanham, Md.: Scarecrow Press.

———. 1999. "Brittany." In *The Companion to Irish Traditional Music*, edited by Fintan Vallely, 40–43. New York: New York University Press.

Williams, Linda. 2001. *Playing the Race Card: Melodramas of Black and White from Uncle Tom to O. J. Simpson*. Princeton, N.J.: Princeton University Press.

Williams, Raymond. 1985. *Keywords: A Vocabulary of Culture and Society*. Rev. ed. New York: Oxford University Press.

———. 1977. *Marxism and Literature*. London: Oxford University Press.

———. 1975 [1961]. *The Long Revolution*. Westport, Conn.: Greenwood Press.

Winick, Stephen. 1997. "The Afro-Celtic Kick." *Citypaper*, March 13, 1997. http://www.citypaper.net/articles/031397/article009.shtml.

———. 1995. "Breton Music, Breton Identity, and Alan Stivell's Again." *The Journal of American Folklore* 108, no. 429. Accessed at http://dolphin.upenn.edu/ ~teachnet/Bretonjaf/bretonjaftoc.html.

Wong, Deborah. 2000. "The Asian-American Body in Performance." In *Music and the Racial Imagination*, edited by Ronald Michael Radano and Philip Vilas Bohlman. Chicago: University of Chicago Press.

Wright, John. 2002. "Morocco: The Last Great Slave Market?" *The Journal of North African Studies* 7, no. 3: 53–66.

Young, Katharine Galloway. 2002a. "The Dream Body in Somatic Psychology: The Kineasthetics of Gesture." *Gesture* 2, no. 1: 45–70.

———. 2002b. "The Memory of the Flesh: The Family Body in Somatic Psychology." *Body and Society* 8, no. 3: 25–47.

———. 1997. *Presence in the Flesh: The Body in Medicine.* Cambridge, Mass.: Harvard University Press.

———. 1987. *Taleworlds and Storyrealms: The Phenomenology of Narrative.* Martinus Nijhoff Philosophy Library. Vol. 16. Boston: Kluwer Academic Publishers.

Zouanat, Zakia. 1998. *Ibn Mashish, maître d'Al-Shadhili.* Casablanca: Najah al Jadida.

DISCOGRAPHY

Aisha Kandisha's Jarring Effects (AKJE). 1993. *Shabeesation* (Rykodisc B00000009Q1).

Amadou and Miriam. 2000. "Si Ni Kénéya." *The Ni Mousso* (Circular Moves 7006).

Boussou, Amhed. 1992. *Gnawa Leila, Volume One: Gnawa Songs and Music from Morocco* (Prod. Antonio Baldassarre and Michel Pagiras. Al Sur).

Bnet Marrakech. 2002. *Chama'a* (l'empreinte digitale).

El 'Abdi, Ouled. 1995. *Le Gnawa du Maroc* (Auvidis/Ethnic).

Ghania, Mahmoud. 1999. *Gnawa Essaouira* (Sounds of the World).

Ghania, Mahmoud, with Pharoah Sanders. 1994. *The Trance of Seven Colors* (Axiom/Island).

Gnawa. 2000. *Morocco: Dances and Trances* (Arbiter).

———. 1992. *Gnawa Leila.* 5 vols. (Prod. Antonio Baldassarre and Michel Pagiras. Al Sur).

Gnawa from Marrakech. 1997. *Song for Sidi Mimoun* (Felmay).

Gnawa of Essaouira. 1993. *Hadra des Gnaoua d'Essaouira* (Ocora, Harmonia Mundi).

Gnawa Music, al-Maghrib. 1997. *The Music of Islam.* Vol. 6 (Prod. David Parsons. Celestial Harmonies).

Gnawa Music of Marrakesh. 1990. *Night Spirit Masters* (Prod. Richard Horowitz and Bill Laswell. Axiom/Island Records).

Hakmoun, Hassan. 1998. *Life Around the World* (Alula Records).

———. 1995. *The Fire Within: Gnawa Music of Morocco* (Music of the World, CDT-135).

———. 1993. *Trance* (Real World).

Hakmoun, Hassan, Don Cherry, Richard Horowitz, Adam Rudolph. 1991. *Gift of the Gnawa* (Flying Fish, 571).

M'allem Sam (Mohammed Zourhbat) and M'allem Hmidah (Ahmed Boussou). 1992. *The Masters of Guimbri Vol. II–V* (Prod. Antonio Baldassarre and Michel Pagiras. Al Sur).

Stivell, Alan. 1988. *Live in Dublin* (Dreyfus Records).

Wanklyn, Christopher. 1966. *Music of Morocco* (Folkways Records).

Weston, Randy. 2005. *Zep Tepi* (Random Chance 7020267).

———. 1994. *The Splendid Master Gnawa Musicians of Morocco* (Verve 521587–2).

———. 1992. "Blue Moses." *The Spirits of Our Ancestors* (Antilles 314–511 896–2).

———. 1990a. *Caravan: Portraits of Duke Ellington* (Verve 841 3122).

———. 1990b. *Well You Needn't: Portraits of Thelonious Monk.* (Verve 841 3132).

———. 1959. *Little Niles.* (United Artists, UAL 4011/UAS 5011).

Weston, Randy, and African Rhythms. 1998. "Creation." *Khepera.* (Verve 314 557 821–2).

Weston, Randy, and The Master Gnawa Musicians of Morocco. 1994. "Chalabati." *The Splendid Master Gnawa Musicians of Morocco* (Antilles 314 521 587–2).

FILMOGRAPHY

Les Maitres Fous. 1992. Directed by Suzanne Baron, Pierre Braunberger, and Jean Rouch, et al. Chicago, Ill.: Interama, Inc.; Facets Multimedia distributor.

Learning to Dance in Bali. 1994. Directed by Gregory Bateson. University Park, Pa.: Penn State University.

Representation and the Media. 1997. Directed by Stuart Hall, Sut Jhally, and Media Education Foundation. Northampton, Mass.: Media Education Foundation.

INDEX

◆ ◆ ◆

Ibn Sina, 31

imagination, 3, 6–8, 28, 31, 87, 204, 210, 215, 250–251n.16; alchemy of, 239, 250n.14; Breton cultural, 198; cultural imaginations, 210, 231, 238–239; filmic, 87; hybrid cultural imaginations, 5, 238; "imaginal world," 28, 31, 110–111, 117, 149, 249n.13; imaginary, 6, 29, 233; musical, 5; phantasms, 253n.23; racial imaginaries, 202, 239; and Renaissance, 253n.22, 253n.25, 253n.27–29

incense, 14, 18, 26, 36, 45–47, 52, 68, 75, 86, 90, 117, 157, 183, 223, 265–266n.35; performativity of, 70

initiation, 80

intimacy, 29

intoxication, 25–26, 29, 42, 45

Jackson, Travis A., 129, 190, 272n.17

jadba, 2

Jakobson, Roman, 69, 83, 85, 185, 187

Jameson, Frederic, 233

Jankowsky, Richard, 246n.14

Jewish Spirits, 113, 235

Jil Jilala, 21, 113, 137

jinn/jnun. See spirits

Johnson, Mark, 65–66, 263n.27

Jones, Etta, 221

Jones, Leroi, 21

Joyce, James, 270–271n.12

Jung, Carl G., 6

Kapchan, Deborah, 42, 57, 85, 140, 143, 185, 231, 246n.16

Kapferer, Bruce, 243n.3

Keil, Charles, 149, 187, 190–191, 262–263n.26, 268n.1; and Steven Feld, 232

Kelley, Robin D. G., 176, 188; and E. Lemelle, 185

Kendon, Adam, 68, 102, 263n.27, 264–265n.31

keying, 1, 51

Kibwe, Talib, 159, 160, 163, 164, 215, 239. See also Blue, T. K.

Kindi (al-Kindi), 31

Kirk, Rahsaan Roland, 218

Kirshenblatt-Gimblett, Barbara, 201, 212, 221, 226, 243n.4, 276n.30; and Backhouse, 182

Kostenbaum, Wayne, 95

Kristeva, Julia, 72–73, 80, 186, 263–264n.30, 265n.32

Laderman, Carol, 256n.37; and Marina Roseman, 105, 256n.37

Lambek, Michael, 1, 3, 142, 203, 243n.3, 244n.9, 246n.14, 248n.21, 252n.18, 256n.44

Langer, Susan K. K., 103, 263n.29

Lapassade, Georges, 277n.7

Larfaoui, Abbass Baska, 22

Laroui, Abdullah, 214, 245n.11

Lawrence, Bruce, and miriam cooke, 3

Lawrence, William, 147; and Randell Barnwell, 147

Lebesque, Morvan, 276n.26

LeCoadic, Ronan, Michel Denis, and Michel Wieviorka, 276n.26

Leder, Bruce, 87, 99

Lefebvre, Henri, 53, 82, 208, 213, 261–262n.22

Leiris, Michel, 136, 267n.13, 269n.5

Lemelle, Sidney J., and Robin D. G. Kelley, 185

Lepecki, André, 60

Lévi-Strauss, Claude, 176, 181

Lewis, I. M., 36, 41, 97, 243n.3, 246n.14

sound symbolism, 102–103

space 82; space of flow 60. See also *fajwa*

spirits, 6, 11, 12, 15–18, 20, 22, 26, 30, 34,
38–42, 46, 49–52, 54, 57, 72, 76–77,
98, 160, 173, 175, 204, 207, 218–220,
227, 228, 230, 234, 240–241, 257n.6,
270n.5; Aisha Qandisha, 15–17, 29,
58, 72, 787, 89, 111, 112, 117, 119, 124,
126, 127, 148, 175, 205, 206, 269n.8;
aiša al-bahariyya, 88, 119, 175; and
gestural economy, 64; Lalla Malika,
107; Lalla Mimuna, 15, 113,
267–268n.6; Lalla Mira, 54, 77, 157;
samawiyya, 119; Sidi Chamharouch,
128; Sidi Hamu, 15, 75, 157, 173;
Sidi Mimun, 15, 28, 50, 54, 87–89,
91–92, 109–110, 116–117, 133, 156,
165, 181–185, 188, 240–242, 257n.6;
Sidi Musa, 4, 5, 15, 49, 160, 177–178,
180, 182–185, 188, 192, 196, 208,
219–221, 227, 228, 257n.6, 275n.24;
spirits and water, 78; "working the
spirits," 39–42, 58–59, 66, 236;
Yubadi, 42

Spyer, Patsy, 276n.27

standing. See gesture

Steiner, George, 101

Stewart, Susan, 78, 81, 95, 103, 252n.16,
257n.9

Stivell, Alan, 199, 275–276n.25

Stoller, Paul, 1, 18, 48, 97–98, 135, 136,
177, 243n.3, 248n.18

Stokes, Martin, 2, 180

style: and "endotropic performance,"
209; genealogy of, 222; and identity,
209, 233; musical, 6, 195, 197, 209

Sufism, 5, 26, 28, 30, 33–34, 42–46,
62–63, 103, 110, 148, 218, 254n.30,
269n.8; and desire, 33; and dreams,
108; and listening, 43; and music,

258n.14; and *sama*, 43, 110; and the
senses, 43; and spectacle, 146; Sufi
masters, 194

Szwed, John, 32, 268n.1, 275n.20

tagnawit, 3, 22–23, 39, 139, 141–142,
144, 214, 215, 220, 228–230, 237

Tamezoujt, Yahya, 132

Tangier, 5, 277n.2

Tatum, Art, 193

Taussig, Michael T., 203, 269n.1,

tawḥid, 111

Taylor, Diana, 250n.16

Taylor, Timothy, 148, 238, 269n.7

Tehuti. *See* Three Initiates

television, 49, 84, 85

Tetrault, Chantal, and Paul Silverstein,
244n.8

Tharaud, Jérome, 182

Thompson, M. J., and Michelle Dent, 55

Three Initiates, 32, 194, 274–275n.19

Tijaniyya, 5, 25

time, 4, 55–56, 60, 78, 83, 103–104, 221;
gestures and temporality, 52, 81;
repetition and, 79; rupture in experience of, 55; sacred time, 53; temporality, 34, 35, 55–56; temporality
acceleration, 103; trance time, 81;
temporal registers, 83

Tomlinson, Gary, 30, 31, 252n.20–21,
253.n.21, 253n.27, 254n.27,
254n.29, 259n.14

tourism, 123

trauma, 3, 34, 35, 204, 236

Tremearne, A. J. N., 246n.14, 268n.5

Trilling, Lionel, 270–271n.12

tropes of trance and possession, 1

Turino, Thomas, 268n.2

Turner, Kay, 222

Turner, Victor Witter, 62, 261n.21

MUSIC/CULTURE
A series from Wesleyan University Press.
Edited by Harris M. Berger and Annie J. Randall
Originating editors: George Lipsitz, Susan McClary, and Robert Walser.

Making Beats:
   The Art of Sample-Based Hip-Hop
   by Joseph G. Schloss
Dissonant Identities:
   The Rock 'n' Roll Scene in
   Austin, Texas
   by Barry Shank
Among the Jasmine Trees:
   Music and Modernity in
   Contemporary Syria
   by Jonathan Holt Shannon
Banda:
   Mexican Musical Life across Borders
   by Helena Simonett
Subcultural Sounds:
   Micromusics of the West
   by Mark Slobin
Music, Society, Education
   by Christopher Small
Musicking:
   The Meanings of Performing and
   Listening
   by Christopher Small
Music of the Common Tongue:
   Survival and Celebration in African
   American Music
   by Christopher Small
Singing Our Way to Victory:
   French Cultural Politics and Music
   During the Great War
   by Regina M. Sweeney

Setting the Record Straight:
   A Material History of Classical
   Recording
   by Colin Symes
False Prophet:
   Fieldnotes from the Punk Underground
   by Steven Taylor
Any Sound You Can Imagine:
   Making Music/Consuming Technology
   by Paul Théberge
Club Cultures:
   Music, Media and Sub-cultural
   Capital
   by Sarah Thornton
Dub:
   Songscape and Shattered Songs in
   Jamaican Reggae
   by Michael E. Veal
Running with the Devil:
   Power, Gender, and Madness in
   Heavy Metal Music
   by Robert Walser
Manufacturing the Muse:
   Estey Organs and Consumer Culture in
   Victorian America
   by Dennis Waring
The City of Musical Memory:
   Salsa, Record Grooves, and Popular
   Culture in Cali, Colombia
   by Lise A. Waxer

ABOUT THE AUTHOR

◆ ◆ ◆

Deborah Kapchan is associate professor of performance studies at New York University. She is the author of *Gender on the Market: Moroccan Women and the Revoicing of Tradition* (University of Pennsylvania, 1996) and has published numerous articles on narrative, music, and other performance genres.